Discourses of Olympism

Discourses of Olympism

From the Sorbonne 1894 to London 2012

Dikaia Chatziefstathiou
Canterbury Christ Church University, UK

Ian P. Henry
Loughborough University, UK

First published 2012 by
PALGRAVE MACMILLAN

Palgrave Macmillan in the UK is an imprint of Macmillan Publishers Limited, registered in England, company number 785998, of Houndmills, Basingstoke, Hampshire RG21 6XS.

Palgrave Macmillan in the US is a division of St Martin's Press LLC, 175 Fifth Avenue, New York, NY 10010.

Palgrave Macmillan is the global academic imprint of the above companies and has companies and representatives throughout the world.

Palgrave® and Macmillan® are registered trademarks in the United States, the United Kingdom, Europe and other countries

ISBN 978-0-230-28957-4

This book is printed on paper suitable for recycling and made from fully managed and sustained forest sources. Logging, pulping and manufacturing processes are expected to conform to the environmental regulations of the country of origin.

A catalogue record for this book is available from the British Library.

A catalog record for this book is available from the Library of Congress.

10 9 8 7 6 5 4 3 2 1
21 20 19 18 17 16 15 14 13 12

Printed and bound in the United States of America

For my father Charalambos, who left us early but has always guided my way, my mother Eleftheria who patiently and tirelessly has always supported all my life and career choices and my two brothers Michalis and Dimitris (and his wife Anna), whose different personalities always enrich my own ways of thinking

For Carol, Alasdair, Amy and James

Contents

Acknowledgements

It is difficult to list all those individuals whose contributions have been significant in the development of ideas for this book and invidious to single out just some. However we would like to place on record our gratitude to colleagues in our respective institutions, Canterbury Christ Church University and Loughborough University, for their collegiality in supporting our endeavour in various ways. We would also like to thank all those friends and colleagues with whom we rehearsed our developing arguments for the book at the various conferences and seminars at which we have presented aspects of the book as germinating ideas over the last four years.

1
Introduction: Developing Discursive Constructions of Olympism

1.1   The nature of Olympism

For the average person in the street the 'Olympics' conjures up images (perhaps both positive and negative) of intense elite sporting competition (sometimes drug fuelled), sporting pageantry (sometimes with political and nationalistic undertones), with instantly and globally recognisable (and commercially exploitable) Olympic symbols such as the Olympic rings and the torch, huge sponsorship deals, and media viewing figures which suggest that a considerable proportion of the world's population has viewed at least some part of the Games. Indeed, Nielsen Media Research (2008) in a study completed for the International Olympic Committee (IOC) claim that 4.7 billion people watched some element of the Beijing Games from a world population of 6.5 billion. Paradoxically, however, despite the global reach of the Olympic Games, 'Olympism' as a set of values, statements or core concepts central to the practice of Olympic sport and to the Olympic movement, which for the most part is intended by its proponents to be global in its application, is perhaps little known beyond a group of scholars, administrators, and other Olympic cognoscenti. It is this, the ideology of Olympism which is the focus of this book. While intended as a 'universal' set of values, Olympism is recognised as a western construct (Chatziefstathiou et al. 2008; Donelly 1996; Segrave and Chu 1981; Segrave 2000) and thus culturally relative, and as temporally bounded, changing over time reflecting shifts in political, economic and cultural contexts. We therefore focus throughout the text on different discourses, from different speakers at different conjunctures, since an understanding of the context and the background of the speaker (or writer) is critical if we are to interrogate the discourse and the interests it may represent.

The term 'Olympism' was first coined by the founder of the modern Olympic Games, Baron Pierre de Coubertin (Segrave and Chu 1981). Coubertin understood, towards the end of the nineteenth century, that sport would become a central point of popular culture and was working towards the definition of a universal philosophy that would have sport and physical activity at its core (Parry 1994). In his *Olympic Memories* (1979, originally published in 1931: 208), Coubertin interpreted Olympism in grand, if occasionally unspecific, terms as a 'school of nobility and of moral purity as well as of endurance and physical energy – but only if … honesty and sportsman-like unselfishness are as highly developed as the strength of muscles' (p. 208). Thus, Olympism, for Coubertin, aimed at the 'harmonious development' of the intellectual, aesthetic and physical aspects of a human being through athletic competition (Segrave and Chu 1981), but also incorporated a clear ethical dimension.

The concept of Olympism and the content of the Olympic philosophy have always been strongly linked with education. In the late nineteenth century Coubertin was working towards an educational reform in collaboration with the French government. While he travelled in England, Germany, America and Canada visiting educational institutions, he was inspired by sport education in England and the intercollegiate competitions in America and Canada (Müller 2000). A number of his biographers (Eyquem 1981; MacAloon 1981; Weber 1970) suggest that Coubertin, after years of study and field research, developed his project for the Olympic Games as a response to political and social crises in his country. He was deeply concerned with rapid industrialisation and urbanisation which resulted in poverty and conflict (Kidd 1996). Thus, Olympism came as a product of a range of different influences and trends but it was also related to Coubertin's concern for the reform of French education (Kidd 1996; Müller 2000). Coubertin viewed education as 'the key to human happiness' and he was convinced that education could provide the most appropriate response 'to the accelerated pace of change in the world' (Müller 2000: 205).

The fundamental principles of Olympism are stated in the Olympic Charter, of which the first version is estimated to have been published around 1898.[1] Since then, the Olympic Charter has been the official 'rule book' of the International Olympic Committee (Loland 1994), and as stated in the Charter itself (International Olympic Committee 1996), it constitutes 'the codification of the Fundamental Principles, Rules and Bye-Laws adopted by the International Olympic Committee (IOC). It governs the organisation, action and operation of the Olympic movement and sets forth the conditions for the celebration of the Olympic Games' (International Olympic Committee 2007: 7). The Olympic movement consists of the IOC, the Organising Committees of the Olympic Games (OCOGs), the NOCs, the IFs, the national associations, clubs and, of course, the athletes. The Olympic Charter provides the following information in relation to Olympism:

> Modern Olympism was conceived by Pierre de Coubertin, on whose initiative the International Athletic Congress of Paris was held in June 1894. The International Olympic Committee (IOC) constituted itself on

23rd of June 1894. In August 1994, the XII Congress, Centennial Olympic Congress, which was entitled the 'Congress of Unity', was held in Paris. (International Olympic Committee 2011: 9)

Olympism is a philosophy of life, exalting and combining in a balanced whole the qualities of body, will and mind. Blending sport with culture and education, Olympism seeks to create a way of life based on the joy of effort, the educational value of good example and respect for universal fundamental ethical principles. (International Olympic Committee 2011: 10)

The goal of Olympism is to place sport at the service of the harmonious development of man [sic], with a view to promoting a peaceful society concerned with the preservation of human dignity. (International Olympic Committee 2011: 10)

Sigmund Loland (1994) has argued that Olympism, from the perspective of the history of ideas, has four main goals: a) to educate and cultivate the individual through sport, b) to cultivate the relation of men (sic) in society, c) to promote international understanding and peace, and d) to worship human greatness and possibility (pp. 36–8). Its definitions have been various (Arnold 1996). It has been referred to as a social philosophy which emphasises the role of sport in world development, peaceful co-existence, international understanding and social and moral education (Parry 1994). It has also been defined as 'sport in the service of man (sic) everywhere' (Lekarska 1988: 73) 'the pursuit of excellence in a chivalrous manner' (Clarke 1988: 99), 'a nebula of speeches, a sea of myths, ideologies and prejudices' (Caillat and Brohm 1984; cited in Landry 1985: 143). Our analysis, therefore, seeks to understand how modern Olympism is defined and understood by key actors in different times and how this understanding reflects and/or reproduces the relations between the individuals who are engaged in the decision-making processes of the movement in conjunction with the economic-political-cultural interests which they represent.

Hoberman (1995) sees Olympism in parallel with other 'idealistic internationalisms' which appeared in three periods that are roughly separated by the First and Second World Wars. The establishment of the Olympic movement in 1894 coincided with the increasing number of a broad range of international organisations, all sharing humanistic and 'universal' values (Hoberman 1995). These organisations were products of late nineteenth-century liberalism, which emphasised values of equality, fairness, justice, respect for persons, rationality, international understanding, peace, autonomy and excellence (Hoberman 1995; Parry 1994). Coubertin's contribution was to locate these values in the milieu of sport. A number of authors identify Olympism with humanism which might explain why socialist societies found little difficulty in incorporating implications of Olympism within their own ideological frames. Boulogne (1999a) makes claims shared by Parry (1994) that 'Coubertinian neo-Olympism asserted itself as a humanism' (p. 37), while Anthony (1992) also supports the idea that Olympism and humanism share the very same purposes. Furthermore, (MacAloon 1996a: 69) suggests that Olympic leaders and dominant Olympic institutions have gone so far as to claim that 'Olympism is Humanism'.

Despite its grand ideals incorporated in the Olympic Charter, Olympism has been subject to major critiques (see for example, Hill 1992; Hoberman 1986; Simson and Jennings 1991). The rise of nationalisms, the involvement of politics with the appearance of successive boycotts, accelerating commercialisation, the professionalisation of athletes, discrimination against race, gender and ethnicity in the Olympic arena, the Eurocentric and western character of the Olympic movement, and the scandals concerning bribery of the IOC members, represent some of the major criticisms levelled against the modern Olympic movement. The Olympic leaders (and their ethical standards) were questioned and subjected to severe scrutiny when certain incidents in the bidding process for hosting the Winter Olympic Games of 2002 in Salt Lake City were revealed. This is perhaps the starkest example of the gap that exists between organisational ideals and organisational conduct within the Olympic movement (Segrave 2000). Simson and Jennings (1991) had accused some Olympic leaders of bribery, hypocrisy and other serious shortcomings, with good reason, though their arguments may have been partially undermined by the 'overblown rhetoric' employed in their account (Houlihan 1994: 109). Seppanen (1984), with a more restrained rhetoric than that of Simson and Jennings, has also criticised the Olympic movement for its inability to promote the Olympic ideals. In similar vein, for others, the Games have become a global business and the values embedded in the Olympic Charter have been neglected (Milton-Smith 2002).

The changing nature of the ideology of Olympism against the broader contemporaneous historical, geopolitical, socio-cultural and economic contexts reflect the principal concerns of this book, and will be discussed in relation to the activities of the Olympic movement and the commentaries of others. An aim of the book is to identify the process of the expression of values associated with this ideology, examining motives, interests and intentions in relation to the promotion of Olympism against the historical, geopolitical, socio-cultural and economic background of the modern Olympic movement. This is done through an analysis of related documentary sources, largely reports, correspondence, articles and speeches written by key actors of the movement. For the period from 1894 up to the end of the twentieth century, three actors or sets actors have been selected for detailed analysis on two criteria: a) the crucial nature of their role in the Olympic movement, and b) their contribution to knowledge and understanding of Olympism in different epochs. The three actors/sets of actors and the sources relating to them are Baron Pierre de Coubertin (1863–1937), founder of the modern

Olympic movement; Carl Diem (1882–1962), close collaborator of Coubertin and initiator of many Olympic innovations (such as the torch relay and the Olympic Village); and selected speakers and visiting lecturers at the International Olympic Academy (IOA) between 1961 and the end of the last century. The first two candidates are rather obvious figureheads who wrote and spoke widely about the movement, Olympism and its aims, and certainly Coubertin's role in promoting Olympism as a philosophy may be regarded as preeminent. The IOA describes itself as an important academic centre established to develop and disseminate Olympic ideals and ideas.

> The aim of the International Olympic Academy is to create an international cultural centre in Olympia, to preserve and spread the Olympic Spirit, study and implement the educational and social principles of Olympism and consolidate the scientific basis of the Olympic Ideal, in conformity with the principles laid down by the ancient Greeks and the revivers of the contemporary Olympic movement, through Baron de Coubertin's initiative. (International Olympic Academy 2011)

Thus all three sets of data covering the first hundred years or so of the modern Olympic movement, form important sources of ideological construction in the sense of consciously seeking to shape debate on the moral dimensions of the Olympic movement and what is claimed to be its core philosophy.

In the discussion of the emergence of key themes relating to Olympism in the early years of the current century up until 2012, we move away from focusing specifically on particular sources to a more eclectic set of voices, to discuss continuities and change in the primary themes emerging around Olympism in the early twenty-first century.

Of course, neither 'Olympism' as a term nor the adjectival conjunction of Olympic with sports and games, was a product solely of Coubertin's activities in seeking to revive the games, and indeed Coubertin was not the sole proponent of the revival of the Modern Games. The Cotswold Olympicks of Robert Dover inaugurated in the early seventeenth century, the Zappas Olympics in Athens in 1859, 1870, and 1875 sponsored by the Greek businessman Evangalos Zappas and the Much Wenlock Olympian Society and Games initiated by Dr. William Penny Brookes in 1860 were perhaps the most prominent other examples of 'revivals'. Indeed some commentators have argued that Coubertin, although the instigator of the first IOC Congress, and the force behind the establishment of the IOC as an organisation, in effect usurped the revival of the modern Games which members of the Greek establishment felt should be permanently staged in Greece (Chatziefstathiou and Henry 2007, 2010). Nevertheless though the discourse on matters Olympic did not begin with Coubertin, for our purpose in reviewing the development of ideas about Olympism, Coubertin and his work represent a compelling start point for evaluating the changing meaning of Olympism from the 1894 Olympic Congress at the Sorbonne up to the present day (though we do also cite some Coubertin material which predates 1894).

Our focus is not however simply on reconstructing the aims, tactics or impact of Coubertin, Diem and the late twentieth century Olympic commentators whose texts we use as the major basis for our analysis of Olympism in this book. Our goal is less one of focusing on subjects, the individuals (Coubertin, Diem and the others) what they say and do, and why they speak, write and act this way (though we do discuss these matters along the way), but rather our primary purpose is to identify the consequences of their speech and actions for the way in which Olympism and Olympic sport are conceptualised, and therefore for the kinds of behaviour which developed across the century and its significance. In other words our concern is with the production of the discourse of Olympism and how this might relate to, or be related by, different types of theoretical tradition.

1.2   Viewing Olympism through the prism of social theory

In addressing the nature of the ideas expressed and their relationship to the historical, political, economic, and cultural context within which they are developed there are perhaps four principal sets of theoretical perspectives which address discursive and non-discursive practices, providing prisms through which to view and evaluate Olympism.

The first of these, the Modernisation thesis argues for the notion of international convergence around scientific and objective 'solutions' to technological, but also social, economic and political problems. This approach first developed in the field of politics and economic development by authors such as Lipset (1959) and subsequently modified to incorporate arguments relating to shifts to post-modern structures by authors such as Ronald Inglehart (Inglehart 1997; Inglehart and Norris 2009; Inglehart and Welzel 2005), who suggest that economic development brings with it the conditions for change in people's knowledge, values and ways of life. Though heavily critiqued in its earlier forms for seeing development as linear, teleological and invariably leading to positive change, more nuanced versions of the thesis emerged in the 1990s (Przeworski and Limongi 1997). The application of a Modernisation thesis approach to developments in sport has perhaps been most cogently expressed in Alan Guttmann's book *From Ritual to Record* (Guttman 1978) which characterises modern sport as converging around a set of key characteristics, namely secularisation, rationalisation, bureaucratisation, equality of the opportunity to compete and of the conditions of competition, specialisation of roles, quantification of performance, and the quest for records. The discourses associated with this type of perspective would emphasise 'progress' and the development of rational, often scientific, approaches to athletic training and performance, which societies and their performance systems will tend to share as they converge around 'optimal' practices.

The second theoretical tradition is represented by neo-Marxist perspectives as reflected in cultural imperialism and dependency theories. Dependency theory characterises the development over time of relations between core and periphery, affluent and poor nations, as being characterised by three primary forms of dependency. The first is colonial (political) dependency evident in the era of imperialism when the colonial power legitimates its expropriation of land, raw materials and labour from its colonies. The second is financial-industrial dependency when capital from the developed world invests heavily in the developing world. The third form is technological-industrial dependency in which the periphery becomes dependent on core countries for access to developing technologies. Thus the relations between rich and poor are characterised by evolving forms and sources of dependency.

The diffusion of sport provides an explanation of the development of a fourth form of dependency namely cultural dependency. Studies of sports diffusions which draw on a dependency theory approach include Alan Klein on baseball (Klein 1995), Darby on the diffusion of football in Africa (Darby 2002), Stoddart on cricket (Stoddart 1988) and Bale and Sang on athletics (Bale and Sang 1996).

The failure of classical Dependency theory to provide an adequate account of the emergence from this dependent set of relationships by certain countries of the periphery has been highlighted by a considerable number of critics (Bauer and Sen 2004; Gold 1986; Haggard 1990; Warren 1980). For example explanation of the emergence of Asia's tiger economies is problematic for this perspective, as, in cultural terms, is the emergence of former peripheral nations in international sport, such as South Korea in football, India, Pakistan and the West Indies in cricket and Algeria, Ethiopia, Kenya and Morocco in athletics. Notwithstanding the significance in the improvement of standards of performance, however, it could be argued that peripheral states still depend on the West for sports technology in the form of coaches, equipment, knowledge, and administration of elite sporting bodies and competitions, and it is certainly the case that membership of the IOC, arguably the preeminent body in contemporary world sport, remains dominated by the West and in particular western Europe (see Figure 1.1), with, in 2011, a disproportionate representation of the titled nobility (11.6 per cent), and of men (81.8 per cent).

From a related position, cultural imperialism explains the replacement of the political and military dominance of colonising powers with the promotion of the former coloniser's interests through cultural means. This implies that, given the demise of some of the world's major imperial projects, and the failure to dominate in particular former colonies by military and political force, dominance and dependency is maintained in part by cultural means and cultural dependency. Thus the control of the Olympic movement by the West is seen as sustaining its power over developing economies and former colonies.

While none of the perspectives outlined represents a simple, single theoretical strand, globalisation theory is particularly diverse and reflects claims

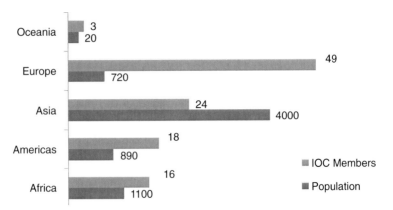

Figure 1.1 Membership of the IOC (March 2011) Compared with Population (millions)

relating to a wide range of phenomena. As we have argued elsewhere different disciplines focus on differing aspects of a multifaceted phenomenon.

> Deregulation and financial liberalisation may be emphasised by economists; the withering of the state by political economists; the decline of the nation state by political scientists and international relations scholars; Westernisation, MacDonaldisation and cultural homogeneity by sociologists; and post-national, post-modern, post-colonial global culture by cultural theorists. (Henry and Institute of Sport and Leisure Policy 2007: 7)

Within the explosion of literature on globalisation there is a tendency which Rosenburg identifies of confusing explanation of the phenomenon with the phenomenon as explanation.

> What presented itself initially as the *explanandum* – globalisation as the developing outcome of some historical process – is progressively transformed into the *explanans*: it is globalisation which now explains the changing character of the modern world. (Rosenberg 2000: 3)[2]

In fact globalising phenomena such as Appadurai's (1990) 'scapes', the global transfer of finance, goods, persons, values, media and services are viewed as both a product of, and ongoing contributory factors in, globalisation processes. The Olympic phenomenon is certainly implicated in such scapes and might be seen as both product and contributory factor, reflecting aspects of both 'glocalisation' (Robertson 1992) and 'grobalisation' (Ritzer 2004), local resistance and global dominance.

The fourth set of theoretical perspectives represents a core focus for the commentary and analysis which follows in this book. We characterise this set of perspectives as post-structuralist in the sense that they reject both structuralist assumptions which appeal to notions of the existence of 'real' underlying and relatively fixed structures that 'cause', shape or at least mediate behaviour; and phenomenological or interpretivist approaches which seek to locate the meaning of behaviour solely in the lived experience of individual actors.

There are perhaps three main schools of post-structuralist enquiry, drawing respectively on Derrida's deconstruction, Foucauldian archaeology of knowledge, and Baudrillard's accounts of hyperreality (Andrews 2000). Derrida's approach employing deconstruction as a method, is a 'parasitic' approach insofar as the deconstruction of the 'colonised' text aims to expose and undermine the oppositions and paradoxes on which such 'texts', including political or social programmes, are constructed. While it offers potentially interesting insights into the construction of Olympic ideology, it has been little exploited in the sports literature. Similarly Baudrillard's work has been less evident in commentary on sport with a few notable exceptions relating predominantly to media analysis (Andrews 1998; Helstein 2005; Silk and Falcous 2005). Foucault's genealogical approach to excavate, or uncover the foundations of, the disciplinary knowledge and institutions of modernity and to note in particular how language operates in the formulation and legitimation of knowledge and thus the instantiation of power, is perhaps the most well developed post-structuralist tradition in the analysis of sport, and is one which we pursue here.

Post-structuralist accounts give primacy to language since our knowledge, whether of 'reality' in the sense of real underlying structures, or of experience in terms of sensory perceptions, can only be gained or expressed via language. Analysis of discourse in the formulation of ideas or conceptions of sport and Olympism is thus very pertinent to the research underpinning this book. In particular Foucauldian approaches have been employed in tracing the roles of discourses in the emergence of new forms of social discipline and in particular of self-regulation, together with structural accounts of the emergence and development of sport, and more specifically Olympism.

1.3   Analysing discourses of Olympism

However, while we look to draw on aspects of each of these four perspectives and their contribution to an understanding of the development of the Olympic movement and its core philosophy, we recognise that these differing types of perspective have different ontological and epistemological domain assumptions. Dependency theory, for example, is seen by many commentators as structuralist with a form of economic determinism built into its assumptions. Modernisation theory also implies a form of techno-economic determinism of cultural outcomes. Globalisation theories incorporate a wide range of approaches, and we should note in particular how some place emphasis on mono and multicausal accounts of global phenomena (globalisation as outcome), while others treat globalisation in itself as a causal factor for other phenomena (globalisation as cause). Thus different accounts imply a world view which is markedly different from that of the post-structuralist. As Hargreaves (2002: 37) argues:

> For [postructuralists], knowledge and truth claims are social constructions, ... so there is a contradiction here between the economic determinism and scientific pretensions of dependency theory, and the ostensible indeterminacy of postmodernism and of Foucault's poststructuralist variant of it.

However, despite Hargreaves' reservations about the compatibility of post-structuralist and structuralist accounts, we wish to underline our claim that analysis of discourse can inform an evaluation of all four approaches, though the ontological significance of the discourse itself, and the epistemological status of discourse analysis is usually viewed very differently by the different perspectives. For advocates of modernisation, neo-Marxist, or globalisation perspectives, language is normally regarded as a reflection of 'reality'. Thus discourse around Olympism will highlight the relationship between Olympism and rationalisation, or dependency, or global-local configurations etc. In the case of post-structuralist accounts, however, discourse is seen as not simply reflecting but rather also as producing reality(ies), and meanings, and thereby relations of power. Language defines the nature of Olympism and thus legitimates social action and relations between those who shape these normative conventions implied by Olympism, and whose life experiences (in sport and wider domains) may be shaped by such conventions. This is achieved most powerfully when these conventions/discourses are internalised and social action is thereby internally regulated in what Foucault terms 'governmentality' (Foucault 1991). Our emphasis is thus on how language constructs reality(ies), and how these realities are formed from assumptions which may be embedded in modernisation, neo-Marxist, or globalisation perspectives and phenomena. In other words we are less concerned with establishing whether modernisation, neo-Marxist or globalisation theories offer better accounts than we are with establishing the extent to which particular discourses of Olympism draw on or reinforce, modernisation, neo-Marxist or globalisation perspectives and explanations.

1.4   Critical discourse analysis as a methodological approach

In the literature a key distinction is made between **power over discourse** (evident in issues such as who can effectively lay claim to legitimacy and authority – in our case in speaking about Olympism – and who, by contrast, represents minority interests, the weaker or the unheard voice); and **power in or of discourse** (how particular discourses of Olympism define, promote or exclude particular forms of behaviour). Our concern in this book is with both of these elements, and each of the theoretical traditions represents a different 'take' on these two dimensions.

To some degree, we have made certain decisions about who exercises power over discourse by selecting our sources, Coubertin, Diem, the IOA speakers and so on. However the discussion of the critics of these sources also implies a consideration of oppositional voices and their efficacy. In terms of power in discourse we can refer to Link's (1982) formulation of discourse as 'an institutionalised way of talking that regulates and reinforces action and thereby exerts power' (quotation translated and cited by Jäger and Maier 2009: 35). As we shall see in subsequent chapters, discourse around Olympism was clearly intended by many to foster or produce certain forms of behaviour in an overtly ideological fashion. Moreover it has also shaped in a more subtle fashion, ways in which sport has impinged on our world view, in for example, moral terms (what constitutes fair play), social terms (aspects of gender and sexuality), or in physical terms (the bodies to which we aspire). Sport has a fairly obvious moral connotation (it implies playing in the context of, if not always by, the rules) but the use of the adjective 'Olympic' provides a prism through which the moral dimension of sport is magnified.

How then is this notion of Olympism produced whether in processes that are, or can be, characterised as modernisation, dependency, globalisation, or as a process of internalised control (i.e. the development of what Foucault terms governmentality)? In the development of Olympism what kinds of ethical standpoints are presented? Whose interests are promoted by such world views? These are issues which will be central to our analysis of Olympic texts, and which can be addressed by adapting Jäger and Maier's (2009) core questions to an analysis of Olympism:

- What constitutes valid knowledge of Olympism at certain places and times?
- How does this knowledge of Olympism and things Olympic arise and how is it passed on? What discursive and non-discursive practices promote such world views? How are such discursive constructions manifest in materialisation of the discourse (e.g. the Olympic stadium)?
- What functions does Olympic discourse have for constituting subjects? What does the discourse tell us about/how does it constitute, the athlete, the fan, the sponsor, the educator etc.? How does it constitute particular historical figures (Coubertin, Diem, Samaranch etc)?
- What consequences does it have for the overall shaping and development of society? Whose interests are promoted by the discourse and what implications does the discourse have for the power of the various parties in wider society beyond the sport domain?

The analysis of the construction of discourse is not necessarily limited to the analysis of texts per se but can also take on two other elements which contribute to the discourse or our understanding of it. These are non-discursive practices, behaviour rather than text (e.g. how the Olympic educator goes about preparing and delivering material, or how the Olympic architect goes about designing an Olympic stadium), and materialisations (material products of non-discursive practices such as the Olympic stadium). This triangular relationship between discursive and non-discursive practices and materialisations connects symbolic and material reality and the connections between them are referred to in Foucault's terms as 'dispositive'. The Bird's Nest and Water Cube as iconic constructions for the Beijing Games of 2008 were intended to convey meanings relating to the arrival of China as a 'super power' not simply in military, but also in cultural and economic terms. The 'no expense spared' approach to the Games and for example its Opening Ceremony linked the great Chinese historical civilisational achievements of the past with the contemporary power of China as potentially the leading nation of the twenty-first century.

Foucault is subjected to criticism in relation to this separation of the material and the symbolic since we can only experience the material through a system of meanings. If we don't recognise a material object then that means we do not have the symbolic means to represent it. Similarly knowledge of non-discursive practices can only be expressed by symbolic means. In other words we can only represent the non-discursive and material through the discourse (of the researcher or of the researched).

For many post-structuralists 'reality' is only defined, or given substance through language. Indeed one can only talk about reality if one has a language to do so (and this implies a language community with which to engage). In effect, describing the physical world in discursive terms gives that world its reality. Thus, to use an example we have employed elsewhere, describing physical phenomena in scientific language develops a 'real' world in which for example the laws of interplanetary motion are what explain the rising and setting of the sun each day. This is a different 'reality' to that which adherents to a 'primitive' religion might experience given a belief that the gods throw the sun over the horizon every day and catch it on the other side of the world each night, and will continue to do so as long as they are appeased. The post-structuralist's concern is not with deciding between the truth value of such systems but rather the underlying conditions of truth within discursive systems. She/he looks to establish the discursive and practical conditions for the establishing of truth (and meaning) within a given discourse.

As we have noted, core to Michel Foucault's thought is the relationship between language and power. To refer back to our previous example, the account of the rising of the sun with reference to laws of interplanetary motion empowers the scientist, defining her as the holder of key knowledge. The account of sunrise by reference to the actions of the gods empowers the priest whose knowledge on how to appease the gods is critically important. In other words no account, no discourse, is neutral in terms of its implications for/instantiation of power.

1.5 Discourse analysis and the evolution of Olympism

It might be assumed that the nature of discourse analytic approaches, and in particular their ontological assumptions which are generally constructivist, militate against any meaningful conversation between this and the three other perspectives. This may indeed be the case for extreme social constructivist positions which deny the possibility of distinguishing between the truth claims of different accounts, or even the possibility of distinguishing between better and worse explanations of social phenomena. However, as critical realists suggest, constructivism and realism are not mutually exclusive (Archer 1995; Bhaskar 1989; Sayer 2000). Social structures may be socially constructed but they also exist independent of individuals and their knowledge of such structures. The strategy of searching for real structures and their relationship to social practices is one which can be common to all four perspectives. Thus though the adoption of a critical realist ontology and related epistemological strategies is not necessarily always associated with the application of critical discourse analysis, we concur with the line taken by Fairclough (2005) that critical discourse analysis is most usefully combined with a realist and constructivist ontology. This implies that the study of Olympism is not reduced solely to a study of discourse but is rather analysis of the relationship between social practices (including discursive practices) and social structures. Such social practices will include the speeches and writings, but also the production of other material forms of action, of key actors. As Fairclough (2005: 924) points out:

> ... a critical realistic discourse analysis is not merely concerned with languages and orders of discourse, it is equally concerned with texts as (elements of) processes, and with the relations of tension between the two.

> Realist discourse analysis ... is based in a dialectical-relational social ontology which sees objects, entities, persons, discourses, organisations etc. as socially produced 'permanences' which arise out of processes and relations ... and which constitute a pre-structured reality with which we are confronted ... . The concern in research is with the relationship and tension between pre-constructed social structures, practices, identities, orders of discourse, organisations on the one hand, and processes, actions, events on the other. People with their capacities for agency are seen as socially produced, contingent and subject to change, yet real, and

possessing real causal powers which, in their tension with the causal powers of social structures and practices, are a focus for analysis.

The 'pre-constructed social structures, practices, identities, orders of discourse, organisations, ... and the processes, actions, and its events' with which we are concerned occur at both global and local levels given the international nature of the Olympic movement, its class and gender make-up. In developing an account of how new discourses on Olympism emerge, how certain among them establish a hegemonic position, influencing through dissemination, or being influenced by, bodies other than the IOC itself, and spreading beyond national boundaries, inculcating (new or established) ways of behaving, one has to reach beyond the discourse per se.

The structure of this book reflects the critical realist approach to discourse analysis described above. The next chapter for example provides an analysis of the material (political, social, and economic) conditions under which Olympism and the Olympic movement have developed. This is followed by three chapters which provide a critical description of the ideas expressed in the writings (and recorded speeches) of three sets of writers across the late nineteenth and the whole of the twentieth century, namely Coubertin, Diem and the IOA guest speakers and writers. The final chapter goes beyond a concern with analysis of discourse at the level of the individual actor or groups of actors, to the identification of the dominant themes in contemporary discourses more generally on Olympism. In particular it seeks to identify the extent to which such discourses represent continuity or change in relation to the evolving discourses of the earlier period. Sport has travelled a long way since the early stages of the modern era and the Olympic movement has had to show great adaptability to maintain its role as the 'moral leader' of the sports movement. The aim of the book is thus in large part to evaluate how Olympism as a 'philosophy' has contributed to and reflected Olympic leadership in the world of sport, and how different discourses have contributed to the reproducing of that leadership.

2
The Discursive Construction of Modern Olympic Histories

2.1 Discourse analysis and approaches to history

The function of this chapter is to provide an overview of the historical context within which the modern Olympic movement has developed, and an evaluation of the nature (and of the different descriptions and explanations, or different histories) of what changes took place within the movement itself. Such an exercise involves drawing on competing historical discourses. Of course given the approach we have adopted in this book we do not simply draw on neutral accounts of historical fact. In a Foucauldian understanding of discourse, representation and meaning as well as knowledge and 'truth' are historicised. Claims about specific phenomena are given a specific meaning and are 'true' only within a specific historical context, or more accurately within particular discursive constructions of a particular period. Olympism is thus not a neutral phenomenon with a common meaning for all. It was only within a particular set of discursive formations that the object, 'Olympism', could develop as a meaningful construct. Olympism in that sense, like all social phenomena is 'constituted by all that was said, in all the statements that named it, divided up, described it, explained it, traced its development, indicated its various correlations, judged it, and possibly gave it speech by articulating, in its name, discourses that were to be taken as its own' (Foucault 1972: 32). But 'Olympism' is also part of a system of symbolic representation which gives meaning to other related phenomena (e.g. the athlete, the fan, the Olympic educator, the sponsor). Although there may be, at particular historical junctures, a dominant discourse of what constitutes Olympism it is important to note two things: first that there will be competing or contested discourses (and thus in this chapter we will be considering contested accounts of events in the Olympic world and/or their significance); and second that strands of discourse will draw on and contribute to overarching societal discourse(s) and thus that histories of the Olympic movement are bound up with societal discourses about wider concerns such as gender, class, ethnicity and national identity, commercialisation and commodification. In this chapter we trace the developing and intertwined nature of these discourse strands.

Of course meanings of Olympism or related phenomena do not remain static over time. The strands of discourse we will trace are not all continuous, and indeed breaks in such strands may be regarded as more significant than continuities in that they signal and explain change. However, to identify such ruptures and/or continuities it is necessary to examine and analyse them over longer periods of time (Jäger and Maier 2009). The chapter therefore covers a period of over 100 years from the inception of the modern Olympic movement allowing for the identification of emerging, growing and discontinued discourse strands.

2.2   Ethical, ontological and epistemological concerns in Olympic historiography

In order to make explicit the nature of our own historical account we undertake two preliminary tasks. The first is primarily ethical, addressing the issue of our view of the values associated with the Olympic phenomenon. The second is epistemological and ontological, indicating how we have constructed our own historical account and its relationship to competing histories.

In relation to the first of these issues we will draw on a simple typology of Olympic studies. Critics have tended to characterise literature on Olympic studies as falling predominantly into one of three categories. The first is that of Olympic apologist: these are commentators who take a generally positive, and sometimes uncritical line on the contribution of Olympic sport to community welfare. Such accounts are often associated with a conservative world view, and one which is unquestioningly western-centric. Examples of this type of work might be Lucas (1992) or Espy (1979). It is not that these authors do not identify difficulties and even crises for the Olympic movement, but that the crises are conceived and evaluated in ways which fall back on a conservative set of concerns such as maintaining the 'purity' of sport.

At the other end of the spectrum is the critic whose work treats Olympic phenomena as irredeemably flawed. Helen Lenskyj's (2000, 2002, 2008) perceptive analysis, or the work of the French Marxist Jean-Marie Brohm (1978) would provide examples here. For these writers there would seem to be no conditions under which support for the Olympic movement or for the staging of the Games could be elicited.

Hoberman (1995: 2) argues in relation to this:

> Historical interpretations of the Olympic movement have generally taken the form of 'either hagiographies or hagiolatries' (quoting MacAloon 1986). [...] Due at least in part to the impassioned and seemingly endless debate between the defenders and detractors of Olympism, with its pronounced

emphasis on ethical values at the expense of historical factors, serious study of the Olympic movement has stagnated.

Between these extremes lies work for which the question of whether the Olympic movement or the philosophy of Olympism represents a positive social element remains a *contingent* issue. Our own approach seeks to occupy this middle ground. Our approach shares with *critical* discourse analysis an emancipatory concern (Fairclough 2005) to highlight the ways in which discourse about Olympism may be linked to the promotion or subordination of sets of interests (e.g. of women, of the West, of humanist principles). We recognise the need to consider the extent to which meaning systems generate positive or negative life chances for particular individuals or social groups at given times, and we therefore argue that the issue of whether Olympism is a progressive or regressive influence at different points in the lives of particular groups is a *contingent* matter to be considered in the light of the dialectical relationship between discourse and other social practices.

The second of the issues we raise relates to epistemological and ontological dimensions of the nature of the historical analysis we adopt. As we have suggested we would wish to distance our approach from one which would emphasise a search for 'neutral' and 'objective' facts, since we would want to argue that histories themselves are discursively constructed. However we would also wish to avoid the dangers of relativism associated for example with some post-modern epistemologies, which can give way to the claim that any account is as valid as any other. We therefore make explicit our approach to historical analysis by reference to Booth's (2004: 13) account (which draws on a typology by Munslow 1997) of three basic models of historical inquiry: reconstruction, construction and deconstruction. The approach of reconstruction is one which seeks to reconstruct the 'real' story of the past based on 'facts' garnered from empirical analysis. In stark contrast, deconstructionists argue that empirical methods cannot provide objective representations of the past. Instead, they perceive history 'as a constitutive narrative' that lacks 'moral and intellectual certainty' (Munslow 1997: 14–15). Hence, they argue that historical understanding implies relativism and believe that there is no single 'real' interpretation of history. The primary concern of deconstructionists is thus simply to unpick the interests which are 'written' or 'sewn' into particular historical accounts. Thus reconstruction and deconstruction offer positivist and post-structural/post-modern epistemologies and realist/foundational and idealist/anti-foundational ontologies respectively.

However if reconstructionists are arguing in effect that 'there is a real world and here is how our empirical evidence helps piece together what the real structures of the historical world are/were'; and deconstructionists are arguing that 'there is *no* privileged account of what historical reality is/was, but simply a set of explanations of relative perspectives on reality that can be subject to deconstruction', the third position of historical construction adopts the argument that to engage in discussion of historical reality the participating parties have to agree on what aspects of a phenomenon it will be important to consider, and what will count as evidence, to support or challenge particular accounts or theoretical frameworks. Thus the constructionist's claim is not that 'my account is objectively and universally true' (reconstructionist), or that 'no "true" account can be developed since all accounts are relative' (the deconstructionist) but rather that 'given the particular theoretically derived premises of my argument, my account is the best available'. This notion of implicit or explicit consensus being required to derive explanation is not as unusual as it might first seem, since for two parties to talk meaningfully to one another at all about any matter whether it is historical interpretation or the price of beans there has to be a tacit shared assumption about the meaning system of the language (in our case English) which is employed, and where there are technical issues to consider (for example what one of the speakers means by the concept of 'price', or the type of bean) then definitions will have to be explicit and generally agreed for meaningful dialogue to take place.

Both reconstructionists and constructionists employ empirical methods and accept historical 'evidence' as building blocks from which they can retrieve or construct the past. A major difference between them is the extent to which they employ *a priori* knowledge from theories and concepts of others, using it as a tool for their interpretation and explanation of relationships between events. Although constructionists accept that the theoretical accounts of others can prove instructive to their understanding of the past, reconstructionists regard such a prospect as contamination.

Approaches relating to reconstruction and construction, seem to dominate Olympic history, and Olympic historians seem to have been sceptical about using deconstructionism, being perhaps reluctant about the validity of non-empirically-based historical evidence. Indeed Booth cites as one of the few Olympic history texts to adopt a deconstructionist approach Douglas Brown's (2001) discourse analysis of Coubertin's *Revue Olympique*. Boulogne (2000) exemplifies a reconstructionist approach in his polemic against ideological involvement in the historical text. Since reconstructionists argue that history exists independently of the historian and they believe they can recover the past with objectivity and without ideological bias, they present history using narrative as a medium, and seek to exclude 'ideological' commentary in historical accounts because they argue that this leads to historical distortion and contaminates historical evidence through the subjectivity of authors. Boulogne (2000), for example, argues that 'feminist leagues', 'radical political groups' and the 'sporting-counter-society' selectively ignore evidence from the historical texts of Pierre de Coubertin, attaching their own ideological perspectives. MacAloon (1981) also reflects the reconstructionist concern to minimise the adoption of *a priori* knowledge from theoretical traditions. He makes it clear that where concepts are borrowed from cultural theory, sociology and psychology, they are 'strategic resources' due to the 'absence' of primary sources (MacAloon 1981: xiii–xvii).

Booth (2004) claims that while most Olympic historians are reconstructionists, they nevertheless adopt concepts outside the field and appropriate them to their study without constructing, testing or confirming formal theories of the modern Olympics or Olympism.[1] The majority of Olympic historians in fact utilise 'organising concepts' which guide their interpretations of the evidence provided. Most common concepts in Olympic history are: classes of objects (e.g. amateur sports, women's sports), general notions (amateurism, professionalisation, commercialisation), themes (nationalism, internationalism), and periods (e.g. age of fascism, post-colonialism, Cold War) and groupings of inter-linked characteristics (e.g. modernity, imperialism, globalisation).

Guttmann (1992), in his book *The Olympics*, seeks to understand the Olympic movement within the context of twentieth-century nationalism and international politics. Guttmann adopts the contextual model developed by Marwick (1998) comprising four principal components: a) major forces and constraints (i.e. structural – geographical, demographic, economic and technological; ideological – existing political and social philosophies; institutional – systems of government, organisations), b) events (First World War, Second World War), c) human agency (politicians, key agents of the Olympic movement), d) convergences and contingencies (interaction between agencies and structures leading to unforeseen events and situations). Ideological forces such as nationalism and fascism, the Cold War and decolonisation are all examined in relation to their impact on the Olympics and the Olympic movement. Human agents, particularly Coubertin, Brundage and Samaranch, and their contribution are also considered in his analysis. Moreover, interrelationships between events and human agencies are also examined as generators of unforeseen circumstances (the end of the Cold War, the success of the 1984 Los Angeles Olympics and a new President initiating a renewed interest in the Olympics). However, although Guttmann (1992) takes into account more complex processes, such as the interrelationship between structures and human agency, in order to increase the validity of his historical account, it is nevertheless the case that this is *his* selection of which forces, which events, which agents, or which convergences to privilege in his analysis. Thus a truly theory-neutral account in the reconstructionist vein is simply not feasible, and historians, bring the biases and judgements of their own discourses when reporting Olympic history, which constructionist versions of history acknowledge. What follows then is our constructionist account of the history of Olympism across the period of the modern Games.

2.3   Chronology of Olympic history: Different approaches

Al-Tauqi (2003) has remarked that researchers who examine changes in the global order employ historical structural methods in order to organise the material in such a way that facilitates the process of investigation. Different researchers have divided world history into slightly different eras depending on the needs of their research focus. Huntington (1996) divides world history into three political spheres: the imperialist period (1500 to the 1920s), the Cold War period (1920–1980s) and the post-Cold War period (1990s to the present). A major limitation of Huntington's (1996) work or at least the way in which it has sometimes been used by neo-conservative interests is its deterministic approach to understanding global change, attributing absolute power to the West as the key determinant of the progression or regression of civilisations. His analysis starts from 'one world' in the 1920s to 'three worlds' of the 1960s and multiple worlds after the 1990s ignoring many variations and dimensions that exist in between (Al-Tauqi 2003). Hoogvelt (1997), in order to examine issues related to the development and capitalist expansion of 'Third World' countries, divides world history into four periods: the 'mercantile phase' (1500–1800), the colonial period (1800–1950s), the neo-colonial phase (from 1950 to 1970s), and the post-colonial phase (1970s to present).

In similar manner, but with slight variations, Maguire's (1999) division of history in order to explain the global diffusion of modern sport adopts Robertson's (1992) model of the globalisation process. Maguire outlines five phases that constitute the 'sportisation process': the initial phase from 1500–1850 when people started to understand the notions of 'humanity' and 'individual' and the early scientific discoveries emerged; the second phase from 1850 to the 1870s where homogenous states started to form and sport became part of them; the third phase ('take-off') from the 1870s to 1920, where globalisation gained momentum and international sport started to develop; the fourth phase (the 'struggle for hegemony') from the 1920s to 1980s where the Cold War and the politics of the opposing ideologies influenced the global politics and the modern sport profile; the fifth and last phase ('the uncertainty phase') in the post-1990s and post-Cold War period where global interconnection increased, different ethnic and cultural identities gained prominence and problems of fragmentation and isolation became central.

Roche (2000) in his account of the history of the Modern Games as a mega-event with global scope also characterises the historical context as falling into four different chronological periods: a period of imperialist politics during the colonial period from 1850s to the 1920s; the inter-war period and the rise of nationalisms ('supernationalisms') from the 1920s to 1945 which witnessed the emergence of ideological absolutisms and the authoritarian regimes of Fascism and Nazism; the political struggle of the Cold War and the competing ideologies of communism and capitalism in the period between 1945 and the late 1980s; and finally the period after the 1990s which he characterises as the rise of globalisation, the dominance of capitalism and the growing ideology of consumerism.

Many researchers, who examine the Olympic movement and the meaning of Olympism, focus on Ancient Greece and the ancient Olympics. Toohey and Veal (2000) divide the modern era and the imperialist era of the late nineteenth and early twentieth centuries; the rise of nationalisms and the emergence of authoritarian regimes in the period after 1920s; the Cold War period and the influence of the two opposing ideologies in the Olympic Games with the new practices of commercialism, professionalism and doping; and the period after the end of the Cold War with the highly competitive ethos of the Games, high profits and the growth in scale of the event across the globe.

Additionally, most studies focusing on Olympism or the Olympic movement make special reference to the period of the early nineteenth century as a highly significant period, providing a starting point for Olympic philosophy in the modern era (Guttmann 1992; Hill 1992; Hoberman 1995; Lucas 1980; Riordan and Krüger 1999; Schaffer and Smith 2000; Schaffer *et al.* 1993; Segrave and Chu 1981; Segrave and Chu 1988; Toohey and Veal 2000). Guttmann (1992), reviewing the history of the modern Olympic movement, focuses on the following historical periods: the years of education and personal development of Baron Pierre de Coubertin with the emergence of the idea of revival of the modern Olympics (1863–1896); the early years of struggle and success of the Olympic movement (1897–1914); the period when the Olympic Games are threatened by the First World War but reach maturity (1914–1932); the period when the emergence of authoritarian regimes have a strong impact on the Olympic movement and the Olympics are hosted in Berlin 1936 ('the most controversial Olympics'); the destruction and recovery of the Olympic movement during and immediately following the Second World War years (1940–1949); the Olympic movement in the shadow of the Cold War (1949–1955); the era of (relatively) good relations (1955–1960); a period of organisational strains (1960–1970s); the troubles of the post-colonial period and the recognition of numerous new National Olympic Committees (NOC) by the IOC (1964–1972); the era of boycotts (1972–1984); and lastly the period post-1988 and the beginning of the post-Cold War era.

Despite the differences in chronology among the different researchers, most approaches identify a similar set of major changes and, according to the purposes of the writer's research, emphasise subsequent trends and flows. In our own account which follows below, we recognise the importance of dividing the development of the Olympic movement into historical periods which have played a significant role in producing forms of knowledge, objects, subjects and practices in the discursive formation of Olympism. First, Olympism as an idea in its modern form takes shape in late nineteenth-century Europe, an important period for the emergence and formation of modern sport culture (with rational recreation and the undermining of forms of traditional popular culture, the establishment of the modern Olympic Games, the foundation of sport federations, associations and clubs, and the inauguration of

Tour de France) (Hoberman 1995; Roche 2000). Subsequently the impact of western imperialism and European colonial control on the Olympic movement is discussed. The role of Baron Pierre de Coubertin as an individual who was able to exercise considerable personal power and influence in his successful endeavour to revive the modern Olympic Games is also highlighted and historical accounts of the early Olympic Games are provided. Second, the late imperialist era and the inter-war period are reviewed, focusing on the consequences of the First World War upon the Olympic movement. Counter currents and resistance against the bourgeois Olympics are also examined, as expressed through the organisation of alternative Games, such as the Workers' Olympics and Women's World Games, and the use of sport as a tool of foreign policy, especially after the emergence of authoritarian regimes. The penultimate section deals with the era of post-colonialism and the ideological conflicts in the Olympic domain during the Cold War period. The rejection by the IOC of political engagement in, or by, the sports world and the paradoxical political significance of the IOC gained through the recognition of NOCs are discussed. The decolonisation process and the use of sport as a binding force of national identity are also examined. Finally, the last section is centred on the post-Cold War era and the consequences of the collapse of the Soviet bloc and the re-making of the world order. The global discourse and the different interpretations of the new global order are provided, and the role of the contemporary 'global' Olympic movement examined.

2.4   Imperialism and the Olympic movement

Many cultural and social analysts attribute a high degree of importance to the late nineteenth century (*fin de siècle, belle époque*) in the formation of the popular culture of western modernity. A number of significant cultural events took place especially in Britain, France, Germany and the United States. Hobsbawm (1992) uses the concept 'invented traditions' to describe the newly emerged cultural manifestations, seeing them as tools used by the middle and upper middle classes to generate consent to their control of the working class.

> To establish the clustering of 'invented traditions' in western countries between 1870 and 1914 is relatively easy. Examples include 'old school ties and jubilees, Bastille Day and the Daughters of the American Revolution, May Day, the Internationale and the Olympic Games, ... the Cup Final and Tour de France as popular rites, and the institution of flag worship in USA. (Hobsbawm 1992: 303)

Hobsbawm's approach to public culture is related to sociological concerns about the nature of western modernity and social dynamics in this period, drawing arguments from neo-Marxist analysis of capitalist dynamics and class struggle. As part of his analysis, he examines the different cultural policies that France and the Third Republic initiated, in an effort to re-establish good relations with its citizens after the loss of the Franco-Prussian War (1870). These policies included the secularisation of education placing emphasis on republican values, and the mass production of public monuments (the female figure 'Marianne', as symbol of French Revolution, the Eiffel Tower, as symbol of technical progress, and the Statue of Liberty, donated to the American republic in 1886). Moreover, there was a growing interest in international expos and thus the Third Republic was responsible for three of the most important of the late nineteenth-century series of International Expositions, namely those staged in Paris in 1878, 1889 and 1900 (Roche 2000). Hobsbawm's analysis of invented traditions provides a comparative account which draws on a number of countries. However, although his approach does allude to some international dimensions, he is mainly concerned with national class relations, and provides limited information about the development of international public culture.

Roche's (2000) approach takes into account international relations and movements, providing a wider picture of international public culture. He argues that the national expos in France in the 1840s and the first international expo in London in 1851 had imperial themes. Britain, through the expos, was demonstrating its industrial and imperial power by displaying its technological and scientific achievements. Late nineteenth imperial expos involved grand parades and impressive spectacles to celebrate the wealth and power of the imperial hosts. Empire had thus been a foundational theme in the approach of Britain and France to the early international expos of the 1850s and 1860s. It rapidly increased in importance as a theme in the expos of the 1880s and 1890s and thereafter, connected with the European nations' 'scramble for Africa' and America's push to extend its influence in the Pacific via Hawaii and the Philippines (Roche 2000: 23).

Apart from international expos, sport events were also organised to generate political benefits. In 1859 and 1870, sport festivals, 'similar' to the Ancient Greek Olympic Games, were held in Greece. Greece owed the staging of these Games to Evangelios Zappas, a rich merchant of Greek origin living in Romania who was passionate about. Inspired by a lecture by the German archaeologist Ernst Curtius delivered on 10 January 1852 arguing that the Games should be revived, Zappas wanted to see Greece regaining its leading position in the western cultural world (Hill 1992). He sought to convince King Otto I that an Olympic contest should be held to reinforce the political image of Greece in the modern world. Since it was entirely financed by Zappas, Otto agreed and in 1858 Zappas gave money to the Greek government to establish an Olympic Trust Fund whose purpose was to organise competitions at four-year intervals. The first festival took place in Athens in 1859 and included a combination of arts, exhibition and athletic events. The second festival, held in 1870, had a similar programme but took place on a site outside Athens which had been acquired by the Fund (Hill 1992). The 1875 and 1889 Games were also held in Greece but are considered by historians to have been less significant.

The English also attempted to revive the ancient Olympics, when in 1849 Dr. W. P. Brookes instituted the *Olympian Games* near Much Wenlock in Shropshire. Brookes had access to leading figures in the country, and through his contacts, obtained 725 subscriptions for the forerunner of the Olympian Society, the Agricultural Reading Society (founded in 1841). It was actually intended for all classes – though there is no record of who actually had access to the library – but one of the main reasons for encouraging people to read was to help them decide how to vote after the extension of the franchise in the Reform Act of 1832 (Hill 1992). Brookes had a passionate interest in physical education in state schools and he found it unacceptable that farm workers, for example, should have compulsory drawing lessons but no physical training; thus, he used the Wenclock Olympian Society as a vehicle through which he would be able to propagate his views. In 1891, the Australian John Astley Cooper proposed a Pan-Britannic and Anglo-Saxon Festival to which athletes from the United States and the British Empire would be invited. Sports would be the means for them to demonstrate Anglo-Saxon superiority and friendship (Guttmann 1992; Hill 1992; Riordan and Krüger 1999).

Nonetheless, the person viewed as responsible for the most successful revival of the ancient Olympic Games was the Frenchman, Baron Pierre de Coubertin. There was a dispute about who should actually be regarded as responsible for the proposal to revive the Ancient Olympic Games. Young (1984; cited in Hill 1992: 16) emphasises that Coubertin 'feigned amnesia about these earlier Games' and, for that reason, the Greek press regarded him as a 'thief' when he claimed the credit for reviving them (Guttmann 1992). Coubertin countered this argument by emphasising that his own project was different, because it was international and not limited to drawing athletes from the Greek world. However, this argument failed to persuade his rivals and those who were suspicious of his plans and ambitions.

2.4.1   Baron Pierre de Coubertin

Coubertin, like many other Frenchmen, wanted to avenge France's defeat and the loss of its provinces of Alsace and Lorraine in the Franco-Prussian war. As a descendant of an aristocratic family, Coubertin might have felt a special responsibility 'to seek *revanche* for the debacle at Sedan' (Guttmann 1992: 8). As with many young aristocrats, Coubertin initially considered a military career. However, after spending some time at the French military academy St. Cyr, he was persuaded that becoming a soldier would not suit him. He subsequently decided to attend classes at the *École Libre des Sciences Politiques*, where the social theories of Fréderic Le Play attracted his attention (Guttmann 1992: 8). In 1883, he joined the *Unions de la Paix*, founded by Le Play, and he wrote a number of essays that were published in Le

Play's journal *La Reforme Sociale*. Although Coubertin studied history, literature, education, sociology and many other subjects, he focused his attention
on education, and in particular on sports education (*pédagogie sportive*) (Hill
1992). Coubertin thought that the defeat in the Franco-Prussian war was a
result, not of the lack of military skills of Napoleon III, but of the physical
inferiority of the average French youth.

In the early years of the nineteenth century, at a time when Napoleon I
had occupied much of Germany, Friedrich Ludwig Jahn had developed a form
of gymnastics underpinned by a strong nationalistic ideology, the 'Turnen'.
Jahn added a patriotic motive to what German educators had developed
at the end of the eighteenth century: to unify the divided German Volk and
to eject the hated Napoleonic invaders from German soil (Hobsbawm 1992).
Turnen became the basis of physical education in German public schools, as
well as the dominant sport in private clubs and sports associations (Guttmann
1992). Coubertin suspected that German soldiers were much fitter than the
French, and that if the latter wished to confront the Germans successfully,
they had to improve their physical capacities. He therefore concluded that the
solution was a sport-based educational reform (Müller 2000), unlike his contemporaries who suggested reform based on educational theory (Hoberman
1995).

Accordingly, Coubertin travelled to Germany, England, the United States
and Canada to inspect the leading approaches to education adopted in
those countries (Kidd 1996). While studying the German approach, he concluded that there were probably better paths to physical development than
the rigid routines of German physical education (Guttmann 1992). In the
United States and Canada, he visited in 1889 the early programmes of intercollegiate athletics, and he was impressed by the excellent facilities that the
colleges and universities had made available to their students. In *Universités
Transatlantiques* (Coubertin 1890a), he wrote enthusiastically of what he had
seen (Guttmann 1992); but still he had not found something that impressed
him sufficiently to advocate its implementation in the French context (Kidd
1996). Therefore, Coubertin travelled to England, knowing that the English
were passionate about sport, as at Eton, Harrow, Winchester and the rest of
the Public Schools, boys engaged in daily practice in activities such as rowing,
running, jumping and ball games (Hoberman 1995).

Coubertin's enthusiasm for English sports education escalated, when, in
1875, he read a French translation of *Tom Brown's School Days* novel in which
Thomas Hughes romanticised his memories of Rugby School (Hughes 1857,
1999). In his study *L'Éducation en Angleterre* (Coubertin 1887, 2000), Coubertin,
at the age of twenty-five, wrote of Arnold, that he 'could not have been English
if he had not loved sport' (Guttmann 1992: 9). Nonetheless, Guttmann (1992)
and Hoberman (1995) argue that Coubertin was misled by Hughes to believe
that Thomas Arnold had been a fervent advocate of sports. In fact, Arnold,
headmaster of Rugby School from 1828 to 1842 (Hill 1992), was far more

interested in boys' moral education than in their physical development (Guttmann 1992). No matter what the real educational focus of Arnold was, Coubertin admired the combination of physical health and character building that was reflected in the sport of the English youth. After visiting Rugby in 1883, Coubertin was totally convinced that the British approach to sport in education would help to invigorate France (Kidd 1996). In one of his memoirs, *Une Champagne de Vingt-et-un Ans* (Coubertin 1909) Coubertin described his visit to the chapel of the Rugby School as a 'pilgrimage' and Arnold became for him an inspirational figure (Guttmann 1992).

His openness to English and American influences brought Coubertin into conflict with his Anglophobic countrymen (Guttmann 1992). Pascal Grousset, organiser of an extremely nationalistic *Ligue Nationale de l'Éducation Physique*, insisted on having French sports with French names. For instance, when league members showed a big interest on playing *football*, he desperately and persistently wanted to rename the sport *la barrette*. In this climate of disapproval and chauvinism, Coubertin steadily and frequently published papers urging the French to emulate the English, as preparation for avenging the defeat by Prussia (Guttmann 1992). Working closely with educators from progressive schools, such as *L'École Monge and L'École Alsacienne*, he propagandised athleticism, a dominant element in British secondary education. Additionally, Coubertin organised or re-organised a number of sports associations, of which the most important was the *Union des Sociétés Françaises de Sports Athlétiques* (USFSA), which was founded in 1890 by Coubertin and his friend Georges St.-Clair. In a letter from Coubertin to Brookes in July 1892, he indicated that he was using the union as the base for reviving the Games. The union had reached 62 member societies with about 7,000 participants and this made him believe that the revival of the Ancient Olympic Games was close. His studies of classical history, as well as his experiences from travelling in different domains comparing educational programmes, had convinced him that 'sport' and 'character' were the ingredients for the successful development of youth. In ancient Greece this combination was said to have been achieved, through a 'triple unity' in Athens gymnasia: between old and young, between different disciplines, and between people of different types (Hill 1992).

It was not until 1889 that Coubertin decided to try to revive the Games, and thus he devoted the next five years to the preparation of the International Congress of Sportsmen in 1894 (Hill 1992). A number of scholars (Hoberman 1986; Kidd 1996; MacAloon 1996a) argue that Coubertin's revival of the Olympic Games aimed at revitalising French society and reducing the imperialist rivalries of the European powers and the growing likelihood of war, with the possibility of further French defeat. To a certain extent, Coubertin changed the focus of his interests over the years. In his early years, his writings were centred on preserving the equilibrium of 'modern' individuals and societies, whereas by 1931, with the publication of his *Olympic Memoirs*, his focus was more on preserving the influence and autonomy of the IOC. Coubertin, in later life, was keener on the survival of the Olympic movement than in engaging with the 'ideological cleavage of the world' (Hoberman 1986: 33).

Coubertin's revival can be interpreted as representing both his nationalist and internationalist tendencies; being traumatised by the defeat of France in the Franco-Prussian war, Coubertin offered a formula for making French youth more robust, healthy and physically fit. However, Coubertin, as an internationalist, perceived sport as a 'pacifier', a means for enhancing peace in the world and fighting controversy (Hoberman 1986: 34). Toohey and Veal (2000) argue that it would not be an exaggeration to acknowledge Coubertin as the driving force and designer of the modern Olympic Games. Most of his ideas are drawn from what was known about Ancient Greece and how Ancient Greeks defined democracy and their values and principles (Hill 1992). His ideal of Olympism, a synthesis of supposed ancient Greek practices and nineteenth-century British sporting ideas, internationalism and peace, underpinned his revival of the Olympic Games (Toohey and Veal 2000; Parry 1994).

2.4.2   Modern Olympic Games: The revival and the early years

Olympism was 'in the air' during the period of the 1890s (Lucas 1980), but it was not until 1894 that it started to take a more specific definition and form. In 1894, Coubertin arranged an international congress, during which the decision was taken to revive the Olympic Games (Hill 1992). This congress in Paris (1894), although it only resulted in the founding of an Olympic Committee and the drawing up of statutes, counts as the first Olympic Congress (Müller 1994). Coubertin took advantage of the fifth anniversary of the *Union des Sociétés Françaises de Sports Athlétiques* (USFSA), held on November 28, to spread the idea of reviving the Games to a group of French and foreign dignitaries. For the first time, Coubertin could express his project publicly before his acquaintances and colleagues (Boulogne 1999a). However, there was a considerable array of opposition from the Ministry of education, professional cyclists, weightlifters, oarsmen and football players (Guttmann 1992). Hill argues that 'a man was a fencer or an oarsman or a cyclist, but did not have the Olympic ideal of being simply a sportsman' (Hill 1992: 17). Different sports clubs and associations were autonomous, and inter-connections and collaborations among them were non-existent at that time. Nevertheless, the idea of Olympism had started to be spread among the sport circles and Coubertin was determined to downplay any opposition (Boulogne 1999a).

During 1892 and 1893, Coubertin wanted to increase the public interest in Olympism and, for that reason, he convinced the USFSA (*Union des Sociétés Françaises de Sports Athlétiques*) that a Congress should be held about the issue of amateurism, the focus of significant debate at that time. He never directly advocated the rebirth of the Olympic Games, but his aim was to strengthen USFSA's internal organisation, to broaden its influence in the French provinces and mostly to establish relations with foreign unions, by raising the issue of amateurism (Hill 1992). As part of the effort to make his ideas known,

Coubertin attended Chicago's Columbian Exposition as an official representative of the French Ministry of Education (Guttmann 1992), and then he spent three weeks at Princeton University as a guest of Professor William Milligan Sloane. Coubertin failed to obtain support from any of the American sport administrators and the biggest disappointment came from failing to win the cooperation of the Secretary of the Amateur Athletic Union, James E. Sullivan, with whom he never succeeded in developing a close relationship (Guttmann 1992).

His ideas did not have much appeal in London either (Hill 1992), but the Prince of Wales and Charles Herbert, Secretary of the Amateur Athletic Association for England and its colonies, expressed their support for Coubertin (Guttmann 1992). On August 1, 1893, Coubertin submitted the preparatory programme, which he had drafted by his own hand, entitled 'Paris International Congress for the Study and Propagation of Amateuristic Exercises (Guttmann 1992). However, despite the efforts he made for Germans to join in, Germany did not wish to participate. As a last resort, Coubertin made an appeal in the Berlin newspaper 'Sport' on June 12, 1894, but this had no effect (Boulogne 1999b). The German government opposed the introduction of English sport in its educational and social systems from 1871 up to 1918 when Germany was defeated in the First World War. Germany perceived foreign cultural practices as a threat to its under-developed self-awareness and identity (Merkel 2000). Thus, the English-oriented concept of amateurism found resistance in German sport circles. Additionally, Coubertin's efforts to persuade Germany annoyed the French who threatened to withdraw if the Germans did join (Hill 1992). Joseph Sansbœuf, President of the *Union des Sociétés de Gymnastique*, refused to take part if the German delegates were invited. As it finally turned out, there were no German representatives at the Congress, except Mr. de Reiffenstein, a personal friend of Coubertin.

The gymnastic clubs also created problems because they argued that 'gymnastics' and 'sport' were one and the same, and thus Belgian gymnasts refused to join (Boulogne 1999b). Notwithstanding the problems, approximately 2,000 members of the aristocracy and bourgeois class participated, but Müller (1994: 29) argues, 'apart from the ten members of the Organising Committee, only 37 sport federations were represented by altogether 78 delegates in Paris. Among them were 58 Frenchmen from 24 sports organisations and clubs', and he emphasises that 'foreign participation was limited to 20 delegates from eight countries'. The Cycling Association was the only international sports federation at the Congress.

The programme adopted by the USFSA included eight Articles, six on Amateurism, one on betting and the last on the possibility of re-establishing the Olympic Games (Hill 1992). However, there is a suggestion that Coubertin misled the delegates of the Congress because he informed them at the last minute that the issue of the revival of the Games would also be discussed (Young 1984; cited in Hill 1992: 19). As a result of the Congress, it was decided that the Games should be held every four years and that an International Olympic Committee (IOC) should be established, having full responsibility for preparing and restoring the Olympic Games (Müller 1994). The Congress decided that the members of the International Olympic Committee were to be representatives overseas of Olympism rather than their countries' representatives on the committee. In addition, each country was to establish a National Olympic Committee and the Presidency of the Committee would rotate, passing after each Games to the country which was chosen to host the next Olympics. The first President was Vikelas, a Greek literary historian, the first Olympic Games would be held in Greece. However, after the end of Vikelas' presidency, Coubertin remained the President for 25 years (Hill 1992).

In July 1894, the first Bulletin of the *International Committee for the Olympic Games* was published, the only available document about the election of the International Committee (Müller 1994). Coubertin determined the composition of the governing body and this raised later questions about the democratic nature of the organisation (Brohm 1978; Gruneau 1984; Guttmann 1992; Simson and Jennings 1991). It is noteworthy that most of the members had not even participated in the 1894 Congress; they had only been listed as honorary members of the Congress (Müller 1994). Coubertin remarked: 'I was allowed a free hand in the choice of members of the IOC. Those proposed were selected without any amendment'[2] (Coubertin 1979; cited in Müller 1994: 36). The fact that, the members of the IOC were expected to pay their travel expenses and to contribute financially to the costs of the IOC for promoting Olympism, meant that such an organisation could only function if its members were wealthy and had free time for IOC work (Toohey and Veal 2000). Consequently, wealth and social status, combined with enthusiasm for the rebirth of the Games, were the criteria for choosing the members (Guttmann 1992). The first thirteen members of the Committee were from the leisured classes: the upper and upper-middle classes, the military aristocracy, wealthy tradesmen and diplomats, the so-called 'haute bourgeoisie' (Boulogne 1999a).

Coubertin had planned the first Olympics to be held in Paris in 1900 as part of the World Fair, but Krüger (1999) argues that the Greeks had come to Paris to claim the International Olympic Games as theirs. Finally, a compromise was reached when it was decided that the first Olympic Games should be in Athens in 1896 and the second in Paris in 1900. However, the choice of Athens was unfortunate, as, after a decade of extreme instability from 1869 to 1879, Greece was politically and financially weak (Lucas 1980; Toohey and Veal 2000). For these reasons, the government opposed hosting the event, and the Greek Etienne Dragoumis, a member of the Zappeion Commission, suggested that the Athens Games should be held in 1900, the beginning of a new century and the year of organising the World Exhibition in Paris (Hill 1992). Finally, after several negotiations the Games were held in Athens, although it is argued that they are best remembered merely for the fact that they took place, as sport results were relatively poor by international standards (Krüger 1999).

The Olympic Games in Paris 1900, St. Louis 1904 and London 1908 were held either within or in support of an international expo event (the international world fair) (Roche 2000). Coubertin's love of expos and the lack of a clear French sport identity seem to have been the main reasons for the association of the Olympics with the international world fair. The USFSA, of which Coubertin was Secretary General, opposed his plans and the French government was not enthusiastic about the Olympics in Paris (Guttmann 1992). Coubertin therefore wanted to ensure that the 1900 Olympics would be staged within the context of the *Exposition Universelle*, and thus hopefully would be able to attract international public interest. In effect Coubertin was seeking to ensure that the Olympic strand of discourse was to be sewn into, or intertwined with the global discourse of empire and industry which underpinned the Expo movement. However, the planners of the exposition were not at all eager to be the hosts of the Games (Guttmann 1992). The director of the Expo, Alfred Picard, who disliked sport, placed the Olympic Games as a marginal cultural activity. Coubertin tried unsuccessfully to gain control but with no luck. As a result, the whole programme was stretched out over the full five months of the Expo itself (Roche 2000). In 1904, the Olympic Games were held in St. Louis, after negotiations between Chicago and St. Louis about which city would finally host the event. In 1901 the IOC formally considered bids from Chicago and St. Louis and decided in favour of Chicago. The great American international expo was scheduled for 1903, so there would be no clash of events. However, the St. Louis event was postponed until 1904 due to delays and, therefore, the Chicago committee asked the IOC to transfer the staging of the Olympics to 1905. The situation became more difficult when the St. Louis group pressurised the IOC by suggesting that they would organise an alternative major athletics event if they did not host the Games in 1904. Finally, the IOC asked the US President Theodore Roosevelt to decide and he chose St. Louis. This caused much embarrassment to Coubertin who had promised the Olympics to Chicago and he chose to boycott his own Games deciding instead to attend the annual dramatic festival of Wagner's music at Bayreuth in Germany.

The 1904 Games had a strong nationalistic, American character with only a few Europeans participating. The biggest absentee was Britain, considered one of the world's strongest athletic nations, because the athletics authorities claimed they could not cover the costs of sending a team (Roche 2000). The Americans used the Olympic Games and the status of modern sport as a sign of 'civilisation' and 'progress' and organised two 'anthropology days', in which various 'primitive' non-western peoples were taught and practised western sports. Their relatively poor performances in sports with which they were not familiar were popularly regarded as confirmation of the theory of white superiority (Goksøyr 1991; cited in Krüger 1999: 8).

After the Games in St. Louis, the Olympic movement faced a major crisis and some argued that 'it was close to disaster' (Guttmann 1992: 27). The situation became more difficult when Rome withdrew from hosting the Games in 1906 and the IOC turned to Britain for assistance. The British Olympic Association (BOA) had just been created (in 1905), but the British agreed to host the Games in London in 1908. Krüger (1999: 9) argues, 'the first modern Olympics in our sense of the word are the ones of 1908 in London', with the English Amateur Athletics Association (AAA) supporting to a great extent the organisation of the event. Additionally, the Games were organised with the support of the financiers of the Franco-British exhibition that was held in London the same year. The expo organisers needed a venue for the purposes of the exhibition, and thus agreed to build a stadium that would also accommodate the Olympics. The spectator numbers were initially low, but nationalistic conflicts between the British and American athletes about the rules attracted the interest of the press and increased publicity (Krüger 1999; Roche 2000). Despite the successful collaboration between the expo organisers and the Olympic group in 1908, the two previous 'problematic' cases of Paris and St. Louis were critical in the de-coupling of the Olympic Games from the expos (Roche 2000).

In the 1912 Stockholm Olympics, the IOC and the sports federations were involved in assuring a unification of standards, rules and by-laws, undermining the local organisers. However, they wished to ensure that the arguments from the London Games between the Americans and the English would not be repeated in Sweden. Coubertin also wanted to ensure that the Olympic Games would be held along the lines of the Olympic philosophy for the 'joyous overflow of manly vigour' and not under the Swedish Gymnastics philosophy of health and equilibrium of strength. With his motto *mens fervida in corpore lacertoso* (an overflowing mind in a muscular body), he wanted to emphasise the differences from the *mens sana in corpore sano* of the medical profession (Krüger 1999). The IOC, starting slowly to accept women's sports, decided to include women as swimmers and divers. This meant an increase in the number of female athletes from 36 in 1908 to 57 in 1912 (compared to 2,447 men) (Guttmann 1992). In terms of racial inclusion, Guttmann (1992: 33) emphasises, 'the irrelevance of skin colour was emphasised by the racial composition of the American team, which included an Afro-American, a Hawaiian and two American Indians'. The inclusion of women and the 'racial inclusivity' of the American team, Guttman argues, could be regarded as signs of gradual democratisation.

In these Games, the Swedes were placed first in the list of medals and the British were so embarrassed that measures were taken to improve their performance in 1916 (Krüger 1999). The *Spectator* claimed in its July 20 issue that specialisation 'has gone too far in America … for many months, sometimes even for years, Americans subject themselves to a professional trainer who takes possession of their lives' (cited in Guttmann 1992: 35). As Day

(2011) points out the British also had professional coaches in their entourage for Stockholm, though the athlete-coach relationship in the British case was rather more class-based such that coaches would not control training regimes but would simply advise. The British press made racist references, complaining about the 'Negroes and Indians' who had competed for the United States (Guttmann 1992). The Swedish were desperate to win for a number of reasons; their king was present in the stadium, they wanted to demonstrate the scientific superiority of their gymnastics system, and they had received money from a special lottery to build the stadium. Krüger (1999) argues that the Swedes can be considered as having introduced the phenomenon of the state amateur, recruiting athletes from the army in their national teams. Nevertheless, the Swedish were accepted as amateurs, but the American Indian Jim Thorpe was stripped of his medals, after admitting that he had been paid to play summer professional baseball while still a student at the Carlisle (Pennsylvania) Indian School (Guttmann 1992; Strenk 1981). Guttmann argues that, since the IOC later punished other athletes whose amateur status was questionable, Thorpe's punishment did not indicate racism but rather reflected prejudice in terms of social class.

Although the Olympic movement was ostensibly promoting a message of universalism, peace, equity and human rights, the exclusionary values of the movement were evident. Roche argues that the Games, similar to other expos of this period, were related to classism, racism and sexism: women, working class citizens, and colonies or ethnic groups, were not allowed or were unable to participate.

> Like the Olympics, expos claimed to promote universalistic and humanistic ideals and world-views as well as internationalist and nationalistic ones. They thus appeared to promote notions of identity and inclusion in nation, the international order and the human race. However, in practice these were mainly aimed at a symbolic cultural inclusion of the white male working class who were, on the one hand, being politically empowered by gaining the new powers to vote and to organise trade unions, and on the other hand, were facing the rigours of work and work discipline in rapidly changing, harsh and debilitating industrial and urban environments. (Roche 2000: 73)

The nineteenth-century expo movement was a product of nation-building and economy-building in modernising western societies, and in principle it was positive, heading towards cultural inclusion, peaceful co-existence and representation of different nations (Roche 2000). However, athletes and those from colonised 'nations' were often excluded or only included as representatives of the colonial power; the working class was excluded from the British version of sport and the ideology of amateurism; women were excluded by means of 'pseudo-scientific theories of feminine physical vulnerability'; and blacks and Asians were excluded for reasons of imperialism and racial inferiority (Roche 2000: 72). At the beginning of the twentieth century, these exclusions diffused internationally with the expansion of the western sport culture. European colonial power increased, and the world had become interdependent politically and economically. Notions of civilisation were associated with a western civilisation that was expanding overseas. Europeans controlled 35 per cent of the earth's landmass in 1800, 67 per cent in 1878, and 84 per cent in 1914 (Huntington 1996). The exclusivist character of the Olympic movement was to be challenged in the inter-war period in a number of important ways.

2.5 Late imperialism: The inter-war period 1914–1944

By the summer of 1914, for many the Olympic Games of the Sixth Olympiad in Berlin were anticipated with enthusiasm, but economic and political conflicts, nationalism, and related crises eventually led to the outbreak of the Great War (1914–1918). One of the major political consequences of the war, was that a number of the old empires collapsed and new states were created, mostly in Eastern Europe. Czar Nicolas II of Russia fell in 1917 (Russian October 1917 Revolution), and Kaisar Wilhem II of Germany and the Emperor Charles of Austria-Hungary left their thrones in 1918. The Ottoman Empire was divided and placed under the control of France and Britain (Culpin 1996). Economically, the war brought 'economic depression' in Europe in the late 1920s and 1930s, increasing mass unemployment and poverty. The distinctions between the social classes were diminishing, as the upper class and the elites eventually began to lose their power and privileges. The 'democratic' countries weakened and extremist political parties emerged, promising in particular to deal with growing economic problems. In Germany, the National Socialist (Nazi) Party was strengthened, and in UK both the Communist Party and the British Union of Fascists gained popularity (Culpin 1996).

In this heavy atmosphere of global political and economic disorder, the 1916 Olympics were cancelled, and the prospects of hosting the Olympic Games in 1920 did not seem promising. During the war, Coubertin moved the Olympic headquarters to neutral Switzerland (April 10, 1915), in order to safeguard the Olympic movement from conflicting interests (Guttmann 1992; Krüger 1999). It was difficult for the IOC to stage the Olympic Games of 1920, as the situation in most countries had been dreadful. Krüger (1999) argues that if there had not been successful Inter-Allied Games in Paris in 1919 under the American General Pershing, 'the IOC would not have dared stage the Olympic Games so shortly after the war' (p. 11). Since the German invasion of Belgium had been the cause that brought Britain into the war, the IOC decided that it was symbolically important for the first post-war Games to be staged in Antwerp (Guttmann 1992), signalling 'a symbolic revival of the Olympic movement and its message from out of the killing fields of Flanders' (Roche 2000: 104). The discourse strand relating to the Games as a vehicle for the pacification of the global community was represented through new symbols, namely the five rings flag, the symbolic release of doves of peace, and the athletes' oath (Roche 2000).[3] Although Germany, Austria and its allies were excluded, the Games were very successful (Krüger 1999) and the main organiser, Henri Baillet-Latour, emerged from the scene as a capable successor to the IOC presidency (Boulogne 1999b).

After the First World War, the international community called for international peace and cultural exchange, demonstrating increased popular awareness for changing the disorganised character of nineteenth century and pre-war international relations (Roche 2000). The establishment of the League of Nations was part of an effort to provide a more secure environment for the global community, institutionalising forms of international communication and cooperation. In this period the IOC was interested in associating itself with the League of Nations, making the movement's own institution-building process appear compatible with wider processes of international institution-building. The values of universalism and humanism, though undermined by the IOC's practices, reinforced such association and helped the movement to establish itself in the interwar period as the primary authority and actor concerned with international sport (Roche 2000). Nonetheless, socialist and women's sport movements emerged and staged their independent sport events, challenging the authority of the IOC and pressurising for some reform and change.

2.5.1   Alternative games: Socialist and Women's Olympics

In various European countries, particularly Germany and states of the Austro-Hungarian Empire, strong socialist, social democratic and workers' movements established large sport organisations on a national basis (Riordan 1999; Roche 2000). In the period after the war, European socialists allied and established an international socialist sport organisation (1920), which was renamed the 'Socialist Workers Sport International' (SWSI). Its emphasis was on mass participation and non-competitive sport, calling for a link between sport and wider political and cultural activities (Roche 2000). In the inter-war period, socialist movements were opposed to the elitism of the Olympic movement, which tended to make sport exclusive and inaccessible for working-class athletes.

The sport movements from the political Left therefore staged their own sport festivals as alternatives to the bourgeois Olympics. SWSI's political profile was reformist and not revolutionary, thus it banned its members from participating in the Soviet Spartakiads, a series of large-scale workers' Olympic-type events organised by the revolutionary Red Sport International (RSI) organisation. The main events that the SWSI organised were the Workers' Olympics in Frankfurt in 1925, in Vienna in 1931, and in Antwerp in 1937. As a counter to both the socialist games of SWSI and to the bourgeois Olympics, the Soviet communist sports movement staged the Worker Spartakiads. The

First Worker Spartakiad was launched on 12 August 1928 by a parade of 30,000 men and women, marching through Moscow's Red Square to the Dinamo Stadium. Despite the boycott by both socialist and bourgeois sport associations, 600 worker athletes from 14 countries were said to have taken part (Riordan 1999). Due to the increasing popularity of the socialist movements, the capitalist governments mobilised and acted against them. When communist workers attempted to stage a Second Spartakiad in Berlin in 1932, all Soviet and some other athletes were refused visas to enter Germany and then, when they finally managed to reach Berlin, the games were banned (Riordan 1999). The last Spartakiad Games, prior to the Second World War, were organised in Moscow in 1932, in opposition to the Olympic Games in Los Angeles in the same year (Roche 2000).

The Olympic Games were also being opposed by women's movements, for the sexist prejudices against female physical capability in sport. Women were not seen as the equal partners of male athletes, and thus were banned from the inaugural Olympics in Athens in 1896 and performed in a few unofficial exhibition events in the expo-related Olympics of 1900, 1904 and 1908. It is important to underline that, during this pre-war period, women in many western countries were given the right to vote, as part of a more active involvement in political life and public culture. In theory, sport offered a sphere of cultural liberation for women who had been oppressed by the restrictive Victorian dress code and 'body culture' (Roche 2000). Nonetheless, the IOC, in contrast to the idealistic claims of their Olympic values, was profoundly sexist, formally banning women from participation in the Olympics in 1912 (Hargreaves 1994). Women's response to this exclusionary attitude was similar to that of working class and socialist organisations discussed earlier, namely they formed their own international association.

A number of European women competed in 1921 in the international *Jeux Féminins* sponsored by the sportsmen of the principality of Monaco, which were repeated in 1922 with great success (Guttmann 1992). In 1921, Alice Milliat, an active member of one of France's upper-class sport clubs (*Fémina Sport*), established the *Fédération Sportive Féminine Internationale* (FSFI) (October 31, 1921). Less than a year later, the FSFI staged their first Olympic-type international sport event in 1922 in Paris, although they changed the title of the games from *Women's Olympics* to *Women's World Games* after the IOC's objections to the word 'Olympic' in the title (Guttmann 1992; Roche 2000). In the same year (1922), the Women's Amateur Athletics Association (WAAA) was founded in Britain. The FSFI World Games were well organised, held every four years, and acted as effective practical publicity for the cause of women's sport internationally (Hargreaves 1994). The main FSFI World Games were staged in Gothenburg in 1926, in Prague in 1930, in London in 1934, and although they were planned for Vienna in 1938, they were cancelled after the Nazi invasion (Roche 2000).

2.5.2   Authoritarian regimes: Supernationalism and the Nazi Olympics

In many European societies in the period 1936–1940 there was support for authoritarian regimes that were promising to solve the difficult economic problems. During this period, both the Soviet communists and the Nazis gained more power and involved themselves in cultural politics, using the mass theatre of festivals, rituals and various forms of populist 'physical culture' as a means of propaganda. Although in different ways, both promoted mass gymnastics and claimed that people should develop a 'body culture' concerned with fitness, open-air activity and work, and dedicated to the creation of the new Nazi or Soviet 'man' (Hoberman 1986). On the one hand, they were critical of the elitist and exclusionary character of modern sport that the Olympic movement was promoting. On the other hand, they were also critical of the growth of professionalised and commercialised forms of sport among the working class, with its 'superficial sensationalism' for spectators, and of the 'rationalistic rule-dominated' type of modern sport (Roche 2000: 103). Therefore, they called for forms of physical culture that, counter to elitist sport, were populist and inclusionary, and, in contrast to spectator sport, were participatory and associated with wider cultural traditions.

The Soviets, as a counterbalance to the revival of 'bourgeois cultural internationalism', staged several, large-scale, cultural and sport events. A special mass re-enactment of the Bolshevik invasion in the Winter Palace in 1917, for example, was held in Leningrad to celebrate the third anniversary of the Revolution. Additionally, two major sport events were staged; the first, a mass sport and gymnastic display in the new Red Stadium in Moscow, involving 18,000 athletes, was staged in order to impress the visiting international delegates at the congress of the Third International; the second, the first Central Asian Games in Tashkent, which involved 3,000 athletes, was designed as a symbol of support for the new Central Asian soviet republics. In addition, as discussed above, the Soviet Union also organised its own sport festivals ('Spartakiads'), which have been described as 'ritualised Marxist demonstrations against the hypocrisy of the bourgeois Olympics' (Jones 1988; cited in Roche 2000: 105).

The Soviets and the Nazis saw the staging of large-scale international sports events as significant resources for conducting foreign policy and international propaganda (Roche 2000). This is particularly evident in the case of the Nazis, who used the 1936 Berlin Olympics to project their image and increase the influence of their ideology internationally. These Games are remembered for the impressive character of their staging, the excellent performance of the black American athlete Jesse Owens, and also for the classic film 'Olympia' made by a controversial figure, the German cinematographer and fascist Leni Reifenstahl. However, they are best remembered for the controversies and political interests of the German organisers. Germany was re-admitted to the Olympics in 1928 and in 1930, at the Olympic congress in Berlin, the Germans suggested that the next Olympics should be held in Berlin (Guttmann 1992). At the 29th IOC session in Barcelona (April 1931), the German organisers successfully convinced the IOC and officially started preparations for the 1936 Berlin Olympics. When the IOC's decision was announced (May 13, 1931), Henring Bruning was Germany's chancellor and an unstable coalition was in power (Weimar Republic). However, by the time the Games were actually held, the National Socialists were in power and Adolf Hitler was chancellor (Guttmann 1992).

Although Hitler was originally opposed to the idea of Germany hosting the Games, he came to understand that staging such an international event would provide an excellent opportunity to project Nazi propaganda to the entire world (Toohey and Veal 2000). Guttmann (1992) argues that the early hesitation derived from the 'problem' that modern sport had developed in England rather than in Germany and thus it was, at least in principle, universalistic rather than particularistic. Among the most important characteristics of modern sport, in theory, was equality and claims that race, religion or ideology should not determine athletic excellence. Nonetheless, such a view could not be officially embraced by the Nazis, whose domestic political agenda included the removal of Jews from all positions of power and influence, including also the removal of world-class athletes from sports clubs and associations (Guttmann 1992; Toohey and Veal 2000).

Hitler and the Nazis were as critical of 'bourgeois' forms of culture as were the Bolsheviks, 'with the added power of their hypernationalism and racist paranoia against all things non-German' (Roche 2000: 116). However, after representations by Theodore Lewald and Carl Diem, leading figures in the German Sport Commission and the Olympic movement, he became enthusiastic about it and invested priority funding in the project. Goebbels and his Ministry of Propaganda were given overall responsibility for the project and he also assigned responsibilities to distinguished personalities such as the architect Albert Speer and the film-maker Leni Reifenstahl, respectively for the architecture of the stadium and for filming the event.

In the early years of Hitler's dictatorship, 1933–36, the Nazi party established an absolute ideological and cultural hegemony in Germany, gaining popularity and attracting the majority of the German people. Hitler's vision included Germany's 'civilising mission' in relation to Europe, mostly inspired by the late nineteenth and early twentieth-century German intellectuals who admired Hellenic civilisation. In these early years of Nazi state-building, the Olympic project allowed the Nazis to appeal to a number of different constituencies (Roche 2000). Among the working-class population, the spectacular and competitive character of the mega-event was popular, while among the German upper- and middle-class circles, the event's high cultural origins and Hellenic connections resonated with their classicism. Roche argues that German Hellenism, through the major achievements and discoveries of its archaeologists in the late nineteenth century, had been an important theme of the Paris Expo of 1889, influencing Coubertin to revive the Olympic Games in the 1890s. Finally, the Olympic event would appeal to both classes through its ritual, theatrical elements that were found in both populist and Wagnerian 'high' culture of German tradition (Roche 2000).

Thus, the hosting of the Games was seen as increasing the potential for disseminating Nazi propaganda, giving Hitler access to 'a symbolic discourse', which was prestigious and influential internationally, and in which the ideological and political meanings of Nazism could be propagated. These underlying interests were evident to many people inside and outside the Olympic movement, and, in response to the German policy, an international boycott of Nazi goods and services was organised, as well as a proposal for transferring the Games to a different site (Roche 2000; Toohey and Veal 2000). This movement fell short, when the IOC announced its faith in Berlin for hosting the Games. However, it had succeeded in exercising pressure on the IOC, and thus the President, Count-Baillet Latour, demanded guarantees from the Nazis that they would abide by the Olympic rules and would reassure the IOC that there would be no discrimination against athletes on the grounds of race or religion (Guttmann 1992; Toohey and Veal 2000). There were debates in the USA about the possibility of a boycott. George Messersmith, USA Secretary of State, arguing against US involvement in Berlin Olympics, declared (November 1935),

> To the party and the youth of Germany, the holding of the Olympic Games in Berlin in 1936 has become the symbol of the conquest of the world by National Socialist doctrine. Should the Games not be held in Berlin, it would be one of the most serious blows which National Socialist prestige could suffer. (Quoted by Roche 2000: 119)

However, after the involvement of the Amateur Athletic Union (AAU, the principal sports federation in the United States) and several 'controversial' negotiations between its president Avery Brundage and the Germans, most criticisms from the American side were muted. Interestingly, it was not a secret that the German team did not include any Jews. In all 21 German Jews from the Makkabi and Schild organisations were nominated as candidates for the team and were invited to a training camp. None was selected (Guttmann 1992).

For its tacit collaboration with the Nazis, the IOC was subject to criticism from many quarters, predominantly for allowing a major Nazi propaganda project to be staged, not only by refusing to acknowledge and denounce Nazi sport policies, but also by resisting the boycotts. The British sport journalist and historian John Rodda argues that the IOC was 'completely insulated from political events within Germany and the strong overtones produced at the Berlin Games' (Killanin and Rodda 1976; quoted by

Roche 2000: 119). Hoberman (1984) regards this period of the Olympic movement as one of at best fascist collaboration and at worst one of ideological domination by fascism. Lucas (1980) also questioned the actions of the Olympic movement in this period, not being able to understand many of the 'bizarre' decisions that were taken (p. 135).

2.5.3 The role of Carl Diem

The nineteenth-century German nationalist movement was associated with mass festivals and rituals, and particularly with popular 'physical culture' movements such as the Turnen gymnastics associations. The connection between nationalism and mega-events continued even after the unification of Germany in 1870 and the Bismarck era in the newly established German state. However, German traditional sport was challenged by the increasing popularity of English competitive sport, French Olympic internationalism and the growth of German sports clubs from the trade-union movements (Roche 2000). This resulted in the foundation of a German state commission for festivals and for sport (Guttman 1994), which, despite the resistance from the gymnastic clubs, was responsible for promoting sport in the educational system (Roche 2000). Carl Diem, a sport historian, was involved with the national German sport commission and the Olympic movement. From his post as a Chairman of the National Sport Commission from 1910 to 1933, he advocated the German sport movement, in preference to his country's 'archaic' Turnen Sport movement (Guttmann 1992; Mandell 1974; Paton and Barney 2002; Roche 2000), but also worked for a unification of these two extreme positions (Haag 1982).

Throughout his life he travelled widely and was active in teaching and sport administration, establishing two schools of physical education: one which opened in Berlin in 1920 and its post-war successor in Cologne which opened in 1947. He offered consultancy services on Olympic matters to several European nations (Mandell 1974; Paton and Barney 2002), and he was the initiator and partial sponsor of the German excavations at Olympia, which were re-started in 1937 (Mandell 1974). Around the time of the 1912 Stockholm Games the IOC decided to give the 1916 Games to Berlin and the building of the Olympic stadium in Berlin (*Kaiserstadium*), using mainly private rather than public finance, was built under Diem's supervision and guidance (Haag 1982). However, the war and the resentment of victors kept Germany out of the Olympic movement for nearly a generation (Roche 2000). Carl Diem, together with Theodore Lewald, also a member of the German state Sport Commission and of the IOC, remained leading figures in German sport and the Olympic movement, keeping the case of Berlin open for a future bid after the successful re-appearance of Germany at the Amsterdam Olympics in 1928. The apex of Diem's Olympic career was his involvement in the organisation of the 1936 Berlin Olympics (Guttmann 1992; Mandell 1974; Paton and Barney 2002).

Diem and Lewald were not very optimistic about Hitler's support for the Olympic project, but after their meeting with him on March 16, 1933, Hitler expressed his tentative approval (Guttmann 1992). Carl Diem was the chief organiser and Secretary General of the Games, initiating many new ideas in the realisation of the Games. For the first time, the notion of the Olympic Village was conceived, bringing most facilities together, a theatre (*Waldbühne*) was also added to emphasise the cultural character of the Games, and a bell tower with a bell calling the youth of the world (*Ich rufer die Jugend der Welt*) was built. Carl Diem also invited 30 students of physical education from every participating country to a youth camp during the Games, and these performed gymnastic displays (Haag 1982). However, Carl Diem's biggest innovation at the Berlin Games was to add to the modern Olympic ceremony a highly symbolic connection between the modern Olympic event site and the ancient site of Olympia by organising a torch relay from Olympia. This represented Diem's connection of Olympic sport with Hellenic idealism, but in the context of 1936 Nazi Germany, it raised suspicions. Roche argues:

> In this new Nazi context of the mid-1930s it [i.e. the torch relay] inevitably carried with it some shadowy and suspect connotations and implications. Olympia had been used by ancient Greek cultures for their sacred games event for around a thousand years. It was a permanent site for what could be conceived of as having been a 'thousand year civilisation'. (Roche 2000: 117)

The idea of the 'thousand year' civilisation through the Olympic project and the connotations of the torch relay was reminiscent of Hitler's vision for the 'Thousand Year Reich'. Diem's role in the organisation of Berlin Olympics in 1936 has raised many questions, concerning his contribution to Nazi propaganda, even if he never joined the National Socialist Party (Guttmann 1992). Mandell (1974: 11) argues:

> Diem's triumphs and the resultant applause and other rewards he received in the first years of Adolf Hitler's Reich seem to have led him into an apparent personality transformation. He tended to see the Nazis as respectable heirs to the grand traditions of German culture. His rhetoric picked up the pseudo-Nietzschian enthusiasm favoured by the official propagandists. In fact, one might believe from much of Diem's writing in the period 1937–1941 that his plans for sport had always been paramilitary, super-patriotic and totalitarian. (Mandell 1974: 11)

There is no evidence that Diem, whose wife was known to have a Jewish ancestor, was an anti-Semite. Due to this fact, but also because his university *Deutsche Hoschschule für Leibesübungen* had appointed several Jews in its faculty, Diem was condemned in the Nazi press as a 'white Jew' (Guttmann

1992; Hoberman 1986). Hoberman points out that it is worth noting that in 1927 he published a list of German intellectuals, including known Jewish poets. However, in many of his writings, he has shown evidence of racism, influenced by the right-wing ideology of the 'Volk', which by the 1920s had achieved widespread respectability within the Republic (Hoberman 1986). In Diem's defence, Paton and Barney (2002) suggest that, even if his role has been controversial, differences from Hitler's Nazi supporters were evident, on the basis of his education, cosmopolitanism and enlightenment. More insights about Diem's role in the Olympic movement and his interpretation of the Olympic values are discussed later in the book.

2.5.4   Colonialism, regional games and the Olympic movement

The late nineteenth-century English ideology of Athleticism (also referred to as *The Games Cult* or *Games Ethic*) influenced to a great extent the English public schools, and eventually wider society in the late Victorian and Edwardian eras. The ideology spread, almost simultaneously, throughout the British Empire, especially after 1850 and with the increasing popularity of Muscular Christianity, the public schools prepared their pupils for imperial roles in the Neo-imperial expansion of the late nineteenth century. Sandiford (1994) argues, 'The Victorians were determined to civilise the rest of the world, and an integral feature of that process, as they understood it, was to disseminate the gospel of athleticism which had triumphed so spectacularly at home in the third quarter of the nineteenth century' (quoted by Mangan and Hickey 2001: 106).

The internationalisation of 'Anglo-Saxon' sport by exporting games, namely cricket, rugby, athletics and squash, to their colonies was done initially on a completely elitist and exclusionary basis. The British colonial administrators and traders of middle and upper middle classes needed these games as means of entertainment and communication among themselves (Roche 2000). Interestingly, in the 'white' self-governing dominions of Australia and New Zealand, cricket and rugby became 'national' games through which people developed their identity (always in relation to the mother country), whereas in the Black and Asian colonies of the West Indies and India, cricket and other sports were initially practised only by native ethnic elites. Guttmann (1994) argues that sport practice, especially in African and Asian colonies, was used as a tool of social control and the reproduction of imperial hegemony. Thus, the classism, sexism and racism of nineteenth British sport culture were reproduced around the world through its colonies.

France also used sport as an element in its imperialistic practices to assimilate the local population into the citizenship of the motherland. Amara (2006) points out that although in the early part of the twentieth century indigenous populations were excluded from sporting organisations in for example Algeria, by the 1930s, policy had been reversed, and 'Metropolitan France' wanted the indigenous populations to practice modern sport and compete as 'French citizens' maximising the potential for national cohesion (Darby 2000). Coubertin believed that French imperialism in Africa represented a 'sacred civilising mission', and he appreciated the efforts of the colonial powers to 'help' in the development of the colonies:

> They [i.e. colonies] are like children: it is relatively easy to bring them into the world; the difficult thing is to raise them properly. They do not grow by themselves, but need to be taken care of, coddled, and pampered by the mother country; they need constant attention to incubate them, to understand their needs, to foresee their disappointments, to calm their fears. (Coubertin 1902: quoted by Hoberman 1986: 39)

Given such overt paternalism, Roche suggests that the IOC's attitudes to race and ethnicity were more closely related to the interests of British and French imperialism than to any real concern for humanism Moreover, in the 1930s even the profoundly imperialistic British Empire Games (later re-named the *Commonwealth Games*) was 'probably a more inclusionary international event in relation to non-European "racial" and ethnic groups than was the Olympics' (Roche 2000: 110).

Coubertin was always keen for collaboration with the colonial powers; when King Leopold of Belgium asked Coubertin to design the programme for a 'colonial preparatory school', he was more than happy to provide his services, although this project was finally cancelled. In 1912, Coubertin published an article, in which he gave advice to colonial regimes on how they could use sport as a tool of administration. He wanted to encourage them to spread sport among the colonised without fearing that victory by local groups could lead to rebellion (Hoberman 1986). However, the biggest link of the Olympic movement with the colonial societies was achieved through the establishment of Regional Games. In the IOC Session in Paris in 1922, discussions took place about initiating Latin American Games, which General Charles Sherill, an American member of the IOC, supported with the condition that they should be controlled by the Roman Catholics (however it was not until 1951 that the Pan-American Games were inaugurated). DaCosta *et al.* (2002) emphasise that a conflict between the interests of the Young Men's Christian Association (YMCA) and the IOC in the development of South American sport did not allow Coubertin to develop action plans in this area. The following year in spring 1923, when the IOC met in Rome, it turned its attention to Africa and invited French and Italian colonial officials to discuss the staging of Regional Games under the IOC patronage and sponsorship. It was decided that the IOC should support the African Games (*Jeux Africains*) for non-Europeans, starting in Algiers in 1925 (Guttmann 1992). Roche argues that the IOC

> ... recommended a version of sport apartheid by proposing a system of two concurrent biennial events, one of European colonisers and one for

colonised 'natives'. However, this was one set of games too many for the colonisers and their lack of support made it ultimately impossible to arrange this event. (Roche 2000: 110)

The African Games were subsequently postponed to 1927, and then again to 1929. They did not actually materialise until the early 1960s, and were first organised by the French government under the name *Friendship Games*. The first African Games organised by Africans themselves were organised in 1965 in Brazzaville (Guttmann 1984).

In terms of participation of non-European 'racial' and ethnic groups during the inter-war period, the Japanese were successful, continuing to organise their impressive displays in expos in the same period, and 'keeping up with' their modernisation process (Roche 2000). Egypt was the first African and Arab country to join international sports competitions, participating in the Olympic Games in 1920, and qualifying for the Olympic soccer semi-finals in 1928. There were also some notable successes by African and Arab athletes, but Guttmann (1994) argues that generally this could be regarded as tokenism. The IOC held its 37th Session in Cairo (Egypt), as part of the preparations for the Olympics in Tokyo (1940) (its first ever attempt to organise the Games on non-western soil). Krüger (1999) argues that the increasing influence of authoritarian regimes over sporting practices in Europe and the political situation that preceded the Second World War were possibly the reasons for the IOC transferring its interests away from Europe.

2.6 Post World War II 1945–1980s: Neo-colonialism and Cold War

Early in the twentieth century, the economic and industrial development of the United States had caught up with industrial economies of western Europe. Its continuous growth was a result of foreign expansion, overseas market outlets, access to raw material resources and foreign investment. It had secured its power over Latin America since the declaration of the Monroe Doctrine of 1823, but could not find a foothold in Asia and Africa which were controlled by the British, French and Dutch. To increase its influence in these territories, the United States implemented the so-called 'Open Door' policy, a non-discriminating international economic system, expressing support to the colonially oppressed (Hoogvelt 2001). The Second World War had significantly altered the pre-war world relationships, as the weakened economies and industrial capacities of the European colonial powers made it important to reassert control over their colonial possessions. At the same time increased nationalism among the oppressed populations of the colonies fuelled a demand for independence. The territorial property of the Third Reich was divided into spheres of control by the Allied Powers, comprising the United States, Britain, France, and the Soviet Union. The Japanese Empire, which had been built up since 1895, was dismantled and occupied, like Germany, by the Allies with primary control in the hands of the

United States (Espy 1979). Among the Allied Powers at the end of the war, the Soviet Union and the United States were the most powerful and influential.

The USA, in exchange for the American lives that were sacrificed in the cause of its European allies, demanded the new international economic order be under US hegemony. This had already been agreed in the early years of the war, when the American Council of Foreign Relations had composed a Memorandum, which described the policy needs of the USA in 'a world in which it proposes to hold unquestioned power' (Hoogvelt 2001: 33). As part of this policy, the USA would acquire military and economic supremacy within the non-German world. This US-led, non-German world was to be called the *Grand Area*. Much of the Grand Area plan was accomplished immediately after the end of the Second World War, when the victorious nations agreed on the need to manage the world economy, and cooperated with international institutions under the acknowledged leadership of the USA (for instance, the Bretton Woods institutions of the International Monetary Fund and the World Bank, 1944, and the General Agreement on Tariffs and Trade in 1947, and the adoption of the European Recovery Plan (the Marshall Plan) in 1948 (Hoogvelt 2001). At a political level, in the adoption of the Truman Doctrine (1947) the USA formally announced its intentions to act as a global policeman, 'defending free people anywhere in the world who were threatened by armed minorities or by outside pressures' (Hoogvelt 2001: 31). Thus the capitalist block in western Europe was formed under US political, economic and military hegemony.

Although the Soviet Union had suffered remarkable human and material losses, it possessed a strong army with which it established its position at home and in Eastern Europe (Espy 1979). It exercised influence and control over Eastern Europe, forming a Communist Bloc which reflected long-standing Russian imperial ambitions, but with a renewed drive in relation to the Marxist-Leninist doctrine of worldwide class struggle. The USSR controlled communist governments in the countries in Eastern Europe, forming the so-called *Eastern or Communist Bloc*. The conflicting interests between the communist expansionism and US neo-imperialist policy fuelled political, economic, cultural and military rivalries between the 'capitalist', western bloc and the 'communist' eastern bloc (Espy 1979). This period of the 'Cold War' is usually seen as having started in 1947 with the establishment of the Truman doctrine, but some commentators trace it back to the Russian Civil War (1918–21) and the western intervention against the Bolsheviks (Heywood 2002).

In consequence of the war, the Allies ultimately joined forces to form the United Nations at the San Francisco Conference (April–June 1945). It was an attempt to establish an organisation that would be more powerful and resilient than the League of Nations, which had proved to be powerless, as Germany, Japan and Italy pursued their expansionist ambitions in the 1930s. Although there were clear interests to extend the anti-Axis alliance of the USA, USSR and the UK in the post-war period, the UN charter laid down the highest standards of international conduct for nations wishing to join the organisation (Espy 1979; Heywood 2002).

The role of the UN as a powerful organisation for economic and military cooperation among the nations was even more evident, when the Cold War manifested itself not only in Europe but became global. Anti-imperialist movements (e.g. pan-Arabism and pan-Africanism) in colonies accelerated in the 1950s and 1960s, and nationalist and liberal movements were striving for independence in the Third World.[4] The Korean War (1950–53) marked the spread of the Cold War to Asia following the Chinese Revolution of 1949. During the 1960s and 1970s, international crises throughout the world, from the Middle East to Latin America and from Africa to Indo-China, were incorporated into the struggle between the USSR and the USA, which represented the broader clash between communism and capitalism. During the period of decolonisation, the UN acted as a sounding board for the independence movements and provided a forum for cooperation, although often criticised for giving more power to the core countries and the US (Tipton and Aldrich 1987).

From the late 1940s to the 1960s the influential role of US-based transnational companies in the world economy was growing, deepening the gap between core and periphery. Hoogvelt (2001) argues that these multinational companies and international governmental organisations were used by the core as tools for controlling the peripheral areas. Despite the formal recognition of political independence of the new emerging countries, there still existed a system of neo-colonialism, neo-imperialism, as a continuation of the orthodox colonialism of the previous period. Throughout the early post-war period (until 1970) the flow of profits from former colonies was maintained through direct exploitation of raw materials resources by multinational capital.

From the 1970s onwards, the bipolar nature of the Cold War became less evident, as the communist world became more fragmented (evidenced for example in the increasing hostility between Moscow and Beijing), and the capitalist world incorporated Japan and West Germany as resurgent 'economic superpowers'. One of the consequences of this reduced bipolarism was *détente* (relaxation of tension) between East and West, which was reflected in President Nixon's historic visit to China in 1972 and the Strategic Arms Limitation Talks between 1967 and 1979 (SALT I and SALT II agreements). The Cold War ended with the fall of Berlin Wall (1989), the meeting in Paris (1990) between representatives of the Warsaw Pact and NATO, and the collapse of the USSR (1991) (Heywood 2002).

2.6.1   Cold War, opposing ideologies and the Olympic movement

Despite the controversy over the Nazi Olympics, the IOC did not seem concerned to exercise caution when it selected Tokyo to host the Games in 1940. Japan's aggressive foreign policy had raised international concern, especially after its invasion of Manchuria in 1931. However, the IOC members stayed firm in their decision, even when the Japanese invaded China in 1937. Guttmann argues that 'In the eyes of the committee, the peaceful diffusion of Olympism to Asian shores was far more important than the ruthless expansion of the Japanese empire' (Guttmann 1992: 73). Awarding the Games to Japan was regarded by many as an important step in IOC policy, as it was the first occasion that the Games were to be held in an Asian country (Toohey and Veal 2000). The IOC was in some doubt about the decision as late as 1938, with the Indo-Chinese war and it could not receive assurances from the Japanese Olympic Committee that the Games would be unaffected by the hostilities. Pressure came from the Chinese members that the Games should be postponed, but the IOC refused to move forward with such a decision. The Games were finally transferred to Helsinki, when the Japanese themselves decided that the Games would be too costly at a time when they needed to invest funds for military purposes (Guttmann 1992). However, in May 1940, the IOC President, Baillet-Latour, issued a statement saying that these Games would be cancelled because of the Second World War.

Just as it had affected other pre-war international organisations, the Second World War interrupted the activities of the committee and forced it to suspend its operations during the war. In an atmosphere of world disorder and in the ruins of war, the IOC began to plan the post-war revival of the Olympic Games. It resumed its work quickly, holding meetings in London from August 21 to 24, 1945, in order to decide the site for the 1948 Olympic Games. The cities of Baltimore, Los Angeles, Minneapolis, Philadelphia, Lausanne, and London had submitted bids. The IOC favoured the cities of the United States because of their great influence in the post-war period, but for practical reasons (distance and expensive transport) they were rejected. London, which had already been chosen to host the cancelled 1944 Games, had begun the preparations for the Games before the war. The IOC, therefore, awarded the Games again to London, allowing the British to continue with their preparations (Espy 1979). However, the choice of London as a site for these Games was controversial from the beginning, both on an international level and within Great Britain. Many considered London an unfortunate choice because of the damage the city had suffered as a consequence of German bombing during the war. The British economy was near collapse, as the country had gone from being a pre-war creditor to a post-war debtor not being able to maintain the heavy overseas commitments of its empire. Moreover, awarding the Games to London portrayed the IOC, supposedly a non-political body, as supporting the Allied Powers of the Second World War (Toohey and Veal 2000).

The IOC, between the time of site selection and the Games themselves, had to deal with various issues. In the post-war period the Soviet Army occupied most of Eastern Europe and constructed governments in those countries, which were largely controlled by the Soviet Union. Germany had been divided into zones according to the pre-arranged plans of the Allied Powers, but by July 1948 the Western Allies – the United States, Britain and France – had joined forces in Germany, in opposition to the Soviet East German zone. The result was the formation of two separate German states, West and East Germany, under the control of the Western Allies and the Soviet Union respectively. In Asia, Korea was split in half, the North controlled by the Soviet Union and the South by the United States. By July 1948 the Chinese civil war was coming to an end, with the Chinese Communists emerging as winners. In South-east Asia and the Middle East decolonisation processes were in progress; the French were striving for control over Vietnam, Indonesia was about to gain its independence from the Netherlands, and India (divided into Moslem Pakistan and predominantly Hindu India) gaining its independence from Britain. The prevailing issue in the Middle East was Palestine, the partition of which, and the subsequent declaration of the State of Israel, provoked tension with ensuing military conflict between Israel and the surrounding Arab countries.

The participation of the Soviet Union in the Olympic movement was one of the many issues that the IOC had to consider in the post-war period. The Russians had not participated in the Olympic Games since 1912, showing more interest in the internal competitions of the Red Sport International (Workers' Olympiads) than the bourgeois Olympics (Riordan 1999). However, after the Second World War, the Soviet Union became interested in participating in international sport, as part of its wider involvement in the world's political and military fields. By October 1946, they had already participated in numerous sporting events and sought to join a number of international sport federations. However, Soviet Union made demands as a condition for their entry. They demanded that Russian should be an official language, that Russian officials should be placed on the executive board, and representatives of pro-fascist organisations of Franco's Spain should be expelled (Espy 1979). Brundage's assessment of Soviet intentions was expressed to Edström quoting the letter of a colleague:

> My own guess is that the real object of the Russians is to humiliate the West ... every time they force a Federation to break its own rules in order to let them compete, Russian prestige is increased and western prestige is decreased. The trouble at the moment ... is that about half the countries don't want to annoy Russia, and any country, which is anxious to obtain a World Championship or a World Congress, is reluctant to annoy the Eastern bloc. (Espy 1979: 28)

The issue of Soviet participation was easily solved when the Soviets failed to form an NOC and under the IOC charter this meant that they were ineligible to participate. Similarly, the issue of recognising Germany and Japan did not pose a problem since no NOCs had been formed in these countries. The recognition of Palestine, however, did pose a serious problem, as the Arab countries threatened to withdraw if the new State of Israel were to take part under the Zionist flag. As an article of the New York Times indicated (24 July, 1948), 'in Egypt's opinion, admission of the Israeli team would imply partial recognition of the Jewish state' (cited in Espy 1979: 29). The general issue of recognition was to play an important role in the future. Espy expresses it thus:

> The IOC, by recognising a country's committee or by recognising a certain name, in effect was conferring political recognition although the IOC had no formal diplomatic status. An Olympic participant was competing in the name of his country by virtue of his affiliation with the national committee, which in turn was affiliated with the IOC. The Olympic Games, grand and world-renowned, were providing a superb forum for the countries of the world. Each country that participated thereby received de facto recognition, even though formal affiliation was not with the state apparatus. (Espy 1979: 29)

The formative years of the post-war Olympics were also the formative years of the post-war world. The increasing tension between the capitalist and Eastern blocs reflected in the concerns of the IOC to invite the Soviets to participate in the Olympic Games.

The process of decolonisation, producing new patterns and establishing new relationships, troubled the Olympic movement in the post-war period. In 1948 this was reflected in the context of the Palestine issue. In the 1952 Olympic Games, which were awarded to Helsinki as compensation for the cancelled 1940 Games, tension was mainly illustrated in the recognition of the two Germanies and two Chinas. Before the Second World War, Germany had one NOC, however, because of the post-war division of the country, committees were formed in both East and West Germany. Consequently, each approached the IOC for recognition, but, according to the IOC regulations, there could not be two committees for the same country. The present composition of the West German committee was the same as that of the former, pre-war German committee but the IOC thought that it would cause trouble to grant full recognition at that time. Thus, the IOC granted provisional recognition to the West German Committee, calling the Germans to attempt to form a single team. The East Germans, who were insisting on two separate committees, refused to take part in the 1952 Games (Espy 1979; Hill 1992; Toohey and Veal 2000).

Parallel to the recognition problem with the Germans was the question of whether to recognise Communist China or Nationalist China. China asked that Taiwan (also referred to as *Formosa*) should not be recognised as an independent country (Hill 1992). The IOC refused the People's Republic of China's request and as a result it withdrew from the Games in 1952 and only rejoined the movement in 1980 in the Lake Placid Winter Olympic Games. In 1959 the IOC agreed that the Taiwan committee could not continue under its present name, since it did not administer sport on the mainland. This decision was misunderstood by the press, which assumed that Taiwan had been expelled. In 1960, it was suggested in the IOC that since Taiwan was recognised by the United Nations as the Republic of China, its committee should also be called *Olympic Committee of the Republic of China*. This was accepted by the IOC but not for the Olympics in Rome (1960), where the team paraded as Formosa but expressed its dissatisfaction carrying a board 'under protest'. In 1968 the name Olympic Committee of the Republic of China was officially recognised by the IOC (Hill 1992). With regard to the problem of the two Chinas, the IOC was criticised for its failure to recognise that sport was no longer divorced from politics, refusing to acknowledge a potentially explosive situation (Espy 1979).

The IOC's 'non-political' policy was criticised in the Olympic Games of 1956, when it failed to acknowledge the impact of the Hungarian and Suez crises on the conduct of the Games. Immediately after the Soviets invaded Hungary, the Netherlands and Spain withdrew from the Games. In the case of the Netherlands, the President of the NOC criticised the IOC for claiming that the Olympic ideal should prevail over political matters. He cynically wondered, 'How can sports prevail over what happened in Hungary? How would we like it if our people had been atrociously murdered, and someone said that sports should prevail?' (cited in Espy 1979: 54). Despite the Hungarian and Suez incidents, the period of 1952 to 1956 was marked by a lessening of tension and a general consolidation between East and West.

The period 1956 to 1968 witnessed the end of the colonial system and the emergence of newly independent states from the former colonies in Asia and Africa. In the Olympic movement this was evident in the issue of South African participation in the Games. The opposition of the African states to South Africa's participation portrayed both actually and symbolically the rift between the developing and the developed world, and anticolonial resistance. During the de-colonisation process, nationalism prevailed which provoked the non-aligned orientation of the emerging areas in Africa and Asia. The East and West sought to extend their influence in developing nations through the activities of multinational corporations. However, the emerging nations sought to avoid implication in the East-West division, with its implicit political dependency, and to resist economic dependency upon the new system of multinational corporations (in effect a form of neo-colonialism). Thus, the Organisation for African Unity (OAU) was established in 1963 and the Supreme Council of Sports in Africa in 1966 (comprised of 32 African states) in large part as a response to these concerns. In the Olympic movement, similar trends were reflected in the establishment of Regional Games. Guttmann argues:

> [the Regional Games] are valuable as a kind of mini-Olympics at which nations unlikely to have their flags hoisted in the victory ceremonies of the regular games might nonetheless enjoy their triumphs, gain experience, and imbibe the lessons of fair play and good sportsmanship. Cities from the Third World, which acted as hosts of the Regional Games, acquired organisational, know-how that enable them to stage the real thing one day. (Guttmann 1984: 222)

The best known Regional Games were: the Pan-American, the Mediterranean, the Asian, the Pan-Arab, and the Pan-African Games, as well as the Games of the New Emerging Forces (GANEFO). Guttmann (1984) argues that these games had a paradoxical nature, strengthening Olympism but also raising conflicts against it. Of all of these, the GANEFO movement was the most threatening for the Olympic movement. In the summer of 1962, when the Asian Games were to be held in Indonesia, the Indonesian government refused to grant visas for the athletes of Taiwan and Israel. Israel had already been banned from the Mediterranean Games in 1952 and this practice was not new. In February 1963 the IOC suspended the Indonesian Olympic Committee for not reacting against its government's discriminatory policy. Within a month the Indonesian Olympic Committee withdrew from the Olympic movement.

As a result, Indonesian President Sukarno proposed the establishment of GANEFO. The purpose of GANEFO, as announced at a preparatory conference in April 1963, was to be 'based on the Olympic ideals, and was to promote the development of sports in new emerging nations so as to cement friendly relations among them' (Espy 1979: 81). Nonetheless, the major aim of the GANEFO movement was to divide and fragment the Olympic movement, to highlight the political realities of world structure, and to materialise the political plans of the new and non-aligned states (Espy 1979). However, the history of the GANEFO movement was short, as the IOC and the International Federations undermined the legitimacy of the games by threatening to use sanctions against athletes participating. Interestingly, although the IOC and the International Federations took measures to prevent NOCs and national sports federations from taking part in GANEFO, applying severe punishments such as the suspension of athletes, the GANEFO organisers permitted athletes to participate in the games of both organisations. Indeed, the leaders of the GANEFO movement were criticised in terms of their tactics for failing to adopt a strong line in relation to the international Olympic system (Kanin 1981). The short life of the GANEFO movement can also be attributed to the fact that the major supporters of the Games withdrew. Sukarno's successor Suharto did not support the movement, Egypt withdrew its bid to host GANEFO II after declaring war with Israel, and China could not support the movement when the Proletarian Cultural Revolution began (Luton and Fan 2007).

The 1968 Olympic Games, held in Mexico, produced a number of incidents and scandals, which reflected wider conflicts and trends in the world. Espy (1979) argues that the Olympic Games was witnessing such 'dark' and 'intense' incidents for the first time (though the 1936 Berlin Olympics is seen by many to have been the Olympic movement's darkest hour up to that moment, and in addition Espy was writing well before the Salt Lake City scandal broke). Three political trends or conflicts can be identified during the 1968 Games in Mexico. The first trend was the increasing commercialism of sport, and the increasing role of business as a semi-independent actor in international affairs. This was reflected in the track shoe scandal of the Summer Games and the conflict about ski manufacturers' names being 'advertised' by skiers in Winter Games. At the Summer Games, it was revealed that many manufacturers, especially the rival shoe companies Adidas and Puma, were paying athletes to use their equipment, contrary to Olympic rules and principles. At the Winter Games, the International Skiing Federation came into conflict with the IOC about the amateur rules, raising concerns that certain skiers were professionals, earning money by advertising equipment brands. Second, a major political trend was that of the emerging voices of opposition to the established order and world power structure. This was reflected at the Summer Games in several ways: when Mexican students rioted over internal government policies; when black American athletes, Tommie Smith and John Carlos, saluted to black power from the victory stand and protested against the United States policies; and when the Mexican government, counter to the IOC, did not allow athletes with Rhodesian passports to participate, as opposition to the white-dominated government of Rhodesia. Finally, the third element that was reflected in the 1968 Games was the deepening Cold War estrangement between East and West, especially after the invasion of Czechoslovakia by the Warsaw Pact countries. Although the Czechoslovakian invasion did not have the same effect on the Games as the Hungarian invasion had had in 1956, apprehension arose in the Olympic circles when there was a clamour to ban the Warsaw Pact countries.

It is also noteworthy to mention that the 1968 Mexico Games marked the beginning of drug-testing in the Games. After the televised death of cyclist Tommy Smith in the Tour de France, the IOC decided to take action against doping. Thus, an IOC committee reached consensus on a definition of doping and outlined a list of banned substances. However, it was not until 1974, that the IOC declared steroid use to be illegal, and the lack of positive tests raised suspicions that the IOC and some organising committees were suppressing positive results (Dimeo and Hunt 2009; Toohey and Veal 2000).

In 1968 the United States' involvement in Vietnam had lost popular support in the US and the new President Nixon declared the USA could no longer perform the role of world policeman (Espy 1979). In the interim, China had emerged as a powerful nation in military terms, claiming for itself a position as a third power alongside the United States and the Soviet Union. In the Middle East, although the United States had always been supportive of Israel, a growing western European dependence on Arab oil 'froze' the relationships between the United States and Israel. By 1971, the United States could not suppress the growing significance of the Middle East that was expanding its influence in Europe, Japan and the United States as a result of oil revenues. These elements represented aspects of the development of a new world power structure, replacing the bipolar arrangement of the post-Second World War settlement (Heywood 2002).

Many nations made use of the Olympic movement as a tool for gaining political benefits and/or undermining opposing ideologies. The 1972 Games have remained notorious for two major political incidents: the Arab terrorist attack against the Israeli team and the South African and Rhodesian questions. As a result of the terrorist attack, eleven Israeli Olympic team members were killed and the Games were overshadowed by the shock of this tragedy. Although many IOC members pressed for the immediate calling of an IOC session in order to decide whether the Games should be cancelled, the President, Avery Brundage refused to accede to this request (Guttmann 1992). According to Killanin, Brundage's attitude caused much reaction in the Olympic circles, and the French Olympic stalwart, the Comte Jean de Beaumont is reported to have complained that 'to Brundage ... he is the IOC – no one else, just he!' (cited in Guttmann 1992: 139). Brundage himself finally took the historical and controversial decision that the Games should continue:

> The Games of the Twentieth Olympiad have been subject to two savage attacks. We lost the Rhodesian battle against naked political blackmail. We have only strength of a great ideal. I am sure that the public will agree that we cannot allow a handful of terrorists to destroy this nucleus of international cooperation and goodwill we have in the Olympic movement. The Games must go on ... (cited in Guttmann 1992: 140)

Brundage makes reference in this extract to the 'Rhodesian battle', the second major political incident of the 1972 Olympic Games. During the 1960s many countries restricted their sporting links with South Africa, as well as Rhodesia, because of their apartheid policies. In December 1968 the United Nations General Assembly proposed a resolution calling for all countries to break off sporting relations with South Africa. At the executive board meeting in April (1969), the IOC condemned the South African National Olympic Committee (SANOC) for using the Olympic symbols in the regional white-only South African Games. South Africa was finally expelled from the Olympic movement for violation of Section 3 of the Olympic Charter (Toohey and Veal 2000).

In March 1971, Rhodesia received an invitation to the 1972 Summer Games in Munich. However, the African countries had raised concerns over Rhodesian participation because of racial discrimination. After investigation, the IOC decided that the teams were multiracial and there was therefore no reason to suspend Rhodesia. Nevertheless, the central issue was not discrimination in sport but general dissatisfaction with the race relations situation more broadly in Rhodesia (Espy 1979; Guttmann 1992). Thus, many African nations boycotted the Games, prior to the opening ceremony (Guyana, Ethiopia, Ghana, Zambia, Tanzania, Sierra Leone, Liberia and Sudan). Espy (1979) argues that Kenya was also threatening to boycott, and that if neither Kenya nor Ethiopia had participated, men's track and field would have lost at least ten potential medallists in 24 events.

Despite the South African expulsion from the movement and the United Nations General Assembly's request to all its members to suspend any sporting links with this country, the New Zealand rugby team competed against South Africa in 1976. Subsequently, the African countries, under the auspices of the Supreme Council for Sport in Africa, refused to participate in the Montreal Games (1976) unless New Zealand was expelled (Guttmann 1992; Hill 1992; Toohey and Veal 2000). The IOC supported New Zealand's participation in the Games, taking into account the claim that rugby was not an Olympic sport and, thus, that the New Zealand Rugby Federation had acted independently from the New Zealand Olympic Committee. As a consequence, New Zealand took part in the Games, but 30 African and Middle Eastern countries boycotted the Montreal Games in 1976 (Toohey and Veal 2000). The notion of the boycott as a forceful and efficient political weapon was again in evidence in the two following Olympic Games of Moscow (1980) and Los Angeles (1984).

By the 21st Olympiad of Montreal, politics and nationalism not only had become a prominent feature of sport and of the Olympic Games, but commercialism had also grown. When Montreal began its planning for the Games in 1969, Mayor Jean Drapeau estimated the costs at $US120 million, but by 1976 the total cost had escalated to $US1.6 billion. The Quebec provincial government initiated investigations for charges of corruption among the official organising committee and officials of Montreal city. To finance and save the Games, Drapeau turned to firms such as Coca Cola and Adidas (Espy 1979). However, fear of facing the same kind of economic crisis as Montreal had done, resulted in few cities wishing to host the Games in the early 1980s, so that Los Angeles, with its private sector-led funding approach, was the only city to bid for the 1984 Games (Guttmann 1992; Toohey and Veal 2000).

In December 1979, the Soviet Union invaded Afghanistan and in response, the US President, Jimmy Carter, called on the world nations to impose sanctions on the USSR and boycott the imminent Moscow Olympic Games. However, many countries, among them some close allies of the US, were reluctant to participate. With the exception of some Muslim nations of Asia and North Africa, which were eager to express support for the Muslim population of Afghanistan, Carter's campaign was not relatively ineffectual (Guttmann 1992; Toohey and Veal 2000). Interestingly, some leaders appeared inconsistent and perhaps even insincere in relation to their participation in the boycott and its relation to politics. Although Malcolm Fraser of Australia had emphasised the need to maintain a separation of sport from politics, when the Australian Olympic Federation announced that it was sending a team to Moscow, his government withdrew all financial support for the Australian Olympic team. Similarly, the British team went to the Games without governmental support but was funded by private contributions. Eventually 26 nations boycotted the Games, most notably the United States, West Germany, the People's Republic of China, Japan and Canada. Kanin (1981) argues that this was 'the most extensive diplomatic effort ever connected with an Olympic celebration and demonstrated unequivocally that nations saw the Olympics as an effective tool to try to influence the foreign policy of other nations, those with opposing ideologies' (cited in Toohey and Veal 2000: 88).

The following Games, held in Los Angeles, were also affected by opposing ideological forces. The Eastern Bloc countries boycotted the Games in retaliation for what had happened at the previous Olympics. The Russian NOC declared that the participation of Soviet athletes in the Games was impossible due to 'chauvinistic sentiments and an anti-Soviet hysteria [that] are being whipped up in the United States' (Guttmann 1992: 157). Although safety concerns were put forward as the major reason for their action, it is suggested that the chance of embarrassing the American hosts was certainly a key element of their agenda.

Guttmann (1988) suggests that while the absence of the USSR in 1984 did not damage the image of the Los Angeles Games, which anyway made tremendous profits from the TV broadcasting rights, by contrast, the Moscow Games lost a significant amount of international legitimacy due to the American boycotting (though this is of course the view from an American commentator's perspective). In relation to the US boycott in Moscow, Nafziger disagrees with Guttmann and emphasises that Carter's political manoeuvres for initiating a wider boycott movement against the USSR, 'divided athletes, threatened to destabilise the International Olympic movement, aggravated a global public, worried persons with a business stake … and threatened to isolate the United States from some of its important allies' (Nafziger 1985: 256).

The Los Angeles Games are seen as having ushered in a new era of commercialisation and commodification of the Games. The President of the Los Angeles Olympic Organising Committee (LAOOC), Peter Ueberroth, sold television rights to ABC for $US225 million; the European networks, Eurovision and Intervision, together paid $US22 million and the Japanese added some $US11 million to the total revenues. The LAOOC raised another $US130 million from thirty corporate sponsors, including American Express, Coca Cola, Levi's, IBM and SANYO. There were also forty-three companies licensed to sell 'official' Olympic products. MacDonald's marketed the official hamburger of the 1984 Olympics; the Mars bar was the official snack food, and Coca Cola the official drink. When the Olympic Games ended, the LAOOC had raised so much money from the sale of television rights and from its sponsorship scheme that it had an excess of some $US200 million (Guttmann 1992).

Despite the increasing exposure to the masses through the media, Gruneau argues from a neo-Marxist perspective, that the highly specialised, elite sport that was being promoted in Los Angeles signified the domination of corporate capital in people's lives. He claimed that the involvement of private, commercial funding of the Games came as a result of 'resistance' against public expenditure.

> ... there has been a considerable degree of resistance to sport's absorption into capitalism's universal market. Not only the lingering anti-professional traditions of amateurism, but also community and trade union groups have objected to the excesses and spending priorities of the Olympic circus ... Yet the result of the resistance was to clear the way for the Hamburger Olympics [Los Angeles] and another stage in the commodification of international sport. (Gruneau 1984: 13; cited in Toohey and Veal 2000: 124)

Roche (2000) also suggests that the TV broadcasting of the Games creates an advantage for powerful countries that have an appropriate technology to personalise media images for their particular national interests, whereas poorer countries are not in a position to enhance their identity through such media messages. The prominence of commercial companies in the staging of the Games and in international sport also accelerated the process of professionalisation of athletes whose commercial interests some commentators argued, undermined Olympic ideals (Espy 1979). The IOC throughout the 1950s and 1960s had defended the amateur code, but evidence of its violation was apparent even before the two World Wars, with the Swedish recruiting athletes from the army and other western European nations and the United States recruiting coaches (Day 2011; Riordan and Krüger 1999). In 1971, the IOC decided to eliminate the term amateur from Article 26 of the IOC Charter, and in 1981 the IOC President Samaranch recognised the shift to professionalism (Lucas 1992) and by the time of the Los Angeles Games (1984) this shift had been reaffirmed with 'professional' athletes able to participate in those sports where the IF responsible permitted.

Nevertheless, despite the criticisms of the new political economy of the Olympic movement, the new economic practices contributed to an enormous growth of the Games, transforming the IOC from an organisation that was funded by wealthy aristocrats to one of the richest organisations in the world (Lucas 1992). Overall, the Games opened to a mass audience, increasing the interest in international sport and creating a worldwide spectacle (Roche 2000).

At the Olympic Congress held in Baden-Baden in 1981, the IOC decided to award the Games of the 24th Olympiad to the Asian city of Seoul. Seoul, however, was a risky choice, since South Korea was ruled by an authoritarian government, it was the capital of a divided nation, and it had been involved in war with its communist neighbour North Korea (Guttmann 1992). Boycott threats started as soon as Seoul had been chosen and calls for the venue to be changed began soon after the Baden-Baden conference (Hill 1992). The leaders of North Korea reacted and after threatening a boycott, they demanded that half of the sporting and cultural elements of the Games should be held in North Korea. President Fidel Castro of Cuba promised to help, and Moscow told IOC President Samaranch that a movement towards sharing would also help the Soviet bloc to participate (Hill 1992). Samaranch, seeking a compromise, offered to allow North Korea to host the whole of the archery and table tennis competitions and some of the cycling and soccer. However, such an offer had a double negative effect, displeasing the South Koreans, and failing to placate the North Koreans who in the end boycotted the Games (Guttmann 1992).

On September 1, 1983, a Korean civilian airliner was shot down by the Soviets and the Seoul Olympic Organising Committee (SLOOC) had to deal with the reaction of public opinion (Hill 1992). The situation worsened after the boycott of the Los Angeles Games (1894). However, a fourth major boycott in a row was avoided after Mikhail Gorbachev made it clear that the Russians intended to rejoin the Olympic movement. Moreover, the Assembly of the Association of National Olympic Committees (ANOC) supported Seoul as the host city (Guttmann 1992; Hill 1992). Due to the complex political negotiations between the North and South Korea, Samaranch visited South Korea eleven times from April 1982 to September 1989. In Korea, he became such a popular figure for his efforts to safeguard the Games that he was awarded the first *Seoul Peace Prize* of 300,000 UK sterling, which he donated to the new Olympic museum's construction fund (Hill 1992).

The Seoul Olympics also experienced the implementation of a new marketing plan, the Olympic Partners Programme (TOP). The TOP-I sponsorship programme, was established in 1985, and was developed by International Sports and Leisure (ISL), a marketing and management company jointly owned by the sport company Adidas and a Japanese advertising agency, Dentsu. The association of Adidas with the Olympic Games has been highly significant, largely due to the influential role of its owner Horst Dassler in the Olympic movement. It is suggested that by the 1968 Olympic Games, 83 per cent of medal winners used Adidas equipment, clothing and shoes (Hill 1996; cited in Toohey and Veal 2000: 108). TOP operates by selling to sponsors world-wide rights to utilise the Olympic logo in advertising and promotion during the period of an Olympiad. Partner companies, such as Coca Cola, IBM and MacDonald's, buy exclusive sponsorship rights related to product categories such as soft drinks, computers or credit cards.

The partnership between the IOC and the TOP sponsor companies formed a new culture in the promotion of the Games, which transformed the Olympic movement into a profitable business operation. Klein (2001) argues that in the 1980s multinational companies altered their marketing strategy from 'promoting a product' to 'promoting a brand'. The Olympic Games, therefore, provided an ideal field for associating cultural ideas to the brands of multi-national companies, offering a marketplace for international capitalism. The TOP programme and the commercialisation of the Olympic movement also enabled the IOC to end dependence on government funding and broad-casting rights (Toohey and Veal 2000). The conservative commentator John Lucas predicted in 1992 that the commercialisation of the Olympic Games would be a temporary phenomenon:

> The Olympic movement, especially the IOC, is bedazzled by its newfound avenues of financial opportunity and will continue exploring them for some years to come. By the millennium year 2000, the IOC will have accu-mulated properties, investments, credits, and cash in sufficient billions of dollars so that it can 'ease off'. It will pull back appreciably from this financial focus and be able at last to devote nearly all of its vast power, influence, and new wealth to educational and altruistic efforts at an even higher level and though a more universal presence than are now possible. (Lucas 1992: 80)

Notwithstanding Lucas' predictions, the commercial interests of the Olympic movement were not reduced after the millennium, but the profits from TOP sponsors escalated in the Sydney Olympics. With the end of the Cold War and its impact on the global economic order, the Olympic movement was transformed into a global capitalist business (Milton-Smith 2002).

In sum, the period of the Cold War was characterised by nationalism, not the chauvinistic nationalism most evident in the early Olympic Games, but nationalism related to sovereignty and political independence. The Olympic movement experienced the engagement of politics in sport, and although the IOC resisted this, it is undeniable that the issue of recognition of NOCs in the post-colonial context provided a source of political power for the IOC, with the result that it gained a leading role in global diplomacy and the conduct of foreign affairs during that period. In addition, the Olympic movement witnessed the shift from amateurism to professionalism and commercialism. The amateur code became more flexible, allowing athletes to earn money by advertising, and once breached full blown professionalism could not be resisted and the Olympic movement adapted quickly to its new, commercialised role, initiating new marketing plans to allow it to consolidate its position as a global business.

2.7   Post-Cold War 1990–2000s: Twenty-first century world order

The end of the Cold War came in the late 1980s, when relations between the East and West began to improve, and the internal tensions within the USSR resulted in its political implosion. There are perhaps two principal perspectives on the causes of the demise of the USSR. The first attributes the end of the war to Ronald Reagan's politics and the instigation of a renewed US military strategy in the early 1980s (the Strategic Defence Initiative of 1983, SDI), which forced the USSR to respond with an analogous scheme that its fragile economy could not sustain. The second attributes the demise of the USSR to Mikhail Gorbachev's inefficient reform of the central-planning system, which provided the space for non-communist governments to come to power in a number of Eastern European states. The Gorbachev reforms, initiated in 1985, brought about the collapse of the Soviet economic system, which although inefficient, was still functioning. The Communist Party lost popularity and centripetal forces were unleashed which led by the end of 1991 to the collapse of the Soviet Union. Some commentators indeed have argued that the Cold War and hostilities against the US policy and particularly against Reagan's government helped to prolong the life of the USSR (Heywood 2002).

The beginning of the post-Cold War era was accompanied by a climate of optimism and idealism that saw the end of East-West rivalry as ushering in a new dawn. With the collapse of the Communist Bloc and the weakening of Soviet power both domestically and internationally, it seemed that the United States would be left as the sole world superpower. The 'new world order', as expressed by the US President, George Bush Sr., was going to be based not on ideological conflicts and shaky international relations, but on a common recognition of international forms and standards (led of course by the US). Central to this new world order was the recognition of the need to tackle international crises peacefully, to resist expansionism and aggression, to control and minimise the production of weapons, and to secure the equal and just treatment of individuals around the world through respect for ('universally recognised') human rights. In the early years of the post-Cold War period, it appeared that the above practices could be applied for resolving major world conflicts. The invasion of Kuwait by Iraq in August 1990 led to the construction of a broad alliance of western and some Muslim countries that worked together to remove Iraqi forces. Although the Soviet Union and China did not participate in the war, they did not oppose the use of military force against Iraq. The Gulf War reinforced to a great extent the role of the United Nations as an international peacemaker, but also as an organisation dominated by American interests (Dodds 2000). Moreover, the *Conference on Security and Cooperation in Europe* (CSCE), which had been created at the Helsinki Conference of 1975, was put into practice in Paris in November 1990, when representatives of the Warsaw Pact and NATO met together and produced the treaty that brought a formal end to the Cold War. The disintegration of the former Yugoslavia in 1991 also saw the use of the CSCE (renamed the *Organisation for Security and Cooperation in Europe*, OCSE), as a mechanism to settle international disputes (Heywood 2002).

The new world order appeared to many to be unipolar, with the USA as the only power which had the military, political and economic capacity to control international affairs, having assumed once more the role of 'world's police force'. The US supported trends towards democratisation in parts of the world such as Latin America and Asia where authoritarian regimes had flourished. It carried out several 'humanitarian interventions', namely the military expulsion of Iraq from Kuwait, its collaboration with NATO to remove Serb forces from Kosovo in 1999, and the bombing of Afghanistan and Iraq in 2002. The USA, promulgated a discourse of liberal democracy, promoting its actions as effecting the spread of political freedom and respect for human rights. Nonetheless, this image of US-sponsored international fraternity and world peace was questioned by some both within and beyond the West. Chomsky (1994) argues that the USA was camouflaging its national interests by proclaiming its support for international law and national sovereignty. For instance, the anti-Iraq coalition of 1990–91 was seen by some as representing the US and wider western concerns about oil supplies. Similarly, US intervention in Kosovo might be seen as an action that, instead of spreading the notion of respect for national sovereignty, fuelled regional disputes (cited in Heywood 2002: 135).

With the end of the Cold War, newly independent states emerged and the world global economy changed dramatically. The collapse of communism in the eastern European revolutions of 1989–91 was seen by some to have given way to a process of democratisation that drew upon the western liberal model and was accompanied by a process of economic transition to capitalism. However, such a transformation from a central-planning system to liberal economies, advocated by the International Monetary Fund (IMF), resulted in insecurity fuelled by the growth of unemployment and inflation, and significantly increased social inequality (Hoogvelt 2001). During the 1990s there was a long period of crisis and transformation of the world capitalist system, with many significant issues remaining unresolved. Such issues included: the political economic consequences of the new world development; just treatment of individuals; equal rights for women, and for ethnic and religious minorities; sustainability of the environment; and debt reduction.

It is argued that the countries of the developed economies have been slow to meet the developing world's demands for assistance in solving socio-political and environmental problems. Moreover, the new nations of the former Soviet Union and Yugoslavia began to compete with other countries of the developing world for aid, with funds provided by the World Bank and other international organisations proving to be insufficient to meet development needs. In the face of such problems, 113 nations (mainly African, Asian and South American) met at the 11th summit of the Non-Aligned movement (NAM) in 1995 in Cartagena. They supported democracy, human rights, economic globalisation and free trade. They called for reform of the International Monetary Fund (IMF) and the World Bank, and positioned themselves against terrorism and against industrial nations' practices such as trade restrictions, blockades and embargos (Dodds 2000).

2.7.1   Unipolar or multipolar new world order?

Since the collapse of the Soviet empire and the democratisation processes in the late 1980s and early 1990s, different intellectual trends emerged in an effort to interpret the geopolitical consequences of the new global world order. It was uncertain whether the end of the bipolar superpower era was characterised by western, US-dominated, unipolarity or by a new multipolar world order. The most characteristic thesis of a unipolar interpretation of the end of the Cold War is provided by Fukuyama (1990, 1992). His article *The End of History?* (Fukuyama 1990), which he later developed into the *End of History and the Last Man* (Fukuyama 1992) generated much controversy. Fukuyama went as far as to proclaim that the history of ideas and the ideological debates had effectively ended with the worldwide triumph of western liberal democracy as the final form of human government. He argues that although there have been unstable liberal democracies, 'liberal democracy remains the only coherent political aspiration that spans different regions and cultures around the globe' (Fukuyama 1992). In his view, all societies strive for economic modernisation, but that this is only likely to materialise in liberal democracies. He argues:

> The only parts of humanity not aspiring to economic modernisation are a few isolated tribes in the jungles of Brazil or Papua New Guinea, and they don't aspire to it because they don't know about it ... But the aspiration to economic modernisation is one of the most universal characteristics of human societies one can imagine. Though the tendency toward capitalism has historically been much less universal than the desire for economic modernisation per se ... technology necessarily points toward market-oriented forms of economic decision-making,

What is even less universal than capitalism is the preference for liberal democracy. Nonetheless, as a purely empirical matter, there is an extraordinarily strong correlation between high levels of industrial development and stable democracy. (Fukuyama 1995: 32)

Fukuyama's assertion of the 'end of history' incited long debates and fundamental controversies. Lawler (Lawler 1994) emphasises that the main deficiency of Fukuyama's thesis is that it does not really make clear what the end of history must necessarily be, thus leading to incoherence in his argument. Among the major criticisms of his account is that it conflates the heuristic/empirical and the normative levels of analysis. In addition, his approach has been criticised for affirming the universality of the liberal democratic ideal from a western-centric, and in particular American-centric perspective. Disputing previous accounts that democracy was the product of the specific cultural and social milieu of western civilisation, he argues, 'it was the most rational possible political system and "fit" a broader human personality shared across cultures' (pp. 220–1). However, he offers no evidence of indigenous non- western liberal democracies. Von Laue claims that this is because 'none exist ... Liberal democracy spread as a result of the Westernisation of the world; its appeal is based on a wide range of factors, all derived from superior power' (Von Laue 1994: 26).

In contrast to Fukuyama and his teleological theory of monolithic diffusion resulting in a liberal-democratic convergence, other intellectuals have raised concerns about 'resistance' in forms of ethnic, cultural or regional nationalism. Samuel Huntington (1996) developed the most radical thesis of this kind, warning about the future 'clash of civilisations'. His thesis is based on the belief that twenty-first-century conflicts will not primarily be ideological or economic but rather cultural; thus these will be conflicts between nations and groups from 'different civilisations'. He argues,

The post-Cold War world is a world of seven or eight major civilisations. Cultural commonalities and differences shape the interests, antagonisms, and associations of states. The most important countries in the world come overwhelmingly from different civilisations. The local conflicts most likely to escalate into broader wars are those between groups and states from different civilisations. The predominant patterns of political and economic development differ from civilisation to civilisation. The key issues on the international agenda involve differences among civilisations. Power is shifting from the long predominant West to non-western civilisations. Global politics has become multipolar and multicivilisational. (Huntington 1996: 29)

Huntington (1996) argued that the major civilisations (Western, Chinese, Japanese, Hindu, Islamic, Buddhist, Latin American and Orthodox Christian) would become, in reaction to globalisation, the major actors in world affairs.

He asserts that western civilisation, though most powerful so far, is in decline and will be challenged by non-western civilisations.

> The West is, and will remain for years to come, the most powerful civilisation. Yet its power relative to that of other civilisations is declining. As the West attempts to assert its values and protect its interests, non-western societies confront a choice. Some attempt to emulate the West and join or to 'bandwagon' with the West. Other Confucian and Islamic societies attempt to expand their own economic and military power to resist and to 'balance against the West. A central axis of post-Cold War politics is thus the interaction of Western power and culture with the power and culture of non-Western civilisations. (Huntington 1996: 29)

Neo-conservative interpretations of Huntington's account suggest that the next world war would be between civilisations rather than states, most likely between China and the West, or between the West and Islam. George W. Bush's declaration of a 'war on terrorism' following the attacks on New York and Washington in September 2001 might be seen as evidence of the latter. Huntington's thesis has nevertheless been widely criticised. It is argued that Huntington does not establish the link between cultural difference and rivalries, and thus does not provide adequate explanation for the fact that most wars take place between states of the same civilisation. Moreover, it is suggested that conflict between civilisations is based more on perceived economic and political inequalities than on cultural incompatibilities (Heywood 2002).

2.7.2   The contemporary global Olympic movement

The Olympic movement in the 1980s, and especially in the 1990s, formed an integral part of global culture through the diffusion of meanings and images in the global media. Media, and particularly television, is one of the most highly commercialised sectors of contemporary culture and constitutes a central element of consumer culture (Roche 2000). Gruneau examines 'media hegemony', specifically in the context of relationships between the institutions of sport and the media. He argues:

> Television's elaboration and selection of preferred emphases and meanings, its favoured narratives, its 'management' of contradictory themes and values (e.g., between unbridled individual success and obligations to team, nation or community), can all be seen as part of a complex process through which some understandings of sport, the body, consumer culture and the pursuit of excellence are naturalised while others are marginalised, downgraded, or ignored. (Gruneau 1989: 28)

Since the 1980s and the IOC's decision to commercialise aspects of the Olympic movement, the Olympic Games have became a global entertainment spectacle; television broadcasting, and other forms of cultural mediation by the media have transformed the Games into a truly global event (Roche 2000). Such transformation is evident at both global and local levels, examining the impact of the Olympic Games as a localised event in space and time, and as a global mega-event of our times.

At the local level, the Summer Olympics of the 1980s and 1990s contributed to major infrastructure development in most of the host cities. Urban development is normally a necessary 'task' of the Olympic cities, which needs to develop an appropriate socio-economic and planning context for staging the Olympic event, while also being capable of transforming the Games from a 'local event' into 'global spectacle' experienced through the media. The Olympic Games are perceived by many as potentially capable of leaving (though not necessarily achieving) a positive material legacy for host cities with the construction of sport facilities, development of transport systems and revitalisation of urban areas. Perhaps the outstanding modern example of urban development due to Olympic hosting is the case of the 1992 Barcelona Games. Garcia (1993) suggests that the city's Olympic Games' project emerged as an attempt to revitalise the city's economy after a period of economic crisis and industrial decline (cited in Roche 2000: 144). It is argued that the most significant feature of the Games was the role they played in the economic, physical, and political regeneration of the city (Roche 2000; Toohey and Veal 2000), including refurbishment of the main stadium, a new museum of contemporary art and a remodelled Catalonian arts museum, and various other buildings, as well as transport and service infrastructure improvements. Local interests and regional modernisation needs are connected with the Olympics, which appeared, especially in the 1990s, as a great opportunity for development of the potential Olympic cities.

Notwithstanding the clamour to join the bidding for hosting the Games the level and range of criticisms of the impact of staging the Games has grown considerably. The criticisms are along six principal dimensions, the cultural, economic, political, social, environmental and sporting (Henry 2012). In cultural terms the games are perceived as Euro-centric promoting western sports, and proposals to introduce additional sports from the non-West, such as wushu, have met with resistance (Brownell 2008; Ren 2008). In addition the incorporation of requirements concerning women's (and subsequently men's) clothing (or the lack of it) in beach volleyball demonstrates a willingness to sacrifice sensitivity to the requirements of modest dress of some cultures which would thus exclude them effectively from participation, to the demands of the media to use athletes' bodies to promote viewing figures (Brooks 2001).

In economic terms critics have focused on the cost of the Games. With the exception of Atlanta, in Olympic Games since 1984 new, purpose-built facilities have predominated, resulting in considerable overspends, with public sector funding meeting the deficits (Cashman 2006; Henry 2009).

Post-games under-utilisation of facilities is also a target of critics in particular for Athens but also in the cases of Sydney and Beijing. In political terms the controversy over human rights issues in relation to China tended to overshadow accusations about the human rights abuses perpetrated by the West in terms of detention without trial in Guantanamo Bay, and the use of torture interrogation techniques on prisoners. Nevertheless western critics pressed the case for a boycott of the Beijing Games (Worden 2008). A major criticism in social terms of the costs of staging the Games has been the impact on local populations who are displaced to make way for facility construction and/or associated infrastructure development (Centre for Housing Rights and Evictions, 2007), while the environmental costs of the huge development and infrastructure projects and the pollution caused by transporting participants, officials and spectators around the world represent another important critique. Finally claims that hosting the games can generate a sporting legacy in terms of increased participation in the home nation with an associated health dividend have also been challenged (Veal and Frawley 2009; Weed *et al.* 2009).

Despite these criticisms however, since 1992, when perception of the various *potential* economic and other benefits of hosting the Olympics had become evident, and the event had become established as a global media-event, the inter-city competition to be selected as host has become more intense. Roche argues that the preceding bidding competition during the pre-war and early post-war periods was not as strong because states' and cities' interest in the Olympics varied and in many cases it was the IOC that invited a city to host the Games and not the other way round (for example, 1896 Athens, 1904 St. Louis, 1920 Antwerp, 1928 Amsterdam). However, he points out that the situation by the end of the century was very different:

> It is true (by definition) that most of the competitors in this global Olympic city bidding game must be losers, and it is also true that the competition can be expensive to enter. However, participation in this global inter-city game in the 1990s at least enables cities to achieve the status of being potential Olympic cities and thus to associate themselves with Olympic mythology and the (positive aspects of the) Olympic story. (Roche 2000: 152)

The selection of Olympic cities is a process, which is led by the IOC and involves interests of NOCs, national governments and local authorities. The 'Bidding Cities' make their bids to the IOC, which evaluates them and shortlists from among the bidders, cities who thus gain the status of 'Candidate Cities' which submit more detailed candidature files for review by an Evaluation Commission. The Commission reviews the files and undertakes a single visit to the Candidate cities before submitting a report to the IOC Session which is charged with making the final selection.

The selection process in its earlier form, had long been criticised for its secretive character and association with political interests that had led to problems of bribery and corruption. In November 1998, the Olympic movement faced one of the most serious crises in its history, when a Salt Lake City television station revealed that the city's Bid Committee had paid for an IOC member's daughter to attend the American University in Washington D.C. Following this revelation, the Swiss IOC member Marc Hodler announced that he believed that there was 'massive corruption' in the IOC. These allegations led to an IOC inquiry in 1998–9, establishing an *ad hoc* Commission of Inquiry under the chairmanship of IOC Vice-President, Dick Pound of Canada, together with a number of other inquiries by relevant organisations. The findings from these investigations (the *Pound Report*) led the IOC in 1999 to the historic decision of expelling six of its members. Additionally, another three resigned, some received official warnings and another remained under investigation. The scandals of corruption and bribery between the local organisers and the IOC members were considered to be a major problem for the public image of the Olympic movement. It was believed that the corporate sponsors might withdraw investment in Olympic-related activities if the reputation of the Olympic movement was tarnished. The IOC underwent a major reform (MacAloon 2011), which among others included the revision of the bidding process and the establishment of an Ethics Commission, in an attempt to safeguard the image of the movement (DaCosta *et al.* 2002; Milton-Smith 2002; Roche 2000; Toohey and Veal 2000).

The IOC reform can also be seen as a response to the challenges that emerge from the 'global citizenship' of the contemporary Olympic movement. Clearly the Olympic movement in its various facets and different levels is involved with international diplomacy and cultural politics in relation to nation-states, international governmental organisations (IGOs), and international non-governmental organisations (INGOs). Roche (2000) argues that the Olympic movement, outside the sphere of religion and science, is the biggest and probably the most important cultural INGO in the international system. Although FIFA plays a very important role in soccer, nevertheless in terms of sport ideology it constitutes part of the Olympic movement, since FIFA is an IOC-recognised international federation and FIFA's President is an IOC member. Because of the major role of the Olympic movement in the international governance system, the corruption crisis surrounding the IOC's global inter-city bid competition induced strong reaction from the sports ministers of various governments, NOCs and major corporate sponsors who pressed for structural reform. In this context, and following the Salt Lake City scandal, the US Senator George Mitchell, an internationally respected figure for his role in the peace process in Northern Ireland, chaired an enquiry on the part of USOC which called for radical new fair and transparent practices within the IOC (United States Olympic Committee 1999).

The Olympic movement has always claimed to support sport as a means to the promotion of such ideals as freedom, fair play, equality, health and peace (though the mix and expression of these ideals has changed over time as we shall see in the forthcoming chapters). However, the discrepancy between its rhetoric and its practices has attracted severe criticism (Hoberman 1986; Milton-Smith 2002; Roche 2000). The intensification of competition in the professional sports world, enhanced by mediatisation and commercialisation, put pressure on the athletes for whom victory would have a tremendous impact on their economic and social status. This has increased the pressure for 'victory at any costs', including doping and the artificial enhancement of physical capabilities. The effectiveness of the IOC in tackling the problem had been called into question (Dimeo and Hunt 2009) and the conflict between its commercial interests and anti-doping responsibilities attracted criticism. Although the problem of doping is fundamentally different from that of corruption, both are considered to be the product of rampant economic and political interests (Hoberman 1992).

In response to the worldwide waves of criticism about doping, commercialism, professionalism and inequalities, the IOC has become increasingly interested in connecting its work with well-established world organisations. The IOC's interest is being connected with the work of the World Health Organisation (WHO), based upon the link between sport and health, which was recently undermined by drug abuse and sport injuries. Thus, in 1998 the IOC supported the WHO's annual *Day Against Smoking* campaign, and it continued to participate in the WHO's *International Working Group on Active Life*. Additionally, the IOC refuses to accept sponsorship from tobacco and alcohol industries, supporting WHO's health policies.

The IOC has also been criticised for the limited extent to which it has contributed to the promotion of the ideal of peaceful coexistence. Despite the idealistic universalism and political independence of its ideology, the Olympic movement has been an active player in world politics throughout its history. However, it has been condemned for its submission to authoritarian regimes (Nazi Olympics) and its use in the Cold War as an international terrain of ideological disputes (Hoberman 1986; Riordan and Krüger 1999). Although it has contributed to the defence of human rights, especially with the isolation of South Africa for its apartheid policy against the Black citizens from 1970 to 1992, the same cannot be said in relation to the regimes that have hosted the Games. The IOC has often awarded the Games to regimes that have been heavily criticised for their record on human rights, such as the 1968 Mexico Olympics, the 1980 Moscow Olympics, the 1988 Seoul Olympics (Roche 2000), and the Beijing Games in 2008.

In an effort to establish itself as an organisation which plays an important role in the sphere of international civil society and governance beyond sport, the IOC has acted together with the UN to promote the concept of the Olympic Truce. Roche (2000) argues that the Olympic movement and the United Nations have been parallel in their actions in the international sphere during the post-war and post-colonial period. Both provided international arenas in which the new nations could strengthen their national identity and worldwide recognition through displays and public appearance. Although their interests clashed in the past (in particular in the 1970s when UNESCO, under the influence of the USSR, tried to take over the running of the Olympics), today they cooperate closely in several matters. The IOC often collaborates with UNESCO and UNICEF and other bodies of the UN, on issues of education, environmentalism and human rights. Nevertheless, its democratic and peace-making profile has been recently undermined by the selection of Beijing as a host city for the 2008 Olympics. Despite the 1989 Tiananmen Square massacre and the allegations of human rights abuses by the Chinese state, the IOC persisted in awarding the Games to Beijing (Roche 2000), though with controversy surrounding alleged torturing of prisoners and detention without trial at Guantanamo Bay, some western states have not been immune from such criticisms. Thus, the future of the IOC might be challenged by the clash of its politico-economic interests and global ethical imperatives, and we return to such questions in the final chapter which deals with discourse themes on sport for development, sport and multiculturalism and the growing role sought for sport in international development.

2.8   Conclusion: Olympic histories and moral agendas

In our introduction to this chapter we stressed the point that the discourses evident in the various histories of the modern Olympic movement would invariably intertwine with societal discourses. What are these strands and how have accounts of the development of the Olympic movement drawn on, or been impacted upon, by these discourse strands? We have highlighted several in our discussion to date: nationalism and internationalisation; gender and the place of women; politicisation of the Olympic movement and of sport in terms of East-West relations in the Cold War period and in relation to the post-colonial period between the core Olympic nations (essentially the West) and the newly emerging nations; debates on amateurism and the implicitly class-based control of the Olympic movement; commercialisation and commodification of sport.

Our approach does not seek to adopt a neutral approach to such social phenomena. Indeed we argue explicitly elsewhere and tacitly in this chapter, for example, in favour of gender equity promoted within, but also by, the Olympic movement (Henry 2007; Henry and Robinson 2010; Henry *et al.*

2004). We acknowledge the importance, indeed the necessary relationship, of politics to sport and the importance of sport in politics, and have argued against the Orientalist (and Occidentalist) tendencies of some Olympic and sporting discourses both historical (Chatziefstathiou *et al.* 2008) and contemporary (Amara and Henry 2010). We identify the positive and negative aspects of commercialisation and commodification, which privilege some and disadvantage others. Our list of discourse themes is not intended to be exhaustive. Scant reference has been made here, for example, to the themes of new technologies which are so costly that they militate against participation on an equal footing (e.g. the requirement of water-based artificial turf hockey pitches for international competition; or the development of hi-tech boat and cycle design), of environmentalist discourse, of the increasing prevalence of social media, or of discourse on youth identity (though this is in part the concern of later chapters).

However while positions adopted in all of these discourse strands are important in the contemporary context one such strand would seem to be core to an understanding of the concerns of a global organisation that has aspirations of universal cultural significance, and this is the debate couched in terms of Huntington's *Clash of Civilisations* and Fukuyama's concept of monocentric cultural diffusion. If we concur with Huntington's analysis of a world made up of 'silos' of essentially mutually incompatible values, or Fukuyama's notion that one political and economic model has a monopoly on wisdom and is likely to supplant all others, then we have a recipe for conflict and mutual antagonism which is dangerous for more than simply the sporting world. Neo-conservatives employed this kind of argument (that value sets of different cultures were incompatible, that the West's values are inherently superior, but that the protection and promulgation of western values may require force) in justifying action in recent conflicts which many have argued ran counter to international law. However we would argue that both Huntington's and Fukuyama's arguments are flawed. As Bassan Tibi (2001) has argued, the differences within cultures are often greater than the differences between cultures. To use an illustration which we have employed elsewhere:

> consensus in western societies about the approach to gender equity will continue to be difficult to achieve because of the problems of incorporating anti-feminist opinion which views gender differences implicitly or explicitly as a product of biological difference. By contrast, building some level of consensus between feminists in Chinese, Muslim, or Hindu civilisational blocks (despite difficulties) is likely to be more straightforward as, for example, the United Nations World Conferences on Women have demonstrated. Here programmes of action have been agreed despite the considerable heterogeneity of world views represented at these Conferences. (Henry 2007: 203)

Generalising what western (or even American) political and economic values might be is far more difficult given the diversity within such societies, than either Huntington or Fukuyama and their proponents would care to accept. This is an absolutely critical point for an international body for which inter-cultural engagement and pluralism are central requirements. The IOC has defined its primary role as one of moral, rather than simply administrative, leadership of the world of sport. Its programme is set out (if perhaps somewhat vaguely) in the introductory section to the Olympic Charter and its aspiration is to provide universal leadership and engagement in its programme. While we might disagree about the likelihood of *universal* cultural engagement we do believe that sport can provide a vehicle for coming to some aspects of *general* consensus across cultures on values to be promoted through sport. Sport, especially where it purports to be guided by ethical concerns provides a domain in which important cultural questions – how we behave to one another, what forms of dress we might wear, which forms of activity are going to be incorporated in international games, and so on, are rehearsed. In effect this provides a practical forum for discourse ethics, though one which deviates from Habermas's (1990) intended approach of universal (rather than general) consensus (Henry 2007). The chapters which follow seek to outline ways in which particular voices sought to shape that discourse and to promote particular sets of values and the apparatus for their internalisation.

3
Coubertin: Patronage and Paternalistic Discourses of Olympism (1887–1937)

3.1 Introduction

While discourse on matters Olympic did not begin with Coubertin, for our purposes in reviewing the development of ideas about Olympism, Coubertin and his work represent a compelling start point for evaluating the changing meaning of Olympism from the 1894 Olympic Congress at the Sorbonne up to the present day. In this chapter we identify the implications of Coubertin's speech and actions for the ways in which Olympism and Olympic sport were conceptualised in late nineteenth-century Europe, as well as in and beyond Europe in the twentieth century (1887–1937). The chapter seeks to examine and understand Coubertin's shaping of the discourse of Olympism and the interests it promoted as expressed in the founder's correspondence, publications and personal records. As Coubertin's conception of Olympism was an outcome of processes which started before the Sorbonne Congress in 1894, we begin by considering the precursors of Olympism (1887–1894). Then we move to discourse around the official establishment of the IOC and the early years of the development of Olympism (1894–1918), and finally we conclude with the years of the expansion of the movement beyond Europe (and Coubertin's death in 1937).

3.2 Precursors of Olympism (1887–1894)

Pierre de Coubertin, during his life, experienced the defeat of France in the Franco-Prussian war, and a succession of social changes, as part of the modernisation processes of his era. His native country, France, experienced the victory of democracy, the industrialisation of its economy, the spread of socialist values and establishment of socialist structures, the secular-isation of civil society, the absorption of provincial cultures into a strong dominant national culture, the linkage of individualism and nationalism but also the interconnectedness of the world due to an increasing tide of cosmopolitanism (MacAloon 1981). Pierre de Coubertin thus lived in an era which experienced distinctive dynamic processes and the social, economic and cultural mobility, observing such processes from the privileged perspective of a French aristocratic background. MacAloon emphasises that,

> Genealogy is linked with much larger social interests than simple ancestor reckoning. In most social groups – peoples, classes, castes, movements, and so on – a family tree is not a mere map of blood ties, but an index and icon of the fundamental values which 'blood' represents to that group. (MacAloon 1981: 10–11)

Hoberman (1992) also argues that Coubertin must be understood as a representative of his noble class and an exemplary citizen of the French Third Republic. In this context, Coubertin's values might be seen to a certain extent as a reflection of the conservatism of his class. Interestingly, his desire for success through important endeavours, such as pedagogical reform in France or the Olympic Games, can also be attributed to the high expectations derived from his aristocratic background. In his 1908 memoir *Une Campagne de Vingt-et-un ans,* Coubertin, commenting on his resignation from the military French academy St. Cyr, had said that he wished to change a career and associate his name with a great educational reform. Inspired by Philhellenism and influenced by the rising cosmopolitanism of his era, Coubertin was committed to initiate educational reforms that would 'modernise' the French educational system.

3.2.1   The need for social reform

Coubertin aligned himself with the liberal, republican classicist intellectuals by writing in the journal *La Reforme Sociale* (1883), a combined organ of two organisations, the *Société d'économie sociale* and the *Unions de la paix sociale*, where his first thoughts and expressions about *l'education athlétique* and *la pédagogie sportive* can be found. Both organisations were founded and led by Frédéric Le Play, a sociologist and social philosopher of the mid-nineteenth century who Coubertin admired and many of whose views he shared. Le Play's work had raised much criticism but also received much recognition for its emphasis on the methods of 'fieldwork' and 'observation' with the modern meaning of the terms in sociological research (MacAloon 1986).

His social philosophy was centred on values of social peace, workers' rights, family, Catholicism and decentralisation. He founded first the *Societé d'économie sociale* that was open to amateur sociologists who wanted to learn his methods. However, after the historical events of 1870–71 (the Franco-Prussian War and the Commune) and the need for an ideological orientation, he founded the *Unions de la paix sociale* and established the journal *La Reforme Sociale*, which had a conservative character and promoted the values of family, Catholicism and social classification. Pierre de Coubertin related strongly to Frédéric Le Play because they both shared a desire to reform French education. Coubertin's biggest ambition in the 1880s was to improve the use of recreation time and introduce sport in schools. Coubertin wrote the following in *La Reforme Sociale* (1888):

> Other ties of even greater significance unite the Committee with the Unions, the goal that it aims to achieve being first and foremost among them. Many a time, Frederic Le Play dwelt on the deplorable tendencies of our current academic regimen, and on the need for immediate reform. We are going to try to achieve one of the points in his programme. Were he still alive, we would certainly enjoy his support and assistance. In our view, improved use of recreation time and the spread of sports among school children are but means to an end. We have set our aim higher. The reason we are using these means is that observation and experience have shown that they are effective in giving young people the precious qualities of energy, perseverance, judgment and initiative that, among us, are the prerogative of only a few. Much can be expected of a generation brought up in this way. (Coubertin 1888, 2000: 75)

Frédéric Le Play's influence on Coubertin is reflected not only in their common plans for social reform, but also in the use of the methods of 'observation' and 'experience' as reliable measurement tools. In common with Le Play, Coubertin believed that social reform should start from education and the young population of France.

> Social reform must be achieved through education. Our efforts must focus not on adults, but on children, in order to ensure our success. We must give those children qualities of mind that will make them capable of understanding, and qualities of character that will render them capable of performing the transformation in which your illustrious founder saw France's salvation. (Coubertin 1888, 2000: 76)

On July 1, 1888 the *Committee for the Propagation of Physical Education* was founded, the Secretary General being Coubertin, and it aimed at the transformation of French education. In a letter on behalf of the Committee to the members of *Societé d'économie sociale* and *Unions de la paix sociale*, asking for their help in the efforts towards social reform through education, he uses the word 'crusade' to describe their attempts.

> In effect, our work is shielded from any political quarrels. It is purely social, and that is one more consideration for you. We are confident that you will assist us in the crusade that we have undertaken, against a system of education that is so ill-suited to the needs of the present day,

and that has proven incapable of producing the true citizens that France needs. (Coubertin 1888, 2000: 77)

Their social reform, characterised here as 'apolitical', aimed to change the conditions of the relationship between the individual and the state, giving more rights to individuals and limiting the authority of the state. In a speech in Boston adopting the discourse of both liberal individualism and of traditional conservatism (in a manner redolent of the British Conservative Party's incorporation in the late twentieth century of the neo-liberalism of the New Right and of patrician One Nation Conservatism), Coubertin argues that:

> We want free-minded self-governing men, who will not look upon the State as a baby looks on his mother, who will not be afraid of having to make their own way through life. Such is the work that our Association has pointed out to French teachers as being the most important part of their duty. It involves practically what I call the training for freedom. (Coubertin 1890b, 2000: 139)

Coubertin, as a social theorist of the French Third Republic promoted the value of 'freedom', hoping for social peace and harmony. Particularly if seen in their French translation *'liberté'* (freedom) and *'ésprit libre'* (free-minded), they appeal to the values of freedom and democracy, upon which French social structures were established after the French Revolution (1789) (Hoberman 1986). Coubertin's ideological framework in this period is predominantly and classically republican with an emphasis on the values of 'freedom, God and country'.

> And so I have the right to say, and to repeat, that we expect this transformed education to produce [...] active and determined citizens who will adopt as their own the motto of the minister of whom I spoke earlier: citizens who will love God, country, and freedom. (Coubertin 1889b: 68)

Nonetheless, he promotes a more cautious, more flexible form of conservatism that allows changes for the betterment of French society, thus his vision for reform(s). His disappointment with the so far unsuccessful attempts of a social reform is evident below:

> At times I have wondered – and certainly I am not the only one who has asked this question – how it is that the doctrines that form the overall social reform programme have not had any clear impact on French society so far. These doctrines were proclaimed by an illustrious man whose name is familiar to everyone. They have been supported by

societies whose simple, ingenious machinery makes it easy to propagate them. Now, these doctrines are defended by devoted citizens thoroughly persuaded of their value. What is missing from these doctrines that keeps them from gaining the upper hand and revitalizing the country? The reason is that the doctrines of Frédéric Le Play are eminently reasonable, and that they are addressed, when all is said and done, to a people that is not. (Coubertin 1888, 2000: 75)

This statement illustrates a number of themes: Coubertin's disappointment at the humbling of France in the Franco-Prussian war and a yearning for reinstatement of lost international power and influence, his personal aspiration to attach his name to a pedagogical reform, and the influence on his thinking of the liberal republican classicist Frédéric Le Play promoting a successful social reform through education. These factors motivated him to dedicate himself during this period to the project of French educational reform. As part of this project, Coubertin travelled to England, America and Canada in order to gain ideas about how to initiate successfully physical education in schools. However, it was English education that impressed him the most and provided the model on which he wished to develop French educational reform.

3.2.2 The English education system

The birth of modern sport is credited to England, dating from the middle of the nineteenth century. Although at this time, games and sports were not the exclusive privilege of the British, Britain has been acknowledged as the society that developed them into their current forms. Many of the rules of sport were first codified in nineteenth-century England, where their governing bodies were also established (Guttman 1978; Guttmann 1994). Thus, Coubertin visited the English and Irish schools and universities in order to make observations on their educational efficiency. Using Le Play's method of 'observation', which was still new, Coubertin was willing to discover those qualities of English education that were highly regarded at that time, and then transfer them to the French educational context. He visited many places and compiled his work in a 326-page book entitled *Education en Angleterre*, which was comprised of an introduction and 16 chapters. He also wrote a large number of articles, many based on the findings of his observations of educational practice (Müller 2000).

A critical formative influence in the evolution of sport in England was exercised by the Greater Public Schools, elite private boarding schools, where team sports were initiated as a means of social control (Toohey and Veal 2000). Key to this model of sport was the notion of amateurism, that is playing the game for intrinsic rather than extrinsic rewards, which reinforced the social distinction between the so-called 'gentleman amateur' and 'professionals' from the lower classes of society who traded on their physical sporting capital (Bourdieu 1989; Gruneau 1993). As an important component of the curriculum, sport was linked with religion in an attempt to develop 'Muscular Christians'. These individuals, mostly representatives of the privileged classes, supposedly exhibited the positive qualities of both sport and religion, following the ancient Greek ideal, and core concept of Muscular Christianity, that of a 'sound mind in a sound body'. However, the pantheon of gods had been replaced by a Christian monotheism, appealing to a notion of chivalry, which, it was purported, could be traced back to the Middle Ages (Toohey and Veal 2000). Three elements of English education drew Coubertin's attention: a) the centrality of sport in the curriculum, as based on the concept of body and mind harking back to an English construction of the ancient Greek ideal, b) the 'elastic' relationship between the Church and the State in the domain of education, and c) the English Public School preparation of individuals for maintenance and expansion of the British Empire.

3.2.3   Athletic education

Coubertin has continuously emphasised in his writings the major role that sport played in English education. He noted in *La Reforme Sociale* (1887):

> Gentlemen, I now come to what seems to me the most noteworthy aspect of English education: I mean the role that sports plays in that education. This role is physical, moral, and social, all at the same time. We have a two-fold reason to consider it here, because I believe that, although we may hope for certain reforms in our system, it is only through sports that they can be introduced. (Coubertin 1887, 2000: 114)

It was believed that some of the virtues required for sound, masculine, muscular Christian practice could be learnt through participation in sport. These included qualities such as sportsmanship, leadership, teamwork, the ability to be a good winner and loser, as well as a work ethic. The strong bond between body and mind, the combination and cultivation of both physical and mental qualities were central to an holistic development of individuals. Coubertin wished to reform French education on the basis of this view of physical culture, bound up with a set of values inspired by the Hellenic civilisation and the English Public Schools culture.

> Minds, like bodies, are constantly occupied by that passion which carries them away and subjugates them. This is, I repeat, encouraged as much as possible. The English believe in the need for enthusiasm at this age. But they think, too, that it is not easy, even if it is a good thing, to engender in children such enthusiasm for Alexander or Caesar. They must have something more alive, more real. The dust of Olympia is still what stirs their healthy competitive spirit the most, and the most naturally.

They gladly pursue honours for which they see grown men proud to compete [...] It has been said that the life of the thinker and that of the athlete are utterly opposed. For my part, I have often seen that those who were the leaders in physical exercises were also leaders in their studies. Their excellence in one area gives them a desire to be first in everything. There is nothing like the habit of victory to assure success. (Coubertin 1887: 116)

The focus of French education was on exhausting intellectual readings and 'non-beneficial', 'wasted' recreation time. In relation to French education he argued once, 'boredom and weakness, those purveyors of immorality, hold sway pretty much from top to bottom in French education. In the public high schools, add to that the absence of moral instruction and the poor utilisation of holidays, and you have the formula for creating a high school student' (Coubertin 1889a, 2000: 71). In contrast, the English education, having achieved equilibrium between theory and practice through sport, prepared its pupils for their demanding roles in society.

If you are familiar with the English, you know that life is untenable for the timid, the weak, and the lazy. In the tumult of existence, such persons are driven back, overwhelmed, and stepped on. They are tossed aside, seen merely as impediments. Nowhere is selection more pitiless. There are two distinct races: the race of men with frank expressions and strong muscles, with a self-assured stride, and the race of weaklings with resigned and humble faces, a vanquished air. Well, what holds true in the world holds true in the schools as well! The weak are tossed aside. The benefits of this education apply only to the strong. (Coubertin 1887, 2000: 119)

One of the foremost and most famous exponents of such educational doctrine was Thomas Arnold, a clergyman and director of Rugby College for 14 years, from 1828. Arnold transformed the school as an institution by attaching to sport a central role in the curriculum (Müller 2000). Coubertin began his '21-year campaign' having a vision to transfer to France Arnold's athletic education, the approach Arnold used in order to produce Muscular Christians.

In a word, one must hurry to create a man, morally and physically, of this child who has bad instincts and passions whose assault he will suffer; he must be given premature muscles and will, what Arnold called 'true manliness'. Initiative, daring, decisiveness, the habit of self-reliance and of taking responsibility for one's own failures ... all these are qualities for which one cannot make up for lost time. It is far more important to cultivate them from early childhood than to strive to inculcate scientific notions in young minds, notions that vanish all too quickly for the very reason that they were placed there too late. (Coubertin 1887, 2000: 115)

Coubertin thought that, if Arnold's athletic education was adopted by the French, it would help France to recover (*rebronzer*) after its defeat in the Franco-Prussian war (MacAloon 1981: 51). As the representative of the French Minister of Public Instruction at the Physical Training Congress in Boston in late 1889, Coubertin visited North America for the first time. There, Coubertin praised in his lecture the work of Thomas Arnold and revealed that the French Educational Reform Association had been established upon his principles, 'the English athletic sport system as understood and explained by the greatest of modern teachers, Thomas Arnold of Rugby [should be adopted]. His principles are the ones on which the French Educational Reform Association was founded last year' (Coubertin 1890b: 138).

Guttmann (1992) and Hoberman (1995) argue that Coubertin was misled by Hughes to think that Thomas Arnold had been a keen advocate of sports. In fact, they suggest that Thomas Arnold was far more interested in boys' moral education than in their physical development. Interestingly, there were two relatively well known books written about Rugby school, *Tom Brown's School Days (1857)* and *The Life and Correspondence of Dr. Arnold (1844)*. The first was a fictional account written by Thomas Hughes, a student not much noticed by Arnold, and the latter was written by Arthur Penrhyn Stanley, who although he came late to Rugby, was promoted to the fifth grade due to his intelligence, bringing him to the attention of Arnold who took him into his inner circle. Thomas Hughes described Arnold as a kind, sensitive, open-minded and benevolent teacher. Nevertheless, MacAloon (1981) argues that Thomas Hughes has possibly romanticised the situation in Rugby school and the distant relationship with the master did not allow him to gain a deeper insight. On the other hand, Stanley, having experienced a closer contact with Arnold, expresses a terrible fear and anxiety about meeting Arnold's high expectations. Therefore, MacAloon (1981) argues, 'Coubertin either missed this [i.e. Stanley's perspective], ignored it, or balanced it off against the far healthier portrait of Thomas Hughes, that more ingenuous, airier, and to Coubertin, more kindred soul' (p. 62). As evident in the documents, it seems that Coubertin was aware of Arnold's strict and rigid profile. Nonetheless, he believed that such doctrine, based upon the principle of selection, a core aspect of the popular British ideology of athleticism, was right and fair for the pupils.

One day, when problems had arisen requiring that several students be expelled, showing discontent in the ranks, before the whole school Arnold spoke these words, which have remained famous and which sum up his whole approach: 'It is not necessary that there be 300, 100, or even 50 students here; but it is necessary that there be nothing but Christian Gentlemen'. This passage deals with an error in public opinion, then as widespread in England as it is today in France. The public held that secondary schools were institutions intended to correct bad character, a detestable notion that can only serve to make a school into a correctional institution and consequently, a rotten place for the honest children who happen to be there [...] This corresponds to a very British idea, that of selection. In the physical order, as in the moral order, it is always the elite that is targeted, because a superior phalanx, though few in number, yields infinitely more than very widespread mediocrity. Thus everything tends to be given to those who already have something, as in the Gospel. (Coubertin 1887, 2000: 107–8)

The 'British' idea of selection, as embodied in the strict Arnoldian doctrine appealed to Coubertin, who envisaged a sound youth for France. Such education could prepare adolescents to become future citizens of a stronger State.

3.2.4   Religion and education

The struggle for the French educational system represented the antagonistic side of Church-State relations under the Republic. When the Republic dismantled the clerical monopoly on education, 'it declared that education under the state was to be "lay", or non-sectarian, that is to say not specifically Catholic. The Church chose to interpret neutrality as hostility and branded the new schools as "godless"' (Hoberman 1986: 68). Coubertin, a keen supporter of the new policy of the Republic, stated the following:

One can make an accomplished mind out of a child raised in absolute atheism; but if you manage to make that person an honest man, it comes about through no fault of your own. Whether one is Catholic or Lutheran, Calvinist or Orthodox, religion is not a lesson to be learned, it is an atmosphere to be breathed. That is why government institutions, which necessarily welcome children from different religions, must be day schools and not boarding schools. Other lay, Catholic, Protestant, or even free-thinking institutions should be set up around them. Why not? There must be freedom for all. (Coubertin 1889c, 2000: 107–8)

In an attempt to relax the Church-State tension and maintain social peace, the government often emphasised and publicly appreciated the role of religion. In similar vein, Coubertin also underlined the importance of religion in education.

There has been talk of codifying moral instruction ... Outside of religion, there is no moral instruction to teach to children. There certainly is such instruction for grown adults, which is merely religion with the label removed. Without that label, however, children scarcely understand it and they do not learn it. I do not know where we will be in a hundred years, but today, it is clear that there is no education without religion, i.e. without the idea of God and without the notion of the life to come. (Coubertin 1889a, 2000: 71)

Nonetheless, Hoberman (1992) argues that Coubertin's 'peculiar religiosity' should not be mistaken for Christianity (p. 38). It was comparable to human-itarian doctrines that did not necessarily embrace the notion of the divine. 'I am not one of those', he wrote in a letter, 'who thinks humanity can get along without religion. I am taking the word here in its most general sense, not as a belief in a determinate form of divine reality, but as adherence to an ideal of superior life, of the aspiration to perfection' (cited in Hoberman 1986: 41). Besides, his Olympic campaign had often been opposed for its pagan elements that deviated from Christianity. In a sense, Coubertin's religion was ceremony itself, as is evident in the following text about the 1920 Antwerp Olympics from his Olympic Memoirs.

By holding a public service in the stadium itself, as in Stockholm, before the start of the competitions, we would be forcing the athletes, already grown men, to take part in a religious ceremony that might be displeasing to some. By inviting them, quite outside the Games, to a ceremony in church, we were only associating religion like any other great moral force of mankind with the celebration of the Olympic Games. Then again, it was important that the ceremony should be sufficiently neutral in character to rise above all differences in doctrine. No mass, no priestly address at the altar. (Coubertin 1997k: 474)

Throughout his writings he made many remarks about the Church, some of which were critical. At his most disapproving, he could go so far as to state that 'the Churches, entrenched in their opinions as though in fortresses, have always had too great an interest in isolating themselves and in forgetting what they have been' (cited in Hoberman 1986: 41). In con-trast, Coubertin admired the English education for its 'elastic' relationship with religion.

Nothing could be further from the spirit of English education. Religion plays a large, but separate, part in it. Discipline is understood there as consisting of certain in-house rules of order, no more. What the eminent Bishop of Orleans finds so essential to French secondary schools, the English dismiss as dangerous and contrary to nature. They reject the reg-ulation of every moment which demands nothing more than obedience – a virtue that, as virtues go, they never seem to have made much of a fuss about, or even to have understood its nature. Two things dominate in the English system, two things that are also means for achieving their ends: freedom and sports. (Coubertin 1887, 2000: 108)

He also suggested that protestant religion allowed more freedom to the individuals,

> Protestant religion [is] a very elastic religion that accommodates the most diverse attitudes. Every child is not necessarily led to first communion, or to the act corresponding to it. So here, there is a conquest for the minister to achieve, what Arnold called 'a chess game against Satan'. Religious instruction is given every Sunday before the students, whose attention and respectful behaviour is required, at least. In general, dissenters do not show a desire to have their children not attend these sessions. But when they do, their wishes are faithfully respected. (Coubertin 1887, 2000: 113–14)

Interestingly, Coubertin admired Arnold's educational doctrine, which was profoundly religious. Arnold's student Stanley has remarked, 'his [i.e. Arnold's] education, in short was not based upon religion, it was religious' (cited in MacAloon 1981: 63). The religious character of Arnold's teaching is apparent in his following letter to a cleric:

> If I do get it (i.e. the headmastership in Rugby), I feel as if I could set to work very heartily, and with God's blessings, I should like to try whether my notions of Christian education are really impracticable, whether our system of public schools has not in it some noble elements, which under the blessing of the Spirit of all holiness and wisdom, might produce fruit even unto life eternal. When I think about it, thus, I really long to take rod in hand. (Quoted by MacAloon 1981: 62)

Arnold's teaching could be characterised as conservative and puritan with frequent references to 'monstrous evil', 'vices', 'temptation and corruption' and 'Satan' (cited in MacAloon 1981: 62). Nonetheless, Coubertin overlooked this and focused his attention on the fact that the English Public schools increasingly prepared their pupils for imperial roles in the Neo-imperial expansion of the late nineteenth century (Mangan and Hickey 2001). Besides, the pedagogical reform through the introduction of physical activity in schools, the achievement of body and mind equilibrium, and the restriction of Church served a core purpose for Coubertin: the preservation of French domestic social tranquillity and the revitalisation of French society.

3.2.5   Educational reform and imperialism

The famous English Public Schools were essentially centred on the ideology of athleticism, which emerged in the late Victorian and Edwardian eras.

After 1850 the image of the English public schoolboy regained its status in the circles of middle and upper middle class clientele due to innovatory reforms, substantially associated with newly developed athletic fields. The pupils of these schools were prepared for their dynamic roles in British Empire in the late nineteenth century (Mangan and Hickey 2001). Athleticism was practised, predominantly by the settlers (at least in the early years) throughout the Britain's empire. Horton (2001) argues that the cult of Athleticism coupled with the ideology of Muscular Christianity relentlessly infused the British Games culture into the culture of its colonies. It has even been suggested that 'Victorians were determined to civilise the rest of the world, and an integral feature of that process as they understood it was to disseminate the gospel of athleticism which had triumphed so spectacularly at home in the third quarter of the nineteenth century' (cited in Mangan and Hickey 2001: 106). Coubertin remarks with admiration that physical activity moulded the individuals in Britain and gave them a collective identity.

> Then there are the colonies, that career of expatriation so well suited to the English, who bring their 'old England' with them wherever they go. Whether they are 'squatters' in New Zealand or planters in America, they are better off for having received such a strong physical and moral education in their schools. Muscles and character are objects of urgent necessity in such circumstances. Although the main cause for our own colonial impotence lies with our deplorable system of succession, it seems to me that education also plays its part. (Coubertin 1887, 2000: 118–19)

Coubertin believed that England owed its strength and colonial power to the ethos of Muscular Christianity and its strong physical culture.

> To the merits of this [English] education we may ascribe a large share in the prodigious and powerful extension of the British Empire in Queen Victoria's reign. It is worthy to note that the beginning of this marvellous progress and development dates from the same time which saw the school reforms of the United Kingdom in 1840. In these reforms physical games and sports hold, we may say, the most prominent place: The muscles are made to do the work of a moral education. It is the application according to modern requirements of one of the most characteristic principles of Grecian civilisation: To make the muscles be chief factor in the work of moral education. In France, on the contrary, physical inertion was considered till recent times an indispensable assistant to the perfectioning of intellectual powers. Games were supposed to destroy study. Regarding the development of the character of the youth, the axiom, that a close connection exists between the force of will and

the strength of the body never entered anybody's mind. (Coubertin 1896a, 2000: 308)

Coubertin's interest in revitalising French society was very strong. It is clear from this text that in physical activity, as practised by the Muscular Christians in England, Coubertin saw a 'tool' for maintaining and expanding imperialistic power. Lucas argues that,

> Baron Pierre de Coubertin was convinced that the sport-centred English public school system of the late 19th century was the rock upon which the vast and majestic British Empire rested. In the recondite scholarship of Dr. Arnold and in the ensuing trend toward manly sport at Rugby and in England, Coubertin saw a catharsis, not only for the English, but also for the Frenchmen and eventually all mankind. (Lucas 1980: 23)

Lucas' point is re-affirmed, when one reads the following text from Coubertin's speech addressed to the *Greek Liberal Club of Lausanne* (1918):

> It was left to the great Englishman Thomas Arnold to take up the Greek work at the point where a hostile fate had interrupted it, and to clothe it in an educational form adapted to modern conditions. The world had forgotten how organised sport can create moral and social strength, and thereby plays a direct part in a nation's destinies; had so far forgotten it that the spread of Arnold's doctrines and example first in England and then throughout the British Empire was an almost unconscious process. Rugby School may thus be truly considered as the starting-point of the British revival. (Coubertin 1918c, 2000: 272)

Coubertin has often associated sport with the strengthening of national vigour. He believed that athletics could 'be used to strengthen peace or prepare for war' and that the victory of a nation was often due to its athletic virility (Coubertin 1997d, 2000: 322).

> At fixed periods all the other manifestations of national life grouped themselves around a considered athleticism [...] Thus when the Persian peril threatened Hellenism between 500 and 449 B.C. unexpected armies and navies barred the way to the ambitions of Darius and Xerxes and the greed of their advisers. There had been hesitation before the massive forces of the adversary; more than one city was inclined to submit to the ultimatum. Athens rose up. Victory proved it right. Now if many centuries later – for history has eloquent turnings and sometimes repeats itself strangely – an English General [Wellington] was able to say that the battle of Waterloo had been won on the playing-fields of Eton, how much more accurate still is it to proclaim that the glory of Marathon

and Salamis was forged in the precincts of the Greek Gymnasium. (Coubertin 1918c, 2000: 270)

Coubertin was convinced that Thomas Arnold's methods at Rugby School and the British sport ethic taught in their private elite schools had been responsible for Britain's success as a world super power in the nineteenth century, and therefore that it should be exported to France (Guttmann 1992; Lucas 1980; Toohey and Veal 2000). Thereafter, one of his major tasks was to persuade the French to introduce physical education in schools based on the classical values of the Greek gymnasium. Coubertin believed that if France would emulate this system, then the nation's former glory days could be revived. In 1919, after the end of the First World War and the victory of the *Entente* Powers, Coubertin argued that France owed to a great extent its regained strength to the educational reforms based on Arnold's model of sport ethic.

> This is the kind of sport [the English sport], which I had in mind thirty years ago when I made a pact with Jules Simon for the reinvigoration of France. The conviction of the septuagenarian philosopher was no less ardent than my own, and events have fulfilled our hopes. A manlier and broader education soon begot results as fruitful as those whose benefits the England of Thomas Arnold had reaped some time before. In vain did Frenchmen blinded by party spirit undertake the sorry task of portraying to the outside world a decadence, which existed only within themselves. History will delineate the rising curve which enabled the Republic to write in forty years the most admirable of colonial epics and to guide youth through the dangers of pacifism and freedom pushed to extreme limits right up to that 1914 mobilisation which will remain one of the finest spectacles which Democracy has given the world. (Coubertin 1918c, 2000: 272)

Coubertin speaks with satisfaction about the new situation in France, which is attributed to the new educational system. He refers to his long-term efforts in this direction together with Jules Simon, Minister of Public Instruction from 1870 to 1879 and President of the Committee for the Propagation of Physical Education. Being relieved that France survived the First World War, and most importantly that France appeared stronger than Germany in the post-Franco-Prussian period, Coubertin could not hide his enthusiasm for such results. The value of physical education was emphasised as a principal factor for this national empowerment.

> Recent events have resulted in entirely new circumstances. Sports are on the front lines of the forces that brought about victory. It is to sports that we owe the magnificent innovations that made it possible for England

and the United States to transport unexpected armies to the theatre of war. It is thanks to them that the valiant Sokols covered their homelands with laurels, even before the borders were set and freedom assured. It is through sports that France, as heroic as in 1870 but infinitely stronger, was able to raise a powerful rampart of muscle against the invasion. After helping train incomparable soldiers, athleticism also helped sustain their zeal and console them in their suffering. They played football, they fenced, and they boxed right up by the front lines and far from them, as well, in the sad prisoners' camps. Public opinion is aware of these things, and appreciates them. Well-deserved enthusiasm will guarantee the value of physical education, and proclaim the triumph of sports. (Coubertin 1919a, 2000: 738)

As evident in his early writings, Coubertin was initially interested in the revitalisation of French society merely from a nationalistic perspective. His patriotism and faith in the Third Republic prevailed, thus his devotion to social cohesion and the need for social reform. However, in an era that witnessed a remarkable proliferation of trans-national movements and organisations promoting world peace and a spirit of reconciliation, Coubertin's international interests transcended his initial limited nationalist concerns. Coubertin's revival of modern Olympic Games thus incorporated a reconciliation of his nationalist and internationalist interests.

3.3   The early years of Olympism (1894–1918)

It was not until 1889 that Coubertin decided to try to revive the Games, and thus he devoted the next five years for the preparation of the International Congress of Sportsmen in 1894 (Hill 1992). During the period of 1890s Olympism was 'in the air' (Lucas 1980), but it was not until 1894 that it started to take a more specific definition and form.

3.3.1   The revival of modern Olympic Games

In 1894, Coubertin arranged an international Congress, during which the decision was taken to revive the Olympic Games (Hill 1992). However, he had already prepared the ground for it two years before. On the occasion of the fifth anniversary of the *Union des Sociétés Françaises de Sports Athlétiques* (USFSA), held on November 1892, Coubertin found the chance to spread the idea of reviving the Games to a crowd of French and foreign dignitaries. For the first time, Coubertin could express his project publicly before his acquaintances and colleagues (Boulogne 1999a).

However, objections were raised by the Ministry of Education, and the professional bodies of cyclists, weightlifters, oarsmen and football players (Guttmann 1992). Hill (1992) argues that, 'a man was a fencer or an oarsman or a cyclist, but did not have the Olympic ideal of being simply a sportsman'

(p. 17). As a response to their opposition, Coubertin argued, 'Let us export our oarsmen, our runners, our fencers into other lands. That is the true Free Trade of the future, and the day it is introduced into Europe the cause of Peace will have received a new and strong ally' (Coubertin 1892; reported by Anon. 1992: 198; cited in Hoberman 2004: 177). Hoberman argues, 'this proposal to invent and implement a symbolic version of free trade on behalf of international relations reminds us that Coubertin's Olympic project remains among the most durable monuments of the early phase of what we may call modern globalisation' (Hoberman 2004: 177).

By the end of the nineteenth century, the technological advances and scientific inventions such as the railway and global telegraphy opened new ways of communication and encouraged people to hope for peace and understanding through contact. Nonetheless, Kristof (1999) argues that such developments constitute the first era of globalisation and emphasises, 'perhaps the greatest myth about globalisation is that it is new' (cited in Hoberman 2004: 177). In support of this view, James (2001) points out that during the *fin-de-siècle*, 'the world was highly integrated economically, through mobility of capital, information, goods and people. Capital moved freely between states and continents. The movement of capital would not have been possible without improved mechanisms for spreading news and ideas' (cited in Hoberman 2004: 177). Hoberman (2004) also argues that this first era of globalisation was made possible by steamship lines, free trade and foreign investment that influenced world civilisations. Nonetheless, it should be noted that Robertson (1992) insists that the process of globalisation is not new, that it precedes modernity and the rise of technology. However, the rapidity of communication, and other modern achievements of science and technology in the late nineteenth century increased the pace of globalisation processes during this period. Moreover, the new conditions made it possible for international projects, such as the revival of the Olympics, to be put into practice.

Whenever a new idea has sprung up, assumed a practical form and become a reality, it is not always easy to explain why this particular idea, more than any other, has emerged from the stream of other thoughts, which are as yet awaiting their realisation. This however is, not the case with the reinstitution of the Olympic Games: Their revival is not owing to a spontaneous dream, but it is the logical consequence of the great cosmo-politan tendencies of our times. The XIXth Century has seen the awakening of a taste for athletics everywhere; at its dawn in Germany and Sweden, at its meridian in England, at its decline in France and America. At the same time the great inventions of the age, railroads and telegraphs, have brought into communication people of all nationalities. An easier inter-course between men of all languages has naturally opened a wider sphere for common interests. Men have begun to lead less isolated existences, different races have learnt to know, to understand each other better, and by comparing their powers and achievements in the fields of art, industry and science, a noble rivalry has sprung up amongst them, urging them on to greater accomplishments. Universal Exhibitions have collected together at one spot of the globe, the products of its remotest corners. In the domain of science and literature, assemblies and conferences have united the most distinguished intellectual labourers of all nations. Could it be otherwise, but that also sportsmen of diverse nationalities should have begun to meet each other on common ground? (Coubertin 1896a, 2000: 308)

In ways which parallel the globalisation processes of the last decades of the twentieth century, this early phase of globalisation in the late nineteenth century was facilitated by technological breakthroughs such as telegraphic communication (something like the internet of the late twentieth century). Such global civilisation offered the Olympic movement the political and economic circumstances in which to develop its international vision. Moreover, international mega-events, such as Universal Exhibitions and international sport events like the Olympics, helped to create an 'international public culture' particularly in the West in the late nineteenth century. Roche (2000) argues that the mega-events of this period have helped to develop 'international public culture' by providing aims and rationales, and by creating internationally recognised calendars and cycles in a specific time and place for internationally-based cultural event movements such as the Olympic movement. Imperialism had been a foundational theme in the approach of Britain and France to the early international expos of the 1850s and 1860s. Particularly for France, Hobsbawm (1992) argues, from a neo-Marxist perspective, that the different cultural policies of the Third Republic aimed to reinstate good relationships with the public after defeat in the Franco-Prussian War (1870–1). The Third Republic was responsible for three of the most important of the late nineteenth-century series of international expositions, namely those staged in Paris in 1878, 1889 and 1900 (Roche 2000).

The last decades of the nineteenth century also saw a remarkable rise of trans-national movements and organisations, which served idealistic purposes. Some of the better-known organisations of this period, the so-called 'idealistic internationalisms', include the International Committee of the Red Cross (1863), the Esperanto movement (1887), the Olympic movement (1894) and the Scouting movement (1907) (Hoberman 1995, 2004). All these organisations dealt with anxieties about war and peace, and promulgated promises of emancipation from the international rivalries of this period. The rapidity of communication, the complexity of modern commerce and the interdependencies it created stimulated confidence and optimism in people about international harmony. The optimism of the age is obvious in the speech of the British ambassador to the United States at a banquet held in 1868 in honour of the inventor of the telegraph, Samuel Morse, 'the telegraph wire, the nerve of international life, transmitting knowledge of events, removing causes of misunderstanding, and promoting peace and harmony throughout the world' (Standage 1999; quoted by Hoberman 2004: 179).

In this 'age of optimism', Coubertin wanted to increase public interest in Olympism and, for that reason, he convinced the USFSA that a Congress should be held about the issue of amateurism, a centre of several debates at that time. He never directly advocated the rebirth of the Olympic Games, but his aim was to strengthen USFSA' s internal organisation, to broaden its influence in French provinces and mostly to establish relations with foreign unions, by raising the issue of amateurism (Hill 1992). In this congress in Paris (1894), which counts as the first Olympic Congress (Müller 1994), Coubertin announced the idea of reviving the Olympic Games, as a means of resolving international confrontations and maintaining world peace.

> We must uphold the noble and chivalrous character of athleticism, which has distinguished it in the past, so that it may continue effectively to play the admirable role in the education of modern peoples that was attributed to it by the Greek masters. [...] Reform is necessary, but before it is implemented that reform must be discussed. [...] The project mentioned in the last paragraph, should it come to fruition, would mean appropriately sanctioning the international understanding for which we hope to pave the way. The time for its implementation has not yet come. The restoration of the Olympic Games, on foundations and under conditions that are in keeping with the needs of modern life, would bring together representatives of the nations of the world every four years. It may be hoped that these peaceful, courteous confrontations are the best form of internationalism. (Coubertin 1894a, 2000: 299)

Many scholars (Hoberman 1984, 1986, 1995; Kidd 1996; MacAloon 1996b) argue that Coubertin's revival of the Olympic Games aimed at revitalising French society, but also at reducing the imperialist rivalries of the European powers and the growing likelihood of war. In the late nineteenth century internationalism and cosmopolitanism emerged as popular trends based on trans-national or global cooperation. The nineteenth-century 'Manchester liberals' Richard Cobden (1804–65) and John Bright (1811–89) sanctioned cosmopolitanism in advocating free trade, hoping that it would promote international understanding and economic inter-dependence, limiting the possibilities of a new war.

'Cosmopolitanism' basically refers to the notion of a cosmopolis or 'world state', and thus implies the elimination of national identities and the establishment of a common political adherence of entire humanity. However, the term is used more to describe the efforts toward peace and harmony based upon the principles of mutual understanding, toleration and, above all, inter-dependence (Heywood 2002). 'Internationalism' also refers to international understanding, but it is rooted in universalist assumptions about human nature that puts it in conflict with political nationalism (that is political identity shaped by nationality). It can take the form of 'liberal internationalism', which is grounded in individualism and is reflected in the belief that universal human rights should transcend the sovereign authority of the nation. It can also take the form of 'socialist internationalism' (or proletarian internationalism), which is based on the belief of international class solidarity and follows the assumptions of a common humanity (Heywood 2002). Coubertin has often referred to the new tendencies of cosmopolitanism and internationalism, which both were seen as result of the modern conditions (especially of the rapidity of communication). With respect to cosmopolitanism, he argued that it 'was on the rise in all quarters. The intoxication of speed was beginning to have its effects, and people were already repeating that clever and stupid expression, Time is Money' (Coubertin 1929, 2000: 572). In relation to internationalism, he developed in several writings his own understanding of the concept, always emphasising that it did not contradict or undermine national sovereignty.

> Gentlemen, there are two trends in modern athletics to which I would like to draw your attention. It is becoming democratic and international. Its social revolution which has now been achieved among men – and which might be achieved in terms of things as well – explains the first of these characteristics; the speed of transportation and the frequency of communications explain the second [...] I might say the same regarding internationalism, understood of course as respect for, not destruction of, native countries. It is a trend that grew out of the deep need for peace and fraternity arising from the depths of the human heart. Peace has become a sort of religion, its altars surrounded day after day by an increasing number of faithfuls. (Coubertin 1894b, 2000: 537)

MacAloon (1981) argues that Coubertin's conception of internationalism did not share the euphoric optimism that was evident in this period, but followed a more rational approach. He notes that Coubertin's notion of international harmony 'was fundamentally rationalistic; war and peace were matters of knowledge and ignorance' (p. 262). Coubertin often mentioned that the introduction of the subject of 'World History' in schools would increase awareness among different peoples and cultures, and thus would resolve many international rivalries. Additionally, in support of MacAloon's argument, as the following quote illustrates that, for

Coubertin, international harmony would follow from better 'knowledge' of others.

> Gentlemen, this is the order of ideas from which I intend to draw the elements of moral strength that must guide and protect the renaissance of athletics. Healthy democracy and wise and peaceful internationalism will make their way into the new stadium. There they will glorify the honour and selflessness that will enable athletics to carry out its task of moral betterment and social peace, as well as physical development. That is why every four years the restored Olympic Games must provide a happy and fraternal meeting place for the youth of the world, a place where, gradually, the ignorance of each other in which people live will disappear. This ignorance perpetuates ancient hatreds, increases misunderstandings, and precipitates such barbaric events as fights to the finish. (Coubertin 1894b, 2000: 537)

The rapidity of communication due to the advancement of telegraphic technology over the second half of the nineteenth century, as already mentioned, marked a significant quickening of the pace of globalisation. During this period, international finance became so interdependent and intermingled with trade and industry that political and military power seemed to be overshadowed. Of course, the outbreak of the First World War dismantled this optimism, and raised concerns about the maintenance of world peace. These purely modern conditions of world inter-connectedness, free trade and foreign investments created a whole new situation, which was essentially different from the ancient (Beinart 1997). Thus, the modern Olympic Games would be described as sharing some basic principles with the ancient event and philosophy, but would be reinvented and adjusted to modern international society.

> Wishing to revive not so much the form but the very principle of this millennial institution, because I felt it would give my country and mankind as a whole the educational stimulus they needed, I had to try and restore the powerful buttresses that had supported it in the past: the intellectual buttress, the moral buttress and, to a certain extent, the religious buttress. To which the modern world added two new forces: technical improvements and democratic internationalism. (Coubertin 1997g, 2000: 620)

The revival of modern Olympic Games was thus an extension of Coubertin's plans for an educational reform, and reflected both his national and international interests. Traumatised as she was by the defeat in the Franco-Prussian war, Coubertin offered France a formula for making French youth more robust, healthy and physically fit. However, Coubertin, as an internationalist, also perceived sport as a 'pacifier', a means for enhancing peace in the world and addressing controversy (Hoberman 1986: 34). Hence, his ideal of Olympism represented a synthesis of supposed ancient Greek practices and nineteenth-century British sporting ideas, internationalism and peace (Toohey and Veal 2000; Parry 1994). We pick up the major ideological strands of Coubertin's Olympism in the commentary which follows.

3.3.2   Ideological components of Olympism

The revival of the modern Olympic Games and the emergence of the ideology of Olympism should be examined against the socio-political background of nineteenth-century continental Europe. Modern societies began to emerge in Europe from about the fifteenth century, but *modernity*, in the sense of a complex and distinct form of social life in modern societies, became identified with the Enlightenment project of the eighteenth century (Hall *et al.* 1992). It was enunciated by different historical processes on a number of levels: the political (the rise of the secular state and polity), the economic (free trade, capitalist economy), the social (formation of classes), and the cultural (transition from religious to secular culture). In the nineteenth century, modernity is signalled by industrialism and the broad social, economic, technological and cultural changes associated with it (Hall *et al.* 1992). With the growth of industrialisation, traditional agrarian society was to a significant degree dismantled and new social classes based on factory production were formulated.

After several decades of political, industrial and demographic revolution, at the end of the eighteenth century and the beginning of the nineteenth, Europe was dominated by a different kind of political conflict. The political conflicts between dynasties or emerging nation-states were replaced by the conflicts between social classes for the exercise of political authority and power. Against the traditional aristocratic ruling class appeared the new bourgeois classes of manufacturers, traders and financiers, on the one hand as well as the still unorganised urban workers on the other (Bowen 1989). The newly emerging 'ruling class' of the nineteenth century included 'the higher offices of the royal court, the established church, the army and navy, the judiciary, parliament and the bureaucracy. Included were the masters of university colleges and headmasters of the major public schools' (Bowen 1989: 162). The first International Olympic Committee (IOC), composed at the 1894 International Athletic Congress in Paris, consisted of fourteen men, all members of the ruling class. At the end of the nineteenth century and in the early years of the twentieth century, given the lack of advanced communication technology and the slowness and high costs of international travel, any attempt to establish an organisation with international scope may be seen as a remarkable achievement. The IOC, an organisation which in principle resisted any government subsidy and national interference, could not have succeeded unless its members were independently wealthy and had plenty of leisure time to devote to the project (Leiper 1976). Thus, male members of royal, aristocratic and upper class elites from around the western world dominated IOC membership. Toohey and Veal argue that,

> Such individuals would not have readily thought in terms of democratic or participatory processes; neither would they have travelled third class or stayed in two-star hotels. Out of their own pockets, they established an IOC 'style' which was an extension of their own privileged lifestyles, and which has been slow to change. (Toohey and Veal 2000: 41)

It was Coubertin, however, who determined the composition of the governing body. He was cautious wishing the IOC to be as politically independent as possible. To achieve that goal, the members were asked to be ambassadors from the committee to their respective countries (Guttmann 1992). He regularly emphasised this requirement,

> People ask now and then why the members of the International Committee are not regular delegates nominated by the leading athletic organisation of each country. Indeed they are not. The privilege of the committee nominating its own members is essential. They act in their respective countries rather as 'ambassadors' of the committee, and if I use such an expression, as 'the trustees of the Olympic Idea'. Their independence and stability answer for the great work achieved by the committee. (Coubertin 1908a, 2000: 736)

However, Coubertin's influential role in deciding the composition of the IOC often raised criticisms.

> It has been believed and said – it was an easy way to cast aspersions on us – that they [i.e. the IOC members] had all been 'appointed' by me. Nothing was further from the truth. Only one of all those I have mentioned had been my personal candidate. Elections have always been held regularly, but the actual choice was always preceded by long investigations, sometimes by direct correspondence with the person involved. (Coubertin 1997b, 2000: 432)

Nevertheless, Coubertin also admitted that IOC membership was sometimes and perhaps often awarded to personal friends.

> I have the programme of the 1894 Congress here before me as I write, in two distinct versions between which lies a space of some ten months. At the head, an immovable trinity composed of three members: C. Herbert, Secretary of the Amateur Athletic Association (London), for Great Britain

and the British Empire; W. M. Sloane, professor at the University of Princeton, for the American continent; and myself, for France and continental Europe. *This unusual geography was intended to simplify propaganda for me.* My two colleagues had accepted *mainly in order to please me.* (Coubertin 1997i, 2000: 316)

The members were selected for their wealth, social status, and geographical sphere of influence. Coubertin emphasised that it was the individual that mattered, not the country. Therefore, since the members were expected not only to pay their own travel expenses but also to contribute to the costs of the IOC, most of them were quite affluent.

All, or almost all of them, were sportsmen in the real sense of the word, in keeping with the idea I had formed from the very beginning, that is to say men competent enough to be able to get to the bottom of any particular question, but far enough removed from any exclusive specialisation ever to become its slaves, men international enough not to be blinded in any international question by their strictly national prejudices, men – finally – capable of holding their own with technical groups and who could be counted on to be completely free of any material dependence upon the latter. (Coubertin 1997b, 2000: 432)

All in all, the IOC was an influential group and influence was needed for the promotion of Olympism and the success of the Olympic Games. In achieving this goal and maintaining support from the elites, Coubertin linked Olympism with prestigious themes, equal to their prominent social position in Europe.

What lasting undertaking can be founded on the basis of fashion? It was to buttress the fragile structure that I had just built that the restoration of the Olympic Games – this time on a completely international footing – seemed to me the only timely solution. The only way to ensure any relative long-term survival of the athletic renaissance then still in its infancy was to superimpose the immense prestige of antiquity on the passing fad of Anglomania, thereby undercutting, to some extent, any opposition from the students of classicism, and to impose on the world a system whose fame spread beyond all national borders. The rising tide of cosmopolitanism, which constituted a threat, had to be turned into a rampart and a safeguard. (Coubertin 1929, 2000: 573)

First, Olympism was associated with Hellenism and the ancient Greek values of body, mind and spirit, which had been re-invented in eighteenth- and nineteenth-century Europe. Hellenism, harking back to the origins of Europe, represented a binding power for Europe's unity and authority

(Bowen 1989). Second, Olympism shared values with English athleticism, which had been identified as a central component of the ideology of 'Anglo-Saxonism', and had been related to the nineteenth-century pre-eminence of the British Empire. The doctrine of imperialism had successfully been developed by the late Victorian visionaries who introduced to the 'under-privileged' peoples of the world the spirit of chivalry, fair play and good government through a games-playing code. An eclectic approach to Olympism, which combined the values of the re-invented nineteenth-century Hellenism, and the principles of the popular British 'imperial' athleticism, could not have failed to appeal to the high-status governing body of the IOC and its adherents.

Hellenism, ruling class and prestige of antiquity

Neo-classicism in Britain and France, and Romanticism in Germany brought ancient Greece to the fore of European thought (Prevelakis 2003). Europe in the early nineteenth century valued classical antiquity to such an extent that historians refer to this affinity as a kind of 'Hellenic madness' (Held *et al.* 1999). The Hellenic influence in Britain is reflected in the following:

> The ideal – so pure and so practical, so divine and yet so human – that was the keystone of the Greek system was perfectly designed to captivate the English when they began to link great destinies in the beyond to the clear, simple meaning of life. This is not a rare occurrence with them, this twofold perspective, eyes cast down on the ground yet lost in the heavens, this double current that causes them to seek rest from their business activities in reading Plutarch and Homer. (Coubertin 1890b, 2000: 283)

It was emphasised that the study of antiquity would provide the means to attain that unity of body, mind and soul (the threefold harmony of Hellenism), of community and individual, the Greek ideal of humanity. In similar vein, Coubertin emphasised that full human self-realisation would follow from the encounter with the culture of classical antiquity which transcends modern formations of society.

> My faith in Hellenism, in its future, and in its continued fruitfulness has grown ever more firm over the past forty years. At the eventide of my journey, I see clearly – for evenings are known for their final, brief, but intense clarity – that above and beyond all forms of government, eco-nomic organisations, and diplomatic understandings – above all else, one might say – must reign that threefold harmony first outlined in Hellenism. (Coubertin 1934b, 2000: 278)

The effects of classicism were evidenced in education where the sons of the 'ruling class' were sent to schools in which the classical studies of

Hellenism, Latin and Roman studies were embraced. Although class conflicts were taking place mainly on an economic basis, ideologies, which would guide and inform the new classes, were equally important. Thus, the struggle for power was apparent in Europe's private or boarding schools where the pupils were moulded to become the next generation of the ruling class through the teachings of ancient Greek civilisation. Bowen (1989: 162) attributes this 'wholehearted embracing' of Hellenism to the 'the new and powerful role that Hellenism offered in the ideological maintenance of the ruling class'. Hellenism and Olympism were linked together at the Conference in Paris (1894), where the audience consisted of representatives of the ruling class across Europe. Such linkage opened ways of communication with the addressees and heightened the possibilities for success of the new project.

> A subtle feeling of emotion spread through the auditorium as if the antique eurhythmy were coming to us from the distant past. In this way, Hellenism infiltrated into the whole vast hall. From this moment, the Congress was destined to succeed. I knew that now, whether consciously or not, *no one would vote against the revival of the Olympic Games*. (Coubertin 1997i, 2000: 319; emphasis added)

Later in the same year, speaking to the literary society in Athens, Coubertin recalled his delegates listening to choirs singing the hymn to Apollo, unearthed at Delphi.

> Then in a sacred hush, for the first time in two thousand years choirs sang the hymn to Apollo unearthed at Delphi. The effect was deeply moving. In one of those mysterious glimpses that music sometimes gives us of lost worlds, for a few seconds those gathered at Paris perceived Greek antiquity in all its splendour. From that moment on, Gentlemen, the Greek genius was among us, transforming a modest congress on athletic sports into a quest for moral betterment and social peace. My goal had been achieved. (Coubertin 1894b, 2000: 533)

European enchantment with Greek antiquity drove Coubertin to associate an international sports competition for the purposes of social and educational reform with the ancient Olympic Games and the values of Hellenism.

> Of all measures tending to this desired end, only one seemed to me at all practicable, namely the establishment of a periodical contest, to which sporting societies of all nationalities would be invited to send their representatives, and to place these meetings under the only patronage which could throw over them a hallow of greatness and glory: 'The

patronage of Classical Antiquity'! To do that, was to re-establish the 'Olympic Games'. That name forced itself upon us, it was not even possible to invent another one. (Coubertin 1896a, 2000: 309)

Tomlinson (2004: 148) underscores the point that Coubertin, in an attempt to fulfil his grandiose plans, 'excelled at hyperbole, hailing his 1894 Congress in Paris as the moment when a 2,000-year-old idea was restirred'. By associating the modern Olympic Games with the ancient tradition of Hellenism, Coubertin claimed continuity and expansion of impact and importance of the Olympic movement and Games. Throughout his writings, Coubertin emphasised the perpetuity of classical Greek antiquity using expressions such as: 'Hellenism's immortal glory' (Coubertin 1929: 567) and 'eternal Hellenism' (Coubertin 1936, 2000: 579). In this way, past, present and future were bridged through the event of the Olympic Games, tracing the longevity of Olympism across time.

> I rejoice that I have been given the opportunity to begin preaching the second part of the Gospel of Sport among a Hellenic community, as I did the first in times past, and that I thus have the opportunity once more to place my endeavour under the patronage of that civilizing force whose past merits every honour and whose future deserves every confidence – Hellenism. (Coubertin 1918c, 2000: 269)

Europe, during and after the Enlightenment, was transformed by the dynamics of modernity driving social, political, and economic change. Modernity's dislocations could be seen in the divergences and antagonisms noted by the European intellectuals: antagonisms of nature and culture, life and intellect, individual and citizen. However, in light of such radical discontinuities with the past, a dialectic relation with it, particularly with Greek antiquity, was established (Held *et al.* 1999). Similarly, Coubertin appears to relocate the ancient Greek tradition in the modern era.

> Hellenism again! We used to believe that Hellenism was a thing of the past, a dead notion, impossible to revive and inapplicable to current conditions. This is wrong. Hellenism is part of the future. Its philosophy of life is suitable for and adaptable to modern existence. That is why sport is such an essential element in modern progress. (Coubertin 1938a, 2000: 202)

Nonetheless, it is argued that the single line of development Greece-Rome-Europe is a conceptual by-product of the Eurocentric interpretation of modernity, and we now turn to an examination of the different dimensions of this argument.

Hellenism, modernity and Eurocentrism

With its Hellenic past as a cradle of civilisation and democracy, Greece is associated with the origins of Europe. However, the original mythological Europe (daughter of a Phoenician king) originates from the Orient and bears little relation to the modern Europe, which is situated to the north and west of Greece and was simply considered by the ancient Greeks as uncivilised, non-political and non-human. Dussel and Fornazzari argue:

> What became modern Europe lay beyond Greece's horizon and therefore could not in any way coincide with the originary (sic) Greece [...] By stating this I am trying to emphasise that the unilineal diachrony Greece-Rome-Europe is an ideological construct that can be traced back to late-eighteenth-century German romanticism. (Dussel and Fornazzari 2002: 465)

Its 'Roman' past – the past of the Eastern Roman Empire, of Orthodox Christianity and of Ottoman Rule – as well as its geographical location keeps Greece in the periphery of modern Europe, 'tainting' her modernity with an Eastern character (Soysal and Antoniou 2000). In the late nineteenth century and after the Greek War of Independence, the question of how to define the Greek nation in a post-classical, post-Byzantine and post-Ottoman period had emerged. The debate was transformed into a socio-political and ideological conflict between the liberal ideas of Enlightenment of the West and the Orthodox tradition in the East. The outcome was to create a synthesis of classical Hellenism and Byzantine Christianity, which was called 'Helleno-Christianity' and was used as a term to describe the historical and cultural continuity of ancient Greece, through Byzantium, into modern Greece (Molokotos-Liederman 2003). However, Coubertin links ancient Greece and the Byzantine period with modern Europe, emphasising the need to maintain such bonds with the past for the best interests of Europe and the wider world.

> No one wanted to see the link between antiquity, what was called the Byzantine period, and the unexpected modern era that was dawning. But today, those on the forefront and the least well informed alike are beginning to understand the power of Greek unity, and how the rising sap of present-day Hellenism is similar to that of former times. *Europe and the world need that sap! May it rise, may it be fruitful, and may it be intoxicating! Zito Ellas*! (Coubertin 1929, 2000: 576)

The dichotomised role of Greece in world history can be interpreted through an examination of the two concepts of modernity. The first concept is Eurocentric, localised and provincial. In Europe, this process took place mainly during the eighteenth century. The temporal and spatial dimensions of this phenomenon were described by Hegel and analysed by Habermas (1985) in his classic work on modernity. Habermas' narrative, broadly embraced by contemporary European tradition, posits, 'The key historical events for the creation of the principle of [modern] subjectivity are the Reformation, the Enlightenment, and the French Revolution' (Habermas 1990a: 17). Other cultural processes that are added to this sequence are the Italian Renaissance, the German Reformation and the establishment of the English Parliament. Similarly, Coubertin lays emphasis on events that predominantly happened in Europe or were controlled by Europe (e.g. African colonialism).

> Gentlemen, in the long series of events that have astonished the nineteenth century, from the brilliant era that marked its beginnings to the great social upheaval that is troubling its waning years, there have been three events to which the adjective 'marvellous' can be applied. We have seen Germany and Italy become unified, we have seen the Republic of United States grow in a colossal way, and we have seen the light of civilisation shine on the vast continent of Africa. (Coubertin 1894b, 2000: 540)

Dussel and Fornazzari (2002: 469–70) label this perspective 'Eurocentric', 'for it indicates intra-European phenomena as the starting point of modernity and explains its later development without making recourse to anything outside Europe'. Even when Coubertin refers to civilisations outside Europe, his perspective is always in relation to the West.

> In terms of Japan, a great people believed frozen in the depths of an ancient civilisation has suddenly been rejuvenated, and has entered lock, stock and barrel, so to speak, into the complicated existence of the western world. (Coubertin 1894b, 2000: 540)

King (1995) argues that 'modern' and especially 'modernism', 'modernity' and 'modernist' are terms and concepts predominantly used to describe particular movement and tendencies in the arts, mainly in Europe and the USA, making no reference to the world system as a whole. Giddens (1990) also refers to modernity as a time period with specific geographical locations, 'modernity refers to modes of social life organisation, which emerged in Europe from about the seventeenth century' (p. 1). In this view of modernity, a direct link of classical Greece with modern Europe was assumed. The Eurocentric position – first formulated at the end of the eighteenth century by the French and English Enlightenment and the German Romantic – reinterpreted all of world history (Dussel and Fornazzari 2002).

Conversely, a second view on modernity takes into consideration a world perspective, dismissing the position of the 'modern West' and the 'other' or 'traditional rest' (Preston 2000). This view posits the fact that there was not *world* history in an empirical sense before 1492, as this date marks (at least for Wallerstein) the beginning of the world-system (with the Portuguese expansion and the discovery of America by Spain) (Wallerstein 1974; cited in Dussel and Fornazzari 2002: 470). During what might be described, from a Eurocentric perspective, as the first stage of modernity, which began in the fifteenth century, Spain may be seen as the first 'modern' nation due to the following characteristics: it had a state that unified the peninsula, a top-down national consensus created by the Inquisition, a national military power, one of the first articulated grammars and the subordination of the church to the state. Modern European powers of England and France replace Spain and Portugal as the hegemonic powers in the 'second stage of modernity', that of the eighteenth-century industrial revolution and the Enlightenment.

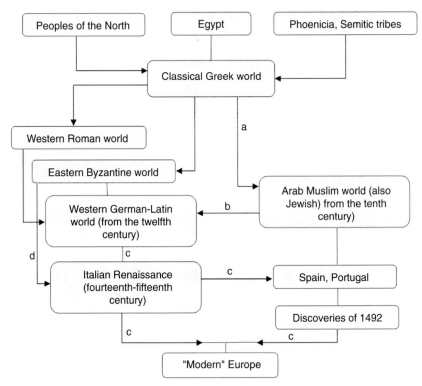

Figure 3.1 A Simplified Model of the Relationship Between Hellenic and Other Cultural/ Civilisation Influences

Note: There is no direct Greek influence on western Latin Europe (it is mediated by both arrows **a** and **b**). There is also no direct link between, either sequence of, **c** of modern Europe and Greece, or the Byzantine world (arrow **d**), but there is a direct link with the western Christian Latin-Roman world. (Adapted from Dussel and Fornazzari 2002)

Within the world perspective of modernity, the Hellenic-Greek identity is differentiated from the modern European, without drawing a linear development from classical Greece to Latin Europe (Figure 3.1). The West consisted of the territories of the Roman Empire where Latin was spoken (the eastern border of which was the area between present-day Croatia and Serbia) and thus included the north of Africa. The West was opposed to the East, the Greek Empire, which spoke Greek and consisted of Greece and Asia (the Anatolia province) and the Hellenist kingdoms.

Prevelakis (2003) argues that during the Ottoman period, the Greek-speaking Christians derived their identity mostly from their religious belonging and not from the classical Hellenes, who were a community of the past, whose significance was re-interpreted by the classicists of western Europe. Interestingly, for the theologians of the Roman Catholic Church the term 'Greeks' referred to the Orthodox Christians, who were often accused of having kept elements of ancient Greek paganism. After the Fall of Constantinople, 'Greeks' carried similar negative connotations to 'Muslims' for some radical Catholics who saw them as schismatic Christians. Metallinos, a Greek theologian, emphasises the centrality of religion in the formation of the modern Greek identity, an element which was completely ignored by the western classicists and Romantics when they re-invented Hellenism in modern Europe.

> Our *a priori* identification with Europe is a mistake. It is a mistake to believe that European culture and our culture are identical and equal. It is not an alliance, a simple socio-political connection with mutual relations. It is a total induction to a new framework of living [...] Europe took ancient Hellenism and altered it within its own standards. Ancient Hellenism is not even preserved within European culture. The Renaissance managed to attain to neither the Hellenic, nor the Roman era, because there was no continuity. The Renaissance was not created by the Romaic people of the West, but by the Franco-German conquerors. *European Man bears no relation whatsoever to ancient man; he has nothing of the relations preserved by the Holy Fathers and Mothers of our Church.* (Metallinos 1995: 1; emphasis added)

Coubertin, being aware of the dichotomy between East and West, once noted,

> From now on, let us let Hellenism do as it pleases. It has numbers, the prestige of history, and the excellence of biology on its side. No other Eastern people has such prerogatives to the world's confidence. (Coubertin 1906, 2000: 250)

Leaving to one side the issue of Coubertin's biological racism, a point to which we shall return later, the problematic identification of modern

Greeks with Europe and their hesitance to see themselves involved in the European project of the modern Olympic Games had concerned Coubertin, who tried to persuade them that their interests would not clash with the interests of Europe.

> People have asked whether it is appropriate to have an international competition held in Athens at a time when Greece is in a rather anomalous position with respect to certain European powers [...] Here Europe is intervening once again to seek your gratitude. It seems that Europe has done everything, and truly when one recalls how late its cooperation was and with what poor grace it provided that cooperation, Europe's claims seem a bit ridiculous in retrospect. I am well aware that you have a Lord Byron, a Santa-Rosa, and a Fabvrier to console you for the ingratitude and indifference of governments. Thanks to them, you can forgive the Austrians for having provided supplies to the Turks, the Lord Commissioners of the Seven Islands for having persecuted your Ionian brothers. (Coubertin 1894b, 2000: 540)

The 'discontinuity' from classical Hellenism to modern Europe, reconstructed by the European classicists and Romantics as 'continuity' and with no references to the linear development from ancient Hellas to modern Helleno-Christianity, may be seen as Eurocentric argument which served national and European interests. Interestingly, Coubertin always emphasised the centrality of internationalism in the revival of modern Games, as opposed to the ancient games, 'which had an exclusively Hellenic character; they were always held in the same place, and Greek blood was a necessary condition of admission to them' (Coubertin 1896b, 2000: 5–7).

He further argued elsewhere that:

> The International Committee, which is at times reproached for having too aristocratic a membership, is certainly more democratic in its procedures. It seeks to spread athleticism throughout the world without cataloguing races; it does not limit the recruitment of its members to Europe and America. Japan is represented on it. China and Siam will be represented soon, regardless of the fact that those countries are not very open to sports. It is quite likely that they will open up to sports eventually. (Coubertin 1913, 2000: 695)

Nonetheless, Coubertin understood and interpreted internationalism from a Eurocentric standpoint, which assumed (and reinforced) the centrality of the West in the Olympic movement.

> The work [of the Olympic Games] must be lasting, to exercise over the sports of the future that necessary and beneficent influence for which I look – an influence which shall make them the means of *bringing to*

perfection the strong and hopeful youth of our white race, thus again helping towards the perfection of all human society. (Coubertin 1908b, 2000: 545; emphasis added)

Therefore, it may also be argued that Coubertin's internationalism was never cosmopolitan but it was tied to the origins of racially exclusive European humanism (Carrington 2004). Evidence of such racial exclusivity is also the distinction Coubertin makes between the Greek race and other 'Eastern' races, 'The Greek race, however, is free from the natural indolence of the Oriental, and it was manifested that the athletic habit, if the opportunity be offered, would easily take root again among its men' (Coubertin 1896b, 2000: 359). Modern Greece was often seen as part of the East, but being associated with the origins of Europe through its classical past, it gave her advantage over other 'Eastern' nations, 'No other Eastern people has such prerogatives to the world's confidence' (Coubertin 1906, 2000: 250).

From Hellenism to Anglo-Saxonism: An alternative source of legitimacy

Coubertin, at the 1894 Congress in Paris turned to Greece and his personal friend Dimitrios Vikelas (also transliterated occasionally as Bikelas) for help concerning the revival of the first modern Olympic Games. The decision was taken for the first Modern Olympic Games to be held in Athens in 1896 and an emphasis on Hellenism was imposed. However, Coubertin's relationship with the Greeks had been very unsettled due to political manoeuvres of the Greek government. Finally, a compromise was reached when it was decided that the first Olympic Games should be in Athens in 1896 and the second in Paris in 1900. However, the choice of Athens was unfortunate, as, after a decade of extreme instability from 1869 to 1879, Greece was politically and financially weak (Lucas 1980; Toohey and Veal 2000). For these reasons, the government opposed hosting the event, and the Greek Etienne Dragoumis, a member of the Zappeion Commission, suggested that the Athens Games should be held in 1900, the beginning of a new century and the year of organising the World Exhibition in Paris (Hill 1992). Tricoupis, the Greek prime minister, had a powerful argument against the Olympic Games believing that the financial state of Greece would not be able to bear the heavy economic burden of the Olympic Games. Finally, after extended negotiations the Games were held in Athens.

Krüger (1999) argues that Coubertin had planned the first Olympics to be held in Paris in 1900 as part of the World Fair, with the Greeks coming to Paris to 'claim' the international Olympic Games as theirs. However, such an argument seems unconvincing when one reads the following:

As to the choice of Athens and the date of 1896, this did not fit in at all with my original plan for the reason that, underestimating like

most of my contemporaries the youthful strength of the recently resusci-
tated Greece, I did not think she was capable of coping with the inauguration of world's sports championships. At one time I had thought
of inaugurating the Games in Paris in the first year of the 20th century,
as I explained in the Revue de Paris dated 15th June 1894, doing everything possible to 'steep in Hellenism' the celebration of the Games.
A number of conversations with D. Bikelas, whose friendship had
charmed me right from the start, led me to change my opinion. For
his part, he wanted them to be held in Greece *but at the same time
hesitated before the responsibility of involving his country in such an adven-
ture. We encouraged each other and Athens was selected to the accom-
paniment of wild applause.* (Coubertin 1997i, 2000: 320; emphasis
added)

Coubertin, as Krüger (1999) correctly notes, had different original plans
for the host city of the first Olympic Games, but there does not appear
any specific evidence of nationalist claims of the Greeks about the paternity
of the first modern Games at this point. These were to emerge later,
when, as a result of the success of the Games, King George of Greece
and other Greek officials had warmed to the idea of holding the modern
Games in Greece on a permanent basis, an idea that Coubertin opposed
strongly.

The group formed by the IOC on either side of the Crown Prince represented the perennial nature of the enterprise and the international character I was determined to preserve at all costs. All around us resounded
the nationalistic fervour of the Greeks intoxicated by the idea of seeing
Athens become the permanent home of the Games, acting as host every
four years to this flattering and profitable influx of visitors. (Coubertin
1997f, 2000: 330)

In his efforts to promote the permanent Olympic Games in Greece, Timoleon
Philemon, a former mayor of Athens and Secretary General of the reconsti-
tuted organising committee of Athens Games, had the full support of new
Prime Minister Deligiannes and the royal family. MacAloon (1981) argues
that at the King's banquet and at the prize ceremony Coubertin was treated
as just 'another face in the crowd' (cited in Guttmann 1992: 19). Lucas
(1980) also argues that Coubertin's name was absent from official Olympic
bulletins, royal proclamations and the Greek press. When Coubertin
claimed to have been involved in the organisation of the Olympic Games,
one Athenian newspaper condemned him as 'a thief seeking to rob Greece
of her inheritance' (cited in Guttmann 1992: 19). Furthermore, Young
(1996) claims that Coubertin did not provide much help to the Greeks
during the preparation of the Games, and he belittled the contributions of

Vikelas, seeking all the credit for himself. This is explicit in his introduction to the booklet for the revival of the Games,

> I claim its paternity with raised voice and I would like to thank once more here those who assisted me to bring it into well-being; those, who together with me, think that athletics will emerge greater and ennobled and that international youth will draw from it the love and peace and respect for life. (quoted by Hill 1992: 26)

Moreover, Coubertin sent a letter of complaint to the editor of the *Times* (July 9, 1908), when they attributed the success of the Games to his joint actions with the Greek Averoff (responsible for the re-construction of Panathenaikos Stadium of Athens). He emphasised,

> I completely fail to see how my plans could have been in any way influenced by Mr. Averoff's decision to reconstruct the Athenian stadium, since when Mr. Averoff decided to undertake this reconstruction, the International Congress *which I had called* forth had already met at Paris Sorbonne (1894) and the revival of the games had already been decided [...] It was that same Paris Congress that chose Athens as the seat of the first Olympiad of 1896; *a marble stadium did not seem at all necessary to make the games a success.* (Coubertin 1908a, 2000: 735–6; emphasis added)

Coubertin's zeal for self-promotion and his fear that the Greeks might succeed in placing the Games under their patronage seem to have been the main factors in his annoyance at the association by the press of a Greek with the success of 1896 Athens Games. It is worth quoting the reply by the editor of the *Times* (July 9, 1908: 23), who remarks that although Coubertin complained of 'a great many mistakes',

> He refers only in one single instance to any alleged error in the article which he criticises. We did not say that his plans for reviving the Olympic Games were influenced by Mr Averoff's decision to reconstruct the Athenian stadium, or that M. Averoff's decision preceded the International Congress at which the revival was decided upon. *We merely observed that it was a combination of M. De Coubertin's plans with M. Averoff's work which rendered the first Olympic Games at Athens a success.* The remainder of this letter deals with matters of opinion. (Quoted by Müller 2000: 736; emphasis added)

It would seem that Coubertin wanted to dissociate himself, and the Olympic Games, from the Greeks, at least until the success of his project was secured. In this uneasy atmosphere, Coubertin displayed his irritation with the attitude of the Greeks, and appeared to adopt more distant and diplomatic language, especially concerning the permanency of the Olympic Games on Greek ground.

> *Above all I had to hold out against the King, whose speech at the final banquet, [which was] attended by all the athletes, had faced me with the famous dilemma: whether to give in or to resign. I had already decided to do neither. But, on the other hand, resistance on such an occasion was hardly possible.* I decided to act as if I were stupid, pretending not to understand. I decided to ignore the King's speech on the pretext of ambiguity; speaking half in Greek, half in French, he had not used identical terms when repeating his proposal to fix the permanent headquarters of the Games in Athens [...] And the very evening the Games closed, I sent the King a public letter thanking him, as well as the town of Athens and the Greek people, for the energy and the brilliance with which, by their support and their action, the call made on them in 1894 had been answered. In it, I clearly specified the continuation of the scheme and the perenniality of the International Committee by alluding to the Games of the second Olympiad which would be held in Paris ... The letter was short and to the point. The German and the English versions appearing at the same time as the French, it became of little importance whether the Greek version was published too or not. (Coubertin 1997f, 2000: 332; emphasis added)

So serious was the situation that some IOC members thought that the IOC would have to disband (Hill 1992). Coubertin, in his *Olympic Memoirs* (1931d), mentions that his letter to the King and his diplomatic manoeuvres against the Greek plans caused a situation which threatened the structure of the IOC.

> The outward form [of the letter] was, of course, perfectly polite and courteous, in accordance with the demands of protocol, but the deed itself was nonetheless of a rare insolence. *The members of the Committee, who were for the most part staunchly monarchist, showed considerable alarm, for I had not consulted my colleagues or submitted anything in advance [...] However nothing happened. The IOC survived the test without resignations or even any cracks in its structure.* (Coubertin 1997f, 2000: 332; emphasis added)

In resolving the situation, Coubertin suggested that the Greeks should host the pan-Hellenic Games spaced between the Olympics, an idea that he did not particularly like but would temporarily stop the Greeks from claiming the modern Olympic Games as their own. Through this skilful compromise, Coubertin succeeded in forestalling the Greek plans for permanent Games in Athens, and continued undisturbed with his own plans for international Games. The Greek officials and the King liked the idea, but it was destined to failure due to the difficulties of raising funds (Guttmann 1992; Hill 1992).

> The Greek committee, which had hoped to celebrate intermediate Games at the foot of Acropolis in 1910 – to which we would have extended our help as loyally as in 1906 – was obliged to give up the idea for lack of money, an economic crisis. From Athens we received an unofficial proposal to include the Athenian series in our own cycle: the Games would be celebrated every eight years in Greece, and every eight years in another country. It was impossible to agree to this proposal. It would have meant torpedoing our own work without any real benefit to anyone. International politics were far too uncertain for the choice of the venue for the Games to be fixed such a long time in advance. (Coubertin 1997e, 2000: 435)

Although Coubertin underlines above that, if the Greeks continued to hold the intermediate games, he would offer his help 'as loyally as in 1906', the next quote provides evidence that he was not content with the Greeks organising parallel games:

> The fear of seeing the launching of this idea [including artistic pro-gramme in the Olympic Games] delayed once again made me decide to summon a 'Consultative Conference on Art, Letters and Sport' for the spring of 1906. *At the same time, I would be able to use this as an excuse for not going to Athens, a journey I particularly wished to avoid.* Even though we were now on very good terms with the Hellenic Committee, the reconciliation was a result more of a conscious effort on the part of both parties than of a serious alteration of our respective position. Finally, what name should be given to these 'additional Games in 1906'? How often should they be held? The idea of an intermediate four-year period, in which I had acquiesced without much conviction, was abandoned. In Athens, they were now thinking of ten-year interval, which would make these two series coincide in 1916 ... All this was very uncertain; the situation would always be a trifle delicate. *In any case, a great deal of friction and many difficulties were bound to arise during contests. It was best for everyone and for everything that I should not be there.* (Coubertin 1997g: 621, emphasis added)

Guttmann (1992) argues, 'an Olympic congress held at Le Havre scotched the Greek attempt to usurp the Games' (p. 21). In order to rescue the inter-nationalism of his project and safeguard it from having a single-nation character, Coubertin turned away from the Greeks. At the 1897 Le Havre conference, Coubertin limited his emphasis on classical Hellenism, which had caused him trouble with the modern Greeks, and highlighted instead an alternative, but equally prestigious, source of inspiration for high values: Anglo-Saxonism.

> *The Le Havre Congress had to do without any help from Greece.* The Greeks were fighting for the independence of Crete and the restoration of the legitimate frontiers, but fate proved hostile. Friends and enemies fighting in the service of their country had no time to turn their eyes towards Normandy. *Therefore, the Hellenism that had permeated the atmosphere of the first Congress in 1894 started to fade before the influence of England, which was closer. It was to Arnold that we turned, more or less consciously, for inspiration.* (Coubertin 1997j: 372, emphasis added)

As noted earlier in this chapter, Coubertin admired England, and saw in it the continuum of Hellenism, 'the virtue of Greek formulae [was] perfected by Anglo-Saxon civilisation' (Coubertin 1918c, 2000: 272). By the middle of the nineteenth century the language and imagery of chivalry had been a core theme in the middle-class discourse of Victorian life. The notion of the 'gentleman', inspired by noble and selfless values, represented a contemporary version of medieval chivalry, which was deliberately promoted by the Victorians in their effort to produce a ruling elite both for the nation and the expanding of Empire. A wider public than simply the English upper classes applauded the emphasis on games in public school education. The English education system was the admiration of continental idealists. Several Frenchmen, in a survey of English (and Scottish) education in 1868, expressed respect for the games, as well as for the freedom and independence of the pupils in Public Schools. In 1876, the German Ludwig Wiese considered the conduct of English upper class youth 'a pedagogic virtue' and praised the way in which 'the germ of manliness' was cultivated (cited in Mangan 2000: 130). In 1897, Edward Demolins published a book entitled *A quoi tient la supériorité des Anglo-Saxons?* (What is the reason for the superiority of Anglo-Saxons?), and appeared quite certain that the answer lay in the centrality of physical exercise in their schools (cited in Mangan 2000: 130).

The emphasis on 'Anglo-Saxon' values at Le Havre Congress (1897) had a twofold purpose: to divert the emphasis from Hellenism to a different civilisational focus thereby safeguarding the Games from too strong an association with the Hellenic nationalism which had arisen, as well as to use positively the rising 'Anglomania' for the best interests of the modern Olympic Games. This balancing of Hellenism and Anglo-Saxon values is evident in a range of Coubertin's writings.

> The only way to ensure any relative long-term survival of the athletic renaissance then still in its infancy was to superimpose the immense

prestige of antiquity on the passing fad of Anglomania, thereby under-cutting, to some extent, any opposition from the students of classicism, and to impose on the world a system whose fame spread beyond all national borders. (Coubertin 1929: 573)

3.4   Expansion of the Olympic movement (1918–1937)

During the 1914–18 war, Coubertin moved the Olympic headquarters, and his own domicile, to Switzerland in order to ensure that the Olympics would survive the threat posed by this crisis of the western world (Riordan and Krüger 1999) since there was no enormous bureaucratic organisation to be repositioned, it was a fairly simple matter (Guttmann 1992). As a result of the war, the 1916 Olympic Games, which were scheduled to be held in Berlin, were cancelled, and the structure of the IOC was challenged by the internal conflicts of its members. The problem of participation of the countries of the defeated powers emerged as a critical issue in the post-war period. Theodore Cook, a British member, demanded the expulsion of the German members, and when his request was not fulfilled, he resigned. It was difficult for the IOC to stage the Olympic Games of 1920, as most of the major western European countries were still coming to terms with the social, political and economic consequences of the war. In relation to the issue of who should participate, the solution was found in the formula initiated at the 1896 Olympic Games, according to which it was left to the organising committee of the host city to decide who should be invited to the Olympic Games. Therefore, the next organisers would not be instructed by the IOC to exclude any of the defeated powers, but they would be encouraged *not to invite them*. In this way, the Germans were not invited to the 1920 Antwerp and 1924 Paris Olympics (they re-appeared at the 1928 Amsterdam Olympics).

The IOC's decision to revive the Olympic Games had been made in April 1919, allowing only one year for the national Olympic committees to make preparations. Since the German invasion of Belgium had been the cause that brought Britain into the war, the IOC decided that was symbolically important for the first post-war Games to be staged in Antwerp (Guttmann 1992), to provide 'a symbolic revival of the Olympic movement and its message from out of the killing fields of Flanders' (Roche 2000: 104). These first Olympic Games after the end of the First World War sought to reflect international unity and peace, which were to be demonstrated through new rituals, such as the five rings flag, the symbolic release of doves and the athletes' oath (Roche 2000). Although Germany, Austria and its allies were not invited, the Games were very successful (Krüger 1999). The resumption of the Games after the First World War in the war-torn Belgium was evidence of the resilience of the Olympic movement (Segrave and Chu 1988; Krüger 1999).

During the years 1912–1927, the Olympic Games grew in size and credibility. More than 2,500 athletes representing 28 nations competed in the

1912 Stockholm Olympics, and nearly 3,000 athletes from 44 countries gathered for the Paris Games of 1924 (Segrave and Chu 1988). In the inter-war period, the IOC established itself as the primary actor and authority in international sport. Increasingly impressive Olympic events were staged at Antwerp 1920, Paris 1924, Amsterdam 1928, Los Angeles 1932 and Berlin 1936, transforming the Olympic movement into a significant international phenomenon. The development of transport and communication, particularly radio in the 1920s, created the potential for the organisation of international sport events on a broader basis. Moreover, after the First World War, the need for international peace and cultural exchange was felt more keenly. The disorganised character of pre-war international relations was seen as problematic, and new ways of international understanding and cooperation were put into practice. The IOC encouraged a close cooperation with the newly established League of Nations, an organisation that hoped to provide stability and security in international relations. Roche (2000) argues that the concepts of universalism and humanism were undermined by the IOC's practices in this period, nonetheless an emphasis on such principles 'made the movement's international institution-building appear compatible and convergent with broader processes of international institution-building. Thus the IOC in this period was interested in associating itself with the League of Nations' (p. 108).

3.4.1   The inter-war crisis: Alternative Olympics

Thus over the inter-war period, both popular and elite interest in international-level sport events increased. Nationalism in relation to sport escalated, and sport victories were used as a means to enhance national pride and prestige in the newly significant international world order. In the inter-war period, such interests were also expressed outside the Olympic movement, and through the establishment of Olympic-type games events, often called 'Alternative Olympics'. These included: a) the 'military Olympics', sport contests between athletes of the Allies on the basis of internationalism and friendship (Inter-Allied Military 'Olympiads'), b) the 'Workers' Olympics', intended to oppose to the elitism, nationalism and sensationalism of the bourgeois Olympics, and c) the 'Women's Olympics' opposed to the sexist prejudices of the Olympic movement. In addition, the inter-war period witnessed the organisation of Regional Games, which often challenged the authority of the IOC, but also contributed to the expansion of the Olympic movement.

Military 'Olympics'

During the early part of America's participation in the First World War, athletics were largely under the control and supervision of the Young Men's Christian Association (YMCA) whose athletic directors did much toward the establishment of a firm foundation for the future development of all types of sports and games in the American Expeditionary Forces (AEF) and among troops in the US. In the pre-war period, team games such as basketball and volleyball were associated with the promotion of Christian values. The YMCA implemented programmes in communities, Sunday schools and in industry in order to spread physical education. However, during the war, the Association's experience and popularity were mostly used in political terms.

> The army drew heavily on the personnel and resources of the YMCA, and 300 athletic directors took charge of the sports programme, operating 836 athletic fields. The YMCA sent scores of these directors overseas and spent between one and two million dollars on athletic equipment ... Under the directorship of Elwood S. Brown, the YMCA carried the burden of athletic activities in France until the General Order 241 made athletics and mass games a matter of military schedule. (Betts 1974; cited in Scharenberg 1999: 94)

On April 18, 1918, with America having joined the Allies and having a rapidly expanding army in Europe, Mr. Elwood Brown, physical director of the YMCA, requested war service and was brought to France as one of the YMCA athletic directors. Becoming a field secretary, Mr. Brown encouraged more widespread and systematic athletic activity in the Army, and for that reason he approached influential figures. It is believed that he aroused the interest of General Pershing and secured full cooperation from the Army and the YMCA headquarters, facilitating the issuance of General Order 241, the first General Order relating to sports in the US Army (issued by the General John J. Pershing, commander of the AEF, on December 29, 1918). The purpose of the order was to encourage the development of sport for the improvement of the physical fitness of the Army. The order called for competition in the AEF including championships in track and field, baseball, football, basketball, tennis, boxing and wrestling. Through the publication of the General Order 241, a closer cooperation between the YMCA and the Army was established (US Army 2004).

Even during demobilisation, the programme for organised sport by the YMCA continued, but was principally with foreign sports aid to promote internationalism (Scharenberg 1999). Sport was thereby promoted through several friendly contests between the athletes of the Allies. The Inter-Allied Military Games, held in Paris, from June 22 until July 6, 1919, signalled the end of the Great War and the beginning of a new era in international relations. Coubertin, when he heard about the YMCA's plans to stage an Olympic-type event in Paris, could not hide his annoyance.

> In Paris, people fuss, they fuss intensely. That could be the refrain of an appropriate song, the verses of which would go on and on. Rather than list the things that people in Paris do fuss about, it would be quicker to

list what they don't. They are also fussing about the Olympic Games. When they learned that the new municipality of Strasbourg was having a stadium built near the Kehl Bridge in order to give the unemployed something to do, the Parisians wanted to hold world championships there in 1920. In addition, the committee of the YMCA, an organisation that gets involved in lots of things because of the great services that it has rendered in many areas, is talking about a 'Super-Olympiad' to be held this spring in the Paris area. What on earth is a 'Super-Olympiad?' When he entered Babylon, not even the victorious Alexander, as eager as he was to Hellenise the East, came up with such a thing. Our friends are growing alarmed *at this disorder, which threatens the Olympic calendar. They are growing alarmed at all these conflicting plans. They should rest assured.* (Coubertin 1919c, 2000: 550; emphasis added)

Coubertin, being aware that the alternative Games could 'lead to cracks in the Olympic structure' (Coubertin 1997a, 2000: 486) did not allow the use of the name 'Olympic' for any other events than the Olympic Games. He believed that the misuse of the term 'Olympic' was intentional, aiming at the interruption of the periodicity of the Olympiads with the organisation of alternative Games.

Reprehensible plots were concocted in which alleged athletes – unaware of the fundamental fairness of frontal attacks in sports – tried to upset the order of the Olympiads and assume direction of them. Not a trace of these plots remains. General Pershing, with a single stroke of his honest pen, crossed out the term 'Olympic' which they wanted to use to deck out allied military games. President Clemenceau, sending a squadron of planes to Lausanne, asked the IOC to see the gesture as an expression of his complete support. (Coubertin 1934a, 2000: 743)

These events were not particularly a threat to the Olympic Games, and 'had been arranged with a view to providing a healthful and enjoyable means of occupying the enforced leisure of the troops of the different armies, whose immediate demobilisation and return home had, for many reasons, not been considered practicable' (Coubertin 1997k, 2000). Interestingly, Krüger (1999) argues that if there had not been successful Inter-Allied Games in Paris in 1919 under the American General Pershing, 'the IOC would not have dared stage the Olympic Games so shortly after the war' (p. 11). Nevertheless, the alleged expedience of the Inter-Allied Games could perhaps have had the reverse effect to the Olympic movement, if Coubertin had not exercised pressure when it was needed.

Here is one that closely concerns Olympism, and to which recent abuses require us to draw the public's attention. A French newspaper, which is at time not afraid to massacre grammar – as is true, alas, of so many others like it – describes the inter-allied military contests led by the head of the American army as the 'Pershing Olympiad'. This is the result of both historical and technical ignorance. An Olympiad is a date on the calendar established, based on fixed and equal intervals of four years. It is therefore absurd to speak of organizing an Olympiad. As the Olympiads were re-established, starting from 1896, nothing can prevent the seventh from starting in 1920, the eight in 1924, the ninth in 1928, and so on. The only issue that arises is that of celebrating these Olympiads with Games. The sixth (1916) could not be celebrated in Berlin as had been intended. The seventh (1920) is expected to be celebrated in Antwerp. Olympiads can, therefore, in no case be likened to the Games with which they are customarily celebrated. For their part, these Games have a programme that is summarised succinctly in the words: all games, all nations. The very essence of the Olympic Games is that they are inter-national and include different types of sports: gymnastic and athletic sports, combat sports, water sports, equestrian sports, etc. The term Olympic is constantly used to describe local or technically limited competitions. This is a mistake. It was necessary to point this out, and explain once more the value of terms that are becoming commonly used. (Coubertin 1919d, 2000: 551)

Some years later, in his Olympic Memoirs, Coubertin refers again to the efforts he made to ensure that the name 'Olympiad' would only be used by the IOC to describe the interval of four years between the Olympic Games.

Naturally, attempts had been made in certain circles to mislead the public by talking of a 'Military Olympiad' and suggesting that it should take the place of the regular Olympiad a year ahead of time. Once again the question of the numbering of the Games and the four-yearly inter-val! I have before me a letter from J.J. Jusserand, giving me an account of the steps he was taking (President Wilson was in Paris at the time) and assuring me that the Americans would never allow use to be made of the terms 'Olympic' or 'Olympiad' for such a purpose. The Inter-Allied Games, as might have been expected, showed moreover that muscular value and sporting enthusiasm were not on the decline. (Coubertin 1997k, 2000: 473)

The Olympic movement itself had a certain degree of recognition among the international circles in the early years. However, in the inter-war period, and through actions such as the resistance against the newly emerged athletic festivals, which carried the name 'Olympic' in their title, the IOC established itself as the primary authority concerned with international sport. Given the fact that the Olympic event is a multi-sport festival, other international sport events which followed the internationally standardised game rules and regulations for international sport could also claim the name 'Olympic'. Nevertheless, Coubertin transformed a situation that could have proved threatening for the future of the Olympic movement to an opportunity for the strengthening of the Olympic structure by drawing the boundaries of the Olympic movement.

The socialist challenge and the 'Workers' Olympics'

The war resulted in the collapse of the old empires and the emergence of new states, mostly in Eastern Europe. In 1917, after a series of revolutions, Russia became the first country in the world to form a communist government (Culpin 1996). In the late 1920s and 1930s, Europe suffered from increasing mass unemployment and poverty, which led to a mobilisation towards social change and re-ordering of the social classes, as the upper class and the elites eventually lost their power and privileges. Due to these social changes, a new form of physical culture was born that would serve the revolutionary purposes of the communists. The communist sport model aimed to introduce sport to all people and employed it for utilitarian purposes that would enhance public welfare. Moreover, it would help to increase national integrity and secure national unity of the people belonging to the communist and authoritarian regimes (Riordan 1999). From 1917 to 1939 a series of 'alternative Olympics' took place, mainly organised by the Soviets. Although the Soviet Union had participated in the 1912 Olympics, it was never invited subsequently to take part in any of the Olympic Games during the inter-war period. Nevertheless, the USSR organised many cultural sport events on a scale even bigger than that of the Olympics (Roche 2000).

In 1917, the USSR organised the Central Asian Games in Tashkent in which 3,000 athletes took part, a significantly larger number than that of the athletes participating in the 1920 Olympics in Belgium (Krüger and Riordan 1996; Roche 2000). The importance of this event lay in the fact that in these games for the first time some of the Russian ex-colonies were summoned together, despite their language, religious and cultural differences. Three years later, in 1920, the USSR celebrated the third anniversary of the 1917 'October revolution' with a mass demonstration of the Bolshevik storming of the Winter Palace involving 18,000 athletes. This event was termed a 'pre-Olympics' as a reference to the 1920 Olympics for which the USSR was not invited to take part. In 1925 and 1928 the Soviets organised the 'Spartakiad Games', a very successful event that combined sport competitions and cultural manifestations. They have been described as a 'ritualised Marxist demonstration against the hypocrisy of the bourgeois Olympics with their apparent discrimination against working class athletes' (Krüger and Riordan 1996). In 1932, the last Spartakiad Games prior to the World

War II were held in Moscow. It has been suggested that those Games were held in this year as part of the ideological opposition to the 1932 Olympic Games in Los Angeles (Roche 2000).

Coubertin asserts in a number of his writings that the changes in the social order, after the end of the war, did not have a major impact on the structure of the Olympic movement. Although he acknowledges that the 'Workers' Olympiads' had achieved remarkable success, he emphasises their weaknesses centred upon the internal conflicts between the socialist and communist organisations, which led to the change of the name of their events.

> Olympia experienced its moments of discord. Olympism survived without going under. Neo-Olympism will evolve in the same way [...] It was in the early days of their revival that they [i.e. the Olympic Games] ran the greatest risks; at present, the sap flows too strongly for it ever to dry up. The 1914–1918 war did not shake them: the social revolution did not affect them either. It is interesting to note, moreover, that alongside the 'capitalist' organisation there is already a 'proletarian' organisation. 'Workers' Olympiads' have been held at regular intervals and not without success. At the time of writing, a gigantic stadium is, I am told, being built in Moscow, where the next are to be held. They are even said to be going to take advantage of the occasion to change the name of this athletic meeting, which – if this were the case – would be infantile and only serve to emphasise an only too frequent failing of revolutionaries the world over: when so many institutions need radical renovation, they limit themselves merely to changing the name: what are needed are deeds not words. (Coubertin 1997h, 2000: 747–8)

The division between the socialist and communist organisations over the leadership and aims of the worker sport movement mounted after the formation of the communist International Association of Red Sports and Gymnastics (better known as Red Sport International – RSI) in Moscow in 1921, as a branch of the Communist International or *Comintern*. Until then, the Lucerne Sport International (LSI – a branch of the Bureau of the Socialist International) had led the worker movement, trying to develop it as a strong independent movement within capitalist society. Thus, the socialists were not trying to make their sport movement into an active revolutionary force. Under the socialist leadership, three 'Workers' Olympics' were held (Prague 1925, Frankfurt 1925, Antwerp 1937). By contrast, the communists wished to organise international sport as a political vehicle of the class struggle, considering that it was not sufficient merely to organise a worker movement within the capitalist order. So they organised the Soviet Spartakiads and banned all their members (RSI) from any activities and contacts with the LSI. Although the two worker sport movements came together again in 1936, Krüger (1999) argues that these internal conflicts of the worker movements, together with the over-politicisation of worker sport and the under-representation of these events in the media led to the diminishing of their popularity among the working classes.

Nevertheless, even though Coubertin did not openly admit that such strong socialist and worker movements threatened the existence of the 'bourgeois' Games, his concerns were obvious.

> A country is not truly sporting until the day when the greater part of its citizens feels personal need for sport [...]. And it is for the adult over-taxed and exhausted by modern life that sport constitutes an essential counterbalance, an almost infallible means of recovery, a discipline that nothing can replace. Now what facilities do our organisations provide for this in this respect? [...] What gymnasium – free or almost free – is open to him? [...] That is the reason why I wish to see a revival in an extended and modernised form of the municipal gymnasium of antiquity. [...] *And let the 'bourgeois' look out for the establishment of which I am speaking could well be built one day at their expense by the proletariat, which is already organising Workers' Olympic Games in which the sporting spirit is superior to theirs.* (Coubertin 1927, 2000: 235; emphasis added)

The above quotation is taken from an open letter to Frantz-Reichel, who was Coubertin's close collaborator in France and had served as Secretary General of the 1924 Olympic Games. Coubertin in this letter warns Frantz-Reichel that, if sport were not to be democratised by establishing institutions such as the public gymnasium, the worker movement would undertake such a project, threatening the existence of the 'bourgeois' sport movement. Such concerns also explain why Coubertin, in his speeches of that period, seemed very keen to promote the principle of social equality and advocates sport for all.

> This new era demands such a change [i.e. federations to adopt a more 'tolerant' policy in matters about class]. For a long time, the renewed interest in athleticism during the nineteenth century was merely an occasional pastime for rich and semi-idle youth. Our Committee has fought more than anyone to make it a habitual pleasure of the youth of the lower middle class. Now it must be made fully accessible to proletarian adolescents. All sports for all people, that is the new goal to which we must devote our energies, a goal that is not in the least impracticable. The recent war was won by the western powers thanks to a 'sacred union', based on the conviction that the two-fold stakes of the fight were the political freedom of States, and the social equality of individuals. If we were to forget the second goal after achieving the first, civilisation

would run the risk of exploding like a boiler without a safety valve. (Coubertin 1919a, 2000: 739)

The above message, with a few alterations, is also included in his Olympic Memoirs.

> It also implies recognition of the vital fact, strongly contested until quite recently, that sport is not a luxury pastime, an activity for the leisured few, nor merely a form of muscular compensation for brain work. For every man, woman and child, it offers an opportunity for self-improvement quite independent of profession or position in life. It is the apanage of all, equally and to the same degree, and nothing can replace it. (Coubertin 1997h, 2000: 748)

In similar vein, he condemns the uniformity caused by industrialisation, of which one product is the working class itself, and emphasises Olympism's social and democratic character.

> Olympism refuses to accept the existence of a deluxe education reserved for the wealthy classes, no shred of which should be handed out to the working classes. It refuses to condense art into pills that everyone will take at set hours and to establish timetables of thought along the lines of railways schedules. Olympism is a destroyer of dividing walls. It calls for air and light for all. It advocates a broad-based athletic education accessible to all, trimmed with manly courage and the spirit of chivalry, blended with aesthetic and literary demonstrations, and serving as an engine for national life and as a basis for civic life. That is its ideal programme. Now can it be achieved? (Coubertin 1918a, 2000: 748)

The Workers' Olympiads were opposed to the exclusionary values of elitism, racism and sexism, which tended to make sport inaccessible for working-class athletes. The IOC Games were criticised for being the preserve of the sons of the rich and privileged through the rules of amateurism and the 'aristocratic-cum-bourgeois-dominated national Olympic committees' (Krüger 1999: 109), as well as the IOC itself (Roche 2000). Coubertin, in order to safeguard the severely scrutinised 'bourgeois' Olympic movement, initiated a new, more democratic, popular and inclusive programme.

> Now, nothing is accomplished when only limited numbers are involved. That may have been sufficient before, but not now. The masses must be touched. In truth, in the name of what can the masses be excluded from Olympism? By virtue of what aristocratic decrees does there exist some link between physical beauty and the muscular power of a young man, between his perseverance in training and his desire to win, on the one

hand, and on the other hand, the list of his forefathers or the contents of his wallet? Such contradictions in terms, which are unfounded in law, lived on after the social organisation that created them. It is morally right that it was an autocratic gesture based on an outburst of barbarous militarism that dealt them the deathblow. [...] Faced with a new world that must be ordered according to principles thought to be utopian until now, and that can now be applied, humanity must find all the strength it can in the heritage of the past in order to build its future. Olympism is one of those strengths. (Coubertin 1919e, 2000: 552–3)

He also wished to introduce this 'inclusive' programme to the educational institutes, mainly universities, hoping that the principles of sport, if applied to all, would contribute to the maintenance of social peace, which had been shaky after the war.

But it is also useful to him [i.e. the university student] in carrying out the social task which will lie ahead of him in the new society [...] All forms of sport for everyone; That is not doubt a formula which is going to be criticised as madly utopian. I do not care. I have weighed and examined it for a long time; I know it is accurate and possible. The years and the strength which remain to me will be employed to ensure its triumph; it will be my contribution to those social reforms whose principle was the basis of the pact of sacred union during this long war and whose achievement will have to be honest and swift if we do not want civilisation to blow up like a boiler without a valve; University students, messengers of knowledge and imagination, will constitute the most active battalions in this great task; let us say if you wish that they will have to be us aviators. Now I have said, and I repeat, that sport by reason of its potent physical and moral effects will be an inestimable instrument in their hands for the establishment of social peace. They must therefore know how to handle it with tact and how to derive the maximum effect from it. *Popular Olympism is about to be born; let the students prepare to serve it.* (Coubertin 1919b, 2000: 172; emphasis added)

As a response to the socialist challenge that the new social order and the worker movement had raised, Coubertin put forward the notion of 'popular Olympism'. He emphasised the necessity of the existence of the Olympic Games as a product of popular culture that would enhance the sense of collectiveness among the individuals of the modern society, increasing the chances of maintaining social peace and unity.

Let us look around us and see what are the general needs of the age. It seems that the primary effort is towards a more just distribution and remuneration of labour, then towards a better delimitation between the area of public services and that of private initiative, whose frontiers are drawn in a frequently vague and sometimes absurd fashion, and lastly towards an education within the range of all and no longer the monopoly of a small number. But all these reforms risk remaining sterile unless we succeed in creating a centre for popular spectacles and enjoyments in which a simple, clear and tangible idea can draw together not only people of all ages and all professions, but of all opinions and all situations. (Coubertin 1918b, 2000: 220)

Thus Coubertin's motto in the post-war era became 'all sports for all people', as part of an effort to establish more sports associations that would serve the interests of the general public. He also expressed the idea of establishing a 'popular university' for the education of all individuals, where members of the working class would be taught world history, science, philosophy, language and other topics.

I expect a great deal of the working class. It is possessed of splendid strengths, and seems to me to be capable of great things. Moreover are we not deluding ourselves a bit as far as that culture, of which we are so proud, is concerned? There is so much dross mixed in with the pure metal, so much incoherence, insipidness, hollow vanity, and thinly disguised pornography! Whatever the case may be, here is how the issue stands, as I see it. *There is not way to link the working class suddenly with high culture, as the previous age understood it. The working class must prepare its own inventory of high culture, so that if the temple that contains the accumulated wealth of civilisation should be entrusted to its care in the future, that temple will be respected and maintained. From this viewpoint, a plan for labour universities was devised [...]* 'What?' you may say, 'you want to teach all that to manual labourers? What foolishness! They have neither the time nor the taste for such studies.' I know; I am familiar with this disdain and these people, when I planned to re-establish the Olympic Games, took me for a madman, too. (Coubertin 1922, 2000: 208–9; emphasis added)

Although Coubertin acknowledges that the working class should not be undermined in its efforts to establish its own culture, his statements are punctuated by paternalist references. He suggests that the 'high culture', as has been so far understood by the bourgeois, cannot be wholly embraced by the working class. The rationale of such a claim is better understood in the following:

Now we come to the third factor that guarantees the stability of athletic sovereignty. I am referring to the conquest of the masses that athletic organisations, as they have existed so far, have been unable to reach. How could they have? We are dealing with the self-baptised, the proletariat, in the pejorative sense of a social have-not. *The hour of proletarian revenge has sounded for; we must acknowledge nothing can be done from now on without it. It is the horde, and a horde overwhelms an elite that has not always remained worthy of its privileges. Yet the proletariat is not ready for its task at all. It has not been instructed.* No one has ever bothered to show it all the riches housed in the intellectual temple, a temple that now depends, in part, on that same proletariat for its very preservation. Above all no one has done anything to dispel the bitterness – no, let us speak frankly, let us use the words that are fitting – to soothe the intense anger, the accumulated hatred that form the disturbing substrate of the new foundations now being laid. (Coubertin 1920, 2000: 225; emphasis added)

Coubertin seems to accept, if not to embrace, the new reality of greater rights and freedom for the proletariat. However, showing once again evidence of paternalism, he emphasises that the proletariat is not capable of carrying out successfully its new tasks in society without the guidance of an elite. In similar vein, the establishment of the popular university may be seen as an attempt by bourgeois interests – and by Coubertin in particular – to 'instruct' the proletariat by organising its education. It may be argued that, since the rising power of the proletariat could not be halted, initiatives such as the popular university could at least assist the bourgeois to maintain some kind of indirect control over the proletariat. This argument sounds more credible, if one reads the following quotation.

There was a confused sense that this war was not going to be like any other, and that, dominated by a new element – the unity of the world – this war was creating unexpected opportunities. Once it was over, accumulated rancour and cramped appetites would clash in a gigantic battle for the conquest of power. *Merely pushing the working class back into its previous status was not an option. The only choices open to discussion were to join forces with it or to submit to it.* Various opinions are in the process of being formed about these alternatives. Some, in light of the flaws in and the breakdown of society, its inability to reform itself, are attached to the idea of a new, more just society – and thereby a more Christian society. Others think that we have what it takes to rebuild, and that it is just a matter of time until that is apparent. *But in the near future, whether the working class is in full control of power or merely involved in the exercise of that power, the issue of preparing that class is just as essential.* Yet there is no such preparation. [...] From this viewpoint, a plan of labour universities was devised. (Coubertin 1922, 2000: 207–8; emphasis added)

All the same, Coubertin, given the new social order, unquestionably made remarkable efforts to reform Olympism and transform it to a more democratic and popular philosophy. This provided evidence that the Olympic movement could develop sensitivity in social matters and that it could be flexible when this was needed. However, the situation was very different in relation to the inclusion of women in the Olympic movement. Although, women's role in contemporary western society was gradually changing by the recognition of more rights (especially in the pre-war period women's right to vote had become a major issue for dispute), Coubertin continued to oppose the participation of women in the Olympic Games. As expected, women reacted to the sexist and exclusivist values of the Olympic movement and organised their own athletic competitions. Thus, the inter-war period of the Olympic movement experienced a further series of 'alternative' games, the so-called 'Women's Olympics' or 'Women's World Games' (as they were later re-named).

The 'Feminist Drive' and the 'Women's Olympics'

Women were never originally seen as equal partners, nor indeed as any kind of partners, in Coubertin's view of modern sport, and consequently in his project to revive the Olympic Games. In his 'Ode to Sport', the centrality of the male athlete was obvious.

O Sport, you are Fecundity!

You tend by straight and noble paths towards a more perfect race, blasting the seeds of sickness and righting the flaws, which threaten its needful soundness. *And you quicken within the athlete the wish to see growing about him brisk and sturdy sons to follow him in the arena and in their turn bear off joyous laurels.* (Coubertin 1912a, 2000: 630; emphasis added)

Classism, sexism and racism were bound up with the organisations and the social structures of the nineteenth-century Europe. Based on the theory of 'separate spheres', the role of women was limited to issues concerning home whereas men dealt with the public affairs. Coubertin shared fully the sexist prejudices of his era which privileged the male physique and male sociability in their conception of sport culture (Guttmann 1992; Hargreaves 1994; Roche 2000). He never hesitated to state clearly his opposition to the prospect of allowing women to participate in the Olympic Games.

The question of allowing women to participate in the Olympic Games has not been settled. The answer cannot be negative merely on the grounds that that was the answer in antiquity; nor can it be affirmative solely because female competitors were admitted in swimming and tennis in 1908 and 1912. So it is clear that the debate remains open. It is good that too swift a decision has not been reached, and that this matter has dragged on. It will resolve itself quite naturally at the Congress of Paris, which will give the Olympiads their final form. Which way will it go? I am not a soothsayer, but for my own part I am not afraid of siding with the no vote. I feel that the Olympic Games must be reserved for men. (Coubertin 1912b, 2000: 711)

Coubertin, in his plans for the Games' revival, had envisaged that they should be reserved for male athletes. In his efforts to explain this position his reasons can be summarised as follows: a) the organisational problems that would follow the inclusion of women due to the increased need for the establishment of separate sport associations and the staging of separate events during the Olympic Games, b) the inappropriateness of viewing women competing with each other in public sports competitions, and c) the limited physical abilities of women which made them 'incapable' of producing records in a highly competitive form of sport such as the Olympics. Those points are evident in the quote below:

First, in application of the well-known proverb depicted by Musset, 'a door must be either open or closed'. Can we allow women access to all Olympic events? No? Then why should some sports be open to them while the rest are not? Above all, what basis can one use to place the barrier between the events that are permitted, and those that are not? There are not just women tennis players and swimmers. There are women fencers, women riders and, in America, women rowers. In the future, perhaps, will there be women runners or even women football players? *Would such sports, played by women, constitute a sight to be recommended before the crowds that gather for an Olympiad? I do not think that any such claim can be made.* But there is another reason, a practical one. Would separate events be held for women, or would meets be held all together, without distinction as to sex, regardless of whether the competition is among individuals or teams? The second of these approaches would be logical, since the dogma of the equality of the sexes tends to expand. Yet this assumes the existence of co-ed clubs. There are hardly any such clubs now, with the exception of tennis and swimming. *Even with co-ed clubs, ninety-five times out of a hundred, elimination rounds favour the men.* (Coubertin 1912b, 2000: 711–12; emphasis added)

Even though the Games were reserved exclusively for male athletes, at the 1900 Paris Olympic Games Charlotte Cooper became the first female modern Olympic victor. There were 1318 men and only 19 women at these Games (a figure which was reduced to eight in the St. Louis Games of 1904). These were females from privileged backgrounds who had the necessary funds and leisure time to enable their participation in socially acceptable sports.

The most popular sport among those classes were archery, field sports, and later in the century, golf and tennis (Guttmann 1992; Toohey and Veal 2000). However, it should be noted that women in these Games performed in a few unofficial events, while the IOC banned women from participation in the Olympics in 1912 (Hargreaves 1994). It is obvious that Coubertin did not want to incorporate women's organised sport into the Games, and, for that reason, he often exaggerated the structural and bureaucratic barriers. Another issue that concerned him deeply was the exposure of female physicality through the public contests.

> Although I would like competitions among boys to be more infrequent, I emphatically insist that the tradition continues. This form of athletic competitiveness is vital in athletic education, with all its risks and consequences. Add a female element, and the event becomes monstrous. The experience of Amsterdam seems to have justified my opposition to allowing women into the Olympic Games. On the whole, reaction so far has been hostile to repeating the spectacle that the women's events provided during the Ninth Olympiad. *If some women want to play football or box, let them, provided that the event takes place without spectators, because the spectators who flock to such competitions are not there to watch a sport.* (Coubertin 1928a, 2000: 188–9; emphasis added)

In similar vein, some years later (1935), he returned to this point.

> I personally do not approve of feminine participation in public competitions, which does not mean that women should not go in for a large number of sports, but I mean to say merely that they should not seek the limelight! In the Olympic Games, their particular role should be that of crowning the champions, as in the tournaments of olden times. (Coubertin 1935, 2000: 583)

Coubertin was able to appeal to, and in some ways to shape, the contemporary view of the concept of chivalry in the Middle Ages. As he described in one of his earlier writings, with reference to the English Dr. Brookes who had attempted to revive the institution of ancient athletics,

> Yet in some ways antiquity was not enough for Dr. Brookes. It did not know of gallantry. So he drew on some chivalrous customs of the Middle Ages. He had the winner of the tournament bend his knee to receive the symbolic laurel from the hands of a lady. (Coubertin 1890b, 2000: 284)

In principle, sport offered cultural liberation for women in terms of the social constraints of the Victorian dress code and 'body culture' (Roche 2000). However, even after World War I, when women had more freedom in many spheres of their lives, they were denied equality of access and opportunity in sport (Birrell and Cole 1994). The culturally appropriate behaviour for women demanded female athletes to demonstrate the principles of modesty, dignity and morality, which defined behavioural and dress standards (Toohey and Veal 2000). With this rationale, Coubertin argued that public competition for women was inappropriate. Instead, a more suitable role for women would be to show their appreciation of the male athletes for their remarkable achievements.

There remains the other possibility, that of adding women's competitions alongside men's competitions in the sports declared open to women, a little female Olympiad alongside the great male Olympiad. What is the appeal of that? Organisers are already overworked, deadlines are already too short, the problems posed by housing and ranking are already formidable, costs are already excessive, and all that would have to be doubled! Who would want to take all that on? *In our view, this feminine semi-Olympiad is impractical, uninteresting, ungainly, and, I do not hesitate to add, improper. It is not in keeping with my concept of the Olympic Games, in which I believe that we have tried, and must continue to try, to put the following expression into practice: the solemn and periodic exaltation of male athleticism, based on internationalism, by means of fairness, in an artistic setting, with the applause of women as a reward.* This combination of the ancient ideal and the traditions of chivalry is the only healthful and satisfactory one. It will impose itself on public opinion through its own strength. (Coubertin 1912b, 2000: 713; emphasis added)

In the above extract, a further reason, explaining why Coubertin opposed women's participation in sport, is also evident. He argued that competitions solely organised for women would lack interest. This relates to his view that women's physical capabilities are limited to physical exercises, and thus women cannot perform successfully in competitive sport.

Let us not forget that the Olympic Games are not parades of physical exercises, but aim to raise, or at least maintain, records. Citius, altius, fortius. Faster, higher, stronger. That is the motto of the International Committee, and the fundamental reason for the existence of any form of Olympism. Whatever the athletic ambitions of women may be, women cannot claim to outdo men in running, fencing, equestrian events, etc. To bring the principle of the theoretical equality of the sexes into play here would be to indulge in a pointless demonstration bereft of meaning or impact. (Coubertin 1912b, 2000: 711–12)

In the nineteenth century, the emphasis for women's physical activity and sport was on graceful movement rather than strenuous competition, which was related to 'masculine' development and loss of 'femininity'. Moreover, a related fear was that strenuous sport competition would damage a young woman's health and in particular her reproductive system. In short, the criteria for women's physical activity were hygienic and aesthetic rather than athletic (Guttmann 1992). Besides, there was the common view that women were frail individuals who just could not cope with the physical exertion that was required in many of the events. Interestingly, Hargreaves (1994) notes that, when the IOC held a conference in 1925 to examine the 'issue' of sport and women, 'its medical report was a reaffirmation of the popular nineteenth century theory of constitutional overstrain ... urging caution about the type and amount of exercise ... with a scientific justification limiting women's participation in track and field athletics during the following years' (p. 213).

> Can the young women I have mentioned before, with justified cruelty, acquire a moral sense through sports, too? I do not believe so. Physical education, athletic physical culture, yes. That is excellent for young girls, for women. But the ruggedness of male exertion, the basis of athletic education when prudently but resolutely applied, is much to be dreaded when it comes to the female. That ruggedness is achieved physically only when nerves are stretched beyond their normal capacity, and morally only when the most precious feminine characteristics are nullified. Female heroism is no phantom. I would even say, more directly, that it is just as common and perhaps even more admirable than male heroism. (Coubertin 1928a, 2000: 188)

Here Coubertin is again concerned with the issue of preserving the characteristics of women's femininity, which could be distorted through sport. He always emphasised that 'the Olympic Games were established to exalt the individual male athlete, whose existence is necessary for the muscular activity of the group, and whose prowess is necessary to maintain the general competitiveness of all' (Coubertin 1931c, 2000: 718). Although Coubertin had no objections to women's involvement in physical activity per se, he felt strongly that women should not take part in competitive sport. Interestingly, Coubertin emphasised that women could also demonstrate a kind of heroism through remarkable achievements, but not in the domain of competitive sport. Evidence of what constituted his perceived 'female heroism' is the following:

> A record. A Swedish woman, Mrs. Wersall, had all six of her sons taking part in the Games in one way or another, the youngest as boy scout enrolled to help in maintaining order and carrying messages. How true to ancient ideals! The IOC awarded her the Olympic medal. (Coubertin 1997e, 2000: 441)

Thus, women were only to be valued for giving birth to Olympic male champions rather than for their own sporting accomplishments. Women's response to this exclusionary attitude was similar to that of the working-class and socialist organisations discussed earlier, namely they formed their own international association. Women from different countries who were interested in sport formed the *Fédération Sportive Féminine Internationale* (FSFI) in October 31, 1921, under the leadership of Alice Milliat, and the Women's Amateur Athletics Association (WAAA) was formed in Britain in 1922. It is also worth mentioning that women's participation in sport was encouraged in the national and international socialist sport movement and in the SWSI Workers' Olympics discussed above (Roche 2000). This group organised a separate female sporting contest, the first 'Women's Olympics', held in 1922 in Monte Carlo, with 300 competitors (Toohey and Veal 2000). However, subsequent to their success and the continued antagonism of the IOC to their proposed term 'Women's Olympics', the event was renamed and the FSFI staged the Women's World Games in 1926, 1930 and 1934 (Guttmann 1992; Roche 2000; Toohey and Veal 2000).

Sigfrid Edström, founder-President of the International Amateur Athletic Federation (IAAF) (1912) and influential member of the IOC' s executive board, in response to the pressure caused by the organisation of the 'Women's Olympics' very close to the Olympic Games, voted in 1924 to sanction women's track and field events but not to advocate their inclusion in the Olympic Games. Finally, after hard negotiations between Edström and Milliat, it was agreed that the FSFI would drop the word 'Olympic' in reference to their sport contests, but in return the IAAF agreed to leave the FSFI in control of women's sport (Guttmann 1992). Just as with the worker movement, women's movement faced internal conflicts because some women wanted women's sport to follow a pattern based more on cooperation, which would be different from that of male competitive sport. Nevertheless, with the success of the 'Women's World Games', the IOC accepted the recommendation of the IAAF to permit the admission of women to a restricted number of athletic events at the Games (on April 5, 1926).

All the same, Coubertin never changed his mind about the participation of women in the Olympic Games, 'as to the admission of women to the Games, I remain strongly against it. It was against my will that they were admitted to a growing number of competitions' (Coubertin 1928b, 2000: 604). Even after the successful organisation of the SFSI successful events in 1922, 1926, 1930 and 1934, his views remained the same, as opposed to the shift he initiated toward the democratisation of Olympism after the analogous rise of the socialist and worker movements that were discussed above. His writings around this period provide evidence of this refusal to change his views.

> Likewise, I continue to think that association with women's athleticism is bad, and that such athleticism should be excluded from the Olympic programme – that the Olympiads were restored for the rare and solemn glorification of the individual male athlete. I believe that team sports are

out of place in Olympiads, unless they compete in associated tournaments held outside the 'Altis' (to use the ancient distinction), in other words, outside the sacred enclosure. (Coubertin 1934a, 2000: 746)

Towards the end of his life, Coubertin explained the rationale for his focus on male adults and adolescents rather than girls.

The average Frenchman's infuriating sense of logic made my friends reproach me: you are working for the adolescent, for the boy ... what are you planning to do for the child, for the girl? ... Nothing at all, was my answer. They are not going to advance my cause. The reform that I am aiming at is not in the interests of grammar or hygiene. It is a social reform or rather it is the foundation of a new era that I can see coming and which will have no value or force unless it is firmly based on the principle of a completely new type of education. (Coubertin 1976, 2000: 753; emphasis added)

The Olympic Games were originally part of Coubertin's envisaged social reform based on a new form of education, in which male sport education would be given priority. The absence of grammar or hygiene from the reformed education reflects his ideas about replacing some aspects of academic discipline with a competitive form of sport. Thus, this form of education based on modern competitive sport, and the Anglo-Saxon model of athleticism, would apply only to the male students who were thought to be physically capable of the rigour of competitive sport. In retrospect, his negative views about the participation of women in the Olympic Games may be seen as a corollary of the original plans and initial reasons for his social reform. Physical exercise, in the form of the Anglo-Saxon model of modern sport, would produce a stronger generation of men, and thus a stronger French army. This would therefore heighten the possibilities for France to become a strong imperialistic force again. Nonetheless, even if socio-political changes took place, it may be argued that his interest in the advancement of the male individual, albeit initially related to an imperialistic *raison d'être*, remained a core belief until the end of his life.

3.4.2 'Olympisation': Power and control over the regional games

In the inter-war period, the power of the IOC as the primary actor concerned with international sport had to be won in the context of the increasing power of other organisations and movements that emerged with the end of the war.

The situation called above all for a declaration of unity, and that is why the pilot at the helm felt that everyone was looking to him to steer a steady course. The danger was not so much that some other body might succeed in taking over Olympism. A French politician and a French journalist were waging a fruitless campaign to hand over the Games to the

League of Nations, which had only just come into being and had not yet found its feet. Such proposals had very little chance of being accepted and it was as easy to fight against them as against the attacks of certain federations, eager to see their delegates sitting at the table of the IOC. (Coubertin 1997a, 2000: 486)

As discussed above, in the inter-war period socio-political interests were principally expressed outside the Olympic movement and through the staging of the 'alternative Olympics', such as the Inter-Allied Military Olympiad, the Workers' Olympics and Women's World Games. These events, albeit short-lived, challenged the authority of the Olympic movement, and succeeded in pressurising the IOC to recognise that it needed to accommodate the growth of popular interest in sport. However, another issue that concerned the IOC during this period was the increasing power of the international federations, which could have an impact on the authority of the IOC as the major decision-making body in international sport.

In a chapter of his Olympic memoirs entitled 'The 1921 Manoeuvre', Coubertin refers to the conflicting interests between the IOC and the international federations. In 1921, the technical Olympic Congress in Lausanne was held, where, among other issues, experts in various sports such as riding, winter sports and mountaineering met to discuss about the technical aspects of the Olympic programme (Müller 2000). The Olympic movement itself had a certain degree of organisation from its early years, being comprised of the IOC on the one hand, and the national Olympic committees (NOCs) on the other. The IOC was a self-recruiting body and viewed its members as diplomatic representatives of the Olympic movement in their home countries, rather than as representatives of their nations. The NOCs organised national teams for the Olympic Games, and when they were the hosts of the event, they would undertake a leading role in the event itself. However, given the fact that the Olympic Games are a multi-sport festival, in addition to this structure it was necessary to develop an international level of organisation in the constituent sports. Such need had already emerged in the early days, when conflicts over the rules and regulations were frequent (especially in 1900, 1904 and 1908 Olympic Games). A number of important international sport governing bodies associated with the Olympic movement were established in this period, including in soccer, *Fédération Internationale de Football Association* (FIFA) in 1904, and in athletics, the International Amateur Athletics Federation (IAAF) in 1913 (Roche 2000).

At the conference in 1921, the IOC had to defend itself against the ambitious plans of the International Federations to establish their world federation, which would act on a relatively independent basis (Müller 2000).

Paul Rousseau did not succeed any better either in creating his super-federation. He had to be content with the maintenance of an 'Office of

International Federations', *which was only very reluctantly granted the minimum rights of intervention and the bare means of existence.* I do not know whether this new body would have come up to it's promoter's expectations, but from the Olympic point of view it would certainly have helped the IOC by freeing it of a technical role that was too extensive and responsibilities, which I had always hoped it might be able to throw off one day. At any rate, the Congress of the International Federations, both at the first meeting, which I was asked to open, and at the final banquet, showed that between them and the IOC the era of misunderstandings had come to an end. (Coubertin 1997a, 2000: 490)

In similar vein, a number of Olympic-related Regional Games, mainly organised by national-level governing bodies, constituted a threat by challenging the power of the IOC as the centre of the Olympic organisation.

The real danger lay in the frittering away of the Olympic idea, which risked being brought about by the proliferation of Regional Games that were the result of the general impatience that seemed to prevail. *They were being created here, there and everywhere or at least we were continually being bombarded with plans, programmes and announcements of the formation of committees and subcommittees.* During the last two years of the war, the threat of secession had hung over Olympism. By indirect and unofficial action I had always succeeded in thwarting any such attempts. The 'League of Neutrals', which had for a while been mooted, had never been more than a project without any real substance. The 'League of Belligerents' of the German group had been nothing more than a vague idea and even if they were to try and carry it through now, it would surely be only very short-lived; Hungary and Turkey would probably be very reluctant to join in. On the other band, if all these 'Games' which were to be organised in Ireland, Poland, Catalonia, the Balkans, India and the Near East were allowed to take root, it might lead to cracks in the Olympic structure. Admittedly all these undertakings looked to us for blessing and depended on our patronage. But largely ignorant of Olympic matters and unfamiliar with the spirit of the IOC, those who conceived them and sought to organise them harboured ulterior motives of a nationalistic or a religious character, which would only upset the whole movement in the end. (Coubertin 1997a, 2000: 486; emphasis added)

In this context, the IOC's main concern was related to the affiliation of each sport to their confederations and federations, and simultaneously to the IOC, thus establishing itself as the primary authority concerned with international sport. Thus, for that reason, DaCosta *et al.* (2002: 98) argue that, 'the "under the IOC sponsorship" expression had a more reactive than hegemonic meaning in the years of 1921, 1922 and 1923'. In light of this, the Regional Games posed a potential threat to the Olympic movement, unless they were to come under the control of the IOC.

> Therefore, I can say that the goal has been reached, and my work is done. Yet in keeping with your wishes, I shall remain as your President until 1924 so that, together, we may celebrate in Paris the Thirtieth Anniversary of the restoration of the Olympic Games on the occasion of the Eighth Olympiad. *Until then, according to my promise, I will work toward the advancement of the Regional Games. Held periodically under your patronage in various parts of the world, these Games will provide valuable human support for Olympism.* Thus it was that the Fourth Far Eastern Games, recently held at Shanghai before a crowd of 150,000 spectators, achieved quite remarkable results in all respects. (Coubertin 1921, 2000: 700; emphasis added)

Thus, given the fact that the Regional Games could constitute a threat to the Olympic movement in the event of the IOC not succeeding in exercising control over them, it is not surprising that Coubertin was relieved when most of these events did not survive the post-war period.

> Of the host of projects produced right after the war and aimed at the creation of 'regional' Games, there remained practically nothing. I was pleased because I had seen no real future in the movement but had thought it best to leave it to wear itself out. Only the Far Eastern Games, now placed under our patronage, survived. They answered a real need. The only other plans I was interested in were those for the African Games, about which I shall speak in a moment, and the South American Games, which Brazil had introduced by inaugurating them the previous year (1922) on the occasion of the centenary celebration of its independence. (Coubertin 1997c, 2000: 496)

In the inter-war period, the IOC was influenced by the increasing current of internationalism and pursued a worldwide profile, by promoting Olympism in colonial societies (Hoberman 1986; Roche 2000). Coubertin encouraged the establishment of Regional Games in different continents for the sake of the expansion of Olympism and based on the principle of universalism, but he made sure first that these games would be limited in number and always under the IOC's control. In this way, he ensured the survival of Olympism in the turbulent post-war years, but also opened ways for its further development. In his speeches and his writings three Regional Games in particular had his support: the Far Eastern Games, the South American Games, and the African Games.

The Far Eastern Games

The IOC aimed to make the Olympic movement universal through the organisation of Regional Games. In the inter-war period, Coubertin had often expressed his interest in the promotion of modern sport in Asia.

> This time, however, it was Asia that experienced the full effects of our restoration efforts – for which they had prepared by periodically holding Far East Games, a sort of 'Olympic kindergarten'. The consequences will be enormous, and are already being felt by those who contemplate the Olympic Games and international championships in general from the vantage point of their own interests, for we are seeing the emergence of new moves. In all likelihood, the Games of the Ninth Olympiad in 1936 will probably not yet provide the means to allow these new moves to develop profitably. In this area as in so many others, power changes hands, principles change form, and centres of gravity shift. A structure comprising independent, interrelated segments is gradually replacing the tutorship system from which Europe has benefited for so long. Europe itself has hastened this demise through its tactlessness in using the system. The power that Olympism retains in the face of the lizards proclaiming its imminent or more gradual collapse derives from its most deeply human, and therefore universal, aspects (as is the case for most institutions rooted in Hellenism). Served by a college of unselfish priests who are haunted by neither ordinary concerns for profits nor a need to rise above their own merits, Olympism withstands the attack of any assailant and emerge unscathed. (Coubertin 1932, 2000: 518)

Although, the interest in promoting modern sport in colonial societies was not officially discussed until the IOC Session in Rome (1923), several Regional Games had already been staged.

> The Far Eastern Games already existed. The educational influence of those Games in China, Japan and the Philippines was swift and profound. At other places around the globe, similar innovations were under way. There was a talk in India of Hindu Games. This was the 'Kindergarten' of Olympism, in which the International Olympic Committee had expressed a special interests from the start. (Coubertin 1931a, 2000: 703)

Coubertin had officially made an agreement with the YMCA in 1920 for the dissemination of the Olympic ideal worldwide through the organisation of Regional Games. However, much earlier, the YMCA had already been involved in the organisation of the Asian Regional Games in Manila, Philippines in 1913.

> We are now in possession of curious accounts of the beginnings of *exotic athleticism*. In truth, these really are not its beginnings. The festivities recently held in the capital of the Philippines did have a precedent. During the competitions of the Third Olympiad, held in St. Louis in 1904, one or more days were reserved for performances by Asians. The Americans clearly see themselves as athletic preceptors in the Far East. The day-long festivities in St. Louis were hardly flattering for the people in that part of the world. *These descendants of such ancient and refined civilisations were called on to compete with the representatives of peoples scarcely refined out of their original barbarianism. This was a mistake.* (Coubertin 1913, 2000: 695; emphasis added)

Coubertin sets against the way the American organisers incorporated in their programme the events in relation to the peoples of Far East (mainly from Philippines). In the St. Louis 1904 Expo, as well as that of Buffalo in 1901, displays of people connected with such places as Hawaii and Philippines took place. Displays of 'Others', such as people from 'exotic' foreign cultures (e.g. Arabia, China, Japan, Hawaii), were often part of the late nineteenth, and early twentieth-century expos. Expo producers found that such displays could enhance the entertainment value of their events, and thus increase participation levels (Roche 2000). Most expos from the 1880s onwards typically presented a diverse range of representations of Others as 'pre-modern', or even as 'uncivilised' and 'savage'. Greenhalgh (1988) emphasised,

> Between 1889 and 1914, the exhibitions became a human showcase, when people from all over the world were brought to sites in order to be seen by others for their gratification and education ... objects were seen to be less interesting than human beings, and through the medium of display, human beings were transformed into objects. (cited in Roche 2000: 83)

These displays included such peoples as Pacific islanders (e.g. Fijians and Samoans), Arctic peoples (e.g. Lapps, Inuit), native Americans (e.g. Sioux, Apache), and tribal peoples of a variety of ethnic and linguistic groups from Africa (e.g. Senegalese, Dahomeans, Zulus, Pygmies) and Asia (e.g. tribes from the Philippines). Roche (2000: 84) notes that these groups remained in Europe and North America, as a kind of professional 'troupe', thus travelling from show to show and from expo to expo.

Interestingly, although the British and French expos also included human displays, the American series of three World's Fairs (Philadelphia 1876,

Chicago 1893 and St. Louis 1904) gave new dimensions of commercialism to the expos, and considerably intensified the entertainment and human display elements, primarily introduced by the Europeans. By so doing, the USA wanted to promote its expansionist and interventionist foreign policy, which had already been extended in the Pacific, the Caribbean and in South America. In relation to the Philippines, Greenhalgh (1988) argues that the importance attached to exposing and legitimating American control over this part of the world can be shown by the fact that a site of 47 acres was provided to the Philippines display at the St. Louis Expo (cited in Roche 2000: 59).

In this context, it can be argued that Coubertin's claim quoted earlier that, 'The Americans clearly see themselves as athletic preceptors in the Far East. The day-long festivities in St. Louis were hardly flattering for the people in that part of the world ... *This was a mistake'* (Coubertin 1913, 2000: 695) may have its roots in a broader rivalry of interests between the emerging 'American empire' (and the new, more commercial profile of the expos) and the European powers. In addition, it should be noted that Coubertin's relations with the St. Louis organisers had been difficult, especially after the latter had pressurised the IOC by threatening that it would organise an alternative major athletics event if the 1904 Games were not to be held in St. Louis, alongside the World Fair. As a result, Coubertin had chosen to boycott his own Games and attended instead the annual dramatic festival of Wagner's music at Bayreuth in Germany (Guttmann 1992; Roche 2000). Nonetheless, despite Coubertin's criticisms of inappropriate treatment of people from the Far East in St. Louis, and the overall effect of these human displays, creating images of 'Otherness' as 'primitive' and 'savage', as opposed to 'we', the 'modern' and the 'civilised', his words also lead to a similar direction,

> The 'yellow men' seem to us to be admirably prepared to benefit from the athletic crusade that is taking shape. They are ready individually and collectively. They are ready individually because endurance, tenacity, patience, racial flexibility, the habit of self-mastery, of keeping silent, and of hiding pain and effort have shaped their bodies most effectively. They are ready collectively, because their young imperialism, which has not yet had its fill of domination, will impel them to taste the fresh joys of athletic victories, as well as the honour this brings to their national flags. For a while still, clearly, athletic Asia will grow and become strong where it is. Yet it is quite probable that contacts with the West will be made and, at Berlin in 1916, the yellow teams will be able to show what they can do. If that comes as a 'revelation', all those who have athleticism and its spread throughout the world close to their hearts must rejoice, with neither second thoughts nor hesitation. (Coubertin 1913, 2000: 697; emphasis added)

The social structures of imperialism that defined colonial relationships produced powerful images of Others, placing them in a binary opposition to the idea of Europe and of civilisation. As the identity of Europe developed during the Enlightenment, humanism became a core ideology, and the notion of 'humanity', though partial and narrow, was constructed (Davies 1997). However, Carrington argues, 'humanism far from challenging European imperialistic expansion and colonial control, actually provided one of the main philosophical justifications for racial error and exploitation' (Carrington 2004: 83). In this context, ideologies of 'race' and white supremacy emerged in European thought, which promoted an ethnocentric, western model of humanism. The French philosopher, Jean-Paul Sartre (1965) argued that, 'there is nothing more consistent than a racist humanism since the European has only been able to become man through creating slaves and monsters' (cited in Carrington 2004: 84–5). The ideological content of Olympism, tied to the same origins of the racially exclusive European humanism, was always skewed in practice towards the interests and perspectives of the 'modern' and 'advanced' western nations and empires (Roche 2000). From this standpoint, Coubertin's references to racial characteristics of the Asians (such as endurance, tenacity, patience and racial flexibility), shares common characteristics with the philosophy of Social Darwinism, which embraced the common interpretation that 'only the strong survive' (Mangan and Nam-gil 2001: 65). In addition, his emphasis on the benefits that the Asians would gain from their contact with the West provides evidence that the movement had retained ethnocentric and racist attitudes, resembling those adopted by the US and European imperial powers.

It is worth noting that the regional Asian Games would return to the agenda of international sports events in 1962, taking place under the auspices of the IOC, and constituting an arena of conflicting interests and diplomatic episodes (the Arab-Israeli, China-Taiwan, India and Pakistan conflicts) (Simri 1983).

The South American Games

Coubertin's interest in the development of sport in South America had been evident from the beginning of the Olympic movement and the establishment of the IOC (1894), which incorporated, among the 79 delegates from 13 countries, Jose B. Zubiaur as the representative in South America. In 1901, he awarded the first Olympic Diploma to Santos Dumont, who had Brazilian nationality, while in several articles (1904, 1909, 1912) he shares positive comments about the practice of sport in South America (with special references to Argentina, Mexico and Chile) (DaCosta *et al.* 2002). In another article, *Le Projet de L' Olympie Moderne et L' Avenir de Lausanne*, published in 1918, Coubertin includes South America as part of his expansion plans (under the name *Les Etats de L' Amerique du Sud*). Eventually, in 1922, the South American Games were held in Rio de Janeiro, Brazil, as part of the International Exhibition.

The only other plans I was interested in were those for the African Games, about which I shall speak in a moment, and the South American Games, which Brazil had introduced by inaugurating them the previous year (1922) on the occasion of the centenary celebration of its independence. Not only had they been placed under the patronage of the IOC, but also the Brazilian Government had sent me an invitation to come and preside over them. Circumstances unfortunately prevented me from leaving in time, but Count de Baillet-Latour was able to replace me. In the course of a journey through most of the South American continent, the delegate of the IOC had not only received the most flattering welcome for the work he represented but had used his time most profitably for the 'Olympisation', to coin a neologism, of these new countries full of as yet unsatisfied sporting ambitions. He had been able, in the meantime, to smooth out difficulties, put an end to conflicts and solve tricky questions. Whether the Games at Rio were to become a really stable regular institution or not, it was worthwhile seeing them renewed in the near future for the benefit of other cities further apart from each other-as a result of inadequate transport rather than actual distance that was the case in Europe. We needed a choice of centres like Mexico, Havana, Santiago, Montevideo and Buenos Aires, where athletes from nearby countries would have an opportunity of competing against each other either in Central America or in South America. This would also be an excellent 'Olympic kindergarten', according to the term used in Manila. (Coubertin 1997c, 2000: 496)

Argentina, Brazil, Chile and Uruguay attended the events as representatives of the Latin American continent and competed in different sports such as athletics, boxing and tennis. A soccer competition also took place but was associated with the Exhibition rather than the Games (DaCosta *et al.* 2002). In 1923, the Count Baillet-Latour, who had attended the Regional Games in Rio as the official representative of the IOC, is reported to have observed in relation to the event:

The Games in Rio, as a whole, were not perfect; however the criticism made of them was extremely exaggerated ... the Games in Rio were also responsible for giving birth to a true wish to maintain the Latin American Games, considered to be the best way to prepare for the Olympic Games (cited in DaCosta *et al.* 2002: 97).

It is worth noting that Argentina and Chile had shown great interest in organising the sport movement in South America by organising the 'South American Olympic Games' in 1910 and 1920 outside the Olympic movement and without the 'IOC patronage'. However, Coubertin opposed these events and demanded that the name 'Olympic Games' should be dropped from the title (DaCosta *et al.* 2002; Torres 2002). Interestingly, the South American Games held in Rio de Janeiro (1922), albeit placed under the IOC patronage, had mainly been organised by the YMCA, as part of a previous agreement between the association and Coubertin (1920) in order to promote the values of Olympism on a larger scale. However, further action of the YMCA was limited when the IOC called for the establishment of National Olympic Committees and the formation of a Steering Committee for the South American Games, thus establishing itself as the primary authority in the organisation of Regional Games. Baillet-Latour, with obvious evidence of paternalism, encouraged the establishment of NOCs, especially in Brazil, Mexico and Argentina, where sport had reached higher levels, and thus their demands were also higher, just like 'a child who has been raised, has grown up, and claims (sic) for a tutor' (cited in DaCosta *et al.* 2002: 99). Nonetheless, Müller and Tuttas (2000) argue that the YMCA was the driving force behind the success of the Regional Games, and Torres (2002) and DaCosta *et al.* (2002) are convinced that the role of the YMCA was much more significant than has broadly been perceived.

The African Games: Athletic colonisation

In the latter part of the nineteenth century western dominance had been extended over almost all of Africa. However, elsewhere by the end of the eighteenth century the pre-eminence of European colonial power had already been challenged when first North America, then Haiti, and then most of Latin America had started to strive for and, finally achieved, their independence. The protection of European dominance over any local expressions of autonomy was of prime concern for the colonial powers (Huntington 1996). It is suggested that through the English ideology of athleticism (also referred to as *The Games Cult* or *Games Ethic*) the public schools prepared their pupils for imperial roles in the Neo-imperial expansion of the late nineteenth century. Thus, often there are links drawn between the success of the British Empire and the dissemination of sport ideal in the colonies (Mangan and Hickey 2001). France also used sport as part of its imperialistic practices to assimilate the local population into the citizenship of the motherland. 'Metropolitan France' wanted the indigenous populations to practice modern sport and compete as 'French' maximising the potential for acquiring national cohesion (Darby 2000).

In this context, Coubertin wished to promote Olympism in the African continent at a time when the most influential European countries were competing for influence in Africa. There were English, French, Dutch, German, Italian and Portuguese colonies where dominant colonial cultures were imposed on the indigenous populations. European powers, for example, coerced native Africans to adopt their language and to adapt to western culture. In that context, Coubertin also turned his attention towards the African continent for the promotion of Olympism and 'the propagation of athletic activity among indigenous youth' (Coubertin 1931b, 2000). To this end, he started a programme with clearly propagandist goals establishing an 'African medal' and initiated the African Games, an idea he proposed in the 1923 IOC Session in Rome (Guttmann 1992).

> In 1923, under the auspices of the International Olympic Committee and thanks to the enlightened generosity of Mr. A. Bolanachi, a member of the IOC for Egypt, an 'African medal' was established for the propagation of athletic activity among indigenous youth. *This was a serious matter that created a storm in some centres of government, a topic to which we shall return.* One side of the medal bears the image of a black man throwing a javelin. The other side shows a stand of bamboo, through which one can read an inscription. The question was what language should the inscription be in. There was no possibility of using African dialects, which are infinitely varied. In Africa, English, French, German, Italian, and Portuguese are regional languages, depending on the nature of local colonisation. Why would we use one rather than another? *Latin, if you will, is not understood by anyone in Africa, but the officers and missionaries know the language and can translate the inscription on the medal into whatever language their subordinates understand. Then there is the matter of the prestige of ancient example.* There was no hesitation. We chose Latin and a whole system of education was carved into the exotic foliage, in just a few words. Here is the text: '*Athletae proprium est se ipsum noscere, ducere et vincere.* – It is the duty and the essence of the athlete to know, to lead and to conquer himself'. Of course, in all the world's languages, it takes twice as many words as the original to express the idea. Yet these words encapsulate a whole lesson in manly athletic education, and that is the main thing. (Coubertin 1931b, 2000: 592–3; emphasis added)

As discussed before, in the late nineteenth and early twentieth century, the classic studies of Hellenism and Latin were taught in the European boarding schools of upper middle classes, emphasising the connections of these civilisations with the origins and history of Europe. Thus, it comes as no surprise that the inscription of the African medal would also be in Latin. This decision had a threefold purpose: a) to impose a European, ethnocentric model of knowledge and set of values on the indigenous people, as translated and delivered by the white, European settlers, b) to gain the support of the colonial officials by associating the development of modern sport in Africa to prestigious themes; a tactic that he has used again in the early history of the Olympic movement, and c) to make the medal a symbol of unity among the European settlers without choosing one language over another, which could be interpreted as acceptance of the superiority of one empire over another.

French and Italian officials were invited to the IOC Session (1923) to discuss the establishment of the African Games. It was decided that the IOC should encourage *Les Jeux Africains* for non-Europeans, beginning in Algiers in 1925 (Guttmann 1992; Roche 2000).

> In the course of the 1923 Session held in the Capitol in Rome under the patronage of the King of Italy, the International Olympic Committee decided to 'conquer Africa' and in order to achieve this purpose created the African Games. They were to be held regularly within the periphery of this vast continent, their aim being to get the natives to realise gradually the beneficial influence they would gain by the practice of sport. All those who later on remembered the peril, which jeopardised the existence of the Negroes, realised the valuable asset the Games would be to them and were surprised at the way this new venture was received. (Coubertin 1931a, 2000: 703)

The IOC however, proposed a version of sport apartheid by recommending the organisation of two biennial events, one preserved for Europeans and one for the colonised 'natives'.

> I will say right away that what became of the project ... What became of it for the moment at least, for I am quite sure the plan will be taken up again. It comprised the holding of 'African Games' every other year, with a very simple programme to start with and which, naturally, would have been almost exclusively regional in character. I would like to have seen these Games reserved for the natives alone. It was preferred however to include competitions for colonials who had been in the country for at least two years. Admittedly, this point of view was quite understandable, but it complicated the proceedings at the start. The cities recognised capable of holding the first Games were Tunis, Rabat, Casablanca and Dakar for French Africa, Tripoli, Benghazi and Asmara for the Italian possessions, Libreville in the Belgian Congo, Luanda and Sumac for Portuguese Africa, Cape Town and Nairobi for South Africa. (Coubertin 1997c, 2000: 498–9)

'Anglo-Saxon' sport, in the form of organised games, such as cricket, rugby and athletics, was already practised in the colonies on a completely elitist and exclusionary basis. The British colonial administrators and traders of middle and upper middle classes needed these games as means of entertainment and communication among themselves (Roche 2000). It is worth noting that, while in the 'white' self-governing dominions of Australia and New Zealand, cricket and rugby became 'national' games through which people developed their identity (always in relation to the mother country), in the Black and Asian colonies of the West Indies and India, cricket and other sports were initially practised only by native ethnic elites. Guttmann (1994) therefore argues that sport practice, especially in African and Asian colonies, was used as tool of social control and reproduction of imperial hegemony.

Nevertheless, Coubertin faced obstacles in establishing the African Games and, thereby expanding the Olympic movement on the continent. The African medal was, as we have noted deemed a serious and controversial issue (Coubertin 1931d, 2000). In an issue of the *Olympic Review* (January 1912) Coubertin, attempted to persuade the colonials who were against the Regional African Games that they had nothing to fear from such an event. Hoberman (1986) argues that Coubertin wanted to encourage them to spread sport among the colonised without fearing that their victory could lead to rebellion. None-theless, the local colonial governments opposed such initiatives fearing that the colonisers' position of power would be undermined in sporting defeat by indigenous groups, though this was by no means universal.

> The January 1912 Olympic Review already dealt with this matter and opposed the view that a victory over the dominant race in the field of sport by the people in bondage may have a dangerous effect and risk to be exploited by the local opinion as an enticement to rebellion. The Germans, settled in their well-equipped African colonies, had not been afraid when they introduced sport practice to the natives. The British in India, although not very much inclined to introduce the Olympic movement among the natives, did not set their face against it. Italy accepted the innovation with good grace although she did not have time to consider the matter thoroughly. It was France who set her face against this idea. Algiers had been honoured with the organisation of the first African Games. The Algerians, supported if not egged on by the Metropolis, declined this honour. In this way the inauguration was put off for two years, when Egypt, in her quality of senior country, was entrusted with the task of organizing the first Games. (Coubertin 1931a, 2000: 703)

Coubertin identifies the French (as opposed to the Germans, British and Italians) as the major opponents of the African Games countering and finally managing to stop the organisation of the proposed first edition of the Games (planned for 1925 in Algeria). Moreover, due to English and French political manoeuvring the inauguration of a stadium in Egypt at Alexandria designed subsequently to host the African Games was denied international exposure and the opening was thus able to attract publicity only on a strictly local scale.

> The mistake I made was to consider (and to reveal this idea to the IOC) the possibility of a more solemn, more magnificent inauguration to be

held in Algiers in 1925. To start with, this decision was greeted favourably in Algeria and Mr. Th. Steeg, who was Governor General at the time, also showed his interest. But it very soon met with opposition, which was all the more formidable as it lacked both direction and a centre. Those against it tried above all to waste time, to blunt good intentions. It was a question of perhaps personal but at any rate administrative rivalries. Eventually the inauguration had to be postponed till 1929 and Alexandria was substituted for Algiers. The preparations at the time were considerable and a very fine stadium was built. Our colleague in Egypt, A. C. Bolanachi, threw himself into this scheme with keenness and a generosity made even more effective by his competence, which was recognised by all ... At the last moment, an English political manoeuvre, in which France joined, rendered ineffective all the work done and King Fouad was left to inaugurate the fine stadium at Alexandria discreetly and on a purely local scale. I am unable to explain this rather annoying matter since, when it broke out, I had already ceased to be President of the IOC. (Coubertin 1997c, 2000: 499)

Coubertin emphasised that the African Games were not inaugurated in Algeria in 1925 because the settlers feared that through the organisation of the African Games the indigenous populations would be given more rights, and thus more power.

We are not concerned with the undercurrents, which caused this failure [of hosting the African Games], but it is now a known fact that the reason, which caused this opposition to fail to understand that truth and loyalty would subsist, is the notion that the prestige of the Metropolis might be jeopardised by colonial successes. (Coubertin 1931a, 2000: 703)

Lack of support from the colonisers made it very difficult for Coubertin to establish the African Games (Benzerti 2002; Dine 1996; Guttmann 1994; Roche 2000). However, Coubertin insisted that the settlers should not delay the introduction of modern sport to the indigenous populations, in order to secure European rule on the African continent.

But at the back of it all, there was the basic conflict, the struggle of the colonial spirit against the tendency to emancipate the natives, a tendency full of perils as far as the general staffs of the mother country were concerned. The arguments used would not have been without value ... earlier on; but they belonged to a past that was completely dead. It was a long time since they were applicable. The Olympic Review had dealt with the fine subject of 'The role of sport in colonisation' in the number for January 1912. Twenty years later, I thought that opinion had evolved sufficiently to allow the idea to be put into effect! It appeared that the time was not yet ripe. *It must be getting nearer now and I remain convinced that before long, in spite of everything, sport will be organised throughout Africa but perhaps less well than if Europe had been clever enough to take over the running of the movement at the right moment.* (Coubertin 1997c, 2000: 499; emphasis added)

The development of sport in Africa, he argued, was inevitable and it was simply a matter for deciding whether that development should take place under the patronage of Europe or develop through the efforts of indigenous groups. In his opinion, if Europe wanted to have more control over the sport movement in Africa (and to foster its interests in other spheres), it should not hesitate to seize such opportunities. His fear that, '… before long, in spite of everything, sport will be organised throughout Africa but perhaps less well than if Europe had been clever enough to take over the running of the movement at the right moment' illustrates the paternalist colonial attitudes of those European interests involved in the management and planning of the sport movement in Africa.

A further theme evident in Coubertin's analysis is that he, in common with the colonial powers viewed the indigenous sporting cultures as 'peripheral' merely providing 'entertainment and recreation'. By contrast, the western sporting model was seen as the only efficient system that, with its rules and regulations could lead to competitive sport performances.

> There are certain forms of sport activities among natives, which localised to a region, sometimes even to a district, should not be discouraged, on the contrary, they ought to be encouraged, but they do not pretend to be anything else but a form of entertainment and recreation. If we want to extend to natives of colonised countries, what we call boldly the benefits of 'sport civilisation', it is imperative that we allow them to belong to the vast sport system, which entails rules and regulations and competitive sports results performances, which form the basis of this civilisation. (Coubertin 1931a, 2000: 704)

The sporting tradition of the imperial powers, predominantly 'modern sport' based on western (mainly Anglo-Saxon) rules and regulations, was imposed on the colonies often with the intention to undermine indigenous sport traditions as an element of a programme with the aim of 'civilising' the colony (Guttmann 1994; Houlihan 1994). In the inter-war period, a number of notable imperialism-oriented expos were staged, where non-European 'racial' and ethnic groups, such as Africans and Japanese, illustrated evidence of their participation in 'modernisation' processes via cultural displays. Major imperial expos were planned in Britain and France in the pre-war period, but these plans were delayed by the war and were restored soon after it. France staged a 'Colonial and International Exhibition' in Paris in 1931 which attracted 33 million visitors which has been described as 'a stunning imperial fantasyland' (Greenhalgh 1988; cited in Roche 2000: 59).

> Three years later, we had the Colonial Exhibition in Paris (1931 Ed.), which commemorated the centenary of French Africa, and showed the progress realised by sport in that country. *Do not be mistaken, however, the situation is not yet frank and definite. Sport there meant chiefly spectacular sport manifestations. It did not mean at all that natives were encouraged to go in for sport, nor did it give them facilities and encouragement for their training in manly games but above all, it failed to make them understand the true philosophical value and pedagogic importance of the motto we alluded to the other day*, in connection with the African medal created in 1923 by the International Olympic Committee as a medal of encouragement, on it were engraved the following words: 'athletae propium est se ipsum noscere, ducere et vincere'. (Coubertin 1931a, 2000: 704)

Coubertin expresses his disappointment that, notwithstanding his efforts to promote organised sport in French colonies, sport practices in those areas remained non-competitive, mostly recreational, activities. However, he had warned the European officials about the forthcoming difficulties in their 'civilising mission' in Africa.

> And perhaps it may appear premature to introduce the principle of sports competitions into a continent that is behind the times and among peoples still without elementary culture – and particularly presumptuous to expect this expansion to lead to a speeding up of the march of civilisation in these countries. Let us think however, for a moment, of what is troubling the African soul. Untapped forces – individual laziness and a sort of collective need for action – a thousand resentments, and a thousand jealousies of the white man and yet, at the same time, the wish to imitate him and thus share his privileges – the conflict between wishing to submit to discipline and to escape from it – and, in the midst of an innocent gentleness that is not without its charm, the sudden outburst of ancestral violence ... these are just some of the features of these races to which the younger generation, which has in fact derived great benefit from sport, is turning its attention. Sport has hardened them. It has given them a healthy taste for muscular relaxation and a little of that reasonable fatalism possessed by energetic beings, once their efforts have been accomplished. But while sport builds up, it also calms down. Provided it remains accessory and does not become a goal in itself, it helps create order and clarify thought. Let us not hesitate therefore to help Africa join in. (Coubertin 1997c, 2000: 498; emphasis added)

A significant element of imperialism was the western perception that indigenous cultures are 'peripheral', 'uncivilised' and 'savage'. Paternalism, hierarchy, conservative and racialist discourse were evident in describing the colonial societies with the notion of assumed superiority of the West over the colonies (Said 1991). It is noted from Coubertin's documents that the African societies were repeatedly described in subordinated terms regarding the spread of Olympic sport in Africa and the development of sport in general.

> Here we consider the matter only in relation to the main precepts of sportive pedagogy. Are these precepts applicable to the native races? Can they be adapted to their often very primitive mode of living? The answer is yes, even entirely so. The beauty of these precepts lies in the fact that they are sufficiently humane to suit all conditions of men from the semi-savage state to that of the ultra-civilised state. Of course, when dealing with men, one must take into account the difference of temperaments. (Coubertin 1931a: 704)

Providing evidence of Social Darwinism again, Coubertin assumes a 'racial' and 'temperamental' superiority of the Westerners, thus legitimating the West's role of 'civilising force' that will bring 'the light of civilisation on the vast continent of Africa' (Coubertin 1894b, 2000: 540).

> The time has come for sport to advance to the conquest of Africa, that vast continent which it has as yet hardly touched and to bring to its people the enjoyment of ordered and disciplined muscular effort, with all the benefits which flow from it. (Coubertin 1923, 2000: 702)

The above quotation is part of the Olympic solidarity campaign that Coubertin had initiated in 1923 but was short-lived due to lack of support (Müller 2000). Interestingly, in the 1960s Olympic solidarity campaign, initiated by the IOC, the African societies were again described in subordinate terms. Al-Tauqi (2003) has cited the following quotation from the minutes of a meeting held by the Commission for International Olympic Aid (CIOA):

> Mr Brundage thought that we should keep ourselves out of all financial considerations, which might put the IOC in an embarrassing position. The President said that above all it was necessary to educate these people and inculcate in them the Olympic ideal. *Any sporting undertaking should be built up the foundation upwards and the people must be taught to help themselves* (CAIO meeting minutes, date unknown: Doc 05; cited in Al-Tauqi 2003: 202, emphasis added).

In a similar vein, Coubertin believed that the colonies should be 'instructed' by the imperial powers.

> They [i.e. colonies] are like children: it is relatively easy to bring them into the world; the difficult thing is to raise them properly. They do not

grow by themselves, but need to be taken care of, coddled, and pampered by the mother country; they need constant attention to incubate them, to understand their needs, to foresee their disappointments, to calm their fears. (Coubertin 1902; quoted by Hoberman 1986: 39)

Thus, in the light of such overt paternalism, it is suggested that the IOC's attitudes to race and ethnicity were more clearly influenced by the imperial paternalism of Britain and France than to any real humanism (Roche 2000; Carrington 2004). Indeed Roche (2000: 110) that even the profoundly colonialist British Empire Games in the 1930s (the *Commonwealth Games* as they were later renamed) was 'probably a more inclusionary international event in relation to non-European 'racial' and ethnic groups than was the Olympics'. However, it should be noted that while, during the period of decolonisation, some ex-colonies rejected the colonial culture, most adapted it to their own cultural ethos. Thus, it can be argued that, although during colonialism modern sport practices were imposed on the indigenous populations, often dismissing their own cultural traditions, in the post-colonial era modern sports such as cricket have often been used by the ex-colonies as a tool to enhance and foster nationalist feelings and racial pride (St. Pierre 1990; cited in Houlihan 1994: 17–18).

It is also worth noting that the original proposals for African Games, which were postponed three times due to lack of support, subsequently came to fruition in the early 1960s, initially under the name 'Friendship Games' (*Les Jeux d'Amitié*). The first African Games organised as such were held in 1965 in Brazzaville (Guttmann 1994).

3.5   Conclusions

Coubertin represents perhaps the classic example of an actor with power over Olympic discourse in the sense that he is able to speak authoritatively as the founder of the modern Olympic movement. His aristocratic patrician background provided him with the cultural and economic resources to propagate his view of how the Olympic idea might be revived even though his was not the only such revival. He also had the intellectual resources to define, colonise and propagate his version of the Olympic ideal. Indeed his careful shifting of Olympic discourse in the early days from an emphasis on its Hellenist credentials to an appeal to an Anglo-Saxon philosophy, implicitly de-legitimising any Greek attempt to lay claim to the 'ownership' of the idea and thus the permanent housing of the Games in Greece, highlights his political astuteness in the discursive construction of Olympism.

Our account of the nature of this construction process has focused on four principle thematic strands which are intertwined with one another, with changing behaviours and with changing material circumstances. These are nationalism and internationalism; changing social structures; changing colonial and post-colonial structures; and gender relations.

In terms of nationalism and internationalism we see the interplay of use of sport for national purposes and its use in the service of a form of internationalism. In the earliest period, particularly pre- and post-First Olympic Congress in 1894, sport is emphasised as a moral project to discipline French youth and to thus halt the decline in French society which had brought about France's ignominious defeat by Prussia in 1870. This element of the discourse plays alongside a growing emphasis on internationalisation, sport as an arena in which cultural interchange can be facilitated and indeed cultural hegemony can be maintained.

In relation to changing social structures there is a subtle change in the nature of the position maintained or promoted in Coubertin's discourse. In the early period before the First World War, his is a patrician, aristocratic position in which, as we have seen, he distances himself from the new industrial bourgeois class as well as the working-class masses promoting the idea of an education in which 'It is always the elite that is targeted, because a superior phalanx, though few in number, yields infinitely more than widespread mediocrity' (Coubertin 1887, 2000: 108). In the post-World War I era however he is at pains to underline that the world has been irrevocably changed. Social equality (of a kind) and 'All sports for all people' are key features of his discourse, since 'Nothing is accomplished when only limited numbers are involved. That may have been sufficient before but not now. The masses must be touched' (Coubertin 1919e, 2000: 552). Here the bourgeoisie is included in the group for whom Coubertin presumes to speak, warning as he does of the damage to bourgeois interests if the masses are ignored. In addition despite the setting up of alternative Workers' Olympics, Coubertin speaks positively of working class self-improvement through sport.

In terms of the relationship of the Olympic movement to colonial and postcolonial forces one might consider Coubertin's approach as being progressive, since he warns against the use of sport by some colonial powers as a means of reinforcing the social exclusion of indigenous groups and the cultural distancing of colonial powers from their colonised peoples. However Coubertin's approach is far from progressive when we see that his call for social integration is legitimated by an appeal to the colonisers' interests, that is, if European colonisers do not admit indigenous groups to the sporting world, they and the Olympic movement will pay the price when those indigenous groups seek to establish their own cultural institutions. The Olympic movement's approach as advocated by Coubertin involves on the part of indigenous groups both deculturation (indigenous sports and games are to be suppressed, by not being included in the pantheon of Olympic sports), and enculturation (the adoption of western culture in the form of Olympic sports and games, and the western rules of international competition). This promotion of western culture is underpinned by Coubertin's appeal to a Social Darwinism which legitimates both the claims of superiority of western sporting culture, and the biological determinism evident in the racist stereotypes he occasionally explicitly rehearses.

While Coubertin's position, or at least the ways in which his interests are expressed, change over time in relation to these first three sets of themes, in relation to the final theme identified here, gender, Coubertin maintained a personal antithetical position in his writings even though women's participation in the Games had *de facto* been agreed following the actions of Alice Milliat and the Women's Amateur Athletic Federation. Here again a major feature of Coubertin's argument is a form of biological determinism – women are 'not biologically adapted' to participation in competitive sport.

The themes with which Coubertin deals relate to all levels of social action from the personal (moral self-improvement) through social groups (social class and gender equity) to the national and global level (national and international issues such as the sustaining of colonialism and decolonisation), and his own confidence in developing a social movement within which one can address such matters is remarkable. Indeed although Coubertin is often referred to as developing a social and educational philosophy, his work does not necessarily manifest the intellectual depth of a major philosopher. His work does however have the political depth as a change agent. While it does not reflect a comprehensive philosophical position, it develops a prescription for behaviour from the personal to the global in a new modernist world order. This is not to say that Coubertin's conception of Olympism is always based on the twin pillars of modernist epistemology, namely rationalism (the emphasis on equality and on his claims around gender manifest a lack of rational coherence) and empiricism (some of his claims concerning an appeal to the spirit of the Ancient Games are based on assumptions which are not necessarily empirically grounded). Despite such inconsistencies Coubertin was remarkably successful in establishing an ideological basis of the support for the fledgling and subsequently growing Olympic movement.

The 'framers', or constructors of Olympic discourse who follow were faced with the challenge of an inherited global, if occasionally fragile, movement rather than one which had to be initiated from scratch, and thus their contribution was always likely to suffer by comparison with Coubertin whose position as the founder of the movement meant that his position as a speaker or a writer on Olympic matters was always likely to be privileged.

Our next key voice on Olympism, that of Carl Diem, is remarkable in other ways, since he was a key and controversial figure in the Olympic history of Germany during the period which spanned the inter-war and the post-war years. This period incorporates the touchstone event of Olympic politics, the 1936 Berlin Olympics, Hitler's Games, and although Diem's reputation is tarnished, if only by association for some, but by more direct implication for others, remarkably he was still able to maintain a position of influence within the movement across the middle of the twentieth century.

4
Carl Diem: Olympism in the Shadow of Fascism and the Post-war Rehabilitation (1912–1961)

4.1 Introduction

In examining Carl Diem's writings throughout this period (1912–1961), we aim to establish an understanding of how the discourse of Olympism, both before, but especially after the death of Pierre de Coubertin on 1937, was reflected in, and shaped by, the ideas of another leading figure in the Olympic movement. This chapter seeks to identify and analyse Diem's discourse of Olympism and to consider the extent to which Diem's dual identity, as an IOC member and as a sporting representative of the Nazi regime might have had an effect on the Olympic movement and his articulation of the nature of Olympism. We examine below the expression of values associated with Olympism, and consider motives, interests and intentions in relation to its promotion, as evidenced in the correspondence, publications and personal records of Carl Diem. Our aim is not simply to reconstruct the aims, tactics or impact of Diem but rather to identify how he reconstructs the expression of Olympism during a period in which he played a key role in the running of the movement and the expression of its philosophy. Ultimately, the chapter will consider the degree to which values bound up with authoritarian regimes impacted upon the meaning of Olympism, not only during the Berlin Games, but also in the period that followed them.

The chapter is divided into three main sections. The first considers the pre-National Socialist Government (Nazi) phase, the early years of Carl Diem's involvement in the Olympic movement (1912–1933). The second deals with the period of the Nazi regime which includes the preparation and hosting of the 1936 Berlin Games (1933–1936), as well as the years leading up to and during the Second World War (1936–1944). The third relates to the post-Second World War period (1945–1961).

4.2   The pre-Nazi phase: The early years of Carl Diem's involvement in the Olympic movement (1912–1933)

Carl Diem was the chief official in charge of the German teams at the 1912 Stockholm Games, and he was appointed as the Secretary General of the German Reich Committee for the Olympic Games one year after the IOC's decision to award the 1916 Games to Berlin (1913). His first experience of the Olympic Games was the 1906 Games in Athens (the interim Games), where he was invited as a sports journalist (Haag 1982).[1] Although not yet familiar with the philosophy of Olympism, his activities in sport, particularly in sport administration and the German sports movement, were various and considerable.

In 1889, he founded together with other friends a sports club in Berlin, the so-called *Markomania*, in an effort to modernise Germany's traditional gymnastic clubs. Among his several administrative posts, he was appointed as the Secretary of the *Deutsche Sportbehörde für Athletik* in 1903 (German Sports Authority for Light Athletics), and as its Chairman in 1908; in 1904 he became a member of the Deutsche *Reichsausschuss für Leibesübungen,* and in 1905 he became the Chairman of the Association of Berlin Athletic Clubs (established in 1904) (Haag 1982; Mandell 1971). For 20 years after 1913, Diem was the Secretary of the German government's Commission for Sport and Recreation (*Generalsekretär des Deutschen Reichanschusses für Leibesübungen*) and during this time he founded and built the principal German school for recreation teachers, *Die Deutsche Hochschule für Leibesübungen* in Cologne. During the years 1925–1935 many books were published under Diem's editorship or with his collaboration, such as the *Handbuch der Leibesübungen (1923–1930), Beiträge zur Turn- und Sportwissenschaft (1922–1929), Taschenbuch der Leibesübungen (1925–1930), Jahrbuch der Leibesübungen (1924–1932)* (Haag 1982).

Because of these activities, the Carl Diem Institute emphasised that, 'it was Carl Diem and his friends who laid the foundations of the German sports movement' (Carl-Diem-Institut 1970: vii). In similar vein, Mandell (1971) has argued that, 'only a fanatically uncritical admirer of Pierre de Coubertin would dispute the claim that Carl Diem is the greatest sport historian and most profound theorist of sport education of this century' (p. 85). However, there is no question that Diem had been significantly influenced by Coubertin, especially in relation to the philosophical bases of sport underpinning the modern Olympic Games. He had studied Coubertin's beliefs in relation to the Olympic Games thoroughly, incorporating a number of aspects in his own account.

Firstly they [the Olympic Games] had to be suited to modern times. Coubertin did not want to build synthetic ruins or to ape antiquity. From the high Hellenic peak of human culture he took over only the Olympic Idea – the idea of a festival sanctified by the sign of peace, by dedication to idealism and to the task of perfecting the human being. For the rest the

Games were to be 'modern', i.e. they were to bear the impress of the age and to serve it; thus they were to be capable of change, so that each future age could in turn make its impress upon them. Secondly, they were to recur with astronomic regularity. This rhythm, echoing the ancient sense of proportion, would quicken delight in the Games ever anew, and at the same time would make manifest the continuity of their sequence. Each festival would be based on the traditions of its predecessors, but would develop these traditions by adapting the past to the future and enriching it, and would thus point towards the future. The Games must be hitched to the future. Whatever else may shake the world, the Olympic Idea must survive indomitably in an 'endless chain'. The Games must therefore be a world festival, in which the youth of all nations can meet in friendship. Thirdly, Coubertin wished what he was reviving to be a genuine 'festival', i.e. an ordered and regulated event of both a sporting and an artistic nature, recognisable and reproducible by its hallmarks of measure in time and space. So he founded the Games, and lived to see them renew their ancient magic; this they did because they revived an eternal human idea, an idea capable like a living cell of developing, dividing and reproducing itself. Thus the Olympic Games are timeless yet subject to time, of their age yet dedicated to the future. (Diem 1957e, 1970: 21)

Diem's discourse is of both continuity (part of an 'endless chain' stretching back to antiquity, but linked to the modern), and of change (as each era makes its own 'impress' adapting the Olympic ideals to the needs of its own time). The games are timeless (they revive an 'eternal idea') but recur with 'astronomic regularity' every four years.

Diem even investigated the Italian origins of the Frédy-Coubertin family and consistently collected Coubertin's edited works (Mandell 1971). He often cited in his articles Coubertin's views, showing considerable respect for the ideas of the founder of the movement.

In Coubertin's words, the Olympic Games are 'celebrations of ambition's passionate endeavour; celebrations of every form of the urge to action in the generation whose feet are on the threshold of life'; and into these exertions, into this ambition, art must enter as a harmonising force, a force promoting harmony by reconciling opposites; it must spiritualise and ennoble the clash of muscular strength by relating it to a high vision of humanity. (Diem 1952, 1970: 17)

His personal admiration to Coubertin was expressed often and openly in his writings,

To Baron de Coubertin, a French nobleman, is due the historic credit of having revived the Olympic Games. Efforts had already been made to this end in the fifties of the last century, but they had met with no success. Yet the representatives of almost all the civilised nations answered Coubertin's call. (Diem 1912a, 1970: 27–8)

Interestingly, in some instances he even adopts the style and tone of Coubertin,

> It seemed as though the gods of ancient Hellas, assembled in the Museum – Zeus and Apollo from the tympanum of the Temple of Zeus, Hermes sculpted by the master hand of Praxiteles, and Paionos' Victory Goddess floating aloft like a breath of air – wished once again to bless the heart, and the community gathered for the interment, with that sign of ennobled humanity which was the attribute of the Greek gods, and with that immortal radiance which we hope may be vouchsafed to Coubertin's work. (Diem 1942b, 1970: 9–10)

However, it should be noted that Diem's expression of admiration toward the well-known and well-connected Coubertin, a leading figure in international sport at that time, also served Diem's personal ambitions. Mandell (1971: 85) contends that 'Diem was an almost slavish admirer of Coubertin. Perhaps this reverential attitude toward the founder was a without-which-nothing prerequisite for admission to international sport's inner council'.

The communication between the two men became more frequent especially after the decision of the IOC to award the 1916 Olympic Games to Berlin. In relation to the hosting of the VIth Olympic Games (1916), Coubertin was ambiguous at the closing banquet of Stockholm (June 26, 1912), 'through our mediation a great people has received the torch of the Olympiads from your hands, and has thereby undertaken to preserve and if possible to quicken its precious flame' (Coubertin 1912c: 448). He expressed the wish that, 'it [the VIth Olympiad] be prepared in the fruitful labour of peaceful times. May it be celebrated, when the day comes, by all the peoples of the world in gladness and concord'. Less than one month later (August 1912) Carl Diem announced in *Revue Olympique* the decision of the IOC to award the 1916 Games to Berlin,

> After some discussion Berlin was unanimously chosen as the venue for the VIth Olympiad. Count Sierstorpff thanked the Committee on behalf of his colleagues and himself, and said he was sure Germany would do its utmost to lend this Olympiad a splendour befitting its importance. The International Committee immediately sent a telegram to His Majesty the German Emperor informing him of the result of the vote. It received in reply the following telegram from His Excellency the Imperial Chancellor 'His Majesty the Emperor has noted with great interest that Berlin has been chosen as the host city for the 1916 Olympiad. He instructs me to

send the Committee his best thanks for this welcome news.' (Diem 1912c, 1970: 44)

In 1914, at the IOC Congress of Paris, the final details and general amendments on the sport programme of the Berlin Games were decided. Carl Diem, from his post as Secretary General of the German Reich Committee for the Olympic Games, participated in the IOC meetings and worked toward the preparation of the 1916 Olympic Games.

> Germany had already worked out beforehand a detailed draft for its 1916 Games, which was one of the basic documents for the Paris discussions. However, it never opposed the well-founded views of the other nations in matters of detail, but always willingly accepted minor alterations to its programme such as were desired here and there by the responsible international sports associations, without wasting the time of the Congress in superfluous debates and votes. This attitude led firstly to a happy recognition of the German contribution such as was expressed inter alia by one of the finest heads of the assembly, the English clergyman Laffan, in the words: 'We admire the integrity, the friendliness and the sporting spirit with which Germany has made its preparations for 1916 and presented them here at the Congress.' Secondly, this attitude had the happy consequence that in the one instance in which Germany took a firm stand upon a matter of principle, the other nations, which originally had shown little sympathy for the German standpoint, gave way in their turn and even helped the German proposal to win acceptance. This happened in regard to the gymnastic programme. (Diem 1914, 1970: 30)

Unfortunately, the European nations were engaged in a more serious contest beyond the realm of sport, and before the congress had reached its end, the First World War had begun with the invasion by Germany of Belgium (3 August, 1914) (Guttmann 1992). Coubertin argues that, two weeks after the invasion, he had received proposals for transferring the Games to another city, but the Germans were too confident that they would have 'a rapid war and a sure victory', thus, 'they did not ask to be relieved of the Olympic mandate' (Coubertin 1997l, 2000: 464). Interestingly, a decision had been taken by the IOC to relocate the headquarters of the IOC every four years to the host country of the next Olympic Games. Coubertin reveals in his *Olympic Memoirs* that he moved the headquarters from Paris in order to protect Olympism in case the Germans invoked their right to transfer the registered office of the IOC to Berlin (Coubertin 1997l, 2000: 465).

The 1916 Games were finally cancelled because of the war. Nonetheless, the Germans had been very keen to host the Games and Coubertin noted that, as soon as the decision was made for Berlin to host the Games 'it [Berlin] was already preparing with the manifest desire to outdo anything that had ever been done before' (Coubertin 1997m, 2000: 460). The cancellation of the Games however brought to an end Diem's architectural plans and detailed scheduling of the events and celebrations. Diem had often made appeals to the public and written articles, as a means to attract spectators and gain wider support for the Games.

In his articles and appeals, he emphasised the importance of the Games for the unity of Germany and the strengthening of German national identity. However, his references to racial or ethno-nationalism have raised questions concerning his ideological leanings during this early period and how this related to Olympic internationalism. For a better understanding of his views and their context, it is instructive to examine the nature of German nationalism, as well as its association with German 'physical culture'.

4.2.1   French and German concepts of nation and national identity

Both Diem and Coubertin exhibit in their discourse the tension between nationalist and internationalist themes. However the two proponents of Olympism were implicated in different national traditions of national identity and citizenship, and the nature of their discourse in intertwining internationalist and nationalist perspectives or considerations is somewhat different. To understand this difference one has to understand the differing origins of national identity and national polity. For Coubertin, French notions of nationhood and of membership of the national community are derived from republican ideals and a political framework forged in the French Revolution, while German tradition forged in the movement for the unification of Germany, which finally took effect under Prussian leadership in 1871, was founded on the 'ideal' of ethnic, linguistic and cultural unity promoted by proponents such as Johann Gottlieb Fichte in his 'Address to the Nation' (1806: 1).

> The first, original, and truly natural boundaries of states are beyond doubt their internal boundaries. Those who speak the same language are joined to each other by a multitude of invisible bonds by nature herself, long before any human art begins; they understand each other and have the power of continuing to make themselves understood more and more clearly; they belong together and are by nature one and an inseparable whole. ...

> Thus was the German nation placed – sufficiently united within itself by a common language and a common way of thinking, and sharply enough severed from the other peoples – in the middle of Europe, as a wall to divide races not akin ...

As we have argued elsewhere (Henry *et al.* 2007), modern French thought in relation to national identity replaced allegiance to a monarchy in the French Revolution with the *voluntary* adoption of republican values of freedom and equality. Nationalism in the French tradition was thus an expression of the willingness of groups with differing cultural, linguistic, religious or ethnic backgrounds to accept a common political project guaranteeing universal rights for all (Kastoryano 2002). However, while the French notion of a national culture depends upon shared political will, the German tradition of nationalism stemming from Herder and Fichte emphasises nationhood as shared culture, language and ethnos. For the French shared culture was a product of political nationalism, in the German tradition political nationalism was seen as the natural consequence of a shared national culture and race (Boswell 2003). Thus while German unification was of a German speaking peoples, French republicanism required non-French speaking communities (Breton Provencal etc.) to give up their linguistic culture. Thus in both cases there is an assertion of a unitary national culture, in the German case this had grown organically among ethno-linguistically related communities, while in the French case it was politically defined by the Republic and signed up to by its citizens. These models of nationalism carry however quite different implications in terms for example of who could represent the nation state in international sporting competition.

German romanticism emerged in the early nineteenth century ironically in reaction to French influence and the values of the French Revolution. The promotion of a membership based on culture and ethnicity stands in contrast to the rationality and the universal values that the Revolution inspired. The German organic conception of a nation and thus of a nation-state, and the exclusive representation of an exclusive citizenship based on ethnic identity of the 'Volk' were put forward as means to fulfil the dream of national identity and unity, and it is within this nationalist tradition that Diem was located.

4.2.2   Tension between German nationalism and Olympic internationalism

With roots in the gymnastics movement of Germany, the so-called *Turnen* movement (based on gymnastics and physical exercises), had been created and developed by Ludwig Friedrich Jahn, a professor at the University of Berlin, in order to prepare German youth for the war against Napoleon. Historical and political events in Germany in the nineteenth century determined the nature of *Turnen*, which by linking the body, discipline, military training, and nationalism became an important source of German national identity (Tesche and Rambo 2001). Jahn is also considered an influential figure in the history of the 'Volkish' tradition, a mystical, integral model of nationalism on the basis of a racial doctrine, a strand of the German nationalist tradition. 'Volkish' thought is based on the idea of the 'Volk' (the people), which from the late eighteenth century 'signified the union of people with a transcendental essence' (Hoberman 1986: 46). Jahn perceived body as a 'politicum', as a means through which to awaken national consciousness and collective identity, and saw physical exercises as a 'public matter' (*Leibesübungen*) (Hoberman 1984: 163).

However, in this period, the traditional German *Turnen* was competing against an Anglo-Saxon model of modern sport, which was popular across Europe and the British colonies, and which had also been introduced in Germany. Although the traditional *Turnen* emphasised mass participation for the reinforcement of a collective identity for those who shared the same language, culture and descent, the Anglo-Saxon model of sport was oriented more towards high performance and sport internationalism, and was spread through the colonies of the British Empire. This rivalry also continued in the early twentieth century, and it was an issue that concerned Carl Diem. In 1914 he wrote an article called 'Peace between *Turnen* and Sport', where he suggested the use of the definition *Leibesübungen* (physical activities) as a joint term for both movements. Haag (1982: 26) argues that Diem, throughout his career in sports administration, worked hard toward 'the unification of these two extreme positions'.

Interestingly, Diem combined in his thought both the nationalism and tradition inspired by the *Turnen* movement, and internationalism and its modern underpinning in Anglo-Saxon modern sport. Mandell (1971: 84) notes that Diem 'was a middle- and long-distance runner at a time when track events as practices among the Anglo-Saxons were almost unknown among his countrymen who were quite devoted to gymnastics'. Hoberman (1986) therefore argues that Diem was familiar with a sport culture that extended beyond the narrow borders of the German sport (gymnastics) movement. This might also provide an explanation of his openness to the internationalism of the Olympic movement, as opposed to the narrow nationalist perspective of other German sport administrators, keen supporters of the nationalist *Turnen* movement.

> The Olympic movement had a curious fate in Germany. Its efflorescence was certainly not helped by the fact that the man who was promoting it happened to be a Frenchman, and furthermore that his invitation to the First Olympic Congress did not reach the only physical education association extant in the year 1894, namely the German Gymnastic Association, but stuck in an embassy pigeon-hole. Another factor was the mistrust felt in German gymnastic circles for all foreign influences, and their both inexplicable and unfortunate aversion to sport itself – sport which has nonetheless become the great driving power sustaining the vitality of the civilised world; thus in Germany the Olympic idea had to fight against the elected officials instead of being helped along by them. (Diem 1920a, 1970: 3)

Some years later in 1933, Diem refers again to the rivalry between the interests of the Olympic movement and the German gymnastics associations.

> Of course this [the development of the Olympic movement in Germany] has not happened without friction. You are aware that in German gymnastic circles there is a widespread aversion to the Games. They are said

to be forcing houses of specialisation and the cult of the ace performer. To say this is to blame them for something, which is a hallmark of the times. These regrettable side effects are of course observable elsewhere than at the Olympic Games, and it would be absurd to assert that they are the result of a Festival recurring once every four years. (Diem 1933b, 1970: 7)

His writings laid emphasis on the internationalism of the Games, often with (explicit or implicit) criticism of those whose narrow perspective was limited to a focus on the national interests of Germany.

Any country of today which wishes to import the Olympic idea into a festival intended for its own nationals only, as we Germans do, must refrain from looking upon itself as the sole perfecter of the antique tradition, for it is actually importing into the Games a restriction which, although quite justifiable in itself, was thoroughly strange to the Greeks. (Diem 1920a, 1970: 3)

Diem travelled to the United States after the Stockholm Games (1912), in order to examine the sport system of the American schools and colleges that had led the Americans to their great success in the recent Games. On his return he brought with him American teachers and coaches that would help Germany develop its sporting system according to the Olympic standards (Haag 1982).

Some countries – particularly the English-speaking countries and Sweden – have reached higher standards in a number of sports than we have. This is because all classes in these countries have had the habit of sport for a longer period of time, because training is more thorough and physical culture better supported. So it is our duty to make such an all-out effort that we can catch up with them in the short time between now and July 1916; for it simply isn't consonant with German prestige to organise the Games and then be consistently beaten in them. (Diem 1942c: 46)

All the same, Diem also acknowledged the value of sport for the strengthening of the German national identity, recognising also that defeat in sport could have a negative impact on the national interests (and prestige) of Germany.

The forthcoming Olympic Games are the sixth of these international Gymnastic and sports occasions, which have to an increasing degree become important cultural events uniting all the civilised nations of the world. With the approval of His Majesty the Emperor, the German

Olympic Committee has declared itself ready to organise the 1916 Games, and the German sports and gymnastics movement feels in honour bound to uphold the German name by organising a festival of classic splendour. For it has become clear that the public of the whole civilised world takes a strong interest in these Games. If the Reich persists in withholding the subsidy, preparations will be seriously hampered, and the Games will lose standing because of the implication that they are a purely private affair and have no government support; the favourable effects on public opinion of state recognition will be lost. The formation of a team worthy to compete with those of visiting countries will also be hampered if the government does not back the Games in the way the Swedish Government did in 1912. (Diem 1942c, 1970: 49)

Interestingly, in his efforts to encourage the Germans to have a positive attitude toward the Berlin Games (1916), Diem often slipped into giving voice to a racial nationalism, which allowed him to appeal to the ideas of the supporters of *Turnen* and the 'Volkish' ideology.

4.2.3   Diem and the Volkish ideology

The Volkish doctrine had gained much popularity among right-wing circles in Germany by the 1920s. Its major themes were: mystical racism (the preservation of German racial identity), xenophobic nationalism, anti-Semitism, anti-industrialism, anti-intellectualism and anti-modernism. In relation to the anti-internationalist outlook of the Volkish mentality, George Mosse (1981) points out that,

The image of the city always conjured up the dread of the rootless elements, their incompatibility with the Volk, and an antagonism to foreign persons or cultures. Volkish thinkers saw the spectre of inter-nationalism in the rapid expansion of the cities. [Wilhelm] Riehl, who was credited with this apocalyptic vision, criticised big cities for wanting to become international urban centres, to achieve equality with all the large cities in the world and form a community of interest. Within such a union, Riehl feared, the world 'bourgeoisie' and 'world proletariat' would recognise their mutual compatibility and exercise a suzerainty over a world in which all that was natural had been destroyed, especially the estates. (cited in Hoberman 1986: 100–1)

The Weimar Republic, after the First World War, became more international and urban in response to the modernisation processes of that period, and the rise of the conservative, right-wing Volkish ideology in the 1920s represented resistance to such developments. In relation to modern sport, there was also resistance to the international trends of this period, an approach that goes back to Jahn, the founder of the nationalist gymnastics movement in Germany. It has been argued that the ideological preconceptions of Nazi sport theory derive to some extent from the doctrine of Jahn (Hoberman 1984, 1986). One contributor to the *Deutsche Turnzeitung* had noted, '*Jahngeist is Hitlergeist*', while Hajo Bernett commented, 'the "fascistoid" spirit of the national [*völkischen*] movement is evident' (cited in Hoberman 1984: 163). The conservative thinkers disapproved of the introduction of technical improvements, of specialisation, the chasing of records and excessive training. Their major concern was that modern sport promoted individualism at the expense of the collective benefits, thus at the expense of the interests of the 'Volk'. The aversion to the competitive and international Olympic Games was often expressed by traditional conservative thinkers adherents to the ideology of the 'Volk', such as Astley and Maurras,

> The real Olympic Games were national to the core, and that was their glory; the international Olympics are rotten to the core. Don't talk to us about the brotherhood of man and those false notions about humanity. The brotherhood of man can be achieved only on the basis of economic agreements. Nationalities cannot be talked out of existence, and they cannot be mixed together (Neuendorff 1910; cited in Hoberman 1986: 101).

Hoberman argues that Carl Diem was influenced by the conservative Volkish ideology, traits of which are often reflected in his writings.

> Diem's writing prior to 1945 is permeated with Volkish themes and a Volkish vocabulary. But how, one might ask, is this sort of nationalism compatible with the internationalist ideals of the Olympic movement Diem served? The answer, as we shall see, is to be found in the profound ambiguity, which marks Diem's relationship to Volkish thought. In some cases Diems simply departs from certain Volkish tenets; on others he plays with Volkish vocabulary, using nationalist terms on behalf of a hidden internationalist doctrine ... One might add that it was most surely Diem's love of sport that modified his Volkish bent. (Hoberman 1986: 47)

Following the line adopted by Hoberman, one can identify further elements of the Volkish ideology in Diem's writings, especially in the period before 1945. However, it is not clear whether Diem uses nationalist terms on behalf of a hidden internationalist doctrine, rather than international terms on behalf of a hidden nationalist one. In other words, his writings are ambiguous and it is not possible to be definitive about whether his prime political interests at any given point of time lay in the advancement of Germany or of the Olympic movement. Nevertheless this does not alleviate concerns about how the conflicting ideological attributes of these two doctrines co-existed in his thought and actions. He often emphasised the benefits to nations of their representation in the large-scale festival of the Olympic Games.

> The Games are more than just a sports festival or a meeting of unemployed sports fans or sports diplomats who are enjoying a pleasant journey. They are a world festival, the only world festival in existence, the embodiment of the only collective world idea, which is visibly and collectively celebrated. That is no trivial thing. To begin with they embrace the whole content of the idea for which all friends of gymnastics since Plato, Vittorino da Feltre, Jahn and v. Schenckendorff have been fighting: *'service to the fatherland through physical culture'*. (Diem 1932, 1970: 58; emphasis added)

In examining Diem's writings in relation to the three major Volkish themes – modernity, nationalism, and race – there is evidence that, especially during the period of preparations for the Berlin Games in 1916, Diem shared tenets of the right-wing ideology.

The anti-modernist view

In the face of the preparations for the 1916 Berlin Games, Diem planned the building of a big stadium that would essentially be used for the Olympics but would also contribute to the promotion of modern sport in Germany. He emphasised in relation to this,

> It is only too well-known that the mighty growth of the German cities is causing, as a disturbing reverse side of the coin, an enervation of the rising generations. Everywhere efforts are being made to combat the looming dangers of this phenomenon by the promotion of gymnastics, sport and open-air play. Only those who are concerned in this work know how slowly it is advancing and how far we still are from the goal. This is not the least of the reasons why all the related efforts in this field tend instinctively or consciously towards an intellectual and physical focus uniting them all and enhancing their driving power. This can however in the last analysis only be a national arena where all those who bear aloft the banner of bodily strength and skill may meet together, and where at regular intervals national, regional and more specialised championships may be held. Who would hesitate to admit the recruiting value of such a centre to the great common crusade? There can be no better way of rousing the laggards and spurring the ambition and dynamism of the active than to create an opportunity for young men from the whole of Germany to compete before the eyes of the nation for the glory of being best of the best. And furthermore, how the sense of unity of the German stocks will be strengthened when youths and men from every corner of the homeland can meet regularly to test their strength und skill! *What*

a chance for North and South, West and East, still largely ignorant of one another and therefore prone to baneful misconceptions about one another, to get acquainted, to learn to understand and respect one another, and to develop a sense of belonging together! Thus the strengthening of a common and healthy patriotism will be a fine fruit of the German stadium. (Diem 1920a, 1970: 4–5; emphasis added)

Two major doctrinal themes of the Volkish ideology can be identified in Diem's words here. First, he expresses distaste for the effects of adopting a modernist view. The Volkish ideology was strongly associated with hostility to industrialisation and an aversion to aspects of the modern age (Hoberman 1986). Diem himself exhibits this hostility, 'passive joys which to some extent signify nothing more than a febrile stimulation of the brain: films, revues, magazines, sport' (Diem 1927; cited in Hoberman 1986: 48). However, he saw in sport a great opportunity to balance the negative effects of industrialisation and of advanced technology, 'so today the civilised nations thereby testify that even in the age of technology and the division of labour they preserve and foster physical culture as the basis of health, strength and hence progress in the life of both the individual and the nation (Diem 1912b, 1970: 38). In similar vein, he argues elsewhere, 'Through sporting activity the human race preserves that intact vitality which is menaced by the effects on the human organism of present-day technical advances' (Diem 1954, 1970: 20).

In relation to the benefits of the Olympic Games in the modern era, he argued, 'Humanity needs this element [of chivalrous contests] in education of youth as a counterpoise to the degenerative effects of civilisation (Diem 1906, 1970: 37), while some years later he also claimed that, 'the Games through their influence on all cultured nations have helped to lift up the human race and to counter the morbid forces in civilised existence' (Diem 1923, 1970: 44). When he witnessed in the 1956 Melbourne Olympic Games the advancement of sport technology and its influence in sport performance, he expressed in frustration,

Can this go on? When will we reach the limits of human capacity? As long as human intelligence continues to improve the conditions of life, and as long as nature responds with enhanced growth and accelerated physical development, so long will there be a natural improvement in physical accomplishments (Diem 1957a, 1970: 95).

Nonetheless, despite his hostility towards technical advances, Diem, as a sports person and a sport bureaucrat, also recognised their benefits on the improvement of sport techniques, 'sport is technology, a refinement of methods and equipment; the very essence of sport implies refinement, that is, the capacity of movement to be "technologised", and yet it is also a flight out of the wasteland of our technologised age. Sport is a tension between technology and romanticism' (Diem 1941; cited in Hoberman 1986: 48).

Nationalism

The second point to be rehearsed in this part of the analysis is Diem's Volkish nationalism, which is found throughout his writings of this period. Diem, in planning to build a major stadium in Berlin, wanted to create a 'national arena' that would contribute to 'the great common crusade'. Central to the Volkish ideology was a need to reinforce the unification of Germany and the need for a collective, 'German' consciousness. Diem encourages the Germans to unify and compete against each other in the sport arena, and he argued this would be a great chance 'for North and South, West and East [Germany], still largely ignorant of one another and therefore prone to baneful misconceptions about one another, to get acquainted, to learn to understand and respect one another, and to develop a sense of belonging together!' (Diem 1920a, 1970: 5). He regularly makes his claims in the context of overtly nationalistic statements, 'to be German must mean to demand the world for Germany' (Diem 1925; cited in Hoberman 1986: 47) or 'we Germans feel more universal' (Diem 1926; cited in Hoberman 1986: 46). It is obvious from many of his writings, as for instance in the quote below, where he encourages the German team to perform well in the 1912 Stockholm Games, that the national interests of Germany were, for Diem, a central concern.

> 'Set foot in the stadium and become men who understand how to conquer'. Thus Philostrate once urged the youth of Greece. We expect no less today from German youth. What is at stake is our ability to demonstrate to the nations the all-round education of our youth and the vitality of our people. It is therefore a patriotic duty to ensure that the German nation, the nation of Friedrich Ludwig Jahn, is worthily represented at this international festival. (Diem 1912b, 1970: 38)

Thus references to Jahn and nationalist ideology mixed with the internationalism of the Olympic idea, demonstrates Diem's engagement with, and mixing of, competing systems of ideas. Thus, while his discourse supports the Games and their international character, he also appeals to his fellow countrymen and women on the basis of the opportunity the Games afford for demonstrating national strength and superiority.

> In the same way there is implicit in the Olympic Idea the triumphant pursuit of that inward delight in life which fills us when we exercise the body; implicit within it at the same time is the awareness that through this exercise we are not only promoting our personal well-being but also

acquitting, a duty to the greater community. *The Olympic athletes compete 'for the honour of their country' as the Olympic oath puts it.* To understand the Games one must see how the competitors expend their last ounce of strength, more utterly than in any other contest. *One must then see the intense emotion with which they salute their country's flag – with which not only they but everyone salutes it, each for the honour of his country, but all in the service of the human ideal which Jahn said animates the gymnastic art.* (Diem 1933b, 1970: 8; emphasis added)

In relation to the Berlin Games (1916), Diem argued that they should be 'treated' as a national affair.

This backing is essential if we are to have an all-round success in the Games. The Olympic Committee wishes not merely total-round success in the Games. The Olympic Committee wishes not merely to gain a few victories, but to field a team of uniformly well-trained and successful athletes. It therefore wishes to draw the team from all classes of the population, the poor just as much as the well-to-do. The Olympic Trials being held in the Army, together with many other proposed events, are in themselves a guarantee that all healthy sons of the nation will be challenged to represent their country in the Olympic Games. (Diem 1942c, 1970: 49)

While in the contemporary context it is perhaps a fairly common claim that 'sport is subject to political regulation by states, is a key source of cultural and national identity and is a tool of international relations as well as a significant sector in the growing service economy' (Henry *et al.* 2003: 296) it would seem that Diem appreciated this from a very early stage.

In these Games it will be up to us to prove German organising capacity, repay the lavish hospitality which we have enjoyed in 1896 and 1906 in Athens, in 1900 in Paris, in 1904 in St. Louis, in 1908 in London and in 1912 in Stockholm, *and show the world our fatherland in its beauty and its industrial, commercial and military might; it will be up to us to demonstrate the unfailing springs of our national vigour and vitality through the prowess of our young men in gymnastics and sport; above all it will be up to us to fill these international Games with a German spirit and use them for our own development.* They must shine like a torch in the twilight of our half-recognition of the need to strengthen our youth through rational physical exercise; we must look upon them as the testing day in preparation for which we must transform all lukewarmness, ignorance and recalcitrance into active cooperation. For will not every mother and father, every authority and every community derive satisfaction and tangible benefit if young people's academic studies are supplemented by a toughening of their limbs and will, through gymnastics, sport, games or walking? (Diem 1942f, 1970: 45; emphasis added)

Nevertheless, despite these nationalistic references, it should be noted that Diem himself was subject to attack from Volkish ideologists, who were critical of his internationalist ideas and his commitment to the Olympic Games. Given this tension between nationalist and internationalist standpoints, it is perhaps inappropriate to characterise Diem as an unequivocal supporter of conservative nationalist ideology. In relation to this, Hoberman (1986) has emphasised, 'Diem's persistent coupling of the national and the international put him at the liberal end of the Volkish spectrum' (p. 47). However, many of his statements regarding the preparation of German youth for the 1912 Stockholm and 1916 Berlin Olympic Games which include strong claims in relation to race and nation would certainly place him at the conservative end.

Race

Given the Nazi position in relation to (amongst others) the Jewish population, there is no compelling evidence that Diem was an anti-Semite. Indeed Diem's wife was known to have a Jewish ancestor, while Diem himself claimed that even before 1933 the Nazis had reproached him as a 'white Jew' on the basis of his international circle of contacts and acquaintances (Guttmann and Thompson 1984; Hoberman 1986). Nevertheless, references to the superiority of the German race and the preservation of German racial identity are relatively frequent in his writings, especially in the period 1912–1914. In the following passage, for example, he emphasises the positive qualities of the German race, (its 'vitality', 'intelligence', 'organising ability', and 'superior qualities') as reflected in the level of sporting performance of the German team in the Stockholm Olympic Games (1912),

German athletics has worn out its baby shoes. It has a sturdy organisation, is recognised by the authorities and public opinion, and most important of all has youth and the army on its side. *It is firmly rooted in the vitality of the German race, and trained and directed by German intelli*gence and organising ability. German athletes are therefore now expected to compete successfully *with the world's best and to wipe out by the superior qualities of the German race, the lead of nations, which took to sport at an earlier date. All of us – the competitors who wear the national colours, we who advise and help them, and the whole German sports community – must put our backs into preparing and executing this enterprise in which the honour of our country is at stake. If we all pull together, if as it were a wave of patriotic enthusiasm carries us along, then success will come, and the black-white-red colours will flaunt gaily in the breeze above the bright sea of* *banners on the topmost mast of the granite stadium in Stockholm.* (Diem 1912b: 39; emphasis added)

Diem's emphasis here is on the importance of 'German unity' and the collectiveness of the 'Volk' in the face of international sporting rivalries. Such a perspective, reflects the objectives of the nationalist Gymnastics movement of Jahn, combined with the elements of racial nationalism reflected in reference to the 'superior qualities of the German race'. In similar vein, in his appeal to the German nation, as part of his efforts to increase the popularity of the forthcoming Olympic Games in Berlin (1916), he emphasised,

The German Stadium, which is to be opened by the Emperor next spring in Berlin as the first and most important achievement of the German Reich Committee for the Olympic Games, *will fill up with skilful and well trained youths who need fear no opponent anywhere in the world; the blessed outcome of the whole movement will be a strong race!* With this aim the German Reich Committee for Olympic Games appeals for the support of the German people. (Diem 1942f, 1970: 46; emphasis added)

When appealing to the German Reich government, he also underlined the benefits of the Olympic Games on the interests of the German race.

German youth has greeted the preparations with enthusiasm. All classes of the population are fired with the Olympic spirit. The clubs and associations are already encountering an ardent response to the challenge of the new and important tasks with which they are confronted, and note with satisfaction the animation and the wave of interest in their work. We appeal to the Reichstag to help in this task. *The underlying purpose of the Olympic Games in [sic] missionary. Their happy fruit will be a sturdy race.* (Diem 1942a: 50; emphasis added)

In promoting the imminent Berlin Games (1916), Diem argued that, 'The effort will be worthwhile, not only because of the successes we may expect in the Games themselves, but because of the popularisation of physical culture, which should give us a healthy and militarily fit race' (Diem 1942c: 46). One might argue that Diem used this nationalistic discourse in order to engage with nationalistic predilections while seeking to promote the Games and the Olympic movement which were genuinely internationalist. Nevertheless it is clear that Diem actually saw the Olympic Games as a great opportunity for Germany to prepare its youth for military purposes. This is of course redolent of Coubertin's early motives in promoting modern sport in France. However, Diem, unlike Coubertin, was appealing to an ethnonationalism (based upon race, culture and ethnicity) and focusing on the preservation of the German racial identity and its further advancement.

Mandell (1974) has argued, 'one might believe from much of Diem's writing in the period 1937–1941 that his plans for sport had always been paramilitary, super-patriotic and totalitarian' (p. 11). However, as we have illustrated earlier in this chapter his writings in the period 1912–1914 also provide evidence of such themes.

Carl Diem's emphasis on race was also linked, via classical Hellenism, to the value of 'perfection'.

> What was the underlying idea of these contests, which enthralled the Greek people for a whole millennium, while they maintained a level of culture, which has never been regained? *They were a hymn of praise to the perfect human being! Their purpose was to ensure that the victor won his laurels 'through work and self-discipline as the noblest and most refined product of his race'* (Diem 1920b, 1970: 2; emphasis added)

Diem's interpretation of Hellenism reflects the German tradition, which stressed the 'Apollonian' calm and clarity of the Hellenic art. 'Beauty' and 'perfection' were central themes to German Hellenistic interpretations (Stephens 1989). This can be explained by the organic character of the German nationality, which, in contrast to the voluntarist ideal of nationality of the French romantics like Renan, the German Romantic ideology was typical for its organicism and determinism centred upon race and ethnicity (Smith 2001). The perfection of the race had become a core value and it is argued that the ideological approach of ethnic nationalism was taken to its logical extreme in the form of biological determinism and ideas relating to the superiority of the Aryan race.

The 'aesthetics of the body' is a theme, which was central to both Jahn's cult of the body and Nazi sport theory. Both ideologies were inspired by an interpretation of the aesthetic values of the ancient Greek civilisation. These ideas focused on 'perfect' bodies and elements of 'physical beauty', thus re-inventing the Hellenic tradition on the basis of their own past and culture. Hermann Glaser characterises the 'German interpretation' of Hellenism as 'an exaltation of the physical which became part of common culture ... a literally maniacal craving for beauty which was coupled with the repression of truthfulness' during the latter part of the nineteenth century, and he goes on to argue,

> [The National Socialists] endowed the 'Greco-National Socialist' body with a 'grace', which really spelled brutality, and with a form of dignity, which reflected racial arrogance. Anatomy was trump ... Classicism was cancelled out in the name of classicism: man was beautiful not to be true and free, graceful or ennobled, but rather to entice race-conscious copulation. (cited in Hoberman 1984: 164)

Diem's references to elements of 'perfection' and 'racial refinement' can thus be seen as connecting with the German interpretation of Hellenism.

This might be taken to imply that his perspective was closer to the racial aesthetic values underpinning both Volkish thought, and that of the National Socialist ideology which flourished under Hitler, than to the values associated with forms of humanism.

4.3   The Nazi phase (1933–1944)

The cancellation of the Games due to the Great War was a major disappointment to Diem, who had worked hard for their realisation. Mandell (1971: 85) describes it as 'a calamity for young Carl Diem ... The war wiped out years of his architectural planning and detailed scheduling of the events and festivities'. However, immediately after the end of the war, Diem returned with enthusiasm to work for the development of the sport movement in Germany. One of his most favoured projects was the establishment of the *Deutsche Sporthochschule für Leibesübungen* in Berlin on May 15, 1920. This institution was under the supervision of the *Deutsche Reichsausschuss für Leibesübungen*. This foundation, being independent of any state influence and help, was a teachers' training school for physical education and a research centre that collaborated with the University of Berlin (Haag 1982). New research possibilities emerged with the development of this centre, and in the years from 1925 to 1935, Diem became particularly active in writing and editing books and articles (Mandell 1971; Haag 1982).

However, in the years that followed the war, Germany had to wait to be readmitted to international sporting circles as it was excluded from all international sporting competitions, including the Olympic Games, as a war aggressor. Since the German invasion of neutral Belgium had been the trigger for Great Britain to participate in the war, the IOC decided that it was important to stage the first post-war Games in Antwerp symbolising the end of the war (Guttmann 1992). Major political issues emerged when the IOC had to decide which countries would be allowed and which should be banned from participating in the 1920 Olympic Games in Antwerp. The authority was finally given to the host city organising committee to decide which countries it would invite. As a result, it was not until 1928 that the Germans appeared again at the Olympic Games and it was not until 1931 that French and German teams competed against each other on the soccer field (Guttmann 1992). Interestingly, during the period of exclusion, Diem introduced the *Deutsche Kampfspiele*, a sport festival appearing every four years between the Olympic Games, for all Germans around the world. The *Deutsche Kampfspiele* was held in 1922 in Berlin, 1926 in Cologne, 1930 in Breslau and 1934 in Nuremberg (Haag 1982).

At the Olympic Congress held in Berlin in 1930, Theodor Lewald, IOC member for Germany and leading figure in German sport circles, and Carl Diem worked hard to demonstrate to the International Olympic Committee that Berlin was a suitable host for the Olympic Games in 1936. Lewald had remarked, 'here [at the congress] we detonated our bombs' (cited in Guttmann 1992: 53). After the successful re-appearance of Germany at the Amsterdam Olympics in 1928, the IOC was convinced that Germany could undertake the role of host for the 1936 Olympic Games. However, when awarding the 1936 Games to Berlin in 1931 (the decision was announced on May 13, 1931) the IOC was in effect awarding it to Berlin under the government of the Weimar Republic, a politically moderate centrist coalition, but when in 1933 the National Socialists came to power and Adolf Hitler became chancellor of Germany, the political context of the 1936 Games changed dramatically. As Guttmann (1992: 53) explains, 'this state of affairs was certainly not what the IOC had expected when Berlin was chosen as the site of the Games'. Both the IOC and the National Socialist government, each for their own reasons, faced the question of whether they should proceed with the hosting of the Games.

4.3.1   The Berlin Games of 1936

Krüger (1972) has pointed out that as long as the Nazis were an opposition party, they could not see any benefit in supporting an Olympiad that would enhance the prestige of their democratic opponents (cited in Hoberman 1986: 103). However, after they seized power, on March 16, 1933, Hitler and his close collaborator Joseph Goebbels met with Theodor Lewald, the Chairman of the German Organising Committee, and confirmed their interest in the Games (Hoberman 1986; Guttmann 1992; Roche 2000). Although they were initially critical and deeply suspicious of the Olympic movement because of its inter-nationalist character which contrasted with their own hyper-nationalist ideo-logy, and their aversion to anything non-German, they subsequently became convinced that the Games could become a great vehicle to demonstrate to the world what Germany had achieved under the National Socialist regime (Haag 1982; Hoberman 1986; Krüger 1999; Roche 2000). To this end, the state gov-ernment granted full financial support and put every effort into making the Games a generator of successful propaganda for the regime. Carl Diem, albeit not officially registered as a member of the Nazi party (Mandell 1971; Hober-man 1986), was the chief organiser and Secretary General of the games. He initi-ated many innovations in the realisation of the Games. For example he wanted all the facilities to be clustered in the same location – for the first time in the history of the Games; he held cultural events in the *Waldbühne* theatre to emphasise the artistic and cultural character of the Games; and he ordered a bell tower to be erected as a symbol of the call to the youth of the world (*Ich rufe die Jugend der Welt*). Another novelty was the torch relay from Olympia in Greece to Berlin. He explained that 'the aim of the relay was to emphasise the spiritual vitality and moral value of the Games both in ancient and modern times, and to show that the same idealism fills the youth of today' (Diem 1942d: 76).

> The fire having once been carried from Olympia to Berlin for the 1936 Games, the idea of such a link refused to die away. For it symbolises

devotion to the common ideal, which the Olympic celebration embodies, and the wish to implicate not only the actual competitors in the Games but the still uncommitted youth of the world. (Diem 1940, 1970: 77)

Despite the appeal here to elements of an internationalised, universalised discourse with reference to a 'common' ideal and the youth 'of the world', such symbolism could be interpreted as representing, not an embracing of common humanity but rather a striving of the elite to manifest their superiority.

In relation to the torch relay, Roche (2000: 117) argues, 'This was a product of Diem's long-standing and probably sincere sporting and Hellenic idealism. However, in this new Nazi context of the mid-1930s it inevitably carried with it some shadowy and suspect connotations and implications'. Olympia had been used as a site for the ancient Greek Games for around a thousand years, representing, as such, a kind of 'a thousand year civilisation'. This inspired Hitler and his 'vision' of a 'Thousand Year Reich' (Roche 2000: 117).

As indicated earlier, elements of Hellenism, such as 'beauty' and 'perfection', were central themes in the German interpretations of Hellenistic values (Stephens 1989), and were related to Nazi ideology based on ethnic nationalism, biological determinism, and the superiority of the Aryan race. Such a discourse is also reflected in the images transmitted in the film 'Olympia' by Leni Reifenstahl, which presented bodies of athletes resembling ancient Greek statues. In this context, therefore, Diem's innovation of the torch relay raises some suspicions, if not about his intentions, then certainly about the message conveyed through the linkage between modern Germany and ancient Olympia. Interestingly, Finley and Pleket (1976) have noted that Hitler held a meeting with the IOC in 1936 during the Olympic Games, where he announced that the Third Reich would finance the completion of the excavations that were taking place in ancient Olympia (cited in Roche 2000: 242), an issue which also concerned Diem with his classicist interests.

A further innovation devised by Diem was the 'Festival Play' (often referred to in the literature as the 'Pageant of Youth'), which included gymnastic displays involving 10,000 participants. The evening festivities ended with a choral performance of Beethoven's Ninth Symphony.

People are expecting Germany to give the long hoped for artistic expression to the Olympic Games, and I believe I am not deluding myself when *I affirm that the Festival Play as at present conceived completely fulfils this wish, represents the climax of the Games, and is a unique opportunity to give the world a notion of German creative power.* If the IXth Symphony is omitted, the Festival Play is reduced to a sporting spectacle in artistic guise, very good in its way, but still commonplace. (Diem 1936b, 1970: 73)

In the Berlin Games, Diem saw an opportunity for Germany to project its image in the international sport arena of the Olympic Games and to be re-established in international political affairs after the disaster of the Great War. For this reason, he appealed to the German sport and gymnastics circles to put aside their rivalries and fight together for a common purpose, the advancement of Germany.

> Despite the German tendency for everyone to make his own Reich policy, we must now be united. The decision on the Games has already been taken. All discussions as to the rights and wrongs of it are now pointless. The need now is to lend a hand, even if one had objections to the Games. *The task now is to stage them in such a way as to win heightened respect for Germany and to show Germany to foreigners.* There are other and more important ways of doing these things. But we have no right to disregard this way, let alone to jeopardise it. *Other countries respect sporting achievements as a visible sign of unimpaired youthful vigour, and sporting organisation as a proof that a nation can close its ranks even in small matters, when its good name is at stake. Germany's reputation in the world depends on many things. If we improve this reputation in 1936, then we will have helped to deepen the world's faith in our mission. This faith, an astonishing faith, is growing. It is no insignificant factor in our struggle for a place in the sun. So let us put all doubts in the pending file for four years and set about the collective task – gymnastic teachers, gymnasts, sportsmen, government, and people!* (Diem 1932, 1970: 63; emphasis added)

In similar vein, Diem emphasised the important national character of the Games, which made it necessary for all Germans to participate and support the event.

> After my experiences in the United States [he refers to the 1932 Los Angels Games] *I am convinced that the 1936 Games will have an international appeal,* which will put all other events in the shade. We must expect more competitors, but the rules set an upper limit to their numbers; on the other hand we must certainly expect tens of thousands of visitors, and above all German emigrants. In this matter we cannot begin too early with preparations and publicity. *The 1936 Games must be both an international and a great German festival. In point of numbers they may well be the greatest pan-German festival in Germany. On the home front this calls for certain solidarity. The Olympic Games are in sober fact an affair not only of the sports movement but of the people.* (Diem 1932, 1970: 62–3; emphasis added)

A further theme evident in his writings is that of the Games as a vehicle to promote Germany's image to the world.

> Thus the Games shape a new outlook and a new generation. The world expects us Germans to stage this world festival impeccably, to carry it

out in a perfect sporting spirit, and to fill it with intelligence and art. We shall have to commit all our talent and to make sacrifices both of time and money. *They must and will be made for the sake of the Olympic Idea and the glory of Germany.* (Diem 1937: 67; emphasis added)

To this end, he planned in great detail every technical aspect of the Games to ensure their success as a positive reflection on Germany. His innovations, while consistent with the international ideals of the Olympic movement, also promoted German interests, reflecting a general effort to demonstrate the power of the new Germany to the world. It is clear that Diem is explicit about his use of symbolism in this respect.

A complete novelty and a graceful way of honouring the victor was introduced by putting into effect a proposal by Mr. Rothe that all victors returning to their native land should be given an oak shoot in memory of their victory in Germany. For this purpose small one-year old seedlings of the German pedicle oak *'quercus pedunculata'* from the Holstein Marshes were taken into horticultural care from the spring of 1935. They were planted in special earth, repeatedly pruned, hardened against weather, treated with special pesticides and cultivated with the utmost care for their later purpose. Having grown into sturdy young plants, they were transferred to special pots decorated with the Olympic Bell and an inscription 'Grow in honour of victory – call to further exploits'. After being handed to the victor they were packed in convenient cartons specially designed for transport to the most distant countries – *a handsome symbol of German character, German strength, German vigour and German hospitality.* (Diem 1937: 72; emphasis added)

Diem incorporated in the programme of the Games a number of theatrical and ritual elements, which had long been part of German nationalist culture and tradition (Roche 2000). However, although Diem was Hitler's festival master, he was 'far less compromised – and far less repentant – than the dramaturge of the Nuremberg rallies' (Hoberman 1986: 49), and as previously indicated, Diem claimed that the Nazis had denounced him as a 'white Jew' because of 'his foreign affinities' (Krüger 1972; cited in Guttmann 1984: 64). In addition, it should be noted that the Nazis, as soon as they seized power, dismissed Diem from all his posts except that of Secretary General of the Games (Haag 1982; Guttmann 1992). In such circumstances one might suspect that Diem's accommodation of nationalistic rhetoric and of aspects of Nazi ideology in his writings, was in part provoked by a fear of losing not simply his last remaining significant official role in sport, but also of the consequences which might stem from this. Mandell (1971) has noted, 'Diem was, then, for a long time one of those in the silent opposition' (p. 240), but Hoberman (1986) concludes that the issue of Diem's relationship with the

Nazis must be 'open to question' (p. 49) and this would seem a more tenable position. After the end of the Games, Diem expressed his enthusiasm and satisfaction with their success.

> Never before has an Olympic Festival been attended by such multitudes of spectators, so much interest been shown in sport or such a degree of enthusiasm for the Olympic ideals. Throughout Germany, and especially in Berlin, the people expressed their joyful interest in the Festival by decorating their dwellings, sincerely hoping that the Olympic Games would constitute a means of establishing understanding and peace, both of which they feel are so necessary. (Diem 1936a, 1970: 75)

Interestingly, Diem, in his writings from that period, did not raise any personal concerns or make any remarks about the political problems that surrounded the Berlin Games, with the exception of some official statements after a session of the IOC regarding issues of team selection and recruitment. In 1935 Germany adopted the Nuremberg Laws, which meant that Jews or those of 'mixed blood' were not eligible for German citizenship. This also meant that Jews could not be admitted to the German team. The ideological discrepancy between the values underpinning the Nazi doctrine and the Olympic Charter had been a major issue in the discussions of the IOC during the meeting in Vienna on June 7, 1933 (Guttmann 1992). In 1933 the Amateur Athletic Union (AAU), the principal sports federation in the United States, voted to boycott the Games unless the treatment of the Jews was improved (Toohey and Veal 2000). The Nazis responded by providing oral or written guarantees confirming that Jews would be allowed to participate in the Games.

> After this declaration Mr. Garland wished to have it known that the American Olympic Committee, who were desirous of having the United States strongly represented at the next Olympic Games in Europe, would have had to give up participation altogether if German Jewish Athletes had not been assured the same terms as members of the same faith in other countries. General Sherrill added that the satisfactory statement made by the President would give great pleasure in the United States. (Diem 1933a, 1970: 64)

Notwithstanding these assurances, the Americans threatened a boycott. A Gallup poll taken in March 1935 showed 43 per cent of the American population to agree with a boycott. Moreover, because the track-and-field team contained many black athletes, Afro-American reactions to the boycott campaign were also quite significant. A 'Committee to Oppose the Olympic Games' was formed in Prague. Russia and Spain announced that they would not participate in the Games (Toohey and Veal 2000). As a response to the world reaction, 21 German Jews from the Makkabi and Schild organisations were invited as 'candidates' for the German team, but in the end none was selected (Guttmann 1992). Avery Brundage, who after his close observation in Germany had 'strangely' re-assured the AAU that there was no difference in the treatment of Jews in comparison with any other German, played an important role in preventing the boycott[2] (Guttmann 1992).

Questions have been raised as to why Diem did not refer to any of these significant issues in his speeches and writings. Furthermore, in his *World History of Sport and Physical Culture* (1960), Diem argued that the critics only started claiming that the Berlin Olympiad was used as propaganda for the Nazis after the collapse of the regime, a claim which Hoberman (1986: 50) has called 'absurd and dishonest' since it ignored the resistance and world-wide expression of disdain which *preceded* the Games. Diem's approach here might be explained as defensiveness about his own role in the production of shameful propaganda. Diem seems to have found it difficult to concede that while aware of the value to the Nazi regime, he still worked with it and contributed to its success. However, in his writings in the post-Nazi phase he fails to express in an unequivocal fashion any regret for his collaboration with the regime. Showing an astonishing selectivity of memory and in the context of the post-war exclusion of Germany from the Olympic Games, he describes Germany's contribution to the Olympic movement through the 1936 Games in glowing terms:

> *If Germany's youth is thinking about taking part in the Olympic Games, it is doing so because it rightly knows that it can be outdone by no one in the world in true devotion to sporting ideals, and because it feels that it belongs when the youth of the world is assembling to honour these ideals.* There is no stain upon its Olympic loyalty. In 1936 we carried out the last Olympic Games faultlessly in accordance with our international mandate. They passed off without anyone daring to deny the Olympic spirit or even to offend against it. That this is so, is irrefutably proved by the fact that at the meeting of the International Olympic Committee in June 1939 in London, Germany by secret written vote unexpectedly received a unanimous request to prepare the 1940 Winter Games in Garmisch-Partenkirchen. Had there been any infringement of the Olympic spirit to complain of in 1936 at least one member of the International Olympic Committee would have handed in a white slip of paper. Even during the whole war we continued up to the collapse to perform without a break the Olympic duties which we had taken over, e. g. the publication of the official International Olympic Review; we loyally preserved the Olympic flame, and as a final gift as late as 1944 endowed the presentation volume for the 50th Jubilee of the Committee, and handed over the reference work, the Olympic Lexikon. (Diem 1948, 1970: 80–1; emphasis added)

Diem presents himself as someone whose genuine love for sport and faith in the development of sport movement in Germany had led him to promote the

Games without reference to the wider political circumstances. The discourse here is one of honouring the Olympic ideal by providing the stage for the highest order of human athletic performance, and it is separated by Diem from the notion of honouring humanity. The notion of a Germany which 'loyally preserved the Olympic flame' and organised Games 'which passed off without anyone daring to deny the Olympic spirit or even to offend against it' is breathtakingly disingenuous. He is writing at a time when the Nazi regime's attempts to demonstrate Aryan superiority, marked by the exclusion of Jewish athletes from consideration for the German team, was known to be a precursor to the Holocaust and the attempt to exterminate Jews, Roma, homosexuals, and these with physical and mental disabilities, but such matters are simply absent from the discourse. His appeal to the 'fact' that nobody in the Olympic movement complained, even if it had been true (and sadly some like Brundage[3] clearly had the opportunity to endorse such complaints but failed to do so) would not constitute an argument for saying that no inappropriate action was taken. Diem here is attempting to shape the discourse as being about Olympic rather than about political matters, as if this distinction were valid, a distinction which his own pre-war statements clearly reject. Hoberman's (1986: 50) criticism of Diem as 'a cunning apologist, if only because he refused to make any apology whatsoever' would thus seem wholly appropriate.

4.3.2   Coubertin and Diem

Coubertin did not attend the Berlin Games, but instead his recorded message was played over the loudspeakers during the opening ceremony. He had also addressed a message to the bearers of the torch relay,

> We are living in solemn hours. Everywhere around us are occurring the most extraordinary and unexpected things. Like a thick morning mist there are taking shape before us the figures of a new Europe and that of a new Asia. It seems that, now more than ever, the crisis that we must face and debate is, above all, a crisis in education. I offer you my message – doubtless the last that I will have the chance to formulate. I hope your course is a happy one. It begins after all in a most illustrious place, under the aegis of an eternal Hellenism that has not ceased to light the way of the centuries and whose ancient solutions remain today as applicable as they ever were. (cited in Mandell 1971: 130)

It seemed that Coubertin had supported the Berlin Games without making any reference to their use as a fascist propaganda. Diem has reported that Coubertin was 'well informed about sports and politics in Germany' and that he 'expected the Olympic Games in Berlin to be a major cultural event' (cited in Hoberman 1986: 43). However, as Krüger (1972) argues Diem cannot be considered a reliable source, as he may have been motivated by a wish to advance the Olympic cause or his own position as a link between Coubertin and the Berlin organising committee (cited in Hoberman 1986: 43). Tellingly however, Coubertin himself, when questioned about the use of the Games as a Nazi propaganda vehicle, made the following vehement defence in the course of an interview during the Games,

> What? 'Disfigured' Games? The Olympic Idea sacrificed to propaganda? That is entirely false! The imposing success of the Berlin Games has served the Olympic ideal magnificently. The French, who alone or almost alone have been playing the Cassandras, commit the greatest injustice by not understanding or by not wanting to understand ... It is good that each nation of the world be granted the honour of putting on the Games and of celebrating them in its own manner, in accordance with its own creative powers and by its own means. In France they are disturbed by the fact that the Games of 1936 were illuminated by a Hitlerian force and discipline. How could it have been otherwise? (cited in Hoberman 1986: 42–3)

It is also worth noting that the interviewer Gaston Meyer remarked that Coubertin seven days after this interview, in a letter addressed to the French sporting paper *L'Auto*, offered 'his congratulations to Mr. Hitler, who he salutes as one of the great constructive spirits of the age, for having preserved the Olympic ideals from distortion and for having served it magnificently' (cited in Hoberman 1986: 43).[4] Coubertin also engaged in correspondence with members of the Nazi regime, in support of its campaign against an international boycott, and the German sport historian Hans Joachim Teichler (1982) has argued that even if Coubertin was not a Nazi, 'he did not criticise – he cooperated'. In his defence, his biographer Marie-Thérèse Eyquem wrote that Coubertin 'would never disavow the Olympic symphony, in spite of the false notes of Berlin. No human work is perfect, not even those, which hold themselves to be divine. The Church has had its heresies, its schisms, its inquisition' (cited in Hoberman 1986: 42). Such an argument is hardly an adequate defence though it may be an explanation of Coubertin's position. To extend Eyquem's analogy, the Church has also had its problems with association with abuse of children and vulnerable adults, but is condemned for these actions even by those who remain committed to their religious institutions. Such phenomena are arguments for reform, rather than excuses for turning a blind eye.

Not long before the Second World War began, Coubertin asked Diem to establish an International Olympic Institute in Berlin for the dissemination of the Olympic ideals and the preservation of the Olympic-related archival material.

> I wasn't able to complete what I wanted to accomplish. What would be dearest by far to me would be the creation of a very modest small institute in Germany, in memory of the Games of the XIth Olympiad, to which I

would leave all my papers, documents, unfinished projects concerning the whole of modern Olympism in order to dispel inaccuracies. I think an Olympic Study Centre, not necessarily in Berlin, would more than anything else support progress of this movement and preserve it from ideological deviation of which I am so fearful. (Coubertin 1938b; quoted by Paton and Barney 2002: 94).

The collaboration between the two men was taken a stage further when Coubertin asked Diem to undertake the editing of the *Revue Olympique,* the International Olympic Committee's magazine of which Coubertin had been the managing director and editor from 1901 to 1914.

He [Coubertin] was very concerned about the spiritual transmission of his work, and always attached importance to the independent cultivation of the educational ideas which are implicit in the Olympic Games, and which had led him to re-establish them. So in 1934, under the impact of the German preparations for the XIth Olympiad, he got into touch with me for the first time and urged me to edit an Olympic Review after the Games were over, as he himself had done for many years. Indeed he had prepared the ideological ground for the revival of the Games by issuing in 1890–91 his own periodical 'La Revue Athletique' in which he already demonstrated the full width of his horizon. After the foundation of the Games he had resumed publication of the periodical under the title 'Revue Olympique'; it appeared sometimes as a monthly, sometimes as a quarterly up to the beginning of the World War. (Diem 1938b, 1970: 34)

Between 1938 and 1944 the Berlin Institute published all 24 issues of *La Revue Olympique* (later renamed as *Olympische Rundschau*), which remained the official organ of the IOC. Diem explains below some details concerning Coubertin's proposal for a 'Centre of Olympic Studies' to the German Reich.

Coubertin expanded his proposal during 1934 with the idea of erecting a second Olympic Museum in Berlin as a counterpart to that in Lausanne. Then in 1937, through the intermediary of his friend the German General Consul in Geneva Dr. Krauel, he made a proposal to the Reich Sport Leader for the foundation of an International Olympic Institute, to which he would bequeath his as yet unpublished writings, in so far as they concerned the educational and psychological problems of Olympism. The Institute was to be a 'Centre of Olympic Studies', and to be devoted to work on all associated historical and educational questions. Coubertin expressly gave as his reason that Germany was the country, which had so well understood his ideas and put them into practice. Reich Sport Leader von Tschammer und Osten, who immediately took up this plan, obtained the consent of the Fuhrer and Reich Counsellor and all the authorities concerned, and thus ensured that the Institute was inaugurated at the appointed time. The International Olympic Committee received the news of its foundation at a meeting that took place in March 1938 on the Nile, and expressed its joyful approbation; it resolved to give up its official announcements through the 'Olympic Review', which was to be published by the new Olympic Institute in quarterly form. (Diem, 1938b, 1970: 34)

Later in the same year (1938), Diem expressed in an article his pleasure at the official inauguration of the International Olympic Institute in Berlin.

We can thus note with satisfaction that as a result of the XIth Olympiad Germany has spontaneously become the intellectual focus of the Olympic effort. The administrative direction of the Olympic Games remains in Lausanne, the seat of the International Olympic Committee. The work in Berlin will begin with the establishment of the Olympic Archive, a documentary centre on world sports organisation. Here it will be possible in future to find data on the sports associations of all nations participating in the Olympic Games, their leaders and their history, and also on laws relating to physical education, state institutions in this field, various methodical principles etc. A second task is research into Olympic history both in antiquity and in modern time, and evaluation of the experience to be gained thereafter. It is clearly unnecessary for every Olympic organiser to start his experience from scratch; such experience can be systematically stored in the Institute and made available to future organisers. This work also covers the principles of construction of Olympic sports facilities, which will turn affect the construction of sports facilities in general. A third question is the educational aspect of the Games. They should even act as a recurrent stimulus to a healthy education of the young, and thus keep them far from professional sport, sensation and theatricality. (Diem 1938b, 1970: 34–5)

The discourse here is focused on the 'scientific codification' of Olympic knowledge (a project later given concrete form in the shape of the IOC's Olympic Games Knowledge Services, established after the Sydney Games in 2000).

In 1938, Diem successfully inaugurated the Olympic Institute in Berlin, but he had not transferred yet from Lausanne to Berlin Coubertin's archival records and papers (Paton and Barney 2002). Within twelve months however, the Second World War had begun, and the future of the Olympic movement was once again threatened with crisis. Belgium was occupied by German troops, which made it difficult for the President Comte Henri Baillet-Latour to continue his work for the IOC. During the winter of 1940–41, Diem, von Halt, and Reichssportführer Hans von Tschammer und Osten visited Baillet-Latour and informed him of grandiose plans by Hitler to take over the international sport movement (Guttmann 1992). From 1937, following the success of the 1936 Berlin Games, Hitler held several meetings with his favourite architect Albert Speer about the design of a huge stadium in Nuremberg, intended to accommodate 450,000 spectators, though this was never built. In a conversation that Speer had with Hitler informing him that the athletic field did not have the prescribed Olympic proportions, Hitler is said to have remarked, 'No matter. In 1940 the Olympic Games will take place in Tokyo. But thereafter, they will take place in Germany for all time to come, in this stadium. And then, we will determine the measurements of the athletic field' (Mandell 1971: 293).

During the war amid disorder and fears for the future of the Olympic movement, Baillet-Latour, who was 'isolated' (Paton and Barney 2002: 97) and 'politically helpless' (Guttmann 2002: 75), died of a stroke on January 6, 1942. However, not long after his death, Diem appeared in Lausanne to initiate the transfer of Coubertin's Olympic papers and records to Berlin. With regard to Diem's visit to Lausanne in early 1942, Madame Zanchi, who had been IOC Secretary since 1927, remarked, 'At the height of the war, I was left alone in Lausanne. When Professor Diem attempted to remove the Olympic headquarters to Germany, I hid the most important documents in the cellar, and convinced the community that Diem was a spy. I alerted Mr. Edström of Sweden' (cited in Lucas 1980: 147; also referenced in Mandell 1971: 241, Guttmann 1992: 75; Paton and Barney 2002: 97). As a result, Edström travelled to Switzerland later in 1942 and locked in a safe place all the IOC records. Paton and Barney (2002), however, argue that, despite Madame Zanchi's resistance, Diem was simply doing what Coubertin had instructed him to do in relation to his archival material. Moreover, Coubertin too, during the First World War crisis, had acted in a similar way by moving in 1915 the headquarters from Paris to Lausanne. Nevertheless, many questions have been raised regarding Diem's motives for such an action, especially given the fact that Berlin was not a safe location at which to store the Olympic records (especially in comparison with neutral Switzerland which had been Coubertin's choice during the First World War crisis).

Mandell (1971) has claimed that Diem's 'pseudo-classical trappings such as the torch run and the shows of the ancient Greek art' aimed at establishing himself as 'the natural successor of the aging Coubertin [and] the leader of the International Olympic movement' (p. 283). In addition, in relation to Diem's actions after the surrender of Germany in 1945, Widlund (1998: 175) has argued that Diem in his memoirs '*Ein Leben fur den Sport*' (A Life for Sports) 'appears as a bitter, reluctant, hostile and uncooperative person'. He continues,

> Diem sees himself as the foremost guardian of the Olympic Idea and takes on the role of Olympian Zeus to condemn what he does not approve of. Besides, he is wrong when he says that the Olympic Flag is handed over by

the Secretary General of the previous Games. This is done by the Mayor of the previous host city. Diem must really have longed to play that part at the 1948 Games in London. Those who study the complex personality of Carl Diem should take notice of this particular part of his memoirs. (p. 175)

Diem's interest in keeping the Olympic archives under his surveillance might be seen as part of a personal ambition to maintain his power and even to succeed Coubertin in the Olympic movement. In similar vein, his dedication to the excavations of the ancient sporting sites in Olympia, especially in the post-Nazi phase, may be seen as an element in his attempts to establish himself in the eyes of the world as a dedicated Hellenist, an Olympic apologist, and as Coubertin's successor. Such claims must however remain speculative.

4.4   The post-Nazi phase: Olympic internationalism?

As with the Great War, the outbreak of the Second World War brought a major crisis in the Olympic movement, and threatened its future existence. Diem had expressed his concerns about the cancellation of the Olympic Games in Tokyo (1940), and also those which were later awarded to Helsinki following the Japanese invasion of China (Toohey and Veal 2000),

> The war has cut across Olympic affairs. Where weapons clash, the Olympic celebration retires. Before the grim struggle for existence, joy in Olympic festivities recedes into the shadows. So the glad hope for a festival in Tokyo paled before the thunder of war in Asia, and the Games in Garmisch-Partenkirchen fell out before the stir of arms in Europe. What will become of the Helsinki festival we shall learn in the near future. At the moment of writing a decision has not yet been taken. It is the task of these pages to rake the Olympic fire so that when peace returns it may blaze up brightly again. (Diem 1940, 1970: 77)

In the aftermath of the Second World War, the IOC started to rebuild the structures of the Olympic movement and revive the Olympic Games. However, the war had heightened the nationalist feelings of the IOC members, even if they were representatives of the IOC in their countries and not ambassadors of their countries in the IOC. For members whose countries had been damaged by the German or Italian occupiers, the presence in the committee of former Nazis or Fascists was more than unpleasant. The presence of Von Halt, for instance, who had been a member of the Nazi party, or of Adolf Friedrich zu Mecklenburg, who had worked closely with Propaganda Minister Joseph Goebbels and of the three Italians – Count Alberto Bonacossa, Count Paolo Thaon di Revel, and General Giorgio Vaccaro – who had all been members of the Italian Fascist party, raised protests among other IOC members (Guttmann 1992). At the first post-war session in Lausanne, it was also decided that Germany and Japan as the war aggressors should not be invited to the 1948 Games.

> Invitations will be sent out by the Organizing Committee to parti-
> cipate in the 1948 'Games' early in the New Year. Germany and Japan
> will not be included. The design for the invitations, which portray
> an athlete running with a flaming Olympic Torch, has been drawn by
> Mr. J. E. Slater of Ribworth, Leicester. (Diem 1947: 80)

Diem was very disappointed by this decision, which he tried unsuccessfully to reverse, right up to the last moment before the staging of the Games in London.

> Roesler has written with such enthusiasm and conviction that his words
> are sure to find a good echo, though in fact Edström needs no urging. It
> was Edström who on receiving the official notification that we intended
> to found a German Olympic Committee, first and forthwith replied that
> he welcomed this intention and that 'the formal condition for an invita-
> tion' was thereby fulfilled. Since he keeps me regularly informed about
> the Olympic deliberations and also sends me the minutes, I know that
> the invitation list of the International Olympic Committee is not yet
> closed and that no decision has yet been taken to exclude Germany (and
> Japan). (Diem 1948, 1970: 81)

Diem seems to have been convinced that Germany would eventually be invited to the London Games. What made him believe this was possibly that good relationships existed between the President of the IOC, Sigfrid Edström and individuals from the German Olympic circles (an official German Olympic Committee was yet to be founded)[5] (Guttmann 1992; Roche 2000). According to Diem at least, he and Edström, communicated with one another freely and in an open manner, and regularly discussed developments in the decision-making processes of the IOC concerning the participation of Germany in the London Games. Edström also showed his support to the German Olympic Committee some years later on the issue of whether Mecklenburg and von Halt, two persons that had been clearly implicated in the activities of the Nazi regime, had the right to represent the newly established Federal Republic of Germany in the IOC session in Vienna (May 1951).

Notwithstanding the protests from a number of members, including Prince Axel of Denmark, General Pahud de Mortanges of Holland, Baron de Trannoy of Belgium, Olaf Ditlev-Simonsen of Norway, and Jerzy Loth of Poland, Edström refused to put the whole issue to a vote. He announced that the Germans were already present in Vienna for the session, stating in response to their reactions, 'these are old friends whom we receive today' (Gutmann 1992: 77). The German National Committee, consisting (among others) of former collaborators of Nazis, such as its President von Halt, subsequently gained full recognition by the IOC. Such actions raised criticisms about the IOC's tendency to be 'completely insulated from political events within Germany and the strong overtones produced at the Berlin Games' (Killanin and Rodda 1976; cited in Roche 2000: 119).[6] However, the decision for the exclusion of Germany from the Olympic Games in London (1948) was not rescinded due to the general outcry in IOC circles.

Interestingly, Diem had emphasised, 'We will not forget, however, that while international sporting relationships grow irresistibly out of the competitive impulse in sport, at the same time they are subject to the general laws of human commerce, namely in this case the need for friendly contacts. Now friendship is always a matter of reciprocity' (Diem 1949, 1970: 83). Diem thus sought to ensure the re-admittance of Germany in the international sport arena through the development of international contacts, at the expense of 'German pride',

> *We must not have any greater urge to resume sporting contacts with other nations than they have to resume contacts with us.* And we note with deep joy that there has already been a rebirth of this sporting friendship in several sporting fields and with several countries. I send greetings from here to our Swedish and Swiss sports friends, with whom we are in close contact. I also greet many other sports leaders abroad who have shown the same will to friendship, and think at this moment of our old sports friend Dan Terns, the intellectual leader, Secretary and Treasurer of American athletics, who from the beginning has urged the reincorporating of Japan and Germany with the fine sentence 'It is my feeling that the athletes of Germany and Japan had no more to do with the war than did our athletes'. We must tackle our preparations for Helsinki today on the assumption that by 1952 conflicts born of the World War will have been resolved. Should this assumption prove wrong in one field or another, our preparations will nonetheless not have been in vain, since as we know from experience they are an inner source of strength for the development in Germany itself. (Diem 1949, 1970: 83–4; emphasis added)

Germany was finally re-admitted to the Olympic movement at the 1952 Helsinki Games, but represented only West Germany due to the problems regarding the recognition of the post-war establishing of East and West German Olympic Committees (Toohey and Veal 2000).

4.4.1   True internationalism or a Eurocentric worldview?

Supernationalism was both 'cause and effect' of the two 'world wars' (Roche 2000: 24). These two periods of ruin and destruction had severe effects in

Europe (and inevitably on the whole world) on political, cultural and economic levels. In terms of their influence on the Olympic movement, they
transformed the event to a mass public festival, which served propaganda
purposes and nationalist interests. Nonetheless, the early-twentieth century
authoritarian states were also responsible for the development of 'super-
nationalist' themes, which extended beyond the national boundaries of the
nation-states, thus developing the implications of the (neo-) imperialist
character of 'international society'. The transformation of the Olympics to
mass public festivals during this period determined the development of
public culture in the late twentieth century. In the post-Second World War
period and the late twentieth century there was an increase in the trends
toward both internationalisation and trans-nationalisation, whereas supernationalism and the notion of international world as a 'world of nations'
had not disappeared. Such trends are identified with recent historical developments in economic, cultural and political spheres and were more visible
after the two 'world wars' (Roche 2000).

Evidence of internationalism

Diem, even in writings during the period of the Nazi regime, made references
to the value of internationalism in the Olympic movement. Both men, Diem
and Coubertin, shared the view that national and international interests
could co-exist in the Olympic Games. Diem, notwithstanding his employ-
ment of a nationalist discourse often emphasised in his writings that sport
was a universal culture.

> The Olympic Congress, like the Olympic Games, is an expression of the
> world-fellowship of sporting ideas and of their world-binding force. Only
> a chivalrous sport, a sport aware both of its strength and its limitations,
> can be a foundation of modern culture. This culture is a web in which the
> individual national elements are the warp, and the things they have in com-
> mon are the woof. International influences penetrate the national cultures
> and in turn draw new strength from their enduring traditions. The Olympic
> Games are an example of this. Here too particular national idioms mingle
> and are permeated in their turn by the universal idea. (Diem 1930, 1970: 33)

Echoing arguments from the thesis of globalisation, Diem explains the
mechanisms of combining the universal with the particular, the national
with the international, in the global sport arena. Having acknowledged
that the Olympic Games should be inclusive of all world nations, he had
raised his objections against the lengthy Olympic programme which was
constraining for the participants of the non-European nations,

> But the Olympic Games are world games, and the intention is that all
> the nations shall participate. Non-European sportsmen would have had

to devote nearly half a year to this programme. For example the Chileans arrived in Holland in the middle of May and left in the middle of August. (Diem 1929, 1970: 54)

Diem emphasised that all the nations of the world should have the right to host the Olympic Games, without any restrictions affecting the smaller nations.

> *The rhythm of the Olympic Games demands that they be organised alternately by large and small countries, and this is the clear intention of the IOC.* The large nations may demonstrate their ability in the Games but they must not in any sense control them, since the smaller nations have the right to imprint their character upon them. An Olympic Festival becomes no less Olympic if its scope is confined, and neither the number of spectators or participants can be regarded as an ultimate indication of success. The determining factor is rather the festive atmosphere. (Diem 1938a, 1970: 79)

Diem in arguing in this text that small nations were capable of hosting the Olympic Games, perhaps had in mind the IOC's decision that Helsinki, the Finnish capital, should replace Tokyo as a host city for the 1940 Olympic Games. When the IOC did not receive any confirmation from the Japanese Olympic Committee that their aggressive foreign policy would not influence the staging and conduct of the Games, they withdrew the offer from Tokyo, replacing it with the offer to Helsinki (Guttmann 1992; Toohey and Veal 2000). The Finns, whose relationship with the IOC had always been good, accepted immediately and provided an attractive alternative at a difficult time. The choice of Helsinki was thus a solution adopted by the IOC *in extremis*, rather than evidence of an 'open' and inclusive policy to incorporate small nations in the staging of the Games.

During the period 1956–1961 in particular, Diem was deeply concerned by the expansion of the Olympic movement beyond Europe, and the interaction between the local, national elements, and the international and global values of the Olympic movement.

> 'Why are they taking the Olympic Games all the way to Melbourne?' is a question often asked in irritation. The simple answer is that it's no further from Berlin, Helsinki, London or Rome to Melbourne than from Melbourne to Rome, London, Helsinki or Berlin. *It is true that the Olympic Games originated once in Europe and were also revived there, but today they are a world festival, to which all civilised nations are invited. Their main content is sporting, and in a world festival good sportsmanship demands geographical fair play. The changes must therefore be rung on all climates and times of year. The classical Games, which began by being purely Greek and*

then became a festival for the whole Mediterranean, did not have to face this problem. But present-day sport has conquered the world, and the Games must therefore be held in the conditions, seasons and places of the various continents, and moreover must take the imprint of their regional cultures. This task has not been approached pedantically or mechanically, but practically and with the aim of promoting the spread of the Olympic idea. The Games have twice been allotted to the New World, i.e. the United States (St. Louis in 1904 and Los Angeles in 1932). Once already it was intended to take them to the Far East (Tokyo 1940), but this was prevented first by the war between Japan and China, and then by World War II. Now it is Australia's turn. No doubt after Rome in 1960 the Games may well be given to East Asia again, and after that to Africa or South America. The initial objection that Olympic Games held too far outside the main World traffic routes would be poorly visited has been disproved by events. The Melbourne Games, with over 70 nations participating, are outdoing all their predecessors, for the good reason that the Olympic Idea has now spanned the globe and taken root everywhere. (Diem 1956, 1970: 91)

In promoting the hosting of the Games in non-European cities, Diem was advocating a kind of equity that would pay dividends to the IOC. He argued that the selection of Melbourne as a host for the 1956 Olympic Games had opened channels of communication with people outside the European cultural sphere, reflecting the international nature of the Olympic movement.

The Melbourne Games were a crucial proof of this. They challenged the world – the world came. Now, however, the world in turn is challenging the Games. I mean that they can and must reflect the intellectual wealth and onward march of the world's cultures. Man's common characteristics, his common needs and perceptions and festal traditions must fuse in them like alloys to create a conducting metal. (Diem 1957b, 1970: 99)

Diem emphasised the need for the local cultures of the different world nations to be reflected in the programme of the Olympic Games.

In Asia national customs have been preserved to the present day in intimate connection with religion. Like Persian athletics, they have frequently survived a change of religions, and appear in Muslim traditions as they formerly did in the rituals of the previous cult; for all physical education is religious in origin and its festivals, whether Olympic or Capitoline, whether the Peruvian races or those of the Hittites and Babylonians, whether Indonesian boxing or Gallic horse-racing, whether Chinese football or the equestrian games of the steppe peoples, are always dedicated to the gods. When these new peoples have had time to consider more deeply the *advantages and disadvantages of modern sport, they will demand that their conception of sport too shall be acknowledged in the Olympic Games. If the Games are to be a universal festival, they must reflect the whole field of bodily culture and of culture through the body.* (Diem 1957b, 1970: 99–100; emphasis added)

Diem's attachment to the multicultural world of sport is in sharp contrast to the nationalist and racist discourse of his earlier years. In arguing that the modern Olympic movement would benefit from understanding world cultures and from including elements of the local traditions in the Olympic Games it might be argued that he was in effect adopting an inter-culturalist approach, though as we shall see such claims would be exaggerated.

This trend is the more likely, in that Asian physical education empha-sises a side whose present neglect in modern sport has led to glaring dis-advantages. *All the defects and perversions attributed to modern sport, its one-sidedness, its exaggeration, its art-for-art's sake attitude and refusal to fit into the framework of life's obligations, and lastly its materialism, all these are rooted in the sensationalism of the prevailing competitive system. We may hope that the Asian systems of physical culture will restore the lost equilibrium.* (Diem 1957b, 1970: 100; emphasis added)

Diem supported in many cases the competitive form of modern sport, 'For one and the other – the great, universal, enduring pageant of life and the modest recurring festival – set man tasks which he must solve as he goes along. In these tasks what matters is not just to take part honourably, but to win!' (Diem 1957b, 1970: 99). However, as we have illustrated, Diem in his earlier writings had been significantly influenced by the Volkish anti-pathy to industrialisation, materialism and competitiveness (Hoberman 1986). Thus for Diem, the inclusion of local cultures in the highly com-petitive Olympic Games could counter-balance the negative effects of modernity.

'High culture' says Nietzsche 'will seem like a bold dance, wherefore great strength and suppleness are needed'. The Indian dances are the flower of all human gymnastics. What a distressing sight, not in itself but by com-parison with the Indian art, is our programme of competitive freestanding exercises, which consists of a large number of acrobatic feats ranging from splits to flick-flack and flying somersault, all strung together with-out rhyme or reason. The whole body of the Indian dance moves in perfect obedience to the secret behests of the soul. Here is the open heaven of our cause. Should these things not form part of the Olympic Games? I saw dances in India, in dance-loving Madras, beginners and women-teachers in the heart of the country at the Amravati Sport School, classes surrendered in self-forgetfulness to the inner rhythm, their black flower-twined pony-tails flying; I saw how the teachers inwardly danced with them, never taking an eye from their chicks, whether their own obviously well-trained bodies were clad in brilliant saris – a dance in themselves – or were enveloped in the severe white robes of the Christian nuns. I ask again: should these things not form part of the Olympic programme? (Diem 1957b, 1970: 100)

The basis of our claim that Diem's construction of a culturally inclusive Olympic Games falls short of a form of inter-culturalism. Diem's perception of inclusion of local cultures in the Olympic Games, echoed that of Coubertin, in being restricted to the peripheral role of cultural displays outside the main competitive programme of the Games.

How can we free mankind from the formalism of an existence with no depth, such as is expressed in our 'modern' dances, if we do not set aside an hour in our only common festival for self-communion and the expression of our highest humanity? It is certainly true that we cannot make any points competitions out of it, any more than a genuine comparison is possible between ice-dancers as the symphony of colour, music and movement plays on the gliding floor. But do the points really matter? Can we not be high-minded and forget any thought of competition for part of the festival, simply offering the game to one another as the Chinese or Indian weapon-dancers do? Doesn't such a spectacle have just as much right as the competitive events to belong to the Olympic festival? Don't the magnificently relaxed movements of competitive events such as the hurdle races and the crawl cry out imperiously for their counterpart in the floating, swift-changing dance? I am inclined to think that both the gymnastic systems and the music and dance of Asia will raise a demand to be incorporated in a genuinely world-wide Olympic Games programme, and that we will derive the same enrichment from them as Goethe did from the songs of Hafts, and Nietzsche from his vision of Zarathustra. From such an Asian contribution we may recover the sense of measure, which is the secret enduring strength of the Olympic story. (Diem 1957b, 1970: 101)

In similar vein, he argued in relation to the cultural displays and exhibitions taking place during the Olympic Games,

Another enrichment is more to the point. The Olympic rules authorise the organiser to invite participating countries to give an exhibition of their native forms of physical education. This was done with complete success in Berlin in 1936. Each light-athletics day ended with a big physical education display, and the smaller teams, which could not be included in the arena, performed before a more restricted public. In 1948 there was a Swedish exhibition and in 1952 a Danish. Since then no further use has been made of this right. But the persistent and perhaps even increasing strength of the desire for deeper methodical study of these matters is shown by the congresses, which take place concurrently with the Games. As new nations flock to join us – many of them, such as the Asiatic nations, having an age-old physical culture – these displays would ensure the preservation of traditional values by the Olympic festival. (Diem 1960, 1970: 106–7)

As discussed earlier, displays of the 'Other', people from exotic foreign cultures, had been popular in the international expos and mega-events such as the Olympics in nineteenth and early twentieth century (Roche 2000). However, even by the early twenty-first century the perception that indigenous sport cultures should only be part of the Olympic Games as peripheral and historically preserved forms of physical culture had not disappeared. Diem argued that Japan for instance 'has a deeply rooted culture preserved through centuries. If its gymnastics and dances were presented in an artistic form they would lend a unique content to such a pageant' (Diem 1960, 1970: 108).

> The Olympic programme must be confined to its essentials and again incorporate all our spiritual and cultural values, weaving them with an artist's hand into a tapestry of man's higher nature, yet remaining within the bounds of our capacity for enjoyment. The tranquillity, the philosophy and the greater nearness to nature of the East must also help to guide the Olympic advance. They cannot fail to make their contribution if the Olympic idea does not merely touch the surface of things and rank as a recurrent tourist adventure, but penetrates more deeply into the thought and the sense of reverence of reflecting men. *Let us therefore hope that the Melbourne Olympic Games and the awaited contribution of Asia to Olympic culture may bear within them the promise of that all-round universal humanism which the Olympic Games as a world festival are capable of attaining.* (Diem 1957b, 1970: 101; emphasis added)

For the critics of the Olympic movement, the so-called 'universal humanism' serves as a smokescreen for western cultural hegemony, which promotes a single sport culture based on the western model of modern sport. The inclusion of indigenous sport forms rather than the exhibition of 'cultural curiosities' would be required to promote what might be regarded as an inter-cultural event.

Evidence of Eurocentrism

Notwithstanding the limits of cultural engagement fostered by Diem, in a number of his writings he sought to promote a 'universal', global sport culture.

> A general physical culture is now recognised throughout the world as indispensable ... the previous systems, Swedish, German, Indian etc.

have blended with one another. Today there is something like a combined selection or 'world system' ... the discoveries of sporting technique have become common property from Alaska to the Fiji islands, from Los Angeles to Rome and Tokyo. (Diem 1957a, 1970: 95–6)

The spread and practice of modern sport in different parts of the world was presented as evidence that the Olympic movement had become universal, but this was a universalisation of western sporting practices.

The development of sporting technique is so universal nowadays that even the new sporting nations can produce top performances, as they have already shown. The great positive feature of the festival was the demonstration of the faith of these new nations in it. The five rings have really become intertwined. Talented sportsmen of every race had come together from every continent, and nothing marred the fellowship, which reigned among them, the sympathy springing from common ideals. (Diem 1960, 1970: 106)

Nevertheless, though perhaps more subtle, Diem's perception of 'world culture' as expressed in his later writings, as with Coubertin, derived from a Eurocentric conception of modernity.

The modern Olympic Games pit the nations-states against one another. In this respect they do not differ so very much from the ancient Games, in which the rivals were the city-states – originally those of Greek extraction, but later those lying within the Greek cultural orbit; *thus the ancient Games embraced the Mediterranean peoples in touch with the then world-culture of Greece just as fully as the modern Games embrace the peoples now in touch with the world-culture-of-the West. The ancient Games were a manifestation of classical culture, just as the modern Games are a manifestation of the western, European culture which now dominates the world, and of which sport has recently become one of the most notable carriers. In both instances the Games have been not merely expressions of the culture in question but its creative agents.* They are a historic force; their contribution to human progress has a unique weight. (Diem 1933b, 1970: 6; emphasis added)

Diem's Eurocentric point of view is also evident below in his references to the origins of the modern Olympic Games,

The Olympic Games bred a spiritual force which made them the focal point of ancient culture and the bond which united firstly the Greek peoples and later the whole Mediterranean. *Thus they became part of the foundations of that western culture out of which modern sport has blossomed.* These foundations are being continually studied and widened today in the world's universities, and especially in those faculties and colleges of education, which point the way of education through the body. (Diem 1961a: 114; emphasis added)

As we have seen, for Coubertin, Hellenism harks back to the origins of Europe, representing a binding power for Europe's unity and authority (Bowen 1989). This is a view which, as Dussel and Fornazzari (2002) argue, is also linked to a Eurocentric conception of modernity. Thus, Diem, by drawing parallels between Hellenic hegemony during classical antiquity and western, European hegemony of modern times, reinforces the notion of the dominance of western culture in the Olympic movement. Nevertheless he did welcome consideration of the inclusion of new elements in the Olympic programme.

Now that these new nations are entering the Games we must not be content merely to teach them modern forms of sport, but we must consider which of their traditional recreations are appropriate to a complete Olympic programme. This is discussed in the official report for 1956. The task still lies ahead and offers extremely interesting comparisons. But one decision has been taken. By resolution of the International Olympic Committee at Rome, 1960, judo is to be included in the list of Olympic sports. (Diem 1960, 1970: 106)

The post-Second World period witnessed the end of the colonial system and the emergence of newly independent states from the former colonial areas of Asia and Africa. As part of the East-West conflict of interests and quest for power, the West sought to gain control over the newly independent Asian and African states, developing a form of neo-imperialism. In the Olympic movement, the opposition of the African states to South Africa's participation portrayed both actually and symbolically the rift between 'core' and 'periphery' and anti-colonial resistance by the 'periphery' (Espy 1979). It was seen as important for the Olympic movement to incorporate the newly independent states into a western Olympic system, before the new states challenged the authority of the IOC through the organisation of their own movements (Al-Tauqi 2003).

In this context, Diem, in paternalist style, emphasised that the Olympic movement should ensure that the new nations would be 'taught' the principles of modern sport. In addition, referring to indigenous local sport cultures as 'traditional recreations', he advised that *the IOC* should decide which of these traditions should finally be incorporated in the Olympic programme (albeit initially arguing that this should be in the margins rather than in the full competitive programme). He also emphasised in relation to the participation of the newly independent nations in the 1956 Melbourne

Olympic Games, 'this was their first experience of the Olympic community, and possibly too of western ways of life. This will have given their youth many new ideas for the future ...' (Diem 1957b, 1970: 99). These kinds of paternalist references within the Olympic movement contributed to pressure for some regional autonomy and resulted in the organisation of the Regional Games.[7] Of these the Games of the New Emerging Forces (GANEFO) represented a real threat to the Olympic movement since these Games had been set up in direct and explicit challenge to the hegemony of the IOC (Luton and Fan 2007; Sie 1978). Interestingly, Diem's paternalistic references in the era of neo-colonialism resemble, to a certain degree, the paternalism of Coubertin in the era of late colonialism. In both cases, the threat, and then the emergence, of opposition played the role of a 'trigger' for the adoption of a more democratic IOC policy.

4.4.2   The International Olympic Academy

Diem had long proposed the establishment of pedagogical centre of Olympism, where young people from around the world would be taught the Olympic values. On a national level, he had been involved with the establishment of the *Haus des Deutschen Sports* in Germany, a major centre for research in physical education and recreation equipped with swimming pools, gymnasiums and classrooms. Moreover, in response to Coubertin's aspiration for the foundation of a Centre for Olympic Studies, he proposed and successfully established, with the cooperation of the Third Reich, the International Olympic Institute in Berlin. However, one of his most ambitious plans involved the continuation of the archaeological excavations in the ancient sites of Olympia. As discussed in the previous chapter, Philhellenism had been a strong intellectual trend in Europe in the eighteenth and nineteenth centuries. In Germany too there was admiration of the ancient Greek models of art, literature, philosophy and science, while many German intellectuals and scholars (such as Johann Joachim Winckelmann, Friedrich Nietzsche, and Ernst Curtius) were inspired by ancient Greek classicism.

The first excavations in Olympia took place in 1829, but in 1875 they became more systematic under the supervision of Ernst Curtius, a German archaeologist and a Philhellene. After six years of continuous works, many temples and artefacts, coins and inscriptions had been unearthed. One of Diem's dreams was to recommence these excavations, abandoned by the Germans in 1881 (Mandell 1971). The Nazis, and Hitler in particular, with his vision of 'the Thousand Year Reich' in part inspired by the thousand years of the sacred ancient Olympic games, supported Diem's plans (Roche 2000). Diem encouraged and convinced the National Socialists to continue the excavations in ancient Olympia, which the Bismarckian Reich had abandoned. Hitler had issued a proclamation in relation to their decision to recommence the excavations,

The philosophical foundations for presenting the revived Olympic Games to the world are of hallowed antiquity. These spiritual forces come out of a sacred city, which for more than a thousand years was the site of festivals expressing the religious feelings and the basic convictions of the Greek Volk. As an enduring monument to the celebration of the XIth Olympiad in Berlin, I have decided to recommence and to see to a conclusion the excavations at Olympia. That these projects will succeed is my and our sincerest wish. (cited in Mandell 1971: 284)

The new excavations started in 1935 and took place until late 1941 when they were interrupted by the war. They were recommenced in 1952 – again at Diem's initiative – and were finally completed in 1961 (Mandell 1971). Diem, from the moment the excavations recommenced, considered the ancient site of Olympia to be the most appropriate place at which to locate the international pedagogical centre of Olympism, the *International Olympic Academy* (IOA), which was finally inaugurated in 1961. In an article published in 1942 (but written in 1939) in the journal *Olympische Flamme*, he had stated,

Soon we shall be able to race and throw the javelin again in the ancient Stadium of Olympia, and – as was agreed during our stay in Olympia and Athens – young Germans and Greeks will celebrate the reawakening of the venerable monument by games in the sacred precinct. Thereafter the stadium will be used only on special occasions and with fitting restraint. But every year the 'Olympic Academy' will meet there, a hundred young students from the whole world, each one chosen and sent by his nation for this high purpose, and will work together for two months under the leadership of teachers who will also be drawn from expert circles in all nations. (Diem 1942e: 113)

Carl Diem, on behalf of the International Olympic Institute in Berlin, had suggested to the Hellenic Olympic Committee (HOC) in 1938 that an Olympic Academy should be founded in Greece. From this point, John Ketseas, Secretary General of the HOC, and Carl Diem became close collaborators in the project to establish the academy. The two men knew each other well from their previous work together in the realisation of the torch relay for the 1936 Berlin Olympics. Moreover, Ketseas and Coubertin, during the latter's 1927 visit to Olympia, had already started discussions about the organisation of a permanent annual sport festival at the site of Olympia (Lucas 1980). At the IOC meeting in Stockholm (19 June 1947), the HOC submitted for the first time the official plan for this *Centre d'Etudes Olympiques* which the President, Brundage, found 'very interesting' (Diem 1961a: 115). In January 1949, Ketseas, with Diem's assistance, submitted a memorandum to the IOC proposing that an Academy should be established in Greece under IOC patronage. On 28th April 1949 the IOC unanimously accepted the Greek proposal but the lack of response from the National Olympic Committees in the difficult post-war period delayed even more the realisation of the project (only four accepted the invitation). It took more than ten years for the HOC to issue formal invitations again and for the academy to be formally inaugurated (Diem 1961a). Diem emphasised that the establishment of the academy also fulfilled Coubertin's dreams for the operation of a pedagogical centre of Olympism.

> We can say simply that the 'Olympic Academy' which is to arise here will be on the one hand a continuation of the old academy – an 'Elis' of our times – and on the other hand the fulfilment of Coubertin's plans to put Olympism on a scholarly basis. (Diem 1961a: 113)

Diem, like Coubertin, considered that the Olympic values bound up with the values of Hellenism, should be taught to the youth of the world, and in particular that an Academy should be located on or adjacent to the ancient Olympic site.

> They will be initiated into classical culture and the idea of the kaloka-gathia, and of course into the question of the possible and desirable function of the Olympic Idea in our time. The sports world is enthusiastic, more or less, and a few able scholars in various countries are willing to take part. I am still wrestling with the Greeks in an attempt to persuade them not to put up an Olympic palace but to adopt my idea of letting participants in the Academy live in tents during the static study period, and spend the rest of the time an (sic) study tours, finishing in Athens, where modest accommodation is still available in the old Panathenaic Stadium. The whole project can only succeed if we find our way back to modesty. (Diem, 1957c, 1970: 111)

Diem emphasised that the students of the academy should be moulded through the Spartan model of life.

> They [the students] will live together in tents like the sportsmen of old, and enjoy the simple communal fare of Sparta ... They will gain living experience of harmony resulting from lofty physical, mental and artistic discipline, which will be of value later in their social tasks. This annual course will bring together sports teachers, artists and young scientists, who will train together in the ancient stadium. Here is the dawn of a hope for the solution of the problem of 'Europe' with which we are now grappling. (Diem 1942e: 113)

Several years later (1957), he insisted,

> If anything modern is to come into existence there, then it will not be an art collection; and if I can prevent it, [it will] not [be] a building

either, but an 'Olympic Academy', to which an international group of specially gifted students will be invited annually. (Diem 1957c, 1970: 111)

He argued that the ascetic mode of life should prevail in the academy, reflecting an anti-modernist attitude.

> We have never considered having an Academy building, least of all in Olympia. The idea is that the students shall as far as possible lead a simple life in tents, as did the Olympic athletes of old. Any 'cosseting' would destroy the educational virtue of the Academy. The spirit of simplicity, which characterised the ancient Games, should continue to pervade the Academy today. Participation is a challenge to the resilience of youth; the Spartan mode of life will be an additional attraction to those we wish to attract, and a discouragement to those who are unsuitable. *The fact that we sleep in tents, wake by the stream and eat under the open sky is part of our Hellenic heritage!* Sportsmen accept the convenience of modern comforts, but are high-minded enough ('megalopsychia', the Greeks called this virtue) to give them up when the word 'Olympic' is heard. If they did not do so the victors of old would jeer at us from their graves ... (Diem 1961a: 116; emphasis added)

The Hellenic connections and resonance for choosing Olympia as the venue of the academy were apparent in Diem's writings.

> They [the students] will revel in the contemplation and study of the noblest artistic treasures, which are housed in Olympia – those already found today, and those, which are confidently awaited. They will enjoy the treasures of the spirit, for which old Hellas was a focal point – the focal point whence western culture was created. (Diem 1942e: 113)

As discussed in the previous chapter, historical Greece and the later cultivation of Greece as a reference point for subsequent philosophy, art and literature in eighteenth and nineteenth century incorporated two different accounts of Hellenism (Dussel and Fornazzari 2002). The narrow confines of western tradition, especially after the discoveries at Pompeii and Herculaneum, recognised in the name of Greece a tradition to define its political existence and modernity (Ferris 2000). This does not mean that the contemporary Greece did not wish to define its own identity in the legacy referred to as 'western tradition'. Thus, the establishment of the IOA in the Hellenistic site of Olympia, on the premises of a constructed ideology of Hellenism, was a promising project for both the Germans and the Greeks. On the one hand, the Greeks would pursue the recognition of a modern identity located in the western tradition that used Hellenism as a cultural and political source for defining its ideology.

On the other hand, the Germans, through the establishment of the academy and the archaeological excavations at the ancient site of Olympia, would continue the legacy of the German intellectuals such as Winckelmann and Goethe, who through their Hellenist interpretations, developed Germany's aesthetic and intellectual production following the example of Greece, elevated as it was to the 'highest example' of western culture (Ferris 2000). Mandell has argued,

> As had been the case with German artists and philosophers since the Enlightenment, since the days of Winckelmann and Goethe, Diem would attempt to legitimise, glorify and sanctify young Germany by establishing her kinship with a fairyland of long ago. This great scholar in Nazi Germany sought to further his own and his nation's ambitions by increasing the world's knowledge of Greek antiquity. (Mandell 1974: 284–5)

Interestingly, the following quotation from Diem, in an article published in *Olympisches Feuer* in 1957, suggests that his enthusiasm for the project of the archaeological excavations was derived to a great extent from his patriotic plans to legitimise Germany, especially in the post-Nazi, post-Second World period.

> It has long since become clear to all who have eyes to see, that our German nation can never again be a world power in the political field. *After our recent historical experiences this is certainly no cause for regret. But in exchange we have a great opportunity to play a leading part in the intellectual and cultural field among the peoples of this restless and peril-ridden earth. If we direct our energies to this end we shall at the same time be linking up with the finest achievements of our past. This, to be sure, is not a 'Programme', which can be dictated and obediently carried out; it calls for the holy zeal of a missionary. Our future depends upon whether we can still find the strength for such a mission. Olympia can be one touchstone. The money spent there will not be without fruit as regards Germany's reputation in the world, and above all it will influence the outlook of coming generations.* What would sport be today without the Olympic Games? What will it be tomorrow if these Games do not keep their quality? What will be the use of building gymnasia in Germany if we cannot preserve the Olympic spirit? 'The things which are truly great lift us above ourselves!' (Goethe I Wilhelm Meister) (Diem 1957d, 1970: 109–10; emphasis added)

Diem, in the name of Olympia, found an opportunity for supporting Germany's regeneration following the intellectual and cultural patterns of Hellenism, which had also been used as a key source by the German Romantics during the Enlightenment. Diem sought to reinstate Germany's reputation in the world, bridging its 'glorious' past with a promising future, just as the unearthed site of Olympia 'constituted a bridge spanning the centuries, a living bond between Olympia of yesterday and today – a call to further deeds' (Diem 1961b: 119). All the same, this should not diminish the significance of Diem's efforts to put into practice his Olympic idealism through the establishment of a pedagogical centre for the dissemination of Olympic values. Nonetheless, it provides further evidence that Diem's Olympic internationalism, even towards the end of his life, was intertwined with a concern for a German nationalist agenda.

4.5 Conclusions

Carl Diem, to this day, continues to be a controversial figure. While Maurice Roche (2000: 120) describes him unequivocally as an active collaborator with the Nazi regime, and Hoberman, 1986 draws similar conclusions, Mandell for example argues that he was part victim, part collaborator.

> Dr. Carl Diem, [was] a good German who had all the qualifications to be ranked as a spiritual hero of sport, ... [who] became unbalanced by his own theatrical constructions. Since he became for while a bad German or at least a co-operator with the worst Germans, he had to be considered part villain, part victim *of the* Nazi Olympics. (Mandell 1971: 291)

The nature of his contribution to Olympic discourse is one which manifested a tension between nationalism and internationalism, throughout his career. Even though his writings in the post-Second World War era were significantly more internationalist, Diem never dealt satisfactorily with criticisms relating to his role as a sports administrator in support of the Nazi regime. His strategy post-war in relation to such matters seems to have been not to apologise or acknowledge guilt at whatever level. The adoption of a relatively silent position is however not a neutral one and the issue of his role and his notion of Olympic ideals is one which continues to provoke controversy.

Diem's rehabilitation was perhaps facilitated by the presence at the head of the IOC of another controversial figure, Avery Brundage, whose sympathies in matters ideological tended towards deep conservatism, and whose recommendation following a visit to Germany before the 1936 Games was to accept the German claim that Jewish German athletes had every opportunity to participate in the Berlin Games, thus averting an American boycott. Diem, in promoting links with the Hellenic ideals of the Ancient Games, seems to have been able in the post-war period, to tap into a rich conservative vein of classical idealism.

Our review of the discourses of Olympism for the later twentieth century now turns to the International Olympic Academy and its invited speakers over four decades. This, as we shall see, manifests a grudging, at first, but growing pluralism. This pluralism is not simply the result of reviewing plural rather than a single speaker, since in the early stages of the IOA speakers reflected a shared orthodoxy. The (limited) opening up to alternative views which occurs in the last decade or so of the century is in part the need of a global movement to adjust to radical and swift moving political, economic, and cultural change.

5

From Bipolar to Multipolar International Relations: Olympism and the Speakers at the International Olympic Academy in the Cold War and Post-Cold War Era

5.1 Introduction

When, after his death and burial in Lausanne in 1937, Coubertin's heart was transferred to be interred in Olympia in March 1938, Carl Diem suggested to John Ketseas the idea of founding an Olympic Academy, which would function as a permanent 'University of Olympism'. The IOC took over the 'overall control of this institution in the service of the Olympic ideal' in June 1939 (IOC archives; cited in Müller 1998: 12). From late 1939, however, the Second World War brought to a halt much of the Olympic movement, and indeed threatened its future. However, Diem, as early as December 1945, began campaigning again for the establishment of an IOA. After Ketseas was elected as an IOC member in 1946, the idea of founding an Olympic academy received more attention in the IOC Sessions. The prospect of building an academy in Greece, which would function as an institution for the spread of the Olympic values, was discussed at the 40th IOC Session in Stockholm in 1947, and at the 1948 IOC Session in London. Finally, the IOC gave its unanimous support in a vote on the Greek proposal at its session in Rome in 1949, though the Academy was only to be officially inaugurated twelve years later because of delays associated with the archaeological excavations in ancient Olympia (Müller 1998). The academy was officially inaugurated on June 14, 1961, a date scheduled to coincide with the official opening of the unearthed archaeological site in Olympia and the 59th IOC Session in Athens. The Hellenic Olympic Committee sanctioned a provisional set of statutes on October 2, 1961, and on January 1962 they elected an Ephoria as the long-term executive body of the International Olympic Academy (IOA) under the presidency of John Ketseas (Müller 1998). The IOA is administered by members of the Hellenic Olympic Committee, but it is also placed under the patronage of the IOC. Ever since its formal inauguration in 1961, the IOA has played a central role in the IOC's promotion of Olympism and the dissemination of its ideals by organising regular sessions for students, athletes, sport administrators, sport journalists, and scholars from around the world at its permanent facilities in Olympia of Greece.

> The aim of the International Olympic Academy is to create an international cultural centre in Olympia, to preserve and spread the Olympic Spirit, study and implement the educational and social principles of Olympism and consolidate the scientific basis of the Olympic Ideal, in conformity with the principles laid down by the ancient Greeks and the revivers of the contemporary Olympic movement, through Baron de Coubertin's initiative. (International Olympic Academy 2011)

The establishment of the IOA contributed to a great extent to a remarkable growth in the educational programmes conducted within the Olympic movement (Kidd 1996). The mission and aims of the IOA are defined in the following manner: to function as an International Academic Centre for Olympic Studies, Education and Research; to act as an International Forum for free expression and exchange of ideas among the Olympic family, intellectuals, scientists, athletes, sport administrators, educators, artists and the youth of the world; to bring together people from all over the world, in a spirit of friendship and cooperation; to motivate people to use the experiences and knowledge gained in the IOA productively, in promoting the Olympic Ideals in their respective countries; to serve and promote the Ideals and principles of the Olympic movement; to cooperate with and assist the National Olympic Academies and any other institutions devoted to Olympic Education; to further explore and enhance the contribution of Olympism to humanity. All this is to be undertaken in conformity with the principles laid down by the ancient Greeks and the revivers of the contemporary Olympic movement, through Baron de Coubertin's initiative (International Olympic Academy 2011).

An 'IOC Commission for the International Olympic Academy' was established in 1968 and its role was to follow the activities of the IOA, to contribute to their success, to receive the periodic reports of the sessions and to keep the IOC informed of the results obtained (Landry and Yerles 1994). Since 1980, representatives of the athletes, members of the NOCs and of the IFs have been appointed to the commission. In 1993, the IOC broadened the sphere of this commission changing its name to the 'Commission for the International Olympic Academy and Olympic Education', implying that more education-related projects would be taken over (Landry and Yerles 1994). With the IOC reform of 2000, the Commission changed its name to the 'Commission for Education and Culture', broadening even more its scope by including culture and expanding its activities beyond a single educational institute (published by the IOC in 2000). Olympic Solidarity also provides funds (gained from the IOC television rights profits) to the NOCs in order to send athletes, coaches, officials, teachers, journalists, artists and graduate students from all over the world to the IOA sessions (Kidd 1996).

In 1969 the IOA opened to meetings of other international sport organisations, resulting in a significant increase in the number of meetings, seminars and congresses that were held in Olympia. From 1962 to the end of the century the total number of participants at the annual sessions for young participants had exceeded 10,000. In addition more than 500 national and international meetings, seminars and congresses took place in Olympia with almost 50,000 participants. As an outcome of the annual sessions, former IOA participants have taken the initiative of establishing national Olympic academies in their own countries, and this has been facilitated by the decision of the Executive Board of the IOC in 1984 to establish an assistance programme for the founding of National Olympic Academies (NOA). Both Commissions (of Education and Culture, of Olympic Solidarity) as well as the International Olympic Academy encourage NOCs to establish their own National Olympic Academies (Kidd 1996). In 1992, the 1st Joint International Session for Directors of NOAs, members and staff of NOCs and IFs was held. Up until 1990, separate Sessions were held for Educators and for Directors and Heads of Higher Institutes of Physical Education, but from 1993, the Sessions have been held jointly. In 1993, another innovation was the establishment of an annual Postgraduate Seminar on Olympic Studies for post-graduate (largely doctoral) students interested in extending their knowledge in the diverse fields of the Olympic movement. Other educational programmes include the sessions for Sport Journalists (initiated in 1986), for Olympic Medallists (from 2007), and the establishing in 2010 of a Master's degree in 'Olympic Studies, Olympic Education, Organisation and Management of Olympic Events' in collaboration with the University of the Peloponnese in Greece (one of the only two masters degrees on Olympic Studies worldwide[1]).

Undoubtedly, the staging by the Academy of this number and variety of sessions, seminars and congresses for over five decades, has established it as a key centre for the exchange of ideas and discussions about major issues in relation to Olympism, the Olympic movement and international sport in general. Moreover, its long-term presence in the service of the Olympic movement has also made the IOA an important source of ideological construction in the sense of consciously seeking to shape debate on the moral dimensions of the Olympic movement and what is claimed to be its core philosophy.

Our concern in this chapter is not to identify particular actors' discourse of Olympism over time, nor even necessarily to capture a single dominant discourse emanating from the IOA. Rather our concern is to identify an indicative range of discourse themes on Olympism as reflected over time in the speeches delivered at this central vehicle for the discussion and promulgation of Olympic values. Thus such an approach allows us to: a) identify multiple ideological constructions of Olympism and examine different interpretations of its moral agenda, and b) identify the issues that have concerned the Olympic community across the span of four decades. Moreover, by examining the major issues that have been raised within the Olympic community, we aim not only to specify and analyse the issues that the lecturers or visiting speakers at the IOA have explicitly considered as key in the domain of the Olympic movement, but also to identify any latent issues that might be understated or absent in such discussions.

It is important to note in relation to this latter point that the speakers at the IOA are selected and invited by the *Ephoria* or Board, and as such are likely to be those most sympathetic to the Ephoria's interpretation of Olympism. As we shall see the IOA as an institution exhibits greater confidence in accommodating critical voices as it matures as an institution but it should be acknowledged there are still those whose critical views make them unlikely to be given a platform in the IOA.

The five decades of the Olympic Academy's history also incorporate some significant events in the development of the Olympic movement. The first three decades were over-shadowed by the Cold War and the struggle for power between the Eastern Bloc and the West. With the demise of communist systems, and the increasing commercialism with growing television rights, the Olympic Partner (TOP) sponsorship programme and the acceptance of professional athletes, a new era was initiated for the Olympic movement which experienced radical change. The chapter is divided into two periods, during and after the Cold War. The first section deals with changes relating to issues such as the involvement of politics in the Olympic movement, amateurism, the rise of commercialism and the shift to professionalism, women's participation, and doping. The second section deals with the period up to the end of the twentieth century and the changes relating to the increase of the power of the West after the fall of the Eastern Bloc, such as the general shift from socialist to liberal polities and economies, and the impact on local sport cultures, while it also highlights the emergence of new concerns such as the issue of environmentalism. (Issues emerging in the first twelve years of the new century are dealt with in the final chapter.)

5.2   The IOA during the Cold War (1961–1989)

The survival of the Olympic movement was threatened on a number of occasions during the years of the Cold War. The formative years of the post-war Olympics were also the formative years of the post-war geopolitical system. The process of decolonisation in Africa and Asia which took place largely in the 1960s and 1970s produced new patterns and established new relationships in international relations (Espy 1979). With regard to the process of the expression of values associated with the Olympic ideology, the Olympic movement during the years of the Cold War witnessed significant changes, as evidenced in the selected sample of IOA lectures against the geopolitical and socio-cultural context of the period. These include: a) the shift from a movement characterising itself as 'non-political' to one which increasingly embraced involvement in world politics and recognised the need for developing its own 'political' programme; b) the shift from amateurism to professionalism and the rise of commercialism; c) the growing technological sophistication of athletic preparation including drug abuse by athletes from communist states and western states, and in the case of some communist regimes, organised by the nation-state itself; and d) the formal admission of female members into the IOC and the rising challenge to male hegemony. Each of these issues is dealt with in turn below.

5.2.1   Politics and the Olympic Games

In contrast to other major international sport organisations, such as FIFA, which though ostensibly not for profit organisations nevertheless generate considerable profits in certain areas of activity, the IOC undertakes to redistribute its profits largely through the Olympic Solidarity Programme to NOCs and IFs and in this respect the IOC is seen as seeking to manifest its commitment to world fraternity and goodwill (Houlihan 1994). The Olympic Games has been defined by the IOC as the terrain where the values included in the Olympic Charter are put into practice. It could be argued that IOC Presidents have always defined the purpose of the Olympic movement in political terms, highlighting the contribution of the Games to world peace, brotherhood and equality. Moreover, the Olympic Charter includes statements of a political nature, which extend far beyond the realm of competitive sport: 'Olympism is a philosophy of life' ... 'The goal of the Olympic movement is to contribute to building a peaceful and better world by educating youth through sport practised in accordance with Olympism and its values' (International Olympic Committee 2010b: 13). Commentators such as Kanin (1981) have emphasised that, 'the Olympic Games were founded with expressly political goals in mind and have thrived on ties to global affairs' (Houlihan 1994: 111).

Nevertheless, although the Olympic movement has invariably promoted an international political agenda, it has traditionally also sought to claim that the movement and the Games must be above politics. Since the years of Coubertin's leadership in the IOC, the members of the committee were characterised as the representatives of the IOC in their respective countries and not as representatives of their respective countries in the IOC. In this way, Coubertin wanted to safeguard the Olympic movement from attachment to political and national interests. Avery Brundage, who succeeded Sigrid Edström to the IOC presidency, and was also known for his strong advocacy against the involvement of politics in the Olympic movement, argued in 1963, in a speech written for the Third Summer Session of the IOA[2]:

> To administer a project of this kind is not a simple task. As it was in the beginning, there are always difficult problems. The natural rivalry of

sport or of nations, with some being stronger and perhaps more important than others, if not restrained, might well have wrecked the Games on many occasions. The solution was found in the International Olympic Committee, composed of individuals who do not represent any country or any sport but do represent, impartially and impersonally, the Olympic movement and only the Olympic movement. This Committee is self-perpetuating and chooses its own members. It was first appointed by the Baron de Coubertin, who charged it to en-force Olympic regulations and to preserve the pure amateur spirit of the Games, free from commercial encroachment, which would soon lead to disapproval, or from political intrusion which would quite obviously be disastrous. (Brundage 1963: 30–5)

...

Amateur sport has become an important part of modern life with millions of followers. Realizing this importance, some misguided persons seem to think that Olympic sport can be made a political tool. This is as erroneous as anything can be. The minute political activities are permitted in Olympic affairs the Games are finished. Never has the world been so peaceful that countries or political systems were not somewhere at odds. If not a hot, there has always been a cold war of one sort or another – sometimes religious, sometimes racial, sometimes political, and the minute distinctions of this kind are permitted, it is quite obvious that the Games will soon come to an end. As it is, the Olympic movement furnishes a conspicuous example that when fair play and good sportsmanship prevail, men can agree, regardless of race, religion or political convictions. (Brundage 1963: 38)

Nevertheless, in the process of recognising the USSR Olympic Committee, Brundage, as an IOC member, had pointed out his reluctance to affiliate the USSR into international federations.

My own guess is that the real object of the Russians is to humiliate the West ... every time they force a Federation to break down its own rules in order to let them compete, Russian prestige is increased and western prestige decreased. The trouble at the moment ... is that about half of the countries don't want to annoy Russia, and any country, which is anxious to obtain a world championship, or world congress is reluctant to annoy the Eastern bloc. (Quoted by Espy 1979: 28)

In addition, as part of the negotiations between the USSR and the IOC, Brundage demanded, as a condition for the Soviet Union to be admitted to the IOC, that his friend and fellow IOC member Karl von Halt (Hitler's *last Reichssportführer*, 1942–5 who was alleged by the US government to have been a war criminal) should be released from a Soviet camp where he had been kept from 1945 to 1949 (Krüger 1999). Moreover, with regard to the recognition of the German Democratic Republic (GDR, East Germany) and the negotiations for the composition of an all-German team in 1956, Hoberman (1986: 54–5) argues that Brundage demonstrated political eccentricity and naivety, portraying himself as the 'Great Reconciler', when in reality he lacked the sophistication required to successfully defend Olympic interests and to handle the contradiction between the anti-communist feelings of the majority of the IOC and their interest in communist sporting achievements.

In similar vein, Ritter, President of the Olympic Committee of Liechtenstein and guest lecturer at the 1978 IOA Session, continued to maintain that sport and politics should be kept separate,

> The Olympic movement has become worldwide. Nations are participating; nations are competing, nations with different political and philosophical aims and structures. Olympia has sometimes become a battleground, even between races. There are, no doubt, positive aspects to the fact that athletes and teams represent their nation. *But one must remember that sport must not offer an alternative for politics. Therefore, political and national interests, other than the representation of the sports movement in the home country, must be put aside, outside the Olympic Games and movement. Political and racial as well as religious problems contradict the aims of the Olympic movement and have to be banned or at least neutralised.* (Ritter 1978: 179–80; emphasis added)

However such a position ignores the fact that the Olympic movement and Games had always been attractive to governmental and non-governmental political interests, and especially during the Cold War, the degree of involvement of political interests in the movement had grown considerably. The increasing tension between the capitalist West and the Eastern blocs was reflected in the concerns of the IOC about which of the newly emerging nations should be invited to the Olympic Games (Guttmann 1992). In 1948, the IOC members received the first draft of a new IOC Charter which had incorporated alterations related to fundamental principles, the statutes of the IOC, the regulations and protocols of the Olympic Games and the general rules of the celebration of the Games. One of the most important decisions taken by the IOC in this period, influencing to a great extent the Olympic movement, and reflecting the changing geopolitical map of the world, concerned the recognition of the NOCs. The new conditions required the NOCs to be formed by independent states (not colonies) and to be autonomous (free from government influence). This caused many problems in the Olympic movement, especially with the recognition of the NOCs from East Germany and Taiwan, resulting in what became known as the problem of the 'two Germanys' and the 'two Chinas'. However, to a degree it also helped the IOC to gain power and become a more influential organisation in world politics, in that it could legitimate the political claims of one side or another in these political disputes, by offering recognition of their 'national' Olympic committees (and thus acknowledging their status as nation states).

Moreover, the participation of the Soviet Union in the Olympic movement was one of the many issues that the IOC had to consider in the post-war period. The IOC President Edström, in an effort to merge the ideologically opposed sport movements, fostered communication with the USSR in order to draw it into the world of 'bourgeois' sport (Krüger 1999). In effect, the IOC found it hard to ignore pressure for Soviet membership since the USSR had emerged from the Second World War as one of the strongest powers in Europe, and it was clear that the IOC leadership wanted to integrate the powerful nations into their organisation, if only to legitimate its claims to be *the* global sporting authority. The USSR, after extended negotiations with the IOC, in which the latter gave in to virtually all of her demands, was admitted to the Olympic movement and participated in the Helsinki Games (1952). However, there were two separate Olympic villages, one for the Eastern bloc and one for athletes of the West, to avoid any potential confrontations (Krüger 1999; Toohey and Veal 2000). The ideological tension was also apparent in granting visas and flag displays. The US and its NATO allies, for instance, between 1957 and 1967 denied visas on 35 times to some communist countries and western officials refused permission for Eastern Germany (GDR) to display its flag and emblem (Riordan 1999). The IOC, however, in its acceptance of the Soviets, had clearly opted to support its universalistic principle (that all countries should participate) over a fundamental principle (that NOCs should be independent of the state).

In the light of this deep involvement of the Olympic movement in world politics, the Dean of the IOA at the time, Nissiotis still felt able to argue that, 'certainly, we cannot ignore the fact that Olympism is unavoidably linked with politics, but we should not allow the interference of international politics in Olympic affairs, as far as we are able' (Nissiotis 1984: 74). Nonetheless, Moltmann, a West German Professor at the University of Tübingen and guest lecturer at the IOA in 1980, maintained that,

> Many athletes and athletic organisations feel themselves to be the 'innocent victims' of the current political crisis, which makes their participation in the Olympic Games impossible. They are right: in sports there is a dimension of the experience of life and luck that has nothing to do with politics and is therefore alienated by political interests and considerations. *But on the other side we have to see that the contemporary Olympic idea was a political idea from the beginning. From the beginning the Olympic idea represented sports and games not for their own sakes but for the sake of other goals.* (Moltman 1980: 81; emphasis added)

Houlihan (1994: 113) shares the view that the Olympic Games and movement are inherently attractive to governmental and non-governmental political interests for a number of reasons. First, as discussed earlier, the successive IOC Presidents and statements in the Olympic Charter reflect the aspiration of the movement to political influence. Second, the structure of the Games offers an ideal terrain for expressions of national interests. Although, from the Coubertin years, it had always been emphasised that the Games are contests between individuals and not countries, the IOC has always perceived issues of participation in terms of eligibility of states rather than the eligibility of athletes (Espy 1979; cited in Houlihan 1994: 111) (see for example participation of Germany in 1936 and South Africa in 1960). Third, the Olympic Games, one of the mega-events of modernity, attract political interests because they have been culturally significant to such a great part of the world. Finally, the high level of publicity of the Games makes them an ideal place for the expression of political interests. The Frenchman Henri Pouret, laureate of the French Academy, reaffirmed in his speech at the IOA in 1970,

> Every time the Games are entrusted to a city, the whole Nation is concerned. The celebration of the Games becomes a political event. Eager to ensure national prestige, politicians have to clear out credits which lie heavily upon the budget of the Olympic city and of the Nation; it is noted then, that will of power leads to expenses which are, more or less, disputed by a part of public opinion because the gigantism of the organisation unfortunately tends to increase. Politicians, however, are anxious to enhance the glory of their country by ensuring perfect organisation and warm hospitality. Behind the celebration of the Games, there is always some very legitimate publicity and tourist activity, which goes on long after the end of the Games. Looking at the recent open competition for the organisation of the 1976 Games and what followed, we may conclude that Olympism is a matter of interest to the political power of several countries. There is, therefore, a very good argument in favour, not only of the organisation of the Games, but also of the Olympic ideal. (Pouret 1970: 104–5)

Nevertheless, the IOC has found it difficult until relatively recently to admit that international politics have a significant role to play in the Olympic Games. Despite the controversy over the Nazi Olympics, the IOC showed little caution or political awareness in selecting Tokyo to host the Games in 1940. Although it was known that Japan had developed an aggressive foreign policy, especially after its invasion of Manchuria in 1931, 'in the eyes of the committee, the peaceful diffusion of Olympism to Asian shores was far more important than the ruthless expansion of the Japanese empire' (Guttmann 1992: 73). With regard to the problem of the two Chinas, the IOC was criticised for its failure to recognise that sport was no longer divorced from politics, refusing to acknowledge a potentially explosive situation (Espy 1979). The IOC's 'non-political' policy was also criticised during the Olympic Games of 1956, when it failed to acknowledge the impact of the Hungarian and Suez crises in the conduct of the Games. Immediately after the Soviets invaded in Hungary, the Netherlands and Spain withdrew from the Games. The President of the Netherlands Olympic Committee criticised the IOC for claiming that the Olympic ideal should prevail over political matters, posing the question, 'How can sports prevail over what happened in Hungary? How would we like it if our people had been atrociously murdered, and someone said that sports should prevail?' (cited in Espy 1979: 54).

As Moltmann (1980) argues, the IOC could no longer dismiss the fact that the Olympic Games were political, and should move beyond this point by developing its own policy on avoidance of political manipulation, as evidenced in the boycotts and the use of the Games for political propaganda. In similar vein, Parry, a guest lecturer at the IOA and an Olympic scholar from the UK, argued eight years later,

> Even though Rule 9 of the Olympic Charter says that the Games are 'contests between individuals and teams and not between countries', and although representatives of the IOC have consistently argued that the Olympic movement is non-political, nevertheless sport has often been used as an instrument of national politics in the world arena. Does this make sport (or the Olympics) a bad thing? The media are often used as an instrument of politicians – does this make the media bad things (in themselves)? *Of course not – but the question is: what can sport do to minimise the effect of external factors? To what extent should it? Does it do enough? Should Olympism be 'neutral', or should it have its own political programme?* (Parry 1988: 85–6; emphasis added)

Ever since the exploitation of the 1936 Games by the Nazis, and the boycotts, the IOC had proved potentially vulnerable to political manipulation. As a consequence of this, the IOC recognised the need to develop the capacity to maintain its own policy objectives and pursue its own independent policy within the international sport community and world politics arena in general. Although the political dependence of many NOCs and IOC members on state governments can still cause political manipulation and thus a potential weakening of the Olympic movement, the IOC has gradually recognised the need to maximise freedom of action and authority in the world of international sport and politics. As the Russian, Stolyarov, emphasised in his speech at the IOA in 1995, 'all those to whom Olympism is dear, cannot, in particular, help thinking about the consequences for the Olympic movement of deep political reforms in the modern world, *and also about whether this movement can itself influence these processes and, if so, how*' (Stolyarov 1995: 76; emphasis added).

The willingness of the Olympic movement to engage in the political sphere has been increasingly evident since the 1990s, with initiatives such as the Olympic Truce, 'reintroduced' in 1992 as a modern equivalent to the ancient *Ekecheiria* or truce (which allowed free traffic of athletes and spectators travelling through hostile territories to attend the Ancient Games). The involvement of the IOC with the UN in developing Sport for Peace initiatives, and more broadly the IOC's involvement with sport for international development has grown considerably. Such pretensions are manifest in, for example, the 'International Inspiration' initiative developed by the UK as a consequence of promises made by Sebastian Coe during his speech to the 2005 IOC Meeting in Singapore at which he was presenting the London bid to host the 2012 Games.

5.2.2   The shift from amateurism to professionalism

The shift from amateurism to eligibility

The issue of amateurism has been subject to many debates in Olympic circles since the early years of the Olympic movement. Ever since the first discussions about the term 'amateur' at the 1st International Congress in Sorbonne (1894), which Coubertin had organised for the promotion of the revival of the Olympic Games, the definition of the term had been problematic. Coubertin (1896) was unsympathetic to professionalism in sport because 'men (sic) give up their whole existence to one particular sport, grow rich by practising it, and thus deprive it of all nobility, and destroy the just equilibrium of man by making the muscles predominant over the mind' (cited in Segrave and Chu 1981: 36). Similarly, Brundage was known for his rigid defence of amateur ideals. He argued in 1963 in a speech written for the Third Summer Session of the IOA,

> Amateur sport is recreation, an avocation and not a vocation, play and not work. To exist and flourish it must be free, without either political or commercial dictation. Professional sport, so-called, is no sport at all, but a branch of the entertainment business like the circus; it is for the spectators whereas amateur sport is for the players. A competitor who is paid is a workman and not a player. The professional takes from sport, while the amateur gives to sport. These are fundamental truths that must always be remembered. We must never forget that 'the most important thing in the Olympic Games is not to win but to take part, as the most important thing in life is not the triumph but the struggle. The essential thing is not to have conquered but to have fought well'. (Brundage 1963: 37)

The debate on amateurism rumbled on in the Cold War period, especially after the re-admission of the Soviets into the Olympic Games of 1952. Andrecs, Director of the Physical Education Department of the Ministry of Education and Arts in Austria, argued in frustration at the IOA Session in 1964,

> I have nothing but contempt for that Olympism which has created the star cult that has placed in the service of business the Olympic idea; that Olympism which enslaves people, in which brotherhood is found only on paper, which has degraded the Olympic Games to another front of

Cold War. I hate those oaths, which must be sworn in order to be able to participate for the sake of national prestige. I despise the games of the rich, the rich who can afford to be amateurs, or the athletes who are paid by the state. I tell you: That is not OLYMPIA! (Andrecs 1973: 188)

'State amateurism' had been a serious problem for the IOC during the Cold War, but it was not until 1962 that a more detailed statement on amateurism was finally approved at the 58th IOC Session.

An amateur is one who participates and always had participated in sport as an avocation without material gain of any kind. One does not qualify: if he has not a basic occupation designed to ensure his present and future livelihood; if he receives or has received remuneration for participation in sport; if he does not comply with the Rules of the International Federation concerned, and the official interpretations of this Rule number 26. (IOC Bulletin 1962; cited in Segrave and Chu 1981: 38)

Nevertheless, two years after the introduction of this new regulation the problem of state amateurism did not seem to have been resolved. Zijjl, an Olympic scholar from the Netherlands, argued in relation to this at the 1964 IOA Session,

If State amateurism is applied consistently and systematically by governments, one can no longer speak of an independent, national and amateur sports movement, by which is meant a sports movement clearly distinguished from undisguised professionalism. The State is interfering directly in the practice of sports to make it serve aims that have nothing to do with sports as such. If crack sportsmen are kept away from the official professional sports and are instead employed by the State, whether wholly or in part, conditions are created that are completely contrary to the idea that in the practice of sports the freedom of the sportsman or woman is the primary consideration. (Zijjl 1964: 217)

As the problems for the amateur code still remained, Lord Michael Killanin, Brundage's successor in the IOC presidency, attempted to modernise and liberalise the existing regulations. In 1974, the IOC passed an amendment to the amateur code, also known as 'Eligibility Rule 26', which allowed reimbursement for loss of salary and legitimised the sponsorship of athletes by International Sports Federations, National Olympic Committees, national sport organisations, private businesses, corporations, and the like (see International Olympic Committee 1978: 16, 47–8). As Nissiotis argued:

Of course, athletes have to be assisted materially as they are sacrificing more and more almost all of their time in their hard training – but we should not allow sports to be the unique financial source of the Olympic athlete's professional life and money the unique purpose of his sports achievement. (Nissiotis 1984: 74)

Despite the modernised and more liberal character of the revised amateur code, many suggested that, although the material support of athletes was acknowledged and encouraged, the distinction between 'amateur' and 'professional' remained ambiguous. Parry argued at the 1988 IOA Session,

> The IOC Rule 26 does not use the word 'amateur' at all, but defines status in terms of eligibility, and leaves it to each International Federation to define eligibility. Most definitions of eligibility refer to the engagement in sport for its own sake, rather than for profit. However, Strenk (1988) demonstrates in detail the absurdities and personal injustices which inevitably follow when each International Federation has a different eligibility rule, and when individuals are banned for seemingly trivial offences. People have been banned for 'contamination' (merely having unauthorised contact with professionals) and for 'personal conduct' offences (such as drinking alcohol or, in the case of Jesse Owens, disobeying an official). (Parry 1988: 89–90)

Parry goes on to provide an explanation of why the issue of amateurism had not been resolved one decade after the new 'Eligibility Rule 26',

> What is in fact happening (with the emergence and success of communist nations) is that such an ideological conception as 'amateurism' cannot survive the struggle of ideas which inevitably occurs when nations with differing political ideologies (and therefore differing conceptions of Olympism) nevertheless have a mutual interest in arriving at a concept of Olympism on which they can all happily agree. (Parry 1988: 90)

After the end of the Second World War and the consolidation of the two opposing ideological factions in the Cold War, the issue of amateurism became more problematic than ever. The amateur code required that an emphasis should be placed on sport's social, moral, educational and aesthetic dimensions, as distinct from the commercial profits that derived from the practice of sport. Thus, the amateur was considered to act because of intrinsic motivation and respect for sport, whereas the professional because of the private and material benefits derived from it. However, although the rules of the IOC on amateurism appeared to have sought clarity and uniformity, they could be subject to different, often widely different, interpretations. Indeed, in the socialist tradition, there is no distinction between shared (common or public), and private, concerns, while the capitalist conception of life pre-supposes the division between public and private concerns in the form of liberal individualism. Osterhoudt suggested that,

> The most notable difference between the socialist and capitalist inter-pretations of modern amateurism occurs with respect to the regulations prohibiting the receipt by athletes of any financial rewards of material benefits in connection with their participation in sport ... The funda-mental difference between the socialist and capitalist interpretations of modern amateurism stems largely from the monistic tendencies of the former, and the pluralistic dispositions of the latter. (Osterhoudt 1981: 42–3)

Thus, it is clear that the amateur ideal could hardly be considered as a 'universal' Olympic principle. The fact of the matter is that although the amateur ideal had been a tenet of Olympic ideology, 'it does seem as though, whatever they say about eligibility, many International Federations of Olympic Sports either allow, tolerate or turn a blind eye to both professionalism and commercialism' (Parry 1988). From Parry's perspective, in an era when the IOC itself was involved in marketing contracts, 'it would seem odd if everyone except the athletes were allowed to profit from their abilities'.

> Some have claimed that amateurism is a necessary and central part of the timeless ideal of Olympism. It still appears in the Olympic Charter as part of the 'fundamental ideals'. *However, I would prefer to say that ama-teurism was an expression of the times of de Coubertin – of the social and eco-nomic structures of the imperialist stage of capitalism operative in western Europe in the late nineteenth century. It was not present in ancient times, partly because the social structures of that time did not generate a bourgeois elite, and it will not (I predict) be present in the twenty-first century, when the Games will be 'open'. It forms part of one conception of Olympism, which is historically and culturally specific – limited in time and space.* (Parry 1988: 90; emphasis added)

The concept of amateurism took form in nineteenth century England and reflects the aristocratic tendencies of nineteenth-century capitalism. Coubertin and his contemporaries, driven by elitist values, ignored the fact that many professional athletes had taken part in the Ancient Olympics (Osterhoudt 1981; Toohey and Veal 2000). Interestingly, Lucas (1992) observed that the term 'amateur athlete' never existed in the ancient Greek language. Similarly, Clarke, Assistant Executive Director of the US Olympic Committee, high-lighted in his speech at the 1988 IOA Session,

> Coubertin conceived the modern Olympics as modern, respecting the Hellenic heritage but representing the cultures of the day. That principle

has been applied since the outset of the XXth Century as well, leading to an 'out-datedness' of some of the original modern Olympic concepts. *The shift from debates on amateurism to debates on eligibility reflects well on the mutability of the 19th century concept of a sportsman. Allowing Olympism to demonstrate its value to all cultures of the world, to experience as well as to extol the fruits of excellence through competition, dropped exclusivity from the system and added significant financial burdens to the aspiring Olympian in the process.* On both accounts, Rule 26 has long been defining eligibility instead of amateurism, having been compromised by the continuing attempt to find rules governing the subsidising of athletes-in-training that are fair (equivalent) for the athletes of all cultures. It need not follow that athletes-in-competition warrant prize money or that rules of eligibility be void of financial considerations. The spectre of the eligible professional is good cause of fear for Olympism, but the fear of the return of the circus gladiator pales against the fear of removing from youth the current realistic opportunity to prepare for becoming an Olympian. (Clarke 1988: 103; emphasis added)

The assertion here is that the application of Olympism has limitations in time and space, with some values becoming outdated, and other new values emerging, as Olympism adapts to the new conditions in society.

If it is indeed true that the commitment to amateurism is dying, it is just as well that amateurism turns out to have been a historically specific element, which is simply becoming an outmoded factor. If, on the other hand, it had been the central universal value of Olympism, this would be indicating that Olympism itself is dying, since its central value is. *Olympism is alive and well, but amateurism is not. This shows that there must be some other source of the values of Olympism than amateurism.* (Parry 1988: 90–1; emphasis added)

As is clear from the debate around amateurism rehearsed by various IOA contributors, what are seen as 'core values' of Olympism at certain points in time, are subject to change as the political, economic and cultural context changes. Notions of 'immutable values', as universals and products of modernity thus appear as naïve constructs. The discursive construction of the 'Olympic athlete'. These were moves from its earlier basis in the English, bourgeois amateur ideal, as it becomes increasingly difficult to deny the existence of state professionals (students, civil servants, members of the armed forces) therefore first clearly evident in the Swedish team in 1912, but subsequently prevalent in the post-war period in the Communist Bloc, to the reliance on IFs to define 'eligibility' in ways which usher in professionals and open commercialism.

Commercialisation and the shift to professionalism

The issue of commercialism was not subject to detailed scrutiny at the IOA until 1992, when a special session was organised on the topic of 'Commercialisation of Sport and the Olympic Games'. Referring to this lack of earlier reference to the issue, the IOA lecturer Milshtein from Russia noted,

> At the very beginning of my lecture I called our session a pioneering act. Why? If you look attentively through what is, in my opinion, one of the unique sources on Olympic history, the monograph 'The International Olympic Academy' by Professor Norbert Müller, IOC historiographer, you will, unfortunately, find no special lecture on the commercialisation of sport or the Olympic movement in the list of the topics of lectures delivered during the 25 years of the IOA history. Even in the supplement to this wonderful book, the dictionary of terms used in the monograph, you will not find this term ... Thus, a long tradition idealising the Olympic movement, world sports and the Olympic Games, as well as our whole way of life, was broken. (Milshstein 1992: 121)

In an attempt to provide an explanation for such an omission, he argues,

> I don't know if it was because of this tradition, or because of the fact that it was not acceptable to speak of such things as 'commercialisation', 'professionalism', or 'politics', not only at the IOA sessions, but at the IOC sessions, as well as in IOC official publications, or for a number of subjective reasons, that it was considered bad form to speak of these phenomena. And, if somebody did speak of the phenomena, it was generally done negatively, which was especially characteristic of the mass media in the entire world. What is the explanation for such an approach? Perhaps [the answer lies] in the fact that until the 1970s the problem of commercialisation was not too urgent in modern world sports and in the Olympic movement. (Milshstein 1992: 123)

Milshtein's claim is that the Olympic movement had not been open to criticism in relation to controversial aspects of Olympism, and that discussion of certain 'uncomfortable' ideas was likely not to have been given a place on the IOA's (or the IOC's) agenda. However, the fact of the discussion of the issue in the IOA programme in 1992 suggests that the IOA had gradually liberalised, and would accommodate at least some controversial themes in relation to the Olympic movement, opening the way to a degree of ideological pluralism.

Prior to 1992, only rare reference had been made at the IOA Sessions in relation to commercialisation. In 1971, Gafner, an IOC member from Switzerland and President of the Swiss Olympic Committee, talked about the noninvolvement of the Olympic movement in economic and commercial interests.

> The Olympic movement draws also its moral strength from its material weakness, from the fact that it threatens no one. Without a police, without an army, until now without any important financial means, as Mr. Avery Brundage, President of the IOC has so often stressed, the efficiency of its action depends entirely on the sympathy it encounters, on the support it raises, and the enthusiasm it arouses. Just like the Red Cross movement, with which, moreover, it has some striking similarities, the Olympic movement is entirely disinterested and justifies its existence only by the services it renders. It is the quality, nature, and extent of these services, which, by forcing the respect of peoples and governments, can make it a beneficial institution, whose intervention is sought by the whole world. (Gafner 1971: 171–2)

Gafner characterises the Olympic movement at this historical juncture as neutral, non-imposing, deficient of substantial economic resources. In his view, its popularity is directly derived from its 'disinterested' qualities that are widely recognised in the international arena. The IOC with little resource but its reputation, had proved to be a strong decision-making body helping to change, as well as reacting to, the post-war geopolitical global order (Riordan 1999; Toohey and Veal 2000). However, although at this point in time the IOC did not have any significant financial means, this did not mean that it was not seeking to find ways to increase its economic resources. Since the 'anachronistic Depression-era Olympic extravaganza of the 1932 Los Angeles Games, which aimed to showcase itself and sport' (Nixon 1988: 240), the Olympic Games became competitions between hosts which intensified the political manipulation of the Games and increased costs and shortfalls. The expansion of the Olympic movement, consisted of the IOC, NOCs and international sport federations (IFs), was also followed by an increase in costs and of commercial pressures. Even from the late 1960s the Games had become a huge business with profits being distributed among the state, industry, the athletes, the sport federations, and the IOC (Espy 1979).

Gafner, in his contribution as a guest lecturer at the 1987 IOA Session, was less ambivalent than in his 1971 lecture in relation to the commercial interests within the Olympic movement.

> 'Olympism and commercialisation'. Of course, our opponents are waging a real war against us in their criticism that we have given in to the temptation of money and turned Olympism and sport in general into an enormous money-making machine. To a certain extent this is true, but first we must take a closer and more realistic look

before deciding that it is scandalous. (Gafner 1987; quoted by Milshtein 1992: 122)

Gafner admitted that the IOC had tried to find ways to benefit financially from the increasing publicity of the Games. However, he emphasised that it searched for sources of financing that would allow the IOC to achieve its goals whilst remaining independent of public authorities. As a result of this, the IOC's cooperation with private bodies such as American TV broadcasting companies and American-based multinational companies transformed the Olympics from an organisation whose future was unclear – after almost bankrupting a city with the enormous debt of $1 billion in the 1976 Montreal Games – into a rich organisation that earned millions. Thus, the situation changed dramatically at the 1984 Olympic Games in Los Angeles, which are often seen as the climax of the ongoing process of commercialisation and commodification taking place in the 1970s (Toohey and Veal 2000). Nixon (1988) shared the view that the 1984 Los Angeles Games 'were a source of controversy and criticism as well as applause' (p. 238). The cooperation between the IOC and the TOP sponsor companies created a new culture in the promotion of the Games. They became more professional, starting a new era with the Olympic movement entering into this entrepreneurial field with interest and developing skill (Lucas 1992). The involvement of multinational companies and the rise of capitalist interests were put forward as major criticisms of the Olympic movement. Nevertheless, the association of commercial interests with the Olympic movement has not been a new phenomenon. Gruneau (1984) noted in relation to this,

> ... The Los Angeles Games are in no way a significant departure from practices established in earlier Olympics. Rather, I believe the 1984 Games are best understood as a more fully developed expression of the incorporation of sporting practice into the ever-expanding marketplace of international capitalism. (Gruneau 1984: 2)

Gruneau thus claims that the commercialisation of the Games, far from being a departure from previous trends, represents a continuity from the early twentieth century, when the Games were associated with trade fairs promoting capitalist trade and commerce (the Paris Exhibition in 1900, the St. Louis World Fair in 1904, the Anglo-French Exhibition in London in 1908). From a similar viewpoint Anthony, President of the British Olympic Association's Sub-Committee for Education, argued at the 1992 IOA Session,

> From the start of the IOC it was established that profits might accrue from such sports festivals (the Olympic Games) and that these profits should be distributed equitably (...) I said the marriage of sport and commerce is not new. Almost one hundred years ago William Penny

Brookes of the Much Wenlock Olympian Society wrote to Pierre de Coubertin. He congratulated him on his brilliant idea to take the Olympic Games round the big cities of the world. 'Your festivals', he said, 'will make a profit – and the proceeds should be distributed among the participating nations'. Olympic Solidarity is making that happen. (Anthony 1992: 158)

Gafner (1987) argued that the major problem for Coubertin was the lack of financial resources, and that the IOC, through contracts with private companies, succeeded in finding resources for multiple Olympic projects, among which has been the programme of the Olympic Solidarity.

Without the income from television and without sponsoring, there would certainly be almost insurmountable problems for the Organizing Committees for the Olympic Games, the work of Olympic Solidarity – about which its Director, Mr Anselmo Lopez, will speak to you in detail – would be reduced to nothing, and few of the International Federations would be able to exercise full or efficient control over the sport. (Gafner 1987; quoted by Milshtein 1992: 122)

Concurring with this view, Clarke, an administrator in the US Olympic Committee, urged that

Commercialism, not to be confused with professionalism, may cause many interruptions in viewing Olympic competition, but without it few peoples of the world would ever be touched by Olympism. Misuse and abuse abound, but harnessed, commercialism can enable the Olympic movement to move through the XXth Century as the global celebration it purports to be. Never before has the IOC had the sources of revenue to distribute in support of Olympism and Olympians through needed programmes and to needy countries. Never before has it been possible for the IOC to continue to expand Olympic opportunities without overburdening the host city. (Clarke 1988: 102)

In similar vein, Barney, an Olympic scholar from Canada emphasised that to view the process of commercialisation in Olympic sport in purely negative terms would be a mistake.

For the most part, IOC financial resources extended to education-related initiatives have been dollars well spent. Subsidies allocated to National Olympic Committees and International Sports Federations, in part, find their way towards the sports and fitness development of youth. National Olympic Academies, of which there are scores in countries around the world, do their part towards the awareness and spread of Olympism, a reputable philosophy of life, irrespective of the type of government, economy or religion that dictates an individual's physical and spiritual environment. And remember Brundage's words in the mid-1950s as to who would pay for what seemed to be a good idea at the time, the establishment of an International Olympic Academy in Olympia, Greece? Television made possible a handsome IOC quadrennial subsidy to the IOA. The information and education-bent IOC publications Olympic Review and Olympic Message have also made an impact on the spread of Olympism. The IOC's Solidarity programme, though criticised by some, has had modest success thus far. Much more must be expected of that programmes' mission. (Barney 1993: 131)

Barney pointed out that 'the ability of the IOC to support each of the projects noted above has increased commensurately with wealth attained largely from television and licensing income' (p. 131). Although, the massive economic benefits for the Olympic movement through its involvement with organisations and companies provided the IOC with the resources to carry out projects, such as the construction and running of the Olympic Museum and the Olympic Study Centre in Lausanne, or support other cultural and educational initiatives around the world for the dissemination of Olympism, it is arguable whether the realisation of the Olympic values is still a primary role in the Olympic movement.

During the twentieth century, the Olympic Games and the Olympic movement challenged the Olympic principles of amateurism, the pre-eminence of the individual athlete, sportsmanship, and international understanding that were promoted so eagerly by Pierre de Coubertin (Espy 1979). The concept of amateurism played a significant role in the post-Second World War period in formulating the political economy of the Olympic movement. The IOC throughout the 1950s and 1960s struggled to defend the amateur code. Nonetheless, the violation of the amateur code was not something new. Moreover, although the principle of amateurism was central in the concept of Olympism, this was a legacy of the bourgeois origins of Olympism. As shown earlier, by 1971, the IOC had decided to eliminate the term 'amateur' from the Article 26 of the Olympic Charter, and by 1981 Samaranch completed the shift to professionalism by leaving IFs free to define eligibility of athletes for the Games (Lucas 1992).

In 1978, long before the big contracts with the multinational companies, Ritter, President of the Olympic Committee of Liechtenstein at the time, expressed his worries about the roles of athletes in relation to commercial interests.

Athletes, known all over the world, are being used as a medium for commercial propaganda. They are becoming more and more commercial symbols. These athletes become dependent on companies and their payments to them. They are no longer athletes, representing sport and the idea of sports, but become, rather, representatives of their commercial interests. As a result, sport becomes a vehicle of commercialism rather than the preserver of a worthwhile human ideal put to practice. If commercialism becomes overriding, sport will cater purely to commercial interests. Such a development is far removed from the aims stipulated by the Olympic idea. (Ritter 1978: 180)

By the late 1970s, growing nationalism, commercialism and professionalism had created an Olympic movement that, it was claimed, was suffering from political manipulation and uncontrolled commercial interests (Nixon 1988). Espy (1979) argues that for all three organisations, the IOC, the NOCs and the IFs, the role of television in the Olympic Games had become a 'bone of contention' (p. 166). These organisations were competing in the name of commercialism and nationalism, thus placing the individual athlete in a secondary position. Milshtein (1992) reminded his audience at the 32nd IOA Session that, while commercialisation and professionalisation processes take place, the *moral* development of the individual athlete should remain the primary goal of Olympism.

While admitting that both the commercialisation of and professionalism in sport are objective and irreversible processes, in my opinion, another thing is important; that is to establish a framework within which these processes may be allowed to penetrate into Olympic sports and the Olympic movement. It is important to work out objective standards for the regulation of such processes which will allow us to keep international sports and the Olympic movement from turning into a means of commerce, of profit, and of exploitation. The moral development of the individual through sports must remain as a goal. The athlete must not become merely the means by which advertising firms, TV companies, and other businesses or any other body or private person seeks to achieve their commercial aims. (Milshtein 1992: 126)

Although the original emphasis of the Olympic Games was placed on the individual athlete, the growth and expansion of the Olympic movement and the structure of the Games shifted the emphasis firmly onto organisations (IFs, NOCs, and ultimately commercial stakeholders in the media and sponsors) for reasons of efficiency and feasibility (Espy 1979). Samaranch is reported as expressing his concern in relation to this.

The enormous progress of top-level sport and the popularity of the Olympic Games are the reasons for much-needed commercialisation. It is our duty to obtain part of the money that sport and our movement generate by means of TV rights agreements, contracts with sponsors and other ways, and to use it for the development of sport, culture and the Olympic movement. This commercialisation must, however, be controlled by the International Olympic Committee, the International Federations and the National Olympic Committees. We must not let young athletes lose their freedom and become dependent on agents who determine where and against whom they should compete. Top-level sport and the Olympic movement have developed so much that they are now vulnerable. Olympism, which is essentially an educational movement, must not allow Olympic sport to become mere show business. (Samaranch's speech to the 97th IOC Session in Birmingham 1991, quoted by Milshtein 1992: 118–19)

Although the IOC President admits here that the growth of the Olympic Games has led to the increased commercialisation evident in IOC policies, placing such organisations in the centre of the movement, he also emphasises, with an implied sense of paternalism, 'we must not let young athletes lose their freedom and become dependent on agents who determine where and against whom they should compete'. This might be taken to reinforce the argument promoted by Espy that in the Olympic movement 'the ideals have been made secondary but have been used as a primary justification for its existence' (Espy 1979: 171).

5.2.3   Doping and the Olympic movement

The growing interests in professionalism and commercialism, which fuelled the competitiveness in the Olympics, were also associated with growing drug abuse particularly during the years of the Cold War. Although the first use of doping in the modern Olympic Games was documented in 1904, drug-taking had been associated with strenuous physical activity and sport for much longer (Toohey and Veal 2000). The Greek physician Galen, writing in the third century BC, reported that athletes in Ancient Greece used stimulants to enhance their performance. In Ancient Egypt athletes followed special diets and took a variety of substances, which aimed to improve their physical competence. Likewise, Roman gladiators, and knights in the Middle Ages, ingested remedies and stimulants that would help them continue in combat after an injury (Waddington 2000). More recently, in the eighteenth and nineteenth centuries all the major commercial and professional sports, such as boxing, cycling and running, have provided evidence of significant drug use. There have been many documented instances of athletes using a wide variety of substances (not always effective) to enhance performance including strychnine, nitro-glycerine, opium, alcohol and caffeine (Hoberman 1992). The Tour de France, for example, has a long history of drug-related incidents with many of the cyclists being reported as using mixed substances that in some cases even led to the death of athletes (Toohey and Veal 2000).

Nonetheless, technological development and the scientific advances of the pharmaceutical industry, together with the emerging need for new drugs that would enhance troops' endurance during wartime, shifted ethical standards concerning the use of drugs. During the Second World War governments organised drug use to strengthen military performance and this ambiguous moral climate continued into the Cold War period (Houlihan 1999). The Cold War experienced significant advances by the pharmaceutical industry, which subsequently designed drugs that would meet the specific requirements of particular sports. Thus, the modern Olympics in the Cold War era saw the introduction of doping as common practice (Toohey and Veal 2000). In the early 1950s, it was rumoured that Soviet scientists had been conducting hormonal experimentation in order to help their athletes increase their sport performance. Voy (1991) argued that at the 1956 World Games in Moscow Dr. Jon B. Ziegler, an American physician who was a member of the medical staff for the Games, witnessed urinary catheters being used by Soviet athletes due to enlargement of the prostate gland from excessive use of steroids. To counteract this, Dr. Ziegler helped the CIBA Pharmaceutical company to develop Dianabol, a very strong anabolic-androgenic steroid, in an attempt to help the western athletes to compete successfully against the Soviets. In the 1952 Winter Olympics in Oslo several speed skaters overdosed on amphetamines and sought medical attention, and in 1960, at the Rome Olympic Games, Knud Jensen, cyclist from Denmark, became the first Olympic athlete to die of a drug overdose during competition.

Until the mid-1960s the issue of doping concerned only a few sport specialists and had not yet become a public affair. As doping became more scientific and more widely practised, the pressures against its use and awareness of its direct or indirect negative effects grew, forcing the issue on to the agenda of both governments and sport bodies. Nonetheless, technical complexity meant that problems arose in detecting and countering drug use given the lack of technology for testing all the classes of drugs in use.

From the 1960s to the late 1980s, the problem of doping was considered to affect only a few sports, and certain countries. Thus only a small number of governments, and up until the mid to late 1980s, few sports bodies, showed a real interest in developing an anti-doping policy (Houlihan 2001). In 1961, the IOC established a Medical Commission and in 1962 it passed a resolution denouncing doping but it was only five years later that this commission was re-established in better premises for developing a sustained anti-doping policy (Houlihan 1999, 2001). In 1963, the Council of Europe established a Committee on Drugs, which provided a definition of doping that was relatively ambiguous and unclear (Houlihan 1999; Toohey and Veal 2000). The *Fédération Internationale de Football Association* (FIFA) carried out some tests at the Soccer World Cup in England (1966) but then it seemed to lose interest in this matter. The International Amateur Athletics Federation (IAAF), following the steps of the IOC, also established a Medical Committee in 1972, and two years later introduced compulsory testing at its championships.

Interestingly, even though drug testing at the Olympic Games started in 1968, it was not until 1988, and the decision of the IOC to disqualify the 100 metres champion, Ben Johnson of Canada, that details of a drug abuse case were broadcast 'live' throughout the world (Toohey and Veal 2000). Similarly, although drug use and drug testing at the Olympic Games had been controversial aspects of the Olympic movement for a long time (and had intensified during the Moscow and Los Angeles Olympics), only a few IOA speakers had occasionally raised concerns in relation to the issue at the IOA Sessions (namely Paparescos in 1970, 1971 and 1976; Silance in 1977; Prokop in 1977; Nissiotis in 1981 and 1982; Kamuti in 1983; Formo in 1983; Powell in 1984; Ford in 1987; Siperco in 1988). It was not until 1989 that the IOA accommodated a Session about 'The Concept of the IOC on Doping as a Counterpoint to the Olympic Spirit'. Read from Canada, an Olympic champion and member of the IOC Athletes Commission, expressed his frustration about the delays in resolving the issue of doping,

Athletes and the Athletes Commission have not been silent on this problem. We have been calling for action for nearly a decade. While we are pleased to see that there is finally some movement in dealing seriously with drugs in sport, we are still frustrated by the slow progress. Why should we be so concerned? Certainly there are the obvious health concerns. But, primarily, athletes want a 'level playing field', so there is no PERCEIVED need to use performance enhancing drugs. We also want to protect the image of and integrity of sport. We all became involved in sport for fun. While some of us were fortunate enough to achieve the level of an Olympic athlete, to the majority of participants in sport, the Olympics represent a higher ideal, of the pursuit of excellence. If this ideal is tarnished, we may never again regain the confidence of the public, sponsors, governments, who make the Olympic Games possible, and cause the destruction of the Games.

... But most important, our sport leaders must provide leadership. Sadly I must agree with earlier speakers, that the problem of doping in sport is not yet taken seriously enough. Perhaps only the imposition of severe penalties such as exclusion from the Games will catch their attention. (Read 1989: 115)

Similarly, Papadoyannakis, Vice-President of the Hellenic Olympic Committee, admitted, 'one might observe, of course, that doping is not something new in the world of sport; however, nowadays it has acquired a new form and dimensions that all of us who are engaged in sport should have reacted earlier to overcome this problem' (Papadoyanakis 1989: 82). Moreover, he emphasised that the early solutions and outcomes of conferences (such as the Council of Europe's Second Conference of European Ministers of Sport on Anti-doping in London in 1975) were not successful enough in controlling the problem.

> Through these texts, attention was drawn above all to the moral and medical risks inherent in the use of drugs and measures were proposed to be taken by the governments and sports associations jointly within the scope of respective competences. There is no mention, however, in these otherwise worthy texts, of any sanctions as a result of which the spreading of the above phenomena would be curbed. It is evident that the first legislative texts aimed at preventing and not at curbing these phenomena in the first place; for this reason sport associations started carrying out doping in their respective countries both at random as well as during competitions of male and female athletes. (Papadoyanakis 1989: 82)

Papadoyannakis proposed that severe penalties should be applied against the athletes and all those involved, including coaches, doctors and physiotherapists. The reluctance of the IOC, and of other event-organising bodies, such as the Commonwealth Games Federation, to develop a strict anti-doping policy can be explained by their interests in maintaining a public perception of their events as healthy and drug free (Voy 1991). When the Olympic Games – assisted by effective electronic media coverage and higher publicity – had become a global success, the commercial interests were far more tempting than the amateur ideals. Admission of the size of the problem could threaten the commercial value of the Games, while the commercial success of the games incited in some interested parties greediness for further profits and success, as evidenced in a number of corruption scandals (see, for example, Jennings and Simson 1992), which militated against the development of strong anti-doping policies.

Although doping is fundamentally distinct from financial corruption, both can be considered as direct products of political and economic interests. Typical examples of a politically determined doping misuse were the doping cases in the former East Germany and China during the Cold War which were state-supported attempts to make ideological gains. The typical example of the association of economic interests with doping is the profitability of big companies, which, by signing contracts to successful athletes for huge sums of money, increase the temptation for athletes to make use of performance-boosting measures (Hoberman 1992).

Heinze, an East German IOC member, and a guest lecturer at the 1989 IOA Session, argued in relation to existing political and commercial interests,

> It is hoped that a miracle drug often recommended by false friends brings quick success. Other people are induced for nationalistic and

chauvinistic reasons to use forbidden agents. But a main reason should be seen in the striving for making the 'great' money, in marketing athletic performances. In order to take part in as many competitions as possible in the course of one year and to be successful in the fight for victory and in order to get the benefit of considerable price money and cash prizes for victories and top ratings, athletes run risks as to their life and health, the consequences and effects of which are often not duly assessed by them. ... In this connection it is particularly fateful to observe that also very young athletes use forbidden drugs in order to achieve fast athletic success and to quickly make money. It is with regret to state that several organisers of international meetings support this process by renouncing carrying out doping controls in a quite light-minded manner. Thus it may obviously be concluded that the increasing application of doping agents is closely linked with professionalisation and commercial abuse of sport. Sport must serve a sound way of life. (Heinze 1989: 64–5)

The interesting point to note here is that, while western critics of doping practices tended to focus on the political motives of those in, or under, communist regimes, this member of the Communist Bloc points to the capitalist search for profit as the primary motive. The modern context of high performance Olympic sport has been a highly commercialised and professionalised activity that attracts the interests of media and multinational companies. Especially for the wealthy western countries, leagues, coaches and athletes, all experience considerable pressure to keep their sponsors happy and maintain the high status of their athletes through sporting success. Sport bodies may therefore fail to cooperate with anti-doping measures and press for short bans to be invoked to limit the financial impact of the loss of their athletes (Moller 2004). Pariente from France, Editor of the newspaper '*L' Equipe*', outlines such pressures in his speech at the IOA,

So, as years went by, scientific doping techniques have progressively taken the place of individual empirical doping. This development has been accelerated by the promise of huge profits and the spectacular increase of amounts involved in top competition sport, be it purely professional, as in the case of football, tennis or basketball, or non-professional, though no longer amateur, as in the case of track and field. You should indeed know, that the salaries of certain players have reached stupendous levels. Naturally the people around them profit substantially from this situation and as a result we witness a proliferation of managers, masseurs, pseudo-technicians and even sham doctors who all eat a big share of this cake which feeds on receipts from advertising, television rights, sponsoring, all part of the sports show. (Pariente 1989: 119)

In similar vein, DeFrantz, an IOC member from the USA, also a speaker at the 1989 Session, alludes to the pressures from those surrounding the athlete.

> People are just beginning to talk about the effects that they have experienced. For too long, steroid use was a sports secret. Medical professionals did not take the time to investigate the consequences of the extraordinarily large dosages that athletes were taking. But now, people are beginning to acknowledge that they have been damaged by steroid use ... sports leaders have failed to take effective steps to stop it. Too many administrators have looked the other way. In fact, some coaches have been directly involved in supplying steroids to athletes, as we are learning from the Durbin inquiry in Canada. (DeFrantz 1989: 108)

Houlihan suggests that the reason for recording relatively few positive results, particularly in the first two decades of anti-doping measures, was not only because the results of the tests were often considered unreliable but mostly because 'there was a marked lack of clarity about where the primary responsibility for the implementation of testing lay' (Houlihan 1999: 132). The high costs of testing and the expenses required for carrying out experimentation about banned substances and new doping practices were substantial economic burdens that all bodies wanted to avoid. Moreover, governments, too, became increasingly aware of the publicity of the Olympic Games and their power to enhance or undermine the prestige of a country. This made it more difficult to introduce effective sanctions against the use of drugs or for national bodies or governments to admit that many of their athletes used them. Houlihan goes on to argue that, 'despite public statements condemning doping, it is accepted that the governments of a number of the most prominent sporting countries were systematically undermining anti-doping efforts, while a further group of countries were allowing policy momentum to dissipate through lack of support' (Houlihan 1999: 98). The East German IOC member, Heinze, suggested that the IOC acting alone would be ineffectual without the cooperation of the International Sports Federations, the NOCs and the governing bodies of the sport organisations of each country.

> The efforts being made by the IOC are aimed at preventing trafficking of prohibited drugs in the field of sport. This is an extremely difficult task, which cannot be fulfilled without the assistance by the governments as this also touches the ideal with medicaments. Without any laws concerning the deal with medicaments and relevant intergovernmental

agreements it is almost impossible to control the illegal trafficking of substances prohibited in sport. (Heinze 1989: 66)

The cases of Dean Capobianco and Antonella Bevilacqua, reveal the complexity of the problem of doping. Both athletes were tested positive by the IOC but their respective domestic governing bodies challenged the IOC decision in their federations' arbitration tribunal (Houlihan 1999; Waddington 2000). These cases illustrate the importance of cooperation between the IOC, governing bodies, international federations and even national governments. Moreover, it illustrates how anti-doping measures now engaged the involvement of lawyers and courts, increasing the level of complexity and the costs involved.

With regard to the ethical dimensions of the doping issue, John Rodda, a British sports journalist for the *Guardian* newspaper and guest lecturer at the 1988 IOA Session, argued that unreliable IOC testing had often exposed 'innocent' athletes. Rodda (1989) raised questions about the IOC's testing system, which had often failed to recognise drug users, but had also raised suspicions in relation to athletes who were not subsequently banned. Rodda, used the example of Linford Christie of Great Britain, a sprinter who had finished third in the 100 metres and who, after Johnson's disqualification, was promoted to second place. The sample, which Christie provided after the 200 metres race, was found to contain a level of pseudo-ephedrine that was 'unsatisfactory'. The IOC, 'giving the benefit of the doubt', did not ban Christie but this accusation, Rodda suggested, had already damaged his public image.

> The case of Linford Christie I would suggest is sufficient to prompt the IOC to conduct an independent inquiry into the whole area of drug testing systems. This is not an implied criticism of those who have worked so successfully in an area of growing difficulty (...) I do not want to leave anyone with the impression that I am opposed to or in any way questioning the validity of drug testing systems. My words today are intended to bludgeon the efforts of those bent on getting the cheats out of sport; my cry is for the innocent, for those who play fairly. (Rodda 1989: 104)

The IOC drug testing system was further questioned some years later, when Don Catlin, the American scientist who was in charge of the testing procedure for steroids at the 1996 Atlanta Games, made it known that four positive results had not been announced. The reason for disregarding the four positive results was that the ultra-sensitive IOC equipment could detect much lower levels of steroid in urine samples, which consequently did not constitute a doping offence. On the basis of this and other similar previous incidents (e.g. at the 1984 Los Angeles Olympic Games nine positive samples were also disregarded), Yesalis, an American epidemiologist, criticised the IOC for failing to invest sufficient funds for anti-doping research, with a subsequent failure to provide valid interpretations of many test results (Houlihan 1999: 16). Nonetheless, the growing phenomenon of doping which threatened the integrity of the Olympic Games forced the IOC to undertake a leading role in developing global policy against doping (Houlihan 1999). One example of this new role was the work undertaken by the IOC in establishing quality standards for accredited laboratories dealing with samples from the Olympic Games.

During the period 1961–1970 the issue of doping had not been raised at all by any IOA speaker, and from 1970 to 1988 relatively few references were made to the nature of the problem. Indeed it was not until 1989 that a special Session on the topic was accommodated. One speaker was openly critical of the IOC approach as reflected in the actions of its President.

> The President of the IOC used the statement 'doping equals death' in the opening ceremony of the 94th Session of the IOC in Seoul. And yet, this April he publicly expressed welcome to one individual to rejoin the Olympics in Barcelona after testing positive in Seoul. With all respect, I would suggest it is inappropriate to welcome back anyone who has violated this trust by cheating. We must be consistent. We must be forceful. And we must act quickly if we are to preserve this trust. (Read 1989: 115)

However, with the exception of Read's comments, there was no direct criticism of the IOC or its anti-doping policy and certainly no reference to its underlying interests and the 'silences' surrounding doping cases or the downplaying of the problem of drug-taking by Olympic athletes. Indeed most speakers applauded the IOC for establishing the Medical Commission, for developing a list of banned substances and for supporting the establishment of accredited laboratories to examine the urine and blood samples of Olympic athletes. Moreover, there was no discussion about serious issues in relation to doping, such as the inequalities generated between the core sporting nations of the developed world, and those of the periphery. Most speakers emphasised the need for further education of athletes and coaches, with particular emphasis on the moral implications and health dangers of doping, and emphasised the commercial and political pressures as the major causes for the acceleration of the problem during the Cold War years. Interestingly, the special IOA Session on doping took place in 1989, one year after the 1988 Seoul Games where the IOC had taken the decision to expose one of the most famous of its athletes, by disqualifying Ben Johnson, in an effort to maintain the integrity of the Games.

Among the interesting features of this theme and the discourses relating to the use of drugs to enhance performance, are the issues of 'motives' and 'blame' – the politics of the Eastern bloc (political ideology) or the morality of the capitalist bloc (individuals motivated by personal gain and profit); the IOC as holder of the moral high ground (establishing an anti-doping policy) or as a part of the problem (positive test outcomes which were not presented through a lack of technical competence, or implicitly through a lack of commitment); of perspectives of speakers from the developing and developed worlds (the latter perhaps tending to be less critical and questioning of the IOC's role).

Indeed in terms of the nature of the way such discourses are shaped or rehearsed at all within the IOA it is significant that for a considerable period up to 1989 the issue was virtually invisible. However, criticisms of the IOC anti-doping policy in general, and the leadership provided by Samaranch in particular, escalated during the years which followed and were fuelled after the revelation of the 2002 Salt Lake City scandal. In the World Anti-Doping Conference in Lausanne in February 1999, fierce criticism of the IOC anti-doping policy was heard from sport ministers and representatives of government anti-doping agencies. These accused the Olympic movement of short-sightedness towards doping and questioned the moral authority of the proposed international agency (initially entitled the 'International Anti-Doping Agency' (IADA), but later re-named as the 'World Anti-Doping Agency', WADA) (Houlihan 2001). The European Commission made it clear that it would not accept the establishing of WADA if this were a body which came under the auspices of the Olympic movement. Thus when WADA was established marking a determined step in the direction of a successful anti-doping policy, it was a body in which the IOC had a large but minority representation and was therefore no longer in the position of primary arbiter in doping cases (Vrijman 2001).

5.2.4   Women and the Olympic movement

Women's under-representation in the Olympic movement, reflected Coubertin's Victorian philosophy about gender and the accepted idea that women were not suited physically or socially to athletics (Sargent 1889; cited in Segrave and Chu 1981: 76). However, during the years of the Cold War, the number of female athletes participating in the Olympics increased, while a few women were also admitted to IOC and NOC administrative posts. The IOC elected to appoint in 1981 its first female members (Pirjo Haggman of Finland and Flor Isava-Fonseca of Venezuela) and in 1990 Isava-Fonseca was elected to the IOC Executive. Speakers at the IOA commented on this change focusing on the period from the early years of the Olympic movement to the first women's co-option to IOC membership in 1981. Despite these relatively modest measures, Lekarska, a member of the Bulgarian Olympic Committee and an IOC member, emphasised in her speech at the 1988 IOA Session, that 'Equality among all has been radically enriched by several new elements' (Lekarska 1988: 75).

As discussed earlier, the story of women's participation in the Olympics has been one of 'struggle and diversity – power and control were fought over, not just between men and women, but between different groups of women' (Hargreaves 1994: 10). The under-representation of women in the Olympics Games can be attributed to cultural, economic, and political factors. The Olympics, as with other sport events, have become a terrain of dispute for different societal values, meanings and ideologies. In the early days of the Olympic movement, at the end of the nineteenth century, power relations based on gender had an impact on athletes' participation placing women in a marginal position (Toohey and Veal 2000). Coubertin, when he revised the ancient concept of Olympism, retained the celebration of male sport, even if, by the first century A.D., girls competed in ancient athletic festivals (Tryphosa and her sisters Hedea and Dionysia, for example, were victors in Pythian and Isthmian Games). Coubertin, reflecting the elitist values of exclusivity of the nineteenth century, argued consistently that in the modern athletic festivals women should not participate.

Nonetheless, even after the World War I, when space in the workplace opened up for women providing them with greater freedom in different spheres of life, the perception that participation in competitive sport projected masculine characteristics onto women still remained (Birrell and Cole 1994). However, with advances of sport research, medical evidence dispelled fears and myths of gynaecological damage through participation in competitive sport. Lekarska (1988) promoted the view that, particularly since 1968 and the submission of the new proposals by the IOC Programme Commission (of which she was a member) for increasing the level of women's participation in the Games, effective efforts had been made to ensure gender equality in the Olympic movement.

> During the last fifteen years of this last period of the 20th century the participation of women in the Olympic Games has reached an unexpected numerical and qualitative standard. At the core of this positive development lies, to begin with, the status of equality among women and men in numerous countries of the world. The image of the helpless woman, dependent on man's commanding will, has largely disappeared. Most women nowadays take their destinies in their own hands with a sense of respective responsibility and this no doubt is duly reflected in their constantly growing sporting activity. (Lekarska 1988: 75)

Lekarska also emphasised that the IOC had recognised the need for women's involvement to go beyond sporting participation and had set an example by electing to co-opt two women to IOC membership in 1981,

> It was rightfully expected that the enlightenment referring to women's equality within the Olympic sphere would not be mainly restricted to the Olympic Games, but that it would logically expand to the Olympic movement too. From 1981 onwards a very good example was set by the

IOC on that matter in electing to IOC membership several ladies, unthinkable in the past, but this had no particular follow-up within the leading bodies of the National Olympic Committees and the International Sports Federations. If I have dwelled more explicitly on that aspect of Olympic equality the reason is that it happens to be one of those topics, which have undergone a very positive development in line with present-day realities. (Lekarska 1988: 75)

In similar vein, Clarke (1988), Assistant Executive Director of the US Olympic Committee, shared Lekarska's optimism about the IOC's progress in the issue of women's representation in the Olympic movement. He asserted the importance of the amending of the official entry of Rule 28 in the Olympic Charter (1984), which stated 'women are allowed to compete according to the rules of the IFs concerned and after the approval of the IOC' (p. 18).

Outdated in practice for many years, but now outdated officially, are IOC reservations about the place of the female athlete in the Olympic celebration. Rule 28, a one-sentence stipulation that allowed women to compete subject to the approval of the IOC, was expunged from the charter on the eve of the 1988 Olympic Winter Games. As in all Olympic sport matters, women will compete according to only the rules of their IF. (Clarke 1988: 103)

Nonetheless, Although Lekarska and Clarke applauded the IOC for its progress to date, Anita DeFrantz, IOC member from the US, argued in frustration,

It is disturbing for me, as an International Olympic Committee member, to acknowledge that, of the 167 Presidents of National Olympic Committees (NOCs) worldwide, in 1992, only six were women (...) only five of the 167 Secretaries General of those same NOCs are women. Perhaps more important is the membership of the International Olympic Committee. There are only seven among the ninety-four members of the IOC. But prior to 1981 there was none. (DeFrantz quoted in Scheinder 1996: 108)

Similarly, Parry (1988), an Olympic scholar from the UK, stressed that although things have changed since Coubertin's time, the achievement of change required much effort and time.

No women competed to begin with (de Coubertin thought that the only role for women was in presenting wreaths to the winners!), but since the early days some progress has been made. Many events from which women had previously been excluded are now open to them, and there is a steady increase in the numbers of female participants and in the number of events open to them. There is, then, no classical parallel to women's participation in the modern Games, which is a response to women's emancipation in the twentieth century. This development has been gained only with great difficulty and over the dead bodies of the (virtually all-male) Olympic hierarchy. (Parry 1988: 87)

Hargreaves (1994) describes women's resistance and struggle to gain a place in the Olympics as having taken place in three phases. The first, from 1896 until 1928 was a period of exclusion and there were only a few efforts to resist this. The second period, from 1928–1952, was a time of struggle for women in the Olympics, when women were accepted in certain sports. The third period, from 1952 until the present, is defined as the period of challenge to masculine hegemony, which was reinforced, with the entry of the Soviet bloc into the Games. Then the 'political medal agenda' overwhelmed the 'gender agenda' and nations became concerned about the number of medals won and not about the gender of the victors. Part of the challenge to masculine hegemony should also be attributed to the direct results of practical and theoretical feminist work from the early 1970s. A wide range of feminist approaches sought to provide explanations about how 'conventional gender relations have been built, reproduced and contested' (Hargreaves 1994: 3) and sport it was argued had played a key role in reproducing the subordination of women's interests. However, Parry (1988) argued that, though there had been a rising challenge to masculine hegemony, real equality had yet to be achieved in the Olympic movement.

Nowadays there is more or less formal (though not actual) gender equality. This is a most important and interesting new dimension for the modern Games. It is possible to gather a few historical fragments which discuss atypical female involvement in the Games, but by and large gender roles were quite clearly laid down (...). Two distinctions are often made to avoid confusion when talking about equality: Firstly, we should distinguish between formal and actual equality. There might well be no legal barrier to women becoming members of the IOC, but there are actually very few who are members. In this case, men and women have formal but not actual equality in regard to their membership of and representation on the IOC. Secondly, we should distinguish between equality of opportunity and equality of treatment. Whilst it is doubtless true that, once on the playing field, everyone is treated equally, it is quite another matter whether everyone has an equal opportunity to make the team, or to make the competition. (Parry 1988: 84)

Parry goes on to raise the following concern,

Women are competing in larger numbers than ever before, and in general the status of women's sport does seem to be improving worldwide. A major

question remains, however, as to whether sport is a means to the emancipation and equal status of women, or whether it contributes to the
perpetuation of existing inequalities. (Parry 1988: 279–353)

Although the IOC modified many of its regulations, women continued to be
excluded from most positions of power and influence in sport organisations,
including the IOC, but also from having the same opportunities as men to
pursue careers in professional sport. Women had to struggle against male hegemony and to challenge sporting attitudes, values and images of male domination, even if the regulations formally allowed them to compete or occupy
higher positions in sports coaching and administration. Nevertheless, limited
opportunities for participation in decision-making processes in male-dominated
leadership bodies in sport continued to exist in societies. Moreover, as feminist
scholars had sought to demonstrate, female socialisation takes place into selective roles, legitimating the dominant ideology of patriarchy (that is the system
of power relations based on male domination) and, thus, maintaining high
ranking positions as a male preserve (Hargreaves 1994). Besides, definitions of
women in sport were always perceived in terms of their 'otherness' from males.
In this sense, 'otherness' implied that the identity of 'woman/feminine' had been
socially constructed in a manner which defined it to be what 'man/masculine'
(the norm, humanity) is not. This indicates that women were constituted as the
'Other' or as peripheral in relation to the 'One' (the male), rather than being
identified in an authentic and personal manner (Ramazanoglou and Holland
2002).

In sum, the IOA speakers promoted the view that positive steps had been
made in order to increase women's representation as athletes and administrators in the Olympic movement. The message was that although in the
early days of the Olympic movement the dominant elitist values of the
nineteenth century bourgeoisie and aristocracy (heavily represented in IOC
membership) prevented women from participating in the Olympic Games,
changes in social, cultural and political values gradually allowed their participation, and raised a challenge to male dominance. There were voices,
such as that of Parry, who suggested a less complacent view of progress but
these were rare. Interestingly none of the speakers made reference to the
Cold War and the subsequent heightened political and economic interests
of nation-states, which is suggested to have brought forward a political
medal agenda, enhancing the value of female sporting victories.

It is also worth emphasising that the under-representation of women in the
Olympic movement was also reflected at the IOA Sessions. The total number
of speeches addressing gender issues was very low, with only nine lectures
related to women's participation in the Olympic movement in a period of
28 years (1961–1989). Moreover, in some Sessions none of the speakers was
female (1961, 1962, 1963, 1967, 1976 and 1993), while the number of female
speakers invited to the Sessions remained low, particularly in the early years,

as the same women were invited to a number of sessions. For example, Monique Berlioux came as a guest lecturer to the IOA 14 times during the years 1968–1985, Liselott Diem, Carl Diem's wife, nine times between 1964 and 1983, Nadia Lekarska from Bulgaria seven times from 1977 to 1994, and Sara Jernigan from the USA four times from 1965 to 1980.

The IOC, in an attempt to increase the levels of women's representation in the Olympic movement, set minimum targets (and not quotas) in 1997 that at least 10 per cent of those in executive decision-making positions in NOCs and IFs should be women by 31 December 2001 and 20 per cent by 31 December 2005 (Henry *et al.* 2004; Henry and Robinson 2010). The IOC's NOC Relations Department's 2010 NOC Annual Review indicates that the average NOC representation on Executive Boards is 17 per cent (although the response rate for this question was only 42 per cent, and may inflate the finding). Thus the minimum targets appear not to have been met. In 2010 out of 205 NOCs, eight had female Presidents and 19 had Secretary Generals. None of the Continental Associations of NOCs had a female President and only one had a female Secretary General. The European Olympic Committee had no elected female representation at all. In 2011 there were 19 of 110 IOC members who were women. Thus despite the dominantly positive discourse in the IOA, and although gains have certainly been made, progress has been slow.

5.3   The IOA in the post-Cold War period

The tense atmosphere of the Cold War, which had existed for nearly four decades, started to fade in the late 1980s. In 1987, the US and the USSR signed the *Intermediate-Range Nuclear Forces Treaty*. This was followed by the withdrawal of the Soviet troops from Afghanistan two years later (1989). In 1990, East and West Germany became a single and united non-communist state, while by the end of 1991 the Gorbachev reforms for democratisation of the Soviet Union and decentralisation of the Soviet economic system brought about the collapse of the USSR as a political system. Communist parties lost popular support and centripetal forces were unleashed leading to the Eastern European revolutions of 1989–91, which triggered processes of democratisation, essentially drawing upon the western liberal model and accompanied by a process of economic transition to capitalism.

In some respects the structure of world power at the end of the twentieth century reflected a return to a traditional model of multipolar politics, but in other respects, it conferred a unique military, economic and cultural status on the US (Held *et al.* 1999). The Olympic movement witnessed the end of the era of boycotts, the formation of new NOCs, such as the Slovenian, Belarusian and Estonian Olympic committees, of teams from Uzbekistan, Latvia and Turkmenistan, but also the emergence of the West as a superpower (Eichberg 2004). Even though the Olympic movement had always been subject to criticism for its Eurocentrism, following the end of the Cold War, it has been suggested that the domination of the Olympic movement by the West increased as signified by political power, economic interests, and the origins of sport on the programme. Indeed, Donnelly (1996) has argued that the Olympics are a form of global sport monoculture. In the sections that follow, guest speakers at the IOA Sessions (1990–1998) reflect upon the new world order and its impact on the Olympic movement and international elite sport. The main themes identified in the selected lectures are: a) the shift to liberal democracy and capitalism, b) the power of the West and the marginalisation of local sport cultures, and c) the emergence of environmentalism as a new element in the values of Olympism.

5.3.1   The shift to liberal democracy and capitalism

In the space of time between the fall of the Berlin Wall and the bombing of the twin towers in New York, there was for many an air of optimism about global relations. For optimists at least. the 'new world order' after the end of the Cold War was going to be based not on ideological conflicts and unstable international relations, but on a common recognition of international forms and standards. Central to this new world order would be the recognition of the need to tackle international crises peacefully, to resist expansionism and aggression, to control and minimise the production of weapons, and to secure the equal and just treatment of the individuals around the world through respect for human rights (Heywood 2002). The spirit of optimism for the beginning of a new era of harmony in global politics after the end of the Cold War was also reflected in the speech by the Russian academic, Vladislav Stolyarov at the 1995 IOA Session.

> Mankind (sic) has entered a world free of ideological grounds for serious national conflict, and, consequently, the use of armed force is becoming increasingly inappropriate. In the modern period of the development of civilisation, the most important thing is no longer confrontation of different social systems and political forces, but the opportunity to increase material wealth and distribute it fairly, and, on the basis of progressive science and high technology, to revive and defend together the resources necessary for the survival of mankind. (Stolyarov 1995: 78)

While at the time such claims might have appeared optimistic, optimism was to some extent the 'order of the day' in the period immediately following the fall of the Berlin Wall. Obviously in the light of events following the '9/11' attacks on the US, such optimism appears hopelessly naïve. Stolyarov also emphasised,

> It is especially important to stress that the global problems and difficulties faced by mankind on the eve of the 21st century have created a desire not

only to proclaim humanistic ideas, but also to try to realise them in practice in all spheres of life, including the Olympic movement. It is increasingly being understood that, if mankind would like to survive, it must place in the foreground civilisation and humanism as reflected by the modern system of values, and aspire not to domination over other people but to solidarity with them. Of course, the social organisation of different states and the behaviour of people, groups and nations do not reflect to the same degree these human ideas, ideals and principles. However, we can hardly deny that any modern society has to make every effort to realise them if it wishes to achieve a high degree of dynamism and stability in its development and a higher level of welfare and comfort for the majority of its members and to make relations between its members more civilised and the member themselves healthier both physically and morally. (Stolyarov 1995: 78)

Stolyarov also points out that Francis Fukuyama and other intellectuals refer to the whole complex of such humanistic ideas, ideals and principles as 'modern western liberalism' and 'western liberal democracy' (p. 77). Fukuyama (1990, 1992) in his 'End of History' thesis claimed that the history of ideas had ended with the recognition of liberal democracy as the final form of human government. The image of a 'world of liberal democracies' suggested the superiority of a specifically western model of development, based perhaps especially on the USA, and it implied that values such as individualism and a liberal economy were becoming virtually 'universal'. However, Stolyarov goes on to invoke the need to recognise cultural plurality in a manner which echoes some of the themes of Huntington's (1996) 'clash of civilisations' thesis.

Of course, Europe, the USA and Canada, embodying 'the West', have played the leading role in the development of humanistic and democratic ideas. However, at the end of 20th century, when the interconnection and unity of world history are most clearly revealed, the conditional character of linking such strong achievements of humanistic and democratic understanding culture only to one region is evident. The contemporary world includes a huge number of countries with rich and varied cultural traditions and intellectual and spiritual strivings. (Stolyarov 1995: 77–8)

Parry (2004) has argued that because liberalism *happened* in the West, this does not necessarily imply it is ethnocentric or less universal. Interestingly, Fukuyama (1992), after disputing previous accounts that democracy was the product of the specific cultural and social milieu of western civilisation, argued, 'it was the most rational possible political system and "fit" a broader human personality shared across cultures' (pp. 220–1). Nonetheless, as discussed previously, Von Laue argues that liberal democracy is primarily associated with the West, as the lack of indigenous non-western liberal democracies suggests that 'liberal democracy spread as a result of the westernisation of the world; its appeal is based on a wide range of factors, all derived from superior power' (Von Laue 1994: 26). However, even though the processes of democratisation in the newly independent states, which were formed after the collapse of the Communist Bloc, were merely drawn upon the western (liberal) model, they should not be seen as indistinguishable from western democracies. First, the values of their communist legacy could not be discarded instantaneously (especially in the case of Russia where the communist system lasted for over 70 years), and second, the transition itself generated very different problems from those of the western democracies. For these reasons, Heywood (2002: 31) has argued 'this liberal-democratic triumphalism reflected the persistence of a western-centric viewpoint, and it may anyway, have been a hangover from the days of the Cold War'.

The post-totalitarian change was also followed by a conversion of the old Soviet Union, and central and southern Europe, to forms of market economy through processes of economic transition to capitalism. Liponski, Vice-President of the Polish NOC and guest lecturer at the 1992 IOA Session, reflected upon the economic differences of the two systems in relation to elite sport,

> What surprises us is that Polish athletes and, I venture to observe, other East European athletes as well demonstrate their pro-commercial orientation in a way incomparably more uncompromising than their western colleagues do. East European countries were for several decades isolated from the outer world not only politically but also in terms of economy. Despite all the ideological pressures, sport in the East Bloc became one of the most attractive ways for young people to go West and to enjoy there some of the benefits of well-developed consumer societies. These benefits were allowed and dosed out to 'communist' athletes hesitantly and in carefully limited quantities in order to immunise them slowly to the 'rotten fruits of the West'. During the first decades after World War II, 'communist' teams sent West were usually guarded by security officers in civilian clothes and 'politruks' i.e. 'educational officers or officials', responsible in fact for the political behaviour of their athletes abroad. Then, in the course of time, restrictions became weaker and at least the separately wired Olympic Village for 'communist' teams so characteristic of the 1952 Games was no longer in existence. (Liponski 1992: 113)

He also argued that the economic restrictions imposed by communism heightened the Eastern European athletes' zeal for money.

> But one factor remained unchanged until quite recently: owing to the well-known economic differences between the eastern and western sides of the Iron Curtain, 'communist' athletes were always poorly endowed

with hard currency. When the era of 'permit-meetings' came into being, money earned by Eastern European athletes was at the beginning entirely, and then to a substantial degree, deducted by their state authorities. While in Poland and some other countries athletes were gradually allowed some percentage of the money they earned (though much less than in the West), in other countries of the East Bloc they did not get anything. As recently as two years ago there was an international rumour that one 'communist' team had been sent abroad without even pocket money and had waited at the airport for the mercy of the organisers and then a voluntary collection of money by other athletes. One can only imagine the psychological frustration of these people, who on the one hand know very well that in competitive terms they are equal to their foreign colleagues and have the opportunity of being in touch with all the luxuries of the contemporary world, usually inaccessible in their home country, while on the other hand they were not able to have easy access to such luxuries, except for the officially paid hotel and meals, and not necessarily even a bus or taxi from the airport. Such psychological factors soon created among East European athletes a kind of wild hunger for western money, technological products and all the other amenities of civilised life. (Liponski 1992: 113–14)

Thus, the 'free' world of the West, and the promising economic system of capitalism attracted many 'Westernisers' in Eastern Europe who wanted to escape from a relatively impoverished, deprived and isolated past. Interestingly, many Westerners, wishing to see the ex-communist societies integrated into the 'winning' western capitalist system, kept inviting them to the West (Liponski 1992). The elite sport system in Eastern Europe and the USSR, it was argued, far from enhancing nationalism and patriotic feelings was rather a source of antipathy or indifference. In particular, Poland, the GDR, Hungary, Romania and Bulgaria rebelled against the communist sport tradition and allowed foreign elements to intrude on their sport culture. In this new culture, elite athletes were no longer seen as part of a shared national heritage or bearers of Olympic success for the nation (Riordan 1999). This resulted in a significant emigration by members of the ex-communist sport elite, including athletes, coaches, PE teachers and sport instructors, to western countries. Such sport trade based on economic benefits unquestionably challenged Olympic ideals.

The more adept individuals, in order to make up for their so obvious financial insufficiency abroad, often metamorphosed into 'trading athletes', who bartered scarce items from their own countries in the West. In such a way they were able to earn money outside the control of their national authorities. In the course of time this became a common sight of East European sport and at the same time an additional element detrimental to the ideals of the Olympic movement, with the effects lasting much longer than the communist economy as such in East European countries. It is true that after the collapse of the East European communist regimes all athletes there obtained much brighter prospects for their normal careers. Para-doxically, however, these newly acquired liberties did not limit their still greedy search for money and other western comforts and benefits. (Liponski 1992: 114)

The early years of the post-Cold War period in particular were characterised by the phenomenon of 'economic escape' from the ex-communist regimes of Eastern Europe and the USSR to the West. Liponski (1992) indicates that, for example, 32 top Polish coaches were employed by foreign national teams during the 1988 Seoul Olympics, and by 1992 this number had increased to 180 coaches. In addition, about 1,100 sport instructors and PE teachers went abroad seeking opportunities to increase their income and improve their sport careers. Thus, although the communist states of Eastern Europe used sport as a contribution to develop a sense of national identity, the trading of sport specialists and athletes in the wake of Soviet collapse raised questions about the effectiveness of sport as a contribution to nation-building. Moreover, the zeal of the East Germans for reunification and the emergence of nationalist movements in the Baltic states, other Soviet republics, and the countries of the former Yugoslavia, provided evidence that East German, Soviet and Yugoslav sense of nationhood might have been superficial (Houlihan 1994).

The collapse of the Communist Bloc, followed by the dismantling of com-munist sport, also meant the end of many progressive practices in the com-munist sport tradition, such as its openness to talent in all sports, to women, and ethnic minorities, as well as its support for the Olympic ideals through participation in the Olympic Solidarity programmes and its resistance to South African apartheid (Riordan 1999). Moreover, the Cold War rivalry itself provided a strong force for the growth of sport in central and Eastern Europe, while it was also an important drive for government support for sport in many countries (including countries such as the USA and Britain). Houlihan (1994) observed that government intervention and support was reduced in the post-Cold War period, referring to the example of Britain where the amount of money spent on sport by local authorities declined by between 30 per cent and 40 per cent during the period 1990–1994, while the budget of the Sport Council had been frozen at its 1992 level (p. 204).

Interestingly, although sport in developed countries retained the lost resources of government intervention from commercial sponsorship, this was not the case in developing economies, whose dependent position increased. More-over, the new nations of the former Soviet Union and Yugoslavia began to compete with developing countries for aid, and thus funds provided by the World Bank and other international organisations were greatly stretched (Dodds 2000). Thus, with the end of the Cold War, the new world order appeared to some commentators as unipolar, with the USA the only power which had the military, political and economic capacity to control international affairs. However, the rapid global political change, which strengthened the power of the West, had its impact upon the Olympic movement and the ideology of Olympism too.

5.3.2   Power of the West: Cultural imperialism and marginalisation of local sport cultures

As we have noted, it has been argued that the modern Olympic movement has, since its inception, been deeply Eurocentric. Eichberg (1984: 97), for example, emphasises that Olympism is a 'social pattern' that reflects the colonial dominance of the West, and the everyday culture of western industrial society. Guttmann (1994) argued that the Olympic programme, the organisation of the Games, the origin of the host cities, and the intense ritualism associated with the Olympic Games have emphasised the European origins of the Games and have imposed a specific character on non-western nations. Thoma and Chalip (1996) reached similar conclusions citing the fact that most world sports, especially the non-European, have been excluded from the programme of the Olympic Games. Several guest speakers at the IOA Sessions, especially in the post-Cold War period, reflected upon the dominance of the West in the Olympic movement, highlighting: a) the problematic dissemination of Olympism and its values in non-European, non-western cultures, b) the suppression of regional cultural (sport) identities, and c) the monopolisation of western interests which have increased the economic differences between core and periphery.

Lalaoui, an Algerian guest lecturer at the 1993 IOA Session, emphasised that Olympic ideology, consisting of values associated with a culture-specific context (that of the West) had failed to be adapted to the needs of the different socio-cultural systems of the world.

> It is rather commonplace to recall that modern Olympism today, through the philosophy, which it conveys, contributes to social and cultural progress throughout the world. What is, however, more difficult is to know the reasons for which it has not been able to reach and transform, in a similar manner, all socio-cultural systems. The answer is that the Olympic idea or the Olympic thinking, which is associated with the historical experience of a human activity (sport), is not inculcated, taught and experienced in the same way in every society. The historical meaning of Olympism, the product of a collective human activity, is therefore quite differently interpreted in each individual national sports system. In fact, if we look back at the history of the sports culture, which Olympism encourages, on the theories, and concepts, which relate to the dissemination of Olympic values, we shall see that the various aspects of this philosophy have developed outside a number of cultural domains. The identification to the Olympic soul, which should generate, in every society, basic sports behaviour, driven

by immovable and trans-cultural values, is given a different interpretation depending on the socio-cultural system concerned ... It is as if modern Olympism and its generous ideas wanted to give, as such, the value of model to the logic of western sports practice, and make it a natural characteristic of sports culture, whilst forgetting that this formal logic of sports practice is also a cultural achievement specific to each country. (Lalaoui 1993: 102–3)

The Olympic movement developed from the Victorian codes of sportsmanship and Muscular Christianity, also incorporating values inspired by the late nineteenth-century interpretations of Hellenic civilisation. Lalaoui's argument is that Olympism, bound up with inherent Eurocentric values (those of Anglo-Saxon sport and of Hellenic civilisation), had not been adjusted to the different socio-cultural systems, and had thus failed to be 'translated' to meet the cultural contexts and needs of non-European, non-western societies. Notwithstanding Lalaoui's claims, it has been argued that cultural identities across the globe have fractured, relativised and 'creolised' in late modernity (Black and van der Westhuizen 2004; McGrew 1992). Thus, although a western global domination might be implied and some 'western' values had been spread, this does not necessarily provide support for the notion of 'western hegemony' (Albrow 1997; Ruuska 1999). Moreover, Parry (2004), taking into consideration Rawls' distinction between concepts and conceptions, argued that the concept of Olympism can be understood at a high level of generality, consisting of values which can be subject to multiple interpretations given different locations in time and space. Thus, although the concept of Olympism might have been formulated in a western context of thought, its differing conceptions can be understood and interpreted in many different ways according to different socio-cultural frameworks. Nonetheless, Lalaoui contends,

In our opinion, the failure of modern Olympism in developing countries is quite evident today: for the simple reason that Olympic values which were, above all, intended to democratise the practice of sport, have failed to reach and change the daily sports reality of youth and thus strengthen ... As a result, for a vast youth population, which lacks the necessary background to decode the civilisation phenomenon which sport represents, *Olympism remains a myth, a muscular technology too advanced and therefore unreachable. In such a context, an Olympiad can only be seen as a show of strength, on the part of rich countries, which come to exhibit their technological advances in the field of sport and their 'muscular power', against the technological poverty and physical destitution of developing countries.* (Lalaoui 1993: 103; emphasis added)

Lalaoui highlights the economic differences between the core and periphery, which are generated from the increasingly commercialised Olympic Games, while in similar vein, Landry, an Olympic scholar from Canada, a guest speaker at the 25th IOA Session in 1985 emphasised,

> The rapid and very considerable growth in the number of countries participating in the Olympic Games has not been paralleled by an equally large increase in the number of national elite, nor in their Olympic successes. In other words, the Olympic sports have diffused widely in the world ... the medals have for their part diffused only little. In fact, we shall see that tendency has even reversed itself (...) The progressive 'universality' of the Olympic sports is accompanied by a growing monopolisation of the success by a handful of countries leading the way in economic and technical terms, two typical characteristics of western culture in the sense described above. (Landry 1985: 147)

Some eight years later, in 1993, Barney, another Canadian Olympic scholar, argued that the economic interests of the Olympic Games, as reflected in the commodification of the Olympics and the high costs required for hosting the event, had widened the gap between the core and periphery even more.

> And though a pragmatist might argue that IOC resources have benefited all, a contending point of view could well be that they have benefited Europeans and North Americans most; Africans, Asians, Latin Americans, and Oceanians, far less. The sports culture that the IOC nourishes most, for instance, is not particularly one indigenous to many countries in those world areas noted above. What might be the destiny of specific culturally oriented sports in Samoa, for example, in the face of a Samoan National Olympic Committee and IOC exertion to foster among Samoan youth greater awareness and participation in Olympic sports, most all of which are culturally bound to Europe? Should Olympism include indigenous cultural sports awareness and preservation as well as sensitivity to Olympic sporting matters? ...

> Will an African, or a Latin American, or a Middle East city ever be able to host an Olympic Games? Even though infrastructures are improving in those world areas, they may, in reality, be falling further and further behind in meeting increasingly high standards set for hosting the great festival. Should the IOC set aside resources to support a guarantee that the Olympic Games will be celebrated from time to time in areas of the world that can only dream of ever serving as host? (Barney 1993: 132)

There has been a reflection of the changing world order here, at least in cultural terms, in that 16 years after this speech the Games of 2016 had been awarded to South America (Rio de Janeiro), and in 2011 the right to host the FIFA World Cup had been awarded to Russia (for 2018) and to the Middle East (Qatar for 2022).

In addition, Barney (1993) raised the issue of the integration of local sport cultures in the Olympic movement, an issue that has been debated ever since the early years of the movement. Landry had voiced a similar concern in relation to this at the IOA Session in 1985,

> Development aid in sport raises some severely practical questions, but also problems of ethics. Because of the present strength of the Olympic movement and of the preponderance of the European and North American sports which are formally (and constantly) valued, the underlying patterns and standards of occidental sporting conduct continues to be exported to many countries where they bring imbalance and even cause the crumbling of local play and physical actively traditions. Thus in the eyes of many, development aid in sport and its international thrust for standardisation has many of the characteristics of a neo-colonialist movement comparable with those of world markets, multinationals, mass-media and global tourism. Example: in a number of African countries where one hoped to serve national prestige by adopting foreign (Olympic) sports and by calling on western coaches, one now observes with regret that the panorama of games and sports and other forms of play activities which were part of the very fabric of these societies have been taken up by occidental games and sports. *The author is of the opinion that the net result here is a regression of cultural identities.* (Landry 1985: 142; emphasis added)

It has been argued that the association between Olympic sport aid and multinational companies (based on the perception that developing countries could well provide potential consumers of sport products, as well as a potential source of workers in the sports equipment industry) has raised many questions regarding benefits to the West from the implementation of sport aid programmes (Al-Tauqi 2003). Moreover, it is often believed that the aim of sport aid programmes is mainly to help talented athletes in peripheral countries to improve their performance by seeking to attain the Olympic standards, thus contributing to the increase of the competitive level of the Games (Donnelly 1996; Dubberke 1986). Lalaoui claimed that the emphasis on competitive success undermined in developing countries the Olympic message.

> In these societies [i.e. the developing countries] you still cannot find a coherent and generous sports programme likely to establish a true pedagogy of Olympism. This is the reason why, for example, the different sports development models, which have been inspired by the West, have failed to introduce an elementary sports education within education and

training institutions ... As a result, we note with bitterness today that, in a number of sport disciplines, the gap is so big that many developing countries devote all their time and money to one or two sports. These countries then have no alternative, if they want to participate in the Olympics, than to sacrifice all available funds earmarked for the development of mass educational sports. It is important, one says, to take part in the Olympic Games, no matter what the results! So, every Olympiad contributes to widening, a little more, the huge gap between North and South in the field of sport. (Lalaoui 1993: 103)

The Canadian, Peter Donnelly, in his speech at the 1995 IOA Session, provided a model of convergence of the two ideologies of Olympism and professionalism, which he named 'prolympism', and claimed that it has an enormous impact on all forms of sport. The impact of this single dominant ideology is that it tends to reinforce and reproduce itself, it marginalises alternatives, and it creates a momentum that tends to draw all sport in a single direction (p. 59). He also emphasised that the Olympic sport aid programmes, also following the principles of prolympism, promote the western model of sport, thus marginalising indigenous sport cultures of the non-western countries.

On a much larger scale, Olympic Solidarity provides similar outreach programmes – coach and athlete development, sports medicine, clinics, facilities, equipment, travel funding – to developing countries in an attempt to avoid the problem, noted previously, of athletes failing to qualify for the Olympics under the new standards. Since this is frequently the only sport development funding available in many new and developing nations, it is eagerly accepted by governments who see membership in the United Nations and marching in the Opening Ceremonies of the Olympic Games as a twin confirmation of nationhood (MacAloon 1986). *However, such interventions have the inevitable consequence of usurping and marginalizing indigenous sport and game cultures.* Various attempts to promote indigenous games (e.g., the GANEFO Games) have been unsuccessful in combating the Olympic juggernaut. The limitations of prolympism become very evident when we see that judo is still the only Olympic sport that is non- western in origin. ...

Is this a perfect hegemony? Has a way of understanding sport become the way of understanding sport? Have all available alternatives been marginalised or incorporated to the point where no new alternatives are apparent or even considered necessary? Has a single sport ideology – prolympism – become the order of the day? (Donnelly 1995: 60–1, 62)

Marxists and neo-Marxists argue that the phenomenon of the Olympic Games has raised many concerns about commodification, global market power, the role of the state, and the question of resistance and the struggle of masses against the powerful forces of capital. However, even outside such an ideological framework it has been argued that the economic interests of the Olympic Games widen the gap between the core nations of the West and the non-western, non-European peripheral nations. This is even more evident when one considers the increasingly high resources required for a city to host the Olympic Games. Moreover, although the organisation of alternative and Regional Games has played a significant role in the global diffusion of modern sport, creating a regional base in which globalised modern sport has penetrated into local communities, it can be argued that most regional and alternative Games either reproduced the same competitive (western) model of the Olympics (e.g. Regional Games), or promoted a political agenda in opposition to the West, but were eventually 'won over' through the political manoeuvring of the IOC (e.g. Workers' Olympics, GANEFO Games). The Olympic Games thus remain a western-dominated movement both in terms of political power and the origin of sports in the programmes (Toohey and Veal 2000).

Nevertheless, as Cashman (2004: 134) points out, this Eurocentric bias does not seem 'to represent a handicap to the global spread of the Olympic Games, since many of the sports in the programme have become cosmopolitan sports, understood by sport communities globally'. Thus many European countries are strong in Asian-origin sport, such as judo, while Asian countries now dominate in sports of European-origin such as archery, badminton and table tennis. Moreover, Donnelly (1995) has emphasised that the developing countries' participation in the Olympic Games has been important for their growth and introduction into the capitalist world, while it has also provided them with a terrain to reinforce their nationhood. He also argues that there are reasons to be optimistic,

> Even within the Olympic movement there is evidence of openness to cultural diversity ... The Olympic movement requires a cultural festival to be held in conjunction with every Olympics. These cultural festivals celebrate local, regional, and indigenous cultures and cultural diversity. Sponsoring cultural diversity in areas such as dance and music, while promoting the development of a sport monoculture represents a contradiction that must be resolved by the Olympic movement. (Donnelly 1995: 66)

The Opening Ceremony of the Sydney 2000 Games provides a good example of how multiculturalism in the Olympic movement has begun to be addressed (Tenenbaum 2000), though the reception of the symbolic message of a multicultural Australia received mixed reviews (Garcia 2007). The Olympic Games are vulnerable in terms of their balance and size, as reflected in the programme of the Games and the unbalanced ratio between new and old sports, as well as 'regional sports'. The achievement of a better balance requires great inter-cultural sensitivity, not affected by the interests of television companies or of sponsors. Thus, Cashman (2004: 134) suggested that it might have been wise for the IOC to include *wushu* in the programme of the 2008 Beijing Olympic Games, as 'it would indicate inter-cultural sensitivity and a recognition of alternative visions of global sport. It would demonstrate that it is possible for the programme of the Olympic Games to evolve to take into consideration the changing global sports system'. Donnelly has also suggested that,

> Organisers of the Games could be permitted to select all of the Olympic events to recognise and celebrate the sporting culture of their country. Olympic Games could be open to a great deal of many different sports. Or, in conjunction with the cultural festival, there could be a parallel sport festival, which celebrated mass participation. The Olympic movement, which is now part of the problem, could also be part of the solution. The available cultural space is going to be colonised, and it is easy to imagine a time when prolympism will be a marginalised alternative. Now is the time to critically examine our current practices in Olympism, and to consider alternatives. (Donnelly 1995: 66)

Barney highlights the responsibility of the Olympic authorities in safeguarding the cultural traditions and maintaining a balance between the core and periphery,

> The IOC should give as much careful consideration to the distribution of their wealth as they most certainly have applied to its creation. IOC coffers are likely to expand greatly in coming decades. So, too, will the ability of the IOC to make an impact on world progress, indeed, to promote peace and harmony, preserve important cultural legacies, and support dreams for which its lack of support will ensure that they remain just that, dreams. (Barney 1993: 132)

In sum, a number of the guest speakers at the IOA Sessions in the post-Cold War period argued that: a) the Olympic movement is western-dominated, b) the monopolisation of western interests has increased the economic differences between the core and periphery, and c) that more indigenous sports should be included in the programme of the Games as a vehicle for multiculturalism. Interestingly, although most IOA speakers cited here originated from the West, they promoted the critique of the Eurocentric character of the Olympic movement, and suggested solutions for the improvement of the movement. This illustrates how, to a certain degree, the IOA as an institution has become more open to critical commentary on the Olympic movement.

Critics from the non-West were less in evidence, though the Algerian, Lalaoui, reflected upon the conditions in developing countries in relation to sport and Olympism, expressing concerns about the problematic dissemination of the

Olympic values in non-European socio-cultural systems, and about the problems surrounding sport aid programmes, and the increasing economic differences between the core and periphery as a result of the competitive nature of the Games.

Thus although the IOA continued to be selective in its choice of speakers, it had begun to provide in more recent years a stage for emancipatory and critical social analysis of the Olympic movement, from the West, and from the non-West. The discourse developed is thus less defensive and celebratory than was the case in the earlier period of its history.

5.3.3   Adaptability of Olympism: New and outdated values

The new value of environmentalism

A further set of issues discussed at the IOA relates to the integration of new values in the ideology of Olympism, such as environmentalism. DaCosta, an Olympic scholar from Brazil explained the significance of this issue at the 37th IOA Session (1997),

> The short period of five years taken by the IOC to be adapted to the main environmental challenges may be contrasted with the long-standing discussion on the gigantism of Games (since 1910s), amateurism (since the 1920s) or the coexistence of IOC with International Federations and National Olympic Committees (since the 1930s). (Dacosta 1997: 102)

Concerns about the negative environmental impact of the Olympic Games came to the fore in the 1992 Winter Games in Albertville. During the opening ceremony, the local community protested that the newly-built infrastructure had damaged many parts of the alpine region. In 1992, the Council of Europe voted for a resolution supporting environmentally-concerned sports and seeking to avoid any recurrence of Albertville's 'environmental abuse'. These rejections led the IOC President Samaranch to recognise publicly the importance of an environmental agenda for the Olympic movement at the Earth Summit, held in 1992 in Rio de Janeiro (United Nations Conference on Environment and Development). The promotion of a 'sustainable development' policy became one of the discourse themes evident in the pronouncements of the IOC. As the environmental lobby gained strength and credibility, the adoption of an approach which engendered sustainable development, defined as meeting 'the needs of the present without compromising the ability of future generations to meet their own needs' (United Nations 1987; cited in International Olympic Committee 2004: 17). The IOC's adoption of sustainable development in sport followed adoption by 178 countries of Agenda 21, a UN action plan for sustainable development at the United Nations Conference on Environment and Development (UNCED) held in Rio de Janeiro, Brazil, in 1992.

The Centennial Olympic Congress held in Paris in 1994 incorporated discussions about sport and the environment and in its final report called for the inclusion in the Olympic Charter of a provision emphasising the importance of protecting the environment. It also called for the establishment of an IOC Sport and Environment Commission. The IOC, in this way, defined its role in promoting 'sustainable development' and officially regarded the environment as 'the third dimension of Olympism, alongside sport and culture' (International Olympic Committee 2009). In 1995 the Sport and Environment Commission was established with a role 'to advise the IOC Executive Board on what policy the IOC and Olympic movement should follow in terms of environmental protection and support for sustainable development, and to coordinate the application of this policy' (International Olympic Committee 2009). Moreover, the Olympic Charter was amended in 1996 adding the following paragraph in rule 2 (role of the IOC):

> The International Olympic Committee (IOC) sees to it that the Olympic Games are held in conditions which demonstrate a responsible concern for environmental issues and encourages the Olympic movement to demonstrate a responsible concern for environmental issues, takes measures to reflect such concern in its activities and educates all those connected with the Olympic movement as to the importance of sustainable development. (International Olympic Committee 1996: Rule 2, paragraph 13)

After several years of preparations, the IOC created its own Agenda 21 based on the model of the UN Conference on Environment and Development (UNCED). It announced the adoption of Agenda 21 at its Session in June 1999 in Seoul, which was later sanctioned by the whole Olympic movement at the Third World Conference on Sport and the Environment in Rio de Janeiro in October 1999. The Agenda 21 for the Olympic movement is bound around three objectives: improving socio-economic conditions, conservation and management of resources for sustainable development, and strengthening the role of major groups.

The IOC, and the Olympic movement, has taken many steps forward since the protests in Albertville (1992). The Olympic Games in Lillehammer (1994) and Sydney (2000) promoted the green profile of the Olympic movement (though ironically the Homebush site in Sydney was criticised for the severe environmental challenges it posed). In addition, the candidate cities for the 2004 Olympic Games presented preliminary or complete environmental impact evaluations at the first selection that took place in 1997 illustrating the increased environmental consciousness in relation to staging the Games. Nevertheless, Lamartine DaCosta has argued,

> Despite these outstanding improvements, the Olympic Family is far from having environmental responsibility as a 'key tenet' of the Olympic

movement or as a 'fundamental principle' of the Olympic Charter in conformity with the 1994 Centennial Olympic Congress recommendations. While the environmental safeguards tend to be better recognised among sport leaders, the decision-making process of sport institutions is often as hidden as it is complex. (Dacosta 1997: 102)

DaCosta goes on to suggest that,

> The judgement of an ideal Olympism rooted in environmental principles can be appropriately made in the Olympic Charter context in which 'Olympism is a philosophy of life, exalting and combining in a balanced whole the qualities of body, will and mind'. Should the 'balanced whole' be scrutinised with an ecological mindset, the interpretation would naturally refer to sustainability. Similarly, the goals of Olympism as proposed by the Charter, fit in quite well with the Olympic family's adaptations to environmental guidelines previously described here. Thus, if 'Olympism seeks to create a way of life based on the joy in effort, the educational value of good example and respect for universal fundamental ethical principles', then the IOC with its commitment to sustainability and the Olympic Games sites' new ecological approaches are in line with both Olympism and environmentalism. Therefore, as a modification of Olympic Charter as mentioned before, a suitable suggestion would be to introduce the expression 'balanced and sustainable whole' in the present definition of Olympism. (DaCosta 1997: 103)

DaCosta, albeit cautiously optimistic about the progress made by the IOC on the issue of environmental protection, acknowledges that a further, more substantial change in the key tenets of the Olympic ideology might not be easily achieved. There are, he suggests, 'deeper processes' to be addressed in achieving change than a mere form of words. However, he suggests that the amendments to the Olympic Charter provide evidence that the Olympic movement is susceptible to the new socio-political pressures and conditions, and he concludes that, 'the IOC's environmental adaptation has proved the capacity-building of the Olympic movement when exposed to external pressures, but equally suggests a lack of strength for resolving internal controversies' (DaCosta 1997: 102). DaCosta perceives the resolution of the environmental issue as a necessary response to external pressures. The IOC, in an attempt to respond to the new demands of global society, has developed links with supra-national organisations such as the EU and the UN, establishing with them a closer cooperation in a number of issues, including the protection of world's environment.

Outdated values

The delays in resolving issues such as amateurism, and women's participation in the Games and in the Olympic movement illustrate how the Olympic movement has been 'slow' to remove outdated elements from the ideology of Olympism. Interestingly, during debates at the IOA Sessions on the meaning of Olympism, discussion has questioned its immutability and suggested that some of its values have become outdated. Lenk, a German philosopher and Olympic scholar, was the first guest speaker to provide an analysis of Olympic values at the IOA, when he argued in the 4th IOA Session that,

> Comprehensive investigation of the system of Olympic values leads to the following conclusions: There has been no essential change in the Olympic value concepts since the beginning of this century. (Strictly speaking, it is this continuity that enables one to speak of the one structure of aims and values). The constancy of values furthered the smooth continuity of the movement and its adhesion to the aims. (Lenk 1964: 210)

Subsequent speakers at the IOA, however, suggested that Olympism had changed through time. Heinz-Egon Roesch (West Germany), for example, argued that:

> Coubertin's illusions of the Olympic idea and of Olympism, which are based on ideality, are nowadays to a large extent outdated and are hardly taken notice any more as it was also the case during his life-time. But nevertheless some agreements are to be found which today have accepted value in a modern interpretation of Olympic idea, Olympism and religion at least in the wider sense. (Roesch 1979: 200)

In a similar vein, Jan Leiper, an Olympic scholar from Canada, argued at the 1980 IOA Session:

> The Olympic Ideal obviously had its foundation in the beliefs of Pierre de Coubertin. Although all the attitudes and beliefs, which may now be seen to comprise Olympism, may have been present in Coubertin's theories at the time of the restoration of the Olympic Games, some were not then stressed in his speeches and writings ... It is doubtful that Coubertin ever sat down and structured the tenets of Olympism before presenting them to the world. However in 1934, looking back 40 years, he contended that 'Neo-Olympism' had been a totality from the beginning when he pointed out that it was not '... an uncertain creation whose stages followed one another timidly and haphazardly'. *Parts of this description of Olympism are still valid today as an ideal but other parts are not. Both the beliefs of people and their behaviours change as society changes. The effects of economic, sociological, scientific and political shifts cause adjustments and adaptations to be made in the ideas and systems under which people live. Olympism has not escaped untouched. Today's sporting*

values are not those of 1896 and sporting behaviours reflect the new attitudes.
(Leiper 1980: 89–90; emphasis added)

Nadia Lekarska of Bulgaria, also echoed the need for the modernisation of Olympism:

> How are we to consider 'Olympism' at the end of this century, a question by no means incidental, as according to a number of sports officials, this concept is apparently in need of modernisation so as to fit the require-ments of present times. In view of the fact that generalisations are more easily assimilated and dissimilated than substantial arguments, it seems necessary to draw the line between what we believe to be immutable and/or in need of change according to today's realities. (Lekarska 1988: 73)

However while acknowledging the need for change Lekarska still wishes to pay homage to, and to protect the integrity of, Coubertin's founding principles,

> I wish to conclude this lecture by expressing my view that the basic Olympic principles, formulated by Pierre de Coubertin, have not been challenged by time. Vigilance seems, however, necessary to prevent trends, which might menace their integrity. Any other changes aimed at modernizing the Olympic Games and movement related to more mortal matters embodied in rules and regulations should be viewed positively. (Lekarska 1988: 80)

Lekarska (1988) argued that Coubertin's ideas about amateurism and women's participation were outdated, but the values of internationalism, excellence and moral development through sport, are still important constituents of Olympism. Thus, she emphasised that any amendments and new elements in the Olympic Charter should not be discouraged, but they should be seen as an integral part of the modernisation processes of Olympism. Sergei Neverkovich a Russian Olympic scholar and guest speaker at the same Session also noted, 'The Olympic idea and the form of its realisation have become part of modern times, enriched and modified by social and historical experience, and will, it is hoped, belong to the future (Neverkovich 1987: 175). With regard to the issue of amateurism, Parry at the same session argued:

> If it is indeed true that the commitment to amateurism is dying, it is just as well that amateurism turns out to have been a historically specific element, which is simply becoming an outmoded factor. If, on the other hand, it had been the central universal value of Olympism, this would be indi-cating that Olympism itself is dying, since its central value is. *Olympism is alive and well, but amateurism is not. This shows that there must be some other*

source of the values of Olympism than amateurism. (Parry 1988: 90–1; emphasis added)

Similarly, Clarke, Assistant Executive Director of the US Olympic Committee, at the 28th IOA Session distinguishes between 'tradition' and values.

> 'Tradition', however, cannot be given the dignity of a value merely because it is a tradition, nor should a problem within Olympism be dismissed as due to an outdated factor just because it is a problem. (Clarke 1988: 99)

He goes on to suggest that 'An ideal is by definition unattainable, and issues thereby evolve continuously' (Clarke 1988: 101). The implication is that values are stable but issues relating to how those values may be realised are changeable.

The shift from amateurism to eligibility, and later professionalism, as reflected in the amendments and new regulations of the Olympic Charter (1974, 1981) provided evidence that the IOC had taken action to remove outdated elements from its underpinning philosophy. Moreover, the promotion of a 'sustainable development' policy as one of the fundamental objectives of the Olympic movement demonstrates the ability of the IOC to adapt its rhetoric at least to meet emergent pressures and needs. Nevertheless, DaCosta warns that incorporating new challenges such as environmentalism through tinkering with the definition of Olympism is unlikely to be a simple matter, the result being a kind of 'concept stretching' in relation to Olympism which renders it less, rather than more comprehensible.

> Although the IOC's environmental efforts are acknowledged, the traditional paradoxes of Olympism soon reappear. Because 'ever upward' is the Olympic creed – that is citius, altius, fortius – the ecological awareness of recent Olympic Games experiences have highlighted the excesses of sport and revisited its necessary limits. This interpretation finds support in Coubertin's memoirs from the beginning of this century; 'sport moves towards excesses … that is the core of the problem but at the same time it is its nobility and even its poetic charm' … But these recommendations [about environment] are ineffective in terms of seeking a binding definition of Olympism or given greater clarification to its philosophy. (Dacosta 1997: 102–3)

Thus, although definitions or concepts of Olympism, have over time been gradually adapted to emergent socio-political, and cultural contexts, issues and value challenges, its inherent paradoxes have still to be resolved.

5.4 Conclusion

The speeches of invited speakers at the IOA illustrate the degree to which the slow pluralising of debate had developed over the last four decades of the twentieth century. While some major critics had not received a platform (and perhaps had not sought one) at the IOA, there is evidence of a growing critical voice. This might take the form of 'critical friends' (though not all of our quoted speakers would be necessarily happy with such nomenclature) but difficult issues such as gender equity, multiculturalism and the Euro-centric nature of the movement, and environmentalism, do receive growing, explicit attention. Clearly as the Olympic family moved towards the end of the twentieth century and was to be faced with a corruption scandal which was particularly threatening for a movement that traded on its image as one with ethical primary goals, the need to become more transparent and accountable was clear. Our final chapter thus deals with the key issues facing the movement in the first dozen years of the twenty-first century, and more particularly with the discursive framing of those issues and of the movement's responses.

6
Technologies of Power, Governmentality and Discourses of Olympism in the Twenty-first Century

6.1   Introduction

In the foregoing chapters we have sought to accomplish three things. First we reviewed in the opening chapter a range of theoretical perspectives through which the nature and impact of Olympism might be evaluated, advocating a form of critical discourse analysis drawing on the work of Michel Foucault to frame our understanding of the development of Olympism as a moral project. Second we introduced the changing global context against which Olympism has developed (and which Olympism itself has to some extent shaped). Third we sought to analyse the discourse strands in, and engaging with, Olympism which are evident in the late nineteenth to the mid twentieth century (through the writings of Coubertin), from the early twentieth century to the second half of the twentieth century (as evidenced in the writings of Carl Diem), and for the later twentieth century (by reference to the speakers and lecturers at the International Olympic Academy). In doing so we have sought to establish the most important discourse themes in relation to these three sources, and to illustrate and analyse ways in which the discourses of Olympism have been enmeshed within, and themselves shaped in symbiotic fashion, the broader local, national and global discourses of the period.

   The Olympic phenomenon has become a common place feature of life for a significant proportion of the global population. The person in the street carries with her an internalised concept of Olympic phenomena, which implies for example a set of propositions about what kinds of person the 'Olympic athlete' is, but also implies aspects of how those athletes and other Olympic actors should behave – a moral agenda which is bound up with the notion of Olympism, indicating aspects such as fair play, generosity of spirit ('it is not the winning but the taking part which matters'), and opposition to doping, and which is also, importantly if less directly, related to ethical issues such as gender equity, multiculturalism and so on. These 'principles' may be seen as more honoured at times in their breach than in their observance, but nevertheless the whole notion of a principle to be broken has to be premised on an ethically-based conceptualisation. In this book we have concentrated rather more on the *production* of discourse by key actors rather than on the *impact* of those discourses on different groups (and in particular different language/cultural/political communities).[1] In this sense we are focusing here rather more on the 'power over discourse', than the 'power of discourse' though we do address issues relating to the latter. An obvious example is our discussion of the failure of Coubertin's discursive construction of the role of women in sport – which was essentially to 'applaud the male protagonists' and 'award the winners' laurels' – to influence the Olympic movement. This was particularly evident after the 1928 'absorption' into the Olympic Games of women's athletics, thus incorporating Alice Milliat's *Fédération Sportive Féminine Internationale* into the Olympic movement. The differences between cultures, and between and within national groupings, in values in relation to Olympism, will be a function of how discourse strands in relation to Olympism engage with other discourses within a given society or group. Thus to take two recent Olympic hosts, Olympic values and their relationship to human rights may be very different in the context of Chinese society with its emphasis on collective rights of the community and society (Chan 2006: 173–202) from those expressed in the 'British' liberal individualist conceptions of human rights (Parekh 1992). Nevertheless despite such apparent contrasts we note that both British and Chinese politicians and commentators have felt able to promote claims of the special relationship of Olympic values to Labour Party philosophy (Jowell 2006) and to traditional Confucian values (Xu 2008).

This final chapter has two major functions. The first is through drawing together the discourse themes addressed throughout the book we look to understand ways in which Olympic concepts, and in particular the moral dimension of Olympism, might be said to have shaped and disciplined our ways of thinking about self, the body, the social milieu, what constitutes a positive way of life and so on. This is largely accomplished through the prism of Foucault's concepts of governmentality and technologies of power. The second is to look forward and to identify examples of the most critical contemporary discourse themes in the Olympic domain in the first two decades of the twentieth century, namely 'youth', 'sport and multi-/inter-culturalism', 'sport and international development', and to consider ways in which such discourses are likely to impinge on the development of Olympism in the twenty-first century.

6.2   Governmentality and technologies of power: The disciplining of self and Olympic values

In the analyses of the discourses developed around Olympism in our three sets of sources covering the period from the late nineteenth to the end of the twentieth century, we have identified ways in which Olympism has reacted to a number of the crises of this period. These crises or critical events and tensions (relations between classes, between genders in modernity, the rise of fascism, the integration of post-colonial nation states in the Cold War and post-Cold War periods etc.) were events that were not centred in the sports domain, as even a brief consideration of Suffragette and feminist campaigns, the Russian Revolution and other class-based struggles, the fight against fascism and the independence struggles of colonised peoples clearly demonstrate. Thus the Olympic movement in addressing related issues did not simply represent a set of sporting institutions responding to sporting matters. The inter-twining of Olympic and other national and international discourse strands means that Olympic discourses have to be understood in the context of these wider social challenges. However on the other hand Olympic discourses do not simply reflect these wider issues, but shape our understanding of these issues and thus frame our actions.

A key Foucauldian concept which contributes to our understanding of these processes is that of governmentality which refers to the notion that 'technologies of power', 'technologies of the self' and 'forms of knowledge' are reciprocally constituted, and this relationship is expressed in the semantic linking of 'governing' (*gouverner*) and modes of thought (*mentalité*).

In Foucault's terms there are four types of technologies:

(1) technologies of production which permit us to produce, transform or manipulate things;
(2) technologies of sign systems which permit us to use signs, meanings, symbols or signification;
(3) technologies of power, which determine the conduct of individuals and submit them to certain ends or domination, an objectivising of the subject;
(4) technologies of the self which permit individuals to effect by their own means or with the help of others a certain number of operations on their own bodies and 'souls', thoughts, conduct, and ways of being, so as to transform themselves in order to attain a certain state of happiness, purity, wisdom, perfection, or immortality (Foucault *et al.* 1988).

Each type of technology 'implies certain modes of training and modification of individuals, not only in the obvious sense of acquiring skills but also in the sense of acquiring certain attitudes' (Foucault *et al.* 1988: 63). However it is the technologies of power and self which together when internalised constitute the notion of governmentality, referring to socio-political contexts where power is decentred and where members of a society play an active role in their own self-government as individuals and groups. The interface between these technologies is thus a primary focus.

Although governmentality will be evident in a range of societies or social contexts, much of the work of Foucault and of political theorists who have engaged with the term, focuses on governmentality in a neo-liberal, modernist context. Neo-liberal individualism is perhaps the dominant form of post-Enlightenment political ideology in the West which engenders a particular form of knowledge, with for example a predisposition to accept market mechanisms and a restricted remit for the state. This implies internalised and reflexive self-governing, and, in addition, has implications for the way we conceptualise 'truth'. As Dean (1999) puts it, we govern ourselves (and others) on the basis of what we take to be true about who we are and how we should behave to achieve appropriate ends, but that also, how we govern ourselves and behave, generates ways of producing truth.

It was no coincidence that Olympism should emerge along with the maturing of neo-liberalism in a post-Enlightenment context in which new relations between classes, genders, and nations (colonial and colonised; West and non-West; capitalist and socialist) were beginning to emerge. Olympism, we wish to argue, in effect operates as a source of governmentality in a post-colonial neo-liberal context. Olympism generates technologies of power 'technologies imbued with aspirations for the shaping of conduct in the hope of producing certain desired effects and averting certain undesired ones' (Rose 1999: 52) as well as technologies of the self, in which Olympism as an overt philosophy of behaviour, of how to proceed in life, provides a set of values, principles, behaviours which both instantiate and legitimate power from the micro inter-personal context, through meso-level contexts (the world of sport, or the Olympic world), to the macro (societal) levels.

We turn now to four sets of discourse themes evident in debates around Olympism in the twenty first century to highlight ways in which governmentality/self-disciplining is involved in each.

6.3   Discourse themes of Olympism in the twenty-first century

6.3.1   Governmentality, youth, sport and the body

Governmentality particularly concerns the political management of bodies (corporeality) in the population as a whole and involves a set of techniques to achieve this. Dean (1994: 171) has argued that 'the rationalities, operation, techniques, strategies, and practices of governmentality are centrally associated with the governance of the social body'. The population's health is regulated through the regulation of their bodies in modern governmentality and, it is argued, sport can play a major role in the process of governance of the health of the social body. Indeed Miller, Lawrence, McKay, and Rowe (2001) have argued that sport should occupy a central place in the history of modern governmentality. Sport, in this interpretation, constitutes a powerful cultural technology and a core disciplining force of a nation.

In contemporary neo-liberal contexts the disciplining of the bodies of the nation is rather obvious at one level in the increasing expansion of 'health industries' in western economies (drugs and vitamins providing treatments of several conditions, health and exercise advice, or surgical body modification techniques). At another, in the heightened emphasis given to health issues in PE and the broader school curriculum especially during the recent years in the USA, UK, Australia and elsewhere (Penney and Chandler 2000; Tinning and Glasby 2002), increasingly privileges, alongside sporting performance, body perfection codes celebrating *responsibility, autonomy and self-control* (Evans and Davies 2004). This is reflected in the UK, for example, in the development of curriculum discourse which relates to Health Related *Fitness* or Health Related *Education*.

Writing about Canada and the USA Fusco (2007: 43) claims that youth are increasingly subject to the invocation 'to engage in healthy living in spaces that are replete with discourses of healthification, civic engagement and consumerism'. Fusco claims that the focus on policies about youth has recently become intense not only as a result of anxiety about obesity and sedentary lifestyles, but also because of concerns relating to crime prevention and 'anti-social' behaviour among the young. Here there is a linking of disciplining the body – eat more carefully, exercise more regularly etc. – with promotion of the wider social discipline of civic engagement.

In the UK also the concern with developing self-regulating citizenry is increasingly evident also in sport and sport-related policy. Green (2007: 64) notes that while, 'historically, government interest in sport, PE and physical activity has at best been one of intermittent action and at worst neglect and indeed outright disdain' there was an unprecedented embrace of policies for sport and physical activity by the government under New Labour. As we saw in policies such as the PESSCAL (Physical Education and School Club Links) and PESSYP (Physical Education and Sports Strategy for Young People) strategies, the British government sought not simply to increase rates of exercise in England, but also to persuade young people to engage in volunteering, and to join community sports clubs outside the education domain. In short government was laying great emphasis on the generating of social capital as a key goal of sport/physical education policy.

In relation to the Olympic movement, the founder of the modern Olympic Games Baron Pierre de Coubertin had always had a primary focus on young people and his interest in the Olympic Games was in part a result of his engagement with the project of social reform through physical activity and sport for the French government. Initially, his aim was the creation of a fit population (and army) for a strong nation through the regulation of the body. In relation to the Olympic movement today, it is rather obvious that a focus on young people has escalated in recent years and this is evident in the policies, programmes and interventions by the Olympic family, targeting young people around the world. The motives for this are expressed as a mixture of moral but also commercial factors.

In an unpublished presentation to the British Olympic Academy in 2006 Giselle Davies the IOC's Director of Communication reported that in studies of Olympic brand recognition commissioned by the IOC, the identification of the Olympic rings as an instantly recognisable brand image was weakest among young people particularly in Asia where for some age segments the rings were rivalled by 'youth' brands such as MTV in terms of levels of recognition. She also noted that while the Games represented the most popular media event its audience was beginning to show some signs of weakening among younger cohorts.

Against this background the IOC embarked on a significant campaign to foster the youth market with new initiatives such as: the introduction of the Youth Olympics; London 2012's International Inspiration Project for young people around the world; the use of new social networking technologies, the development of virtual participation in Olympic Congresses in the digital age (first introduced in Copenhagen 2009), and the addition of 'youth' sports such as snowboarding and BMX bicycle racing in the Olympic programme. The introduction of new youth sports to the Games is particularly striking since Jacques Rogge had made it one of the priorities of his presidency to tackle the problem of gigantism, the increasing size and complexity of the Olympic programme, and while consideration of the Eurocentric nature of the programme did not result in the addition of new sports or disciplines to address this, the priority given to attracting the youth market reflected in the addition of youth events to the Games programme may be seen as even more impressive.

The targeting of the youth market through the use of social media is something which accelerated in the period from 2008. The urgency of dealing with the new media issue was also illustrated when the IOC announced in 2008 a deal to broadcast the Beijing Olympic Games highlights via YouTube on the internet in 77 countries which did not have access to the official provider NBC's internet coverage. Alex Balfour Head of New Media for London 2012 pointed out the IOC had little choice but to conclude a deal because 'The Olympic Games will be played out on YouTube, Facebook and Twitter whether we like it or not' (Techshout 2008). The IOC's Interim Report for 2009–10 entitled *Shaping the Future* reported the launch of multiple social media channels to capture the interest of the youth market

> A further enhancement of the Olympic Games occurred with the IOC's first-ever use of Facebook, Twitter, Flickr and YouTube to engage younger Olympic fans around the globe, who are increasingly difficult to reach through traditional media.

> The IOC launched its Facebook page one month before the start of the Games, enabling fans to stay up to date with activities and events whilst sharing their stories about Vancouver 2010. By the time the Games ended, the page had attracted more than 1.5 million fans and generated

nearly 200 million impressions. (International Olympic Committee 2010a)

Of course special reference should be made to the Youth Olympic Games which have been characterised by the IOC President Jacques Rogge as 'the flagship of the IOC's determination to reach out to young people'. He has emphasised that 'these Games will not only be about competition. They will also be the platform through which youngsters will learn about Olympic values and the benefits of sport, and share their experiences with other communities around the globe' (International Olympic Committee 2008).

6.3.2 The contemporary Olympic movement and multiculturalism in a multipolar world

Engagement of the young is thus one concern but it overlaps with a concern to incorporate cultural diversity. The IOC is an organisation with a self professed global role, which purports in its Charter to promote *universal* values. There is of course debate as to whether such values are universal but such reticence is not evident in the preamble to the Olympic Charter.

1. Olympism seeks to create a way of life based on the joy of effort, the educational value of good example and respect for universal fundamental ethical principles. ...
2. The goal of Olympism is to place sport at the service of the harmonious development of man (sic), with a view to promoting a peaceful society concerned with the preservation of human dignity.
3. The Olympic movement is the concerted, organised, universal and permanent action, carried out under the supreme authority of the IOC, of all individuals and entities who are inspired by the values of Olympism.
   ...
4. The practice of sport is a human right. Every individual must have the possibility of practising sport, without discrimination of any kind and in the Olympic spirit, which requires mutual understanding with a spirit of friendship, solidarity and fair play.

(International Olympic Committee 2011: 10)

Despite these aspirations for universalism, however, the IOC's cultural product 'Olympic sport' is predominantly associated with western cultural forms in the form of western codifications of sport and games, and its membership and principal sources of funding are dominated by western individuals and interests. Thus to meet its aspiration toward universality the IOC would appear to need to embrace some form of multiculturalism. The IOC's traditional approach might be said to have been 'assimilationist' (Henry *et al.* 2007) requiring potential new members to join the movement but on the existing terms of the IOC, with the existing diet of Olympic sports.

The IOC's milieu is in the cultural domain of international relations, and until the end of the Cold War such relations could be characterised as bipolar, and thus comparatively less complicated than the contemporary context since effectively there were two major sets of interests to reconcile. This reconciliation of course sometimes required the conceding of some aspects of the assimilationist position, when for example the IOC turned a blind eye to state intervention in the communist bloc in the appointment of NOC members.

However, in the multipolar reality of post-Cold War international relations the situation has become rather more complex. As indicated in our discussion in Chapter 2, this multipolar system is regarded by some as premised on a world of competing and ultimately incompatible cultures (Fukuyama 1993; Huntington 1996) and that if the West wants its values to prevail they will probably have to be defended by force. We argued that this position is wrong-headed and dangerous. It is wrong-headed because it conceptualises cultures as 'silos' of values, attitudes and behaviours, ignoring the fact that there are often far more significant differences between groups within a culture, than there are between cultures, as we see for example in claims about transnational youth cultures , or transcultural ethics (Evanoff 2000; Giroux 1994). It is also dangerous in that such claims have been used by neo-conservative interests in the West to defend acting militarily outwith UN resolutions, and the detention without trial and the torture of terrorist suspects (Steyn 2003).

Since the bombing of the Twin Towers in New York on 11th September 2001, and the ensuing 'War on Terror', with the bombings in Madrid and London (the latter the day after the IOC awarded the 2012 Games to London), the West's 'Other' has undoubtedly been defined in the popular imagination and in western governments' policies as Muslim. The fact that the perpetrators of this violence command little support among their co-religionists is ignored feeding the politics of the right in the West, and this is as true in the western European heartland of the Olympic movement as it is in the United States.

> Beyond all the noise about Europe's 'Muslim problem' lurks a growing unease about the changing texture of European society. Gone are the days of pure white, Christian Europe. Now Europe is multi-ethnic, multi-religious and multicultural, a fact which many find hard to swallow. Muslims are part of this evolving reality, but the idea that the continent is being Islamised is a figment of the right's imagination.
>
> In a European population of some 540 million, Muslims number between 20 million and 25 million, or about 4%. The majority are underprivileged,

and socially, economically and politically marginalised. Whatever the scaremongers say, Muslim armies are not at Europe's gate preparing to conquer.

Obsession with the question of Britishness in the UK and with les valeurs de la République in France reflects a state of anxiety about identity. The collapse of empire, globalisation and flow of immigrants from the old colonies brought new peoples into Europe's bosom. The Muslim other – the Saracen or Turk, in opposition to whom Europe defined its imaginary geographic and cultural borders – is now located within its frontiers, a sort of internal outsider. From the periphery of the empire in distant overseas colonies in Lahore or Algiers, it has moved to the periphery of capitals and industrial cities in London or Paris. The borders of identity and culture are overlapping, making it impossible to draw rigid boundaries between east and west, Europe and Islam, white and black. (Ghannoushi 2007)

So great is the concern with such issues that both the German Chancellor Angela Merkel and the British Prime Minister David Cameron felt able to declare that multiculturalism as a policy idea had failed (Connolly 2010; Doward 2011).

Within this difficult context the IOC seeks to establish its universalist credentials. A useful illustration within which to discuss related issues is the case of incorporation of women of different cultures (and in particular given current moral panics within western societies, Muslim women) in terms of both participation in Olympic sports and leadership within Olympic organisations. This allows us to illustrate both the difficulties such a position presents and how the Olympic movement is able to facilitate aspects of a progressive discourse in promoting gender equity within the Olympic movement.

Two examples in recent Olympic events are instructive. The first relates to FIFA which placed a ban on the wearing of the hijab at the first Youth Olympics in 2010 which effectively would have excluded the Iranian girls' football team. This was done on two grounds, first, of safety (a player might be choked), and second the rule that no clothing signifying a religious affiliation would be permitted on the field of play. After a period of relatively intense discussion between FIFA, the IOC and the Iranian NOC a compromise was reached with girls wearing a specially designed cap (CNN 2010). However when Iran was due to play Jordan in a qualifying match for the 2012 Games the players appeared on the field wearing hijabs which covered the neck and officials abandoned the match. Ironically three players on the Jordanian team were sitting out the game because they also wore the hijab (Dorsey 2011). The range and fashion styling of hijabs and sports suits available on the market for female Muslims is now considerable and it does not seem beyond the wit of men/women to come up with a solution which meets safety criteria. However the secularist requirements of FIFA (which ironically the organisation had been willing to breach with its solution of the cap to cover hair) is something which is a sticking point in principle.

The differences in positions taken on religious symbolism in dress are clearly highlighted in comparing what have been the traditional British and French attitudes to the wearing of the hijab for Muslim women and the turban for Sikh men. The European Court of Human Rights in 2009 upheld a ban on turbans in France for those in public institutions such as schools or the civil service (Singh 2009), a situation which contrasts dramatically with the traditional position of the UK in which Sikhs can wear a turban not only in mainstream jobs but also in the police, and the armed forces, and where wearing of a turban permits an exemption for the legal requirement to wear a motorcycle crash helmet.

At the Beijing Olympic Games six Egyptians, three Iranians, an Afghan, a Bahraini and a Yemeni competed in sprinting, rowing, taekwondo[2] and archery wearing the hijab. Perhaps the highest profile athlete of those participating was Bahrain's track athlete, Ruqaya Al Ghasara, the 2006 Asian Games 200 metres champion, who made the 2008 Olympic semi-finals and was accomplishing world class times in her event while competing with full body cover clothing including a hijab. In effect these athletes provided rich symbolic messages (non-verbal discourse) in relation to the potential for inter-culturalism within the Olympic movement, the media providing positive images of women as active participants rather than passive 'victims' in sport.

In studies conducted for the IOC on women and leadership in Olympic organisations (Henry and Robinson 2010; Henry *et al.* 2004) it is clear that the evidence in relation to women's position in Olympic bodies is not one of the West as 'progressive' and the non-West as lagging behind. In relation to data concerning the position of women in Muslim countries in the first of these studies, we have argued that:

> While the data for this study, for example, show that women's representation on NOC Executive Committees is lower on average in the countries which are members of the Organisation of the Islamic Conference (7.9% compared to an overall average of all countries of 12.9%), nevertheless to explain this by reference to religion rather than by reference to local cultures is problematic. There are perhaps two principal objections to the 'religion-blaming' strategy. The first is that in the context of the present study, it is not only Muslim societies which manifest gender inequality. When such gender inequality is present in western societies, academic analyses tend to explain this by reference to the concept of patriarchy, but when it is present in Muslim societies it tends to be

explained by western commentators by reference to religious practice. Such an argument applies double standards, and leaves proponents open to the charge of Orientalism (Said 1991; Volpp 2001; Winter 2001).

It is important in this context to differentiate between 'religiosity' (the customs and practices associated with a group practising a particular religion) as opposed to religious beliefs, the fundamental tenets of a religious group. The norms and practices (religiosity) may vary from one group to another within the same religious grouping, even where fundamental beliefs are shared. There is a lively debate within Muslim feminist literature about the distinction between 'revealed truth' in the form of the Q'ran and the Hadith on the one hand, and ijtihad and the opinions of (male) religious scholars on the other (Stowasser 1998). Muslim feminists and feminist commentators such as Fatima Mernissi (Mernissi 1985; Mernissi and Lakeland 1991), Haleh Afshar (1998), Azza Karam (1998) and Saliba *et al.* (Saliba *et al.* 2002) show how, for many, it is not Islam but certain male interpretations of Islam, which promulgate gender subordination.

One of our difficulties as western observers of the non-West is a tendency in our discursive constructions of Muslim women to treat these women as a homogeneous group when this is clearly not the case:

The differences between the societies of some of the Gulf States and those, for example, of North Africa or Turkey are considerable, as reflected in the differing roles played by women in these societies (Haddad 1998), but also studies such as Afshar (1998), Karam (1998), and Al-Ali (2000) show how, even in 'conservative' contexts (Iran and Egypt respectively), different forms of feminism are evident, warning against a simplistic notion of a single unitary perspective on the appropriate roles for women in wider society.

The survey data from the first of the studies highlights the danger of this unitary perspective since two countries which are members of the Organisation of the Islamic Conference (Iran and Gambia) exhibited levels of female membership of NOC Executives which were more than double the average for all countries (Henry *et al.* 2004). While the qualitative data from interviews with women who are members of NOC Executive Committees or Boards further highlights the diversity in positions taken by Muslim women in relation to the issue of clothing (Henry 2007: 204–7).

The Federation of Islamic women's sports was established by agreement brokered between Faezah Hashemi (the Iranian women rights activist, former member of the Iranian parliament, and daughter of former Iranian President Akbar Hashemi Rafsanjani), Ayatollah Hashemi Rafsanjani, Juan Antonio Samaranch, the President of International Olympic Committee (IOC), Sheikh

Ahmad Al-Sabah Alfhd, President of the Olympic Council of Asia (OCA) and in 1993 in Kuwait. Subsequently the Women's Islamic Games have been held every four years in Iran, where international competition takes place in a female-only environment. Samaranch's decision to provide the IOC's recognition of the Games was much criticised and deemed by a number of commentators to be a fairly daring policy move. Support for the Islamic Women's Games within the Olympic family is by no means universal, as illustrated by the response of a sample of Secretary Generals of NOCs who, when asked about their view of this initiative, provided four very different types of response,

- the enthusiastic adoption of the initiative as a good end in its own right;
- outright opposition;
- promotion or at least acceptance of this initiative as providing the only possible form of participation in international competition for some women from Islamic countries;
- acceptance of the initiative as the first step to full integration.

Sport provides a medium through which there is potential for cultures to engage with one another. This may reflect an assimilationist approach (as is exemplified at a national level in the French secular republicanism) in which citizens of a nation state or, in the Olympic case, members of multi-national bodies or movements agree to abide by centrally defined norms; a multiculturalist approach (as has been traditionally associated at the national level with, for example, policy in Britain) in which all cultures and civilisations are seen as being of equal value and should be treated and promoted equally; and an inter-culturalist approach in which the 'best'[3] aspects of various cultures are absorbed within a wider shared world view. Critical to the Olympic movement's positioning of itself in relation to the issue of how to address cultural and political pluralism in a wider world will be the nature of the discourse adopted (assimilationist, multicultural, or inter-cultural) each of which will have distinctive political consequences for the movement.

For one Olympic commentator there is a managerial discourse evident in the highly professionalised administration of the IOC which he associates with the ethical values not of the Olympic movement, but the business values of what he terms 'the Olympic Sport Industry' (OSI). The former sees 'business opportunities as a means to leverage the ethical benefits of Olympic sport, while the latter

> can be thought of as Olympic sport without Olympism, or stated more precisely, the OSI, as an ideal type, reverses the means/ends relationship between sport and the intercultural, diplomatic and educational meanings characteristic of the Olympic movement. For the OSI, Olympic symbols,

values, social projects and histories are mere instrumentalities available for the expansion of Olympic-style competitions, for the 'growth of the brand' as many of its paid professionals like to put it. (MacAloon 2011: 293)

MacAloon was a member of the 2000 Commission (and of the Working Group within the Commission that addressed issues of culture and education). The Commission which reviewed governance of the movement made 50 recommendations to the IOC Special Session of 2009 (all of which were formally accepted). MacAloon describes how he and colleagues were able to shape the recommendations of the working group:

> we framed the RC's [Reform Commission's] consideration of education, culture and ritual issues as being central to renewing the IOC's social legitimacy and moral authority, in other words, its place in the Olympic movement. I would love to go line by line through the two-page preamble and the four recommendations, since I wrote them, with the collaboration of He Zhenliang, Robin Mitchell and Norbert Müller. Suffice it to point out that we caused the RC and the Session to nominally commit themselves to:
> * an anthropological conception of 'culture';
> * a recognition that global interconnection is associated with increasing not decreasing cultural diversity, therefore requiring a more multicultural and inter-cultural approach to Olympic education;
> * continuing Olympic education for all members of the Olympic family, including IOC members; and
> * that (here I cannot resist quoting) 'In the Olympic movement, valuing "universality" should never mean demanding standardised modernisation or cultural homogenisation, much less Europeanisation or Westernisation'.

He goes on however to acknowledge that though incorporated within the recommendations accepted by the IOC Special Session in 1999, this may have had little impact because of its failure to chime with the global managerialism of professional elements in the administration.

> I am hardly so benighted as to claim that these resolutions had at the time or have had since then a major impact on the (overwhelmingly European and business management oriented) IOC centre. Indeed, they were intended in no small part to directly confront the universalising, 'world's best practices' logic through which IOC managerial elites were endeavouring, in this same section of the RC report, to justify and to impose standardised and culturally insensitive practices around the world. Stricter and more transnational accounting standards are one

thing (though imagining a fully standardised and comparable cost-accounting of an Olympic Games in such very different systems as Greece and Australia, much less China or Russia was and remains seriously naive). But the IOC 'brand' managers were moving on to imposing organisational forms, 'knowledge transfer' regimes, and values rhetorics irrespective of cultural contexts, and their soft neo-imperialism required, in our judgement, explicit confrontation from the Olympic movement side of things. (MacAloon 2011: 302)

6.3.3 Sport for development and international relations

The third contemporary discourse theme which we develop here relates to the use of sport for development. This we take to incorporate a range of initiatives and projects relating to sport for peace, sport to promote the millennium development goals, sport for health, and sport as a human right. The movement might be said to have started in the development of sport aid which preceded the establishing of Olympic Solidarity and its forerunner the Committee for the International Olympic Aid (Henry and Al-Tauqi 2008). It brings together aspects of the two other twenty-first century themes identified in relation to a predominant focus on youth and on the integration of developing nations into the Olympic movement.

A major impetus for sport for development was the establishing by the Lillehammer Winter Games Organising Committee of Olympic Aid in 1992 in preparation for the 1994 Winter Olympic Games. The initial focus of Olympic Aid was to provide support for those affected by war and distress in partnership with a variety of other fund raising bodies, and these efforts accompanied the IOC's establishing of the Olympic Truce, an attempt to use the influence of the Games to suppress conflict over the period of the Games. The Olympic Truce was adopted by the UN in 1993, and Olympic Aid continued until 2003 when it was 'rebranded' as the NGO Right to Play.

At the 1996 Games a partnership was developed with UNICEF and $13 million were donated by ten countries to aid the UNICEF vaccination programme allowing them to vaccinate 12.2 million children and over 800,000 women (Right to Play 2011), and the humanitarian effort alongside the Olympic Truce produced some remarkable outcomes:

This vaccination effort was extraordinary as it resulted in two Olympic Truces: one truce in Afghanistan that lasted the duration of the Atlanta Games (16 days) and a second truce in the Kurdish region in northern Iraq for forty-eight hours. All fighting stopped in the regions so the UNICEF staff could safely immunise the children and women of these areas. Olympic Aid further supported these initiatives by engaging Olympians in Olympic Festivals in areas where vaccinations were taking place and by educating these communities as to the benefits of immunisation. (Right to Play 2011: 1)

From 2003 Right to Play developed from a fundraising partner to an implementer of child development programmes using sport with underprivileged children in a wide range of international contexts. It was joined by an increasing number of NGOs using sport to work with children in difficult contexts such as refugee camps, ongoing conflicts or the aftermath of such conflicts.

The United Nations, alongside the development of Olympic Aid/Right to Play which it has worked closely with through its various agencies (in particular UNICEF and UNHCR), developed its programme on Sport for Development and Peace. In 2001 a Special Advisor to the UN Secretary General on Sport for Development and Peace was appointed (Adolf Ogi, a former President of the Swiss Confederation) and a UN Inter-agency Task Force established to evaluate the contribution which sport could make to the achievement of UN goals and in particular the Millennium Development Goals (United Nations 2011). The UN cites as among the key milestones in the rapid evolution of its Sport for Development and Peace approach those listed in Table 6.1.

Table 6.1 Key milestones in the development of UN involvement in sport for development

2003	Landmark report published of the UN Inter-Agency Task Force on Sport for Development and Peace: 'Sport for Development and Peace: Towards Achieving the Millennium Development Goals'. UN General Assembly Resolution 58/5 adopted 'Sport as a means to promote education, health, development and peace', proclaiming 2005 as the International Year for Sport and Physical Education (IYSPE).
2005	International Year of Sport and Physical Education
2008	March Wilfried Lemke, of Germany, appointed as Special Adviser to the UN Secretary General on Sport for Development and Peace Beijing Olympic Games. Publication of the Final Report of the Sport for Development and Peace International Working Group (SDP IWG): 'Harnessing the Power of Sport for Development and Peace: Recommendations to Governments' UN General Assembly resolution 63/135 adopted, 'Sport as a means to promote education, health, development and peace', which 'welcomes the Secretary General's decision to [...] incorporate the Sport for Development and Peace International Working Group into the United Nations system under the leadership of the Special Adviser.' (Table adapted from United Nations 2009: 1)

It is worth quoting in detail the UN's rationale for its engagement with sport.

> ... one may wonder: what does sport have to do with the United Nations? In fact, sport presents a natural partnership for the United Nations (UN) system: sport and play are human rights that must be respected and enforced worldwide; sport has been increasingly recognised and used as a low-cost and high-impact tool in humanitarian, development and peace-building efforts, not only by the UN system but also by non-governmental organisations (NGOs), governments, development agencies, sports federations, armed forces and the media. Sport can no longer be considered a luxury within any society but is rather an important investment in the present and future, particularly in developing countries
>
> ...
>
> Sport plays a significant role as a promoter of social integration and economic development in different geographical, cultural and political contexts. Sport is a powerful tool to strengthen social ties and networks, and to promote ideals of peace, fraternity, solidarity, non-violence, tolerance and justice. ...
>
> From a development perspective, the focus is always on mass sport and not elite sport. Sport is used to reach out to those most in need including refugees, child soldiers, victims of conflict and natural catastrophes, the impoverished, persons with disabilities, victims of racism, stigmatisation and discrimination, persons living with HIV/AIDS, malaria and other diseases. (United Nations Organisation for Sport for Development and Peace 2010: 1)

The focus on low-cost, high impact humanitarian, development and peace building activity focusing predominantly on children proved remarkably attractive to the Olympic movement. Although IOC activity was evident with Olympic Aid well before the Salt Lake City scandal came to the fore, sport for development was certainly attractive in terms of the IOC's concern about its image in the wake of the scandal. In addition it played to the IOC's concern about the integration of youth, and maintained the IOC's centrality in what was an increasing area of activity, namely the use of sport as a development tool. As a consequence when Sebastian Coe in his presentation of London's bid to host the 2012 Games at the IOC Congress in Singapore in 2005 undertook (in what became known as the 'Singapore Promise') that if London were successful in its bid it would ensure that it would use this opportunity '... to reach young people all around the world and connect them to the inspirational power of sport', the British government developed with partners the development of the International Inspiration programme with the goal of reaching through sport twelve million children in 20 countries.

The claims made are that the programme will 'enrich the lives' of young people around the world

> International Inspiration inspires and enables millions of young people in countries around the world to play sport. This changes lives, opening doors to leadership, health, inclusion, excellence or simply the joy of participation. (London Organising Committee of the Olympic Games and Paralympic Games 2010: 3)

The approach adopted by London 2012 has been enthusiastically endorsed by the IOC and in the election of the host city for the 2016 Games, three of the four candidate cities (Rio de Janeiro, Madrid and Tokyo) incorporated an approach which emulated the International Inspiration template (though for reasons of copyright were unable to use the term International Inspiration in naming their projects). Rio having won the bid is presumably committed to its undertaking as a candidate city, while Tokyo, even though it lost the bid has maintained its commitment to international sport for development as a legacy of its bid, to be delivered through the new Jigoro Kano Memorial International Sport Institute, and the associated Centre for Olympic Research & Education (CORE) at the University of Tsukuba.

The discourse of life changing experiences delivered to young people in developing countries has been subject to criticism on a number of levels. Darnell (2007) in a study of Right to Play materials and interviews with personnel argues that there is an implicit post-colonial frame which portrays the provider (the West) as 'benevolent, rational and expert' (p. 574) implying by contrast naiveté and dependence on the part of recipients, while Coalter (2010) points to the difficulties of solving large-scale problems through small-scale local initiatives and the tendency for evaluation to be used as supportive rhetoric for the NGOs and other organisations which promote such programmes. Giulianotti (2004: 356–7) points to the exporting of sports evangelism following its relative failure in 'civilising' the young in western societies, which might be said to illustrate the limits of governmentality through sport.

> in their development and peace work the shift of 'sport evangelists' to locations outside the West may constitute a form of neo-colonial repositioning. Through the twentieth century, sports evangelism at home had sought to promote organised sporting activities to dissipate the lower orders' dangerous energies and to divert them from 'licentious' social practices (such as drinking, gambling, casual sex, and the following of

youth subcultural styles). There is evidence to suggest that such evangelism has not proved wholly successful among young people in the West
over the years. However, it appears to be assumed, the young people in
the old colonies may be more readily organised to receive and internalise
the tendentious, self-controlling messages buried within sports.

The objectives of some funding agencies may also be mixed with the concern
for the image of the funding body or its backers. The British Council for
example has as a major aim the promotion of a positive image of Britain and
British culture and such concerns will inform approaches to projects such
as International Inspiration. Right to Play relies on positive publicity to sustain donations, as will be the case for many other agencies. Thus delivery of
projects and self-reporting of performance will be subject to other pressures.

The depth and sustainability of programmes are also issues to consider.
The International Inspiration programmes target to reach twelve million
children which was achieved in 2011, calculated 'reach' on the basis of a
young person having attended at least one event on one occasion. Leaving
aside any difficulties in calculation, attendance (perhaps even passive attendance) at an event is unlikely to constitute a life changing experience.
In addition sustaining projects beyond the lifetime of externally funded
projects invariably proves challenging.

All this is not to say that truly worthwhile experiences are not generated
for young people in a range of contexts but it does have a bearing on the
way such programmes are discursively constructed. Engagement of the
West and non-West, or the North and South in terms of developing and
developed economies, in a single global family is likely to remain a key
theme. The value of sport is stressed in ways which counter the negative
images – of doping assisted performance, gambling and corruption, over
commercialised activity in which some performers are hyper-rewarded
while others remain exploited. It is therefore not surprising to identify a
note of qualification introduced into sport aid discourse which admits of
potential dis-benefits and the need for evidence-based approaches to achieve
desired outcomes.

Sport is not a cure-all for development problems. As a cultural phenomenon, it is a mirror of society and is just as complex and contradictory.

As such, sport can also have negative side effects such as violence, corruption, discrimination, hooliganism, nationalism, doping and fraud. To
enable sport to unleash its full positive potential, emphasis must be placed
on effective monitoring and guiding of sports activities.

The positive potential of sport does not develop automatically. It requires a
professional and socially responsible intervention which is tailored to the

respective social and cultural context. Successful Sport for Development and Peace programmes work to realise the right of all members of society to participate in sport and leisure activities. Effective programmes intentionally give priority to development objectives and are carefully designed to be inclusive. (United Nations Organisation for Sport for Development and Peace 2010: 1)

6.3.4 Governance and governmentality: The governance of the Olympic movement in the twenty-first century

If governmentality implies self-governance at the level of the individual, it is matched at the organisational level in terms of the principles of organisational self-governance, though this is increasingly an *explicit* set of principles, and it is at this level in recent years that the Olympic movement and other international sporting bodies have had severe challenges to face.

The crisis of governance however has not been limited to sport but rather is a generic crisis of self-regulation. Promotion of good governance may imply the reform of the state, of the private sector or of civil society and thus of different institutions, and the nature of governance indicators used will vary depending on the focus of interest on a particular sector. Thus international bodies such as the World Bank (World Bank 2010), the IMF (International Monetary Fund 2005), the OECD (Organisation for Economic Co-operation and Development 2005), and the UN (United Nations ESCAP 2007) have produced normative guidelines for good governance employing different but related sets of indicators. The development of governance indicators by these international bodies are exercises which have their origin in the incorporation and disciplining of developing economies into a global economic system of trade. However events in the leading economies in the 1990s and 2000s illustrate that governance failure has been even more spectacularly evident in the economically developed world. It is perhaps worth drawing parallels between these broader cases of governance failure and those which are sport specific.

The Enron scandal is a significant example. Enron, an energy business, at one time the seventh largest US company, with wide ranging links with the US administration, collapsed in 2002 following revelations that it had concealed losses through a range of barely impenetrable accountancy manoeuvres such as setting up shell companies to take on company debt (Fusaro and Miller 2002). Arthur Anderson one of the world's five leading accountancy firms which acted as auditor of Enron's accounts was accused of collusion in promoting this inaccurate picture of the company's financial position, and subsequently itself collapsed when it became subject to legal charges and was broken up and largely sold off to its competitors. Enron entered Chapter 11 bankruptcy status in December 2002. The story is thus one of a failure not only of the company per se but also of the checks and balances in the self-regulating system (Eichenwald 2005).

The collapse of Lehman Brothers in the early 2000s was an even more high profile case. It represented the biggest bankruptcy case in US history, with Lehman's holding more than $600 billion in assets. Its downfall was brought about by its level of lending in a high risk sector (the sub-prime mortgage sector) of a housing market which experienced a heavy downturn and a consequent devaluation of its asset base. Lehman Brothers filed for Chapter 11 bankruptcy in September 2008. In a report by the Bankruptcy Examiner, Lehman Brothers was heavily criticised for manipulating the representation of the bank's financial position by accounting manoeuvres at around the end-of-year balance sheet reporting period. Subsequently the US Attorney General laid charges against Ernst and Young, the company's auditors alleging that it had 'substantially assisted ... in a massive accounting fraud' (Lovell and Stokdyk 2010). Thus, as in the Enron case the problem was in large part a crisis of self-regulation within the system.

The problems of major companies were not restricted to failures of financial self-regulation but incorporated failures of environmental self-regulation as well, with the most spectacular example being the BP oil spill in the Gulf of Mexico in 2010 which wrought huge levels of damage to marine life and the regional economy (Guardian Newspaper 2011).

Thus governance failure is not a minor concern in the developed economies, nor indeed is the failure of self-regulation restricted to the general business world. At the turn of the twenty-first century sport was increasingly experiencing its own deep crises which undermined faith in sport's ability for self-regulation, and thus the legitimacy of its governing bodies. Undoubtedly the most significant of these crises, at least in Olympic terms, was the Salt Lake City debacle. In 1998 allegations of bribery were made against IOC members whose votes for Salt Lake City as the venue for the 2002 had been bought by cash and in kind inducements. These allegations were compounded when Marc Hodler, a Swiss IOC member, in a statement during a press interview claimed that such corruption was systemic and not limited to the Salt Lake case. Indeed, such claims were not even new. It later transpired that the Toronto Bidding team in 1991 (whose bid to host the 1996 Games had come third behind Atlanta and Athens) had submitted a report of unethical practices on the part of IOC members during that bid process but had not even received a reply from the IOC (BBC News 1999). Following an open IOC session in March 1999, ten IOC members either resigned or were expelled, and ten others received sanctions. However in December of that year the IOC President, Samaranch, was summoned to appear at a US Congressional hearing as the IOC became subject to public scrutiny in what was seen to be a somewhat embarrassing and uncomfortable process (Jennings 2000).

In addition to the establishing of an Ethics Commission in 1999, the 2000 Commission (widely referred to as the Reform Commission) was set up to address issues relating to governance, and to make recommendations to the IOC Session. The Reform Commission came up with 50 recommendations which dealt not only with the issue of codes of practice for IOC members and their relationships with bidding cities, but also with changes of terms of office for co-opted members (a retiring age of 70), limiting the term of office of the President and formally establishing a quota of places (15 each) to represent the three Olympic constituencies of athletes, International Federation representatives and representatives of NOCs.

The American academic John MacAloon in an ethnographic account of the workings of the Reform Commission (of which he was a member) argued that such was the depth of the crisis that IOC President Samaranch, who had a reputation for strong leadership and tight control of the organisation by centralising power in the Executive Board and in the administration, was forced to open up membership of the Commission to include power-ful, respected external personalities who would command public trust. The invited members thus included Henry Kissinger (former US Secretary of State), Boutros Boutros-Ghali (former UN Secretary General) and Giovanni Agnelli (the Italian industrialist), and MacAloon (2011) points out that this situation caused considerable nervousness on the part of the President and certain factions within the IOC and its administration since predicting the outcome of the Commission's debates was difficult with unfamiliar figures who were unlikely to be easily influenced or manoeuvred. Nevertheless MacAloon observes that to the credit of the IOC the process was broadly an open one and a broad range of views were accommodated in the working meetings of the Commission.

Ultimately the 50 recommendations made by the Commission were accepted *en bloc* by the IOC membership. Reviewing the outcome ten years on, MacAloon notes that not all of the recommendations had been acted upon, however the actions proposed and those taken at the time were sufficient to placate critics who for the most part saw the action taken as appropriate and proportionate.

The IOC's response to the Salt Lake City scandal contrasts significantly with the FIFA governance crisis of 2011. Allegations were made by Lord Triesman a leading member of the Football Association's delegation promoting the England bid to host the 2018 World Cup that he had been approached and asked for inducements by four members of the FIFA Executive to support the England bid. In addition a BBC television documentary just days before the crucial vote aired other allegations of unethical practices on the part of members of the FIFA Executive. Finally allegations of bribery surfaced as Mohammed Bin Hammam, the President of the Asian Football Federation, sought to challenge Sepp Blatter in the 2011 FIFA presidency elections. Hammam and Jack Warner a FIFA Vice President were investigated by the Ethics Committee for offering financial inducements to vote for Hammam, while Blatter was investigated by the Committee in respect of allegations by Hammam that he knew of bribery claims in respect of amongst other things his own candidacy but failed to take action. These were not the first allegations made concerning Blatter's presidency. The Somali Football Federation representative, Farra Ado claimed he was offered $100,000 to vote for Blatter in the 1998 FIFA election and that Blatter had repeatedly failed to investigate serious corruption allegations within the organisation (Prynn 2011), most of which had been raised by the British media, in particular the investigative journalist Andrew Jennings (Jennings 2010) who had also played a significant role in raising corruption claims in respect of the IOC (Jennings 2000; Jennings and Simson 1996).

The outcome of the Ethics Committee's deliberations was that while Blatter was cleared of any wrongdoing, Warner was forced to resign and Hammam was banned for life from holding office within the game. Blatter was thus able to stand for re-election as President unopposed, in an election described by the British Prime Minister in the UK Parliament as 'a farce' (Gold 2011) and there were continuing calls for the imposition of external governance regulation, not least by members of the European and British parliaments (Bose 2011; Honeyball 2011). The tarnished reputation of FIFA and of Blatter thus is an outcome which is in relatively stark contrast to that achieved by the IOC in its reforms of 2000 and the threat of imposition of forms of external regulation still hung over football.

One area in which the IOC's attempts to maintain the primacy of self-regulation have been compromised is the area of anti-doping regulation. WADA (the World Anti-doping Agency) was established in November 1999 as a transnational body to develop a harmonised code of practice at a global level so that uniform outcomes could be achieved across the world in terms of policing doping in sport. With pressure from governmental organisations, and in particular the EU, to develop an effective system of anti-doping control, the IOC was forced to cede majority membership of the Board of WADA to governmental entities. The trigger to action on the part of the EU was the exposure of a widespread doping culture on the Tour de France following the arrest by French customs officials of a member of the support team for the Festina cycling team carrying doping materials intended for the whole team. This discovery led to the uncovering of widespread abuse organised at team level and claims that all leading riders engaged in such practices (the so called 'no dope, no hope' culture). This systematic abuse, and the cycling authorities' failure to deal with it, proved to be the last straw in terms of EU trust in Olympic sport's ability to police itself.

The IOC had introduced anti-doping measures in the 1968 Mexico Games under its Medical Commission which was led by the Belgian Prince Alexandre de Merode, an IOC member without medical qualifications. However the IOC's anti-doping efforts, and Merode's leadership were subject to increasing criticism (Dimeo 2007). In the 1980 Moscow Games there were no positive tests on athletes leading Merode to claim that the Games were 'clean', although in retrospective tests on samples the West German scientist Manfred Donike was able to conclude that 20 per cent of female athletes samples tested had illegal levels of testosterone (Dimeo and Hunt 2009). In 1984, at the Los Angeles Games, the paperwork relating to nine positive samples was 'lost' and in 1996 under Merode's leadership, it was also alleged positive samples were discarded (Dimeo and Hunt 2009). Thus, when in 1998 the Festina scandal became public, the pressure from governments and the EU for reform became intense.

The IOC's response was to stage the First World Conference on Doping in Sport in Lausanne in 1999, with WADA being formed later that year. While within the IOC there were attempts to ensure that control of WADA remained within the IOC's grasp, pressure from governments led to the balance of the Foundation Board being weighted in favour of membership by representatives of the EU, the Council of Europe, and individual governments with 19 members, compared with 18 members from the Olympic movement.

The above examples illustrate the tension which exists between sport as an area of economic activity, subject to the rules and discourse of business and government regulation, and as an area of social, physical and moral self-development of civil society. The special nature of sport, referred to in 'Eurospeak' terms as the 'specificity of sport', is seen as valued and protected by the ability of sport to self-govern in certain critical respects (referred to as the 'autonomy of sport'). Jean-Loup Chappelet and his colleagues in a study commissioned by the Council of Europe defines the areas in which the autonomy of sport is to be recognised (Chappelet *et al.* 2008).

The dimensions of sporting autonomy represent a balancing act which is reflected in the discourse of the European Union in the development and articulation of Article 165 of the Lisbon Treaty which gave the EU a formal competence to engage in sports policy for its own sake. (It already had the competence to engage in sports policy insofar as it impacted upon its other core competences such as competition regulation, social integration, or regional development.) The EU represented the most significant challenge to the 'autonomy of sport' (or more specifically here the autonomy of the Olympic movement). The EU's rulings through the European Court of Justice on sport as an economic activity (perhaps most spectacularly represented in the Bosman ruling, had a major impact on the ability of sporting authorities to impose decisions on sporting bodies and participants. Jacques Rogge, speaking as President of the European Olympic Committee in 2001 at a conference on sport governance which brought together EU actors and representatives of sporting bodies, put the case for the cultural specificity of sport, treating sport as different from other forms of economic activity. Sport he maintained had to establish competitive balance, and to organise on some basis of solidarity represented in the form of shared revenue.

The EOC have therefore repeatedly asked EU institutions to take into account the special characteristics of sports when applying EU rules to sport. There is no doubt that EU competition rules have dramatically influenced sports in the past five years. After the Bosman ruling, fears were great among the sporting community that a strict application of EU competition rules on sports would jeopardise the current structures of sports in Europe. Sports organisations did not contest that EU rules were applied to sport. At stake was that sport could not be considered under EU competition rules as any economic activity. Sports competitors need strong opponents in order to organise a good competition and have no interest in excluding competitors from the market as would be the case in other sectors.

Secondly, sports governing bodies are needed to organise solidarity within one sport. Solidarity may include the redistribution of financial resources from participants to a competition but it may also signify redistribution for development purposes to the grassroots of the sport. The IOC revenues provided by the broadcasting agreements and the sponsoring programme allow the IOC to support the organisation of the Olympic Games, to redistribute funds to IF's and NOC's and also to fund programmes through Olympic solidarity, and all this by ensuring that the games are broadcast on free television. The universality of the Games must remain, even if avoiding pay TV causes a loss of 600 millions USD to the IOC. (Rogge 2001: 20–1)

In fact the IOC had considerable interaction with the EU about developing the EU's role in sport while protecting sporting autonomy. Samaranch was instrumental in the first moves by the EU to legitimate its interest in sports policy expressed in the relatively weak form of an appendix to the Maastricht treaty on European Union (1992) when he negotiated a compromise between those who were against the defining of EU interests in sport and those who felt that this was a necessary requirement if sport was to be protected (Henry and Matthews 1998).

Sporting bodies, and in particular the European Olympic Committees continued to lobby for EU measures to be adopted which would both promote sport and protect it from 'undue intrusion'. A series of reports and declarations, most notably the Nice Declaration on Sport (European Council 2000) and the White Paper on sport (European Commission 2007) were forerunners to the Lisbon Treaty which on ratification in 2010 provided a competence for the EU to intervene in the sports sector for its own sake rather than simply using sport as a vehicle to achieve other policy goals (Parrish *et al.* 2010). The IOC's lobbying proved successful to a significant degree since the Commission has accepted the need to respect the autonomy of sport.

The specific nature of sport, a legal concept established by the Court of Justice of the European Union which has already been taken into account by the EU institutions in various circumstances and which was addressed in detail in the White Paper on Sport and the accompanying

Staff Working Document, is now recognised by Article 165 TFEU. It encompasses all the characteristics that make sport special, such as for instance the interdependence between competing adversaries or the pyramid structure of open competitions. The concept of the specific nature of sport is taken into account when assessing whether sporting rules comply with the requirements of EU law (fundamental rights, free movement, prohibition of discrimination, competition, etc.).

Sporting rules normally concern the organisation and proper conduct of competitive sport. They are under the responsibility of sport organisations and must be compatible with EU law. In order to assess the compatibility of sporting rules with EU law, the Commission considers the legitimacy of the objectives pursued by the rules, whether any restrictive effects of those rules are inherent in the pursuit of the objectives and whether they are proportionate to them. Legitimate objectives pursued by sport organisations may relate, for example, to the fairness of sporting competitions, the uncertainty of results, the protection of athletes' health, the promotion of the recruitment and training of young athletes, financial stability of sport clubs/teams or a uniform and consistent exercise of a given sport (the 'rules of the game'). Through its dialogue with sport stakeholders the Commission will continue its efforts to explain, on a theme-per-theme basis, the relation between EU law and sporting rules in professional and amateur sport. As requested by Member States and the sport movement in the consultation, the Commission is committed to supporting an appropriate interpretation of the concept of the specific nature of sport and will continue to provide guidance in this regard. Regarding the application of EU competition law, the Commission will continue to apply the procedure as foreseen in Regulation (EC) No 1/2003. (European Commission 2011: 1)

Thus the Olympic movement in the European context at least has been able to limit to some degree the incursion of economic and other forms of regulation into its field of action. With the realisation of the commercial value of the Games from Los Angeles in 1984, the advent of huge broadcasting contracts, the TOP sponsors scheme, and admission of professional sportswomen and men into the Games from the 1980s, the Olympic authorities had adopted a more business-oriented approach but they were also having their 'special' position formally recognised. The discourse is one of business, but a form of business which has quite successfully sought a virtually unique position in terms of its protection as described

We are also confident that in bringing our own proposals to public authorities, we will prevent readjustments imposed on us by outside intervention; at the same time, I am also convinced that improving

democracy, transparency and solidarity will strengthen our organisations to the benefits of its stakeholders, mainly the clubs, athletes and
sportsman which must remain our 'core business'. (Rogge 2001: 21)

6.6   Conclusions

In our selection of these four discourse themes as major foci for discursive
constructions around Olympism in the twenty-first century we are intimating
aspects of continuity: concern with the socialisation of the young; assimilation versus multiculturalism or inter-culturalism; the use of sport for development in ways which will tie in developing nations and their young
people to a 'global' (but western dominated) phenomenon which purports
to bring social and physical but also moral benefits; and finally control of
systemic governance of the Olympic system. None of these four themes
is entirely new but each of them is given particular salience by the fact that
the Olympic movement is required to deal with the speed of change in
technological, social and political terms.

Sport as a social phenomenon is neither inherently positive nor negative
in its effects. Its use is defined and legitimated for particular ends, and our
own position has been to argue that developing a critical understanding of
how the use of sport is framed (what kinds of language games are being
played) allows us to consider, in whose interests, and with what kinds of
impact sport is being promoted, and these are central concerns for any
emancipatory approach to analysis of Olympic sport. We would define our
position in line with other analysts of the Olympic movement such as
Bruce Kidd and John MacAloon, as 'critical friends' to the movement, iden-
tifying as far as possible what constitutes positive (or negative) outcomes,
and establishing in what sense they are conceptualised as positive or negative, and how adequate a claim for positive or negative outcomes might
be. This critical conceptualisation of Olympic outcomes is a necessary condition for establishing ways in which the ethical claims for Olympism
might be met.

Our ontological position is not simply constructivist. We do want to refer
to real underlying structures which, though they are socially constructed,
exist independently of the individuals and groups which have participated
(and perhaps continue to participate) in their construction. Thus though
Coubertin may have introduced the term Olympism to the language, to
give that term meaning he, or any other speaker, has to engage in public
discourse and the term may then appear to 'take on a life of its own'. At
the outset it may be easier to impose a meaning on the use of a new term
by being prescriptive about its use, but as Wittgenstein (1967) argued the
meaning of a term is its use, and other speakers will begin to use the term
in their own way. In this sense power over discourse is always likely to be
transient, and we have sought to trace that transience.

This book has been about how speakers have borrowed, shaped and reshaped the concept of Olympism by virtue of their discursive practices. We have adopted, in part, an historical perspective because new uses of the term cannot suddenly be decided by individual speakers without reference to what has gone before (again to cite Wittgenstein 'there can be no such thing as a private language'). New uses of the term Olympism have to be defined with reference to previous meanings. Even where there are 'epistemic breaks' the 'new' has to be defined in ways in which it differs from the 'old'.

While charting the place of changing discourses we have tried to emphasise also that uses of the term will also carry an ethical dimension in their meaning (sometimes explicitly, sometimes implicitly), and that such ethical meanings will be related to deeper value sets (positive or negative). Our own ethical position draws unsurprisingly on a form of discourse ethics (see for example Henry 2007: Chapter 9) which advocates public debate (in a formal or an implied sense) as a vehicle for developing ethical consensus. Such a project is to be regarded as a priority in a culturally plural, globalised world. Tracing of the ethical dimension here is also intended as an engagement with such critical debates. Sport, and Olympic sport in particular, is an important venue for cultural interaction and the development of forms of moral consensus (about the rules, about how to behave in an appropriate manner etc.). Thus with the shift or evolution of meanings which we have been tracing in this text comes a shift of values sometimes subtle, sometimes profound. In seeking to lay these processes bare we hope to have made a contribution to an understanding of the ethical as a well as the social and political dimensions of Olympism.

Notes

Chapter 1   Introduction: Developing Discursive Constructions of Olympism

1   The earliest version held by the IOC Studies Centre, however, dates back to 1908.
2   We are grateful to Marie-Therese Zammit for drawing our attention to this argument.

Chapter 2   The Discursive Construction of Modern Olympic Histories

1   Booth regards John Hoberman's (1995) approach as a rare example, which attempts to invent a concept (idealistic internationalisms) by comparing four international organisations (the Red Cross, the Esperanto movement, the Scouting movement and the Olympic movement).
2   The first bulletin of the IOC contained the following list of IOC members: Bikelas – sometimes spelled Vikelas (Greece, President), Coubertin (Secretary General), Callot (France, Treasurer), Boutovski (Russia), Guth (Bohemia), Balck (Sweden), Cuff (Australasia), Sloane (USA), Zubiaur (Argentina), Lucchesi-Palli (Italy), Herbert (England), Ampthill (England) and Kémény (Hungary). In the second bulletin of the IOC dated October 1894, the list had been modified. Count Lucchesi-Palli from Italy had been replaced by his compatriot Count Andria Garafa because he was too busy with diplomatic tasks (Boulogne 1994), and Count Bousies from Belgium had been added.
3   This strand has been continued in more recent times by the promotion of the Olympic Truce in 1992 when the IOC led an appeal for a Truce and sought UN support for participation in the Barcelona Games of athletes from the war-torn former Yugoslavia.
4   For Pan-Arabism and sport see Henry *et al.* (2003).

Chapter 4   Carl Diem: Olympism in the Shadow of Fascism and the Post-war Rehabilitation (1912–1961)

1   However Mandell (1971) provides the information that Diem also led the German team in 1906 (as in 1912 Stockholm, 1928 in Amsterdam, and 1932 in Los Angeles).
2   Brundage's approach to this issue has raised many concerns about his motives, and any hidden anti-Semitic sympathies. For more see Guttmann (1992).
3   Brundage's approach to this issue both in finding in his investigation at the time that Jewish athletes were not excluded from consideration for the German team, and his subsequent lack of apology for these findings, has been the subject of considerable criticism (see for example Guttmann 1992).
4   However, Gaston Meyer does not make known whether the article was only addressed to *L'Auto* or also published in the journal (Hoberman 1986).
5   Before the Second World War, Germany had one German National Olympic Committee, but due to the post-war division between East and West Germany the

recognition of a single joint German National Olympic Committee was still pending (Toohey and Veal 2000).
6   Even after the intense controversy over the Nazi Olympics, the IOC awarded the 1940 Games to Tokyo, despite the international concerns for Japan's aggressive foreign policy at that time (Guttmann 1992).
7   The best known Regional Games of this period are: the Pan-American Games, the Mediterranean Games, the Asian Games, the Games of the New Emerging Forces (GANEFO), the Pan-Arab Games and the Pan-African Games (Espy 1979).

Chapter 5   From Bipolar to Multipolar International Relations: Olympism and the Speakers at the International Olympic Academy in the Cold War and Post-Cold War Era

1   The other Masters degree was inaugurated in 2010, administered and awarded by a consortium of four universities (the German Sports University in Cologne, Germany; l'Université Claude Bernard, Lyon I, France; Loughborough University, UK; the Autonomous University of Barcelona, Spain).
2   Avery Brundage was unable to attend the Session but the speech he had prepared can be found in the proceedings of the 1963 IOA Session.

Chapter 6   Technologies of Power, Governmentality and Discourses of Olympism in the Twenty-first Century

1   Our work is also limited to the English language community in the sense that we deal with sources in English even of Coubertin's and Diem's work.
2   Interestingly no objection was made even for a contact sport such as taekwondo in terms of fear of choking of an athlete.
3   Of course what will count as the 'best' aspects of given cultures is a problem to be resolved and we have argued elsewhere (Henry 2007) that a form of discourse ethics which seeks *general* consensus (rather than *universal* consensus) on cultural norms to be adopted will be required. In rejecting the goal of a universal set of norms and advocating general agreement we are of course consciously departing from the modernist approach adopted by Habermas (1990a).

Bibliography

Afshar, H. 1998. *Islam and Feminisms: An Iranian Case-Study*. New York: St. Martin's Press.

Al-Ali, N. S. 2000. *Secularism, Gender, and the State in the Middle East: The Egyptian Women's Movement*. Cambridge, U.K.; New York: Cambridge University Press.

Albrow, M. 1997. *The Global Age*. Cambridge: Polity.

Al-Tauqi, M. 2003. *Olympic Solidarity: Global Order, the Diffusion of Modern Sport and the Hegemony of the Olympic Movement*, unpublished PhD Thesis, Loughborough University.

Amara, M. 2006. 'Sport and Algerian nationalism in the "global" era: Within and beyond the nation-state'. *Francophone and Postcolonial Studies*, 4: 88–115.

Amara, M. and I. P. Henry. 2010. 'Sport, Muslim identities and cultures in the UK, an emerging policy issue: Case studies of Leicester and Birmingham'. *European Sport Management Quarterly*, 10: 419–43.

Andrecs, H. 1973. 'The Olympic idea and its realization in schools', ed. International Olympic Academy, *13th Young Participants Session*, pp. 180–9. Olympia: International Olympic Academy.

Andrews, D. L. 1998. 'Feminizing Olympic reality: Preliminary dispatches from Baudrillard's Atlanta'. *International Review for the Sociology of Sport*, 33: 5–18.

Andrews, D. L. 2000. 'Posting up: French post-structuralism and the critical analysis of contemporary sporting cultures', eds. J. J. Coakley and E. G. Dunning, *Handbook of Sports Studies*. London: Sage.

Anon., 1992. *Encyclopædia Britannica*. Chicago: Encyclopædia Britannica Inc.

Anthony, D. 1992. 'The propagation of Olympic education as a weapon against the corruption and commercialization of world-wide sport', ed. International Olympic Academy, *32nd Young Participants Session*, pp. 157–64. Olympia: International Olympic Academy.

Appadurai, A. 1990. 'Disjuncture and difference in the global cultural economy', ed. M. Featherstone, *Global Culture: Nationalism, Globalization and Modernity*. London: Sage.

Archer, M. 1995. *Realist Social Theory: The Morphogenetic Approach*. Cambridge: Cambridge University Press.

Arnold, P. J. 1996. 'Olympism, sport and education'. *Quest*, 48: 93–101.

Bale, J. and J. Sang. 1996. *Kenyan Running: Movement Culture, Geography and Global Change*. London: Frank Cass.

Barney, R. K. 1993. 'Golden egg or fool's gold? American Olympic commercialism and the IOC', ed. International Olympic Academy, *33rd Young Participants Session*, pp. 123–33. Olympia: International Olympic Academy.

Bauer, P. and A. Sen. 2004. *From Subsistence to Exchange*. Princeton, NJ: Princeton University Press.

BBC News. 1999. *IOC 'Ignored' 1991 Corruption Warning*. British Broadcasting Corporation.

Beinart, P. 1997. 'An illusion for our time'. *New Republic*, 20 October.

Benzerti, K. 2002. *Olympism in Africa*. http://www.sport.gov.gr/2/24/243/2431/24312/e243123.html (retrieved 23 May 2003).

Betts, J. 1974. *America's Sporting Heritage, 1850–1950*. Reading, Mass: Addison-Wesley.

Bhaskar, R. 1989. *Reclaiming Reality: A Critical Introduction to Contemporary Philosophy*. London; New York: Verso.

Birrell, S. and C. Cole. 1994. *Women, Sport and Culture*. Champaign, Illinois: Human Kinetics.

Black, D. R. and J. van der Westhuizen. 2004. 'The allure of global games for "semi-peripheral" polities and spaces: A research agenda'. *Third World Quarterly*, 25: 1195–214.

Booth, D. 2004. 'Post-Olympism? Questioning Olympic historiography', eds. J. Bale and M. K. Christensen, *Post Olympism? Questioning Sport in the Twenty-First Century*, pp. 13–32. Oxford: Berg.

Bose, M. 2011. 'FIFA faces MPs wrath over handling of corruption allegations', *Inside the Games*.

Boswell, C. 2003. *European Migration Policies in Flux: Changing Patterns of Inclusion and Exclusion*. Oxford: Blackwell.

Boulogne, Y.-P. 1994. 'The presidencies of Demetrius Vikelas and Pierre de Coubertin'. *The International Olympic Committee – One Hundred Years: The Ideas – The Presidents – The Achievements*. Lausanne: IOC, vol. 1, p. 200.

Boulogne, Y.-P. 1999a. 'Olympism more than ever'. *Olympic Review*, XXVI-25, February–March 1999, pp. 37–9.

Boulogne, Y.-P. 1999b. *Pierre de Coubertin. Humanism et Pédagogie: Dix Leçons sur L'Olympisme*. Lausanne: International Olympic Committee.

Boulogne, Y.-P. 2000. *Pierre de Coubertin and Women's Sport Olympic Review*, pp. 23–6.

Bourdieu, P. 1989. *Distinction: A Social Critique of the Judgement of Taste*. London: Routledge.

Bowen, J. 1989. 'Education, ideology and the ruling class: Hellenism and English public schools in the nineteenth century', ed. G Clarke, *Rediscovering Hellenism*, pp. 161–86. Cambridge: Cambridge University Press.

Brohm, J. M. 1978. *Sport: A Prison of Measured Time*. London: Ink Links.

Brooks, C. M. 2001. 'Using sex appeal as a sport promotion strategy'. *Women in Sport & Physical Activity Journal*, 10: 1–16.

Brown, D. 2001. 'Modern sport, modernism and the cultural manifesto: De Coubertin's Revue Olympique'. *The International Journal of the History of Sport*, 18(2): 78–109.

Brownell, S. 2008. *Beijing's Games: What the Olympics Mean to China*. Plymouth: Rowman and Littlefield.

Brundage, A. 1963. 'The Olympic philosophy'. In International Olympic Academy Proceedings, *28th Young Participants Session*, pp. 29–39. Olympia: International Olympic Academy.

Caillat, M. and J.-M. Brohm. 1984. *Les dessous de l'olympisme*. Paris: La Découverte.

Carl-Diem-Institut. *The Olympic Idea. Discourses and Essays*. Verlag, Germany: Karl Hofmann.

Carrington, B. 2004. 'Cosmopolitan Olympism, humanism and spectacle of "race"', ed. J. Bale and M. K. Christensen, *Post-Olympism? Questioning Sport in the Twenty-first Century*, pp. 81–98. Oxford: Berg.

Cashman, R. 2004. 'The future of a multi-sport mega event: Is there a pace for the Olympic Games in a "post-Olympic" world?', eds. J. Bale and M. K. Christensen, *Post-Olympism? Questioning Sport in the Twenty-first Century*, pp. 119–34. Oxford: Berg.

Cashman, R. 2006. *The Bitter-Sweet Awakening: The Legacy of the Sydney 2000 Olympic Games*. Petersham, NSW: Walla Walla Press in conjunction with the Australian Centre for Olympic Studies, University of Technology, Sydney.

Centre for Housing Rights and Evictions. 2007. *Fair Play for Housing Rights: Mega-Events, Olympic Games and Housing Rights*. Geneva: COHRE.

Chan, G. 2006. *China's Compliance in Global Affairs: Trade, Arms Control, Environmental Protection, Human Rights*. Singapore: World Scientific.

Chappelet, J.-L., with L. Bousigue and B. Cohen. 2008. *The Autonomy of Sport in Europe*. Strasbourg: Council of Europe.

Chatziefstathiou, D. and I. Henry. 2009. 'Technologies of power, governmentality and Olympic discourses: A Foucauldian analysis for understanding the discursive constructions of the Olympic ideology'. *Esporte y sociedad*. Vol. 4, No. 12 (electronic journal – <http://www.esportesociedade.com/>).

Chatziefstathiou, D. and I. Henry. 2007. 'Hellenism and Olympism: Pierre de Coubertin and the Greek challenge to the early Olympic movement'. *Sport in History*, 27: 24–43.

Chatziefstathiou, D. and I. Henry. 2010. 'Hellenism and Olympism: Pierre de Coubertin and the Greek challenge to the early Olympic movement', ed. V. Girginov, *The Olympics: A Critical Reader*, pp. 123–34. London: Routledge.

Chatziefstathiou, D., I. Henry, M. Al Tauqi and E. Theodoraki. 2008. 'Cultural imperialism and the diffusion of Olympic sport', in eds. H. Ren, L. P. Dacosta, A. Miragaya and N. Jings, *Africa: A Comparison of Pre and Post Second World War Contexts, Olympic Studies Reader. A Multidisciplinary and Multicultural Research Guide (Volume 1)*, pp. 111–28. Beijing: Beijing Sports University Press.

Chomsky, N. 1994. *Secrets, Lies and Democracy*. Tucson: Odonian.

Clarke, K. 1988. 'Olympism at the beginning and at the end of the twentieth century – Immutable values and outdated factors', ed. International Olympic Academy, *28th Young Participants Session*, pp. 99–104. Olympia: International Olympic Academy.

CNN. 2010. *Iran's Girls' Football Team Banned from Olympics for Wearing Hijab*.

Coalter, F. 2010. 'The politics of sport-for-development: Limited focus programmes and broad gauge problems?' *International Review for the Sociology of Sport*, 45: 295–314.

Connolly, K. 2010. 'Angela Merkel declares death of German multiculturalism'. *Guardian*, 16. London.

Coubertin, P. 1887, 2000. 'English education', ed. N. Muller, *Pierre de Coubertin 1863–1937 – Olympism: Selected Writings*, pp. 105–20. Lausanne: International Olympic Committee.

Coubertin, P. 1888, 2000. Letter to the Members of the Société de' Économie Sociale and of the Unions de la Paix Sociale, ed. N. Muller, *Pierre de Coubertin 1863–1937 – Olympism: Selected Writings*, pp. 75–7. Lausanne: International Olympic Committee.

Coubertin, P. 1889a, 2000. 'Our students'. In ed. N. Muller, *Pierre de Coubertin 1863–1937 – Olympism: Selected Writings*, pp. 69–74. Lausanne: International Olympic Committee.

Coubertin, P. 1889b, 2000. 'English education in France'. In ed. N. Muller, *Pierre de Coubertin 1863–1937 – Olympism: Selected Writings*, pp. 60–8. Lausanne: International Olympic Committee.

Coubertin, P. 1889c, 2000. 'English education'. In ed. N. Muller, *Pierre de Coubertin 1863–1937 – Olympism: Selected Writings*, pp. 105–20. Lausanne: International Olympic Committee.

Coubertin, P. 1890a. *Universités Transatlantiques*. Paris: Librairie Hachette.

Coubertin, P. 1890b, 2000. 'Athletics and gymnastics'. In ed. N. Muller, *Pierre de Coubertin 1863–1937 – Olympism: Selected Writings*, pp. 138–40. Lausanne: International Olympic Committee.

Coubertin, P. 1892. Speech at a meeting of the Union des Sports Athlétiques in Paris on November 25, 1892.

Coubertin, P. 1894a, 2000. 'The Congress of Paris'. In ed. N. Muller, *Pierre de Coubertin 1863–1937 – Olympism: Selected Writings*, pp. 298–9. Lausanne: International Olympic Committee.

Coubertin, P. 1894b, 2000. The Neo-Olympism Appeal to the People of Athens (November 16, 1894). Lecture Given to the Parnassus Literary Society at Athens. In ed. N. Muller, *Pierre de Coubertin 1863–1937 – Olympism: Selected Writings*, pp. 533–41. Lausanne: International Olympic Committee.

Coubertin, P. 1896a, 2000. 'The modern Olympic games'. In ed. N. Muller, *Pierre de Coubertin 1863–1937 – Olympism: Selected Writings*, pp. 308–11. Lausanne: International Olympic Committee.

Coubertin, P. 1896b, 2000. The Olympic Games of 1896. In ed. N. Muller, *Pierre de Coubertin 1863–1937 – Olympism: Selected Writings*, pp. 350–60. Lausanne: International Olympic Committee.

Coubertin, P. 1902. Notre épopée lointaine. In *Notre épopée lointaine*, Le Figaro. Paris.

Coubertin, P. 1906, 2000. 'The Philhellene's Dutyr'. In ed. N. Muller, *Pierre de Coubertin 1863–1937 – Olympism: Selected Writings*, p. 250. Lausanne: International Olympic Committee.

Coubertin, P. 1908a, 2000. To the Editor of the Times: The Olympic Games (July 13, 1908). In ed. N. Muller, *Pierre de Coubertin 1863–1937 – Olympism: Selected Writings*, pp. 735–6. Lausanne: International Olympic Committee.

Coubertin, P. 1908b, 2000. 'Why I revived the Olympic Games'. In ed. N. Muller, *Pierre de Coubertin 1863–1937 – Olympism: Selected Writings*, pp. 542–6. Lausanne: International Olympic Committee.

Coubertin, P. 1909. *Une Champagne de Vingt-et-un Ans*. Paris: Librairie de l'Education physique.

Coubertin, P. 1912a, 2000. 'Ode to sport'. In ed. N. Muller, *Pierre de Coubertin 1863–1937 – Olympism: Selected Writings*, pp. 629–30. Lausanne: International Olympic Committee.

Coubertin, P. 1912b, 2000. 'The women at the Olympic Games'. In ed. N. Muller, *Pierre de Coubertin 1863–1937 – Olympism: Selected Writings*, pp. 711–13. Lausanne: International Olympic Committee.

Coubertin, P. 1912c, 2000. 'Closing words'. In ed. N. Muller, *Pierre de Coubertin 1863–1937 – Olympism: Selected Writings*, p. 448. Lausanne: International Olympic Committee.

Coubertin, P. 1913, 2000. 'An Olympiad in the Far East'. In ed. N. Muller, *Pierre de Coubertin 1863–1937 – Olympism: Selected Writings*, pp. 695–7. Lausanne: International Olympic Committee.

Coubertin, P. 1918a, 2000. 'Olympic Letter III: Olympism and education'. In ed. N. Muller, *Pierre de Coubertin 1863–1937 – Olympism: Selected Writings*, pp. 547–8. Lausanne: International Olympic Committee.

Coubertin, P. 1918b, 2000. 'Olympic Letter VI: Panem et Circenses'. In ed. N. Muller, *Pierre de Coubertin 1863–1937 – Olympism: Selected Writings*, p. 220. Lausanne: International Olympic Committee.

Coubertin, P. 1918c, 2000. What We Can Ask of Sport. Address Given to the Greek Liberal Club of Lausanne. In ed. N. Muller, *Pierre de Coubertin 1863–1937 – Olympism: Selected Writings*, pp. 269–77. Lausanne: International Olympic Committee.

Coubertin, P. 1919a, 2000. Letter to the Members of the International Olympic Committee (January, 1919). In ed. N. Muller, *Pierre de Coubertin 1863–1937 – Olympism: Selected Writings*, pp. 737–41. Lausanne: International Olympic Committee.

Coubertin, P. 1919b, 2000. 'Olympic Letter XI: The sporting spirit of students'. In ed. N. Muller, *Pierre de Coubertin 1863–1937 – Olympism: Selected Writings*, pp. 172–3. Lausanne: International Olympic Committee.

Coubertin, P. 1919c, 2000. 'Olympic Letter XIII: The periodicity of the Olympic Games'. In ed. N. Muller, *Pierre de Coubertin 1863–1937 – Olympism: Selected Writings*, p. 550. Lausanne: International Olympic Committee.

Coubertin, P. 1919d, 2000. 'Olympic Letter XXI: The pershing Olympiad'. In ed. N. Muller, *Pierre de Coubertin 1863–1937 – Olympism: Selected Writings*, p. 551. Lausanne: International Olympic Committee.

Coubertin, P. 1919e, 2000. 'The twenty-fifth anniversary of the proclamation of the Olympic Games'. In ed. N. Muller, *Pierre de Coubertin 1863–1937 – Olympism: Selected Writings*, pp. 551–3. Lausanne: International Olympic Committee.

Coubertin, P. 1920, 2000. Address Delivered at Antwerp City Hall in August, 1920: Sport is King. In ed. N. Muller, *Pierre de Coubertin 1863–1937 – Olympism: Selected Writings*, pp. 222–6. Lausanne: International Olympic Committee.

Coubertin, P. 1921, 2000. Letter to the IOC Members (1921): 'My Work Is Done'. In ed. N. Muller, *Pierre de Coubertin 1863–1937 – Olympism: Selected Writings*, pp. 700–1. Lausanne: International Olympic Committee.

Coubertin, P. 1922, 2000. 'Between two battles. From Olympism to the popular university'. In ed. N. Muller, *Pierre de Coubertin 1863–1937 – Olympism: Selected Writings*, pp. 203–9. Lausanne: International Olympic Committee.

Coubertin, P. 1923, 2000. Athletics Want to Conquer Africa. An Appeal from the President of the IOC. In ed. N. Muller, *Pierre de Coubertin 1863–1937 – Olympism: Selected Writings*, p. 702. Lausanne: International Olympic Committee.

Coubertin, P. 1927, 2000. 'The truth about sport: The ideas of Pierre de Coubertin. An open letter to Frantz-Reichel'. In ed. N. Muller, *Pierre de Coubertin 1863–1937 – Olympism: Selected Writings*, pp. 235–6. Lausanne: International Olympic Committee.

Coubertin, P. 1928a, 2000. 'Educational use of athletic activity'. In ed. N. Muller, *Pierre de Coubertin 1863–1937 – Olympism: Selected Writings*, pp. 184–94. Lausanne: International Olympic Committee.

Coubertin, P. 1928b, 2000. Message to All Athletes and Participants Meeting at Amsterdam for the Ninth Olympiad. In ed. N. Muller, *Pierre de Coubertin 1863–1937 – Olympism: Selected Writings*, pp. 603–4. Lausanne: International Olympic Committee.

Coubertin, P. 1929, 2000. Olympia. Lecture Given in Paris, in the Festival Hall of the 19th Arrondissement Town Hall. In ed. N. Muller, *Pierre de Coubertin 1863–1937 – Olympism: Selected Writings*, pp. 563–76. Lausanne: International Olympic Committee.

Coubertin, P. 1931a, 2000. 'Athletic colonization'. In ed. N. Muller, *Pierre de Coubertin 1863–1937 – Olympism: Selected Writings*, pp. 703–4. Lausanne: International Olympic Committee.

Coubertin, P. 1931b, 2000. 'New mottoes'. In ed. N. Muller, *Pierre de Coubertin 1863–1937 – Olympism: Selected Writings*, pp. 591–3. Lausanne: International Olympic Committee.

Coubertin, P. 1931c, 2000. 'The Olympic Games and gymnastics'. In ed. N. Muller, *Pierre de Coubertin 1863–1937 – Olympism: Selected Writings*, pp. 716–18. Lausanne: International Olympic Committee.

Coubertin, P. 1931d, 2000. *Olympic Memoirs*. Lausanne: International Olympic Committee.

Coubertin, P. 1932, 2000. 'The apotheosis of Olympism'. In ed. N. Muller, *Pierre de Coubertin 1863–1937 – Olympism: Selected Writings*, pp. 517–18. Lausanne: International Olympic Committee.

Coubertin, P. 1934a, 2000. 'Forty years of Olympism'. In ed. N. Muller, *Pierre de Coubertin 1863–1937 – Olympism: Selected Writings*, pp. 742–6. Lausanne: International Olympic Committee.

Coubertin, P. 1934b, 2000. To My Hellenic Friends. An Open Letter Dated April, 1934. In ed. N. Muller, *Pierre de Coubertin 1863–1937 – Olympism: Selected Writings*, p. 278. Lausanne: International Olympic Committee.

Coubertin, P. 1935, 2000. 'The philosophic foundation of modern Olympism'. In ed. N. Muller, *Pierre de Coubertin 1863–1937 – Olympism: Selected Writings*, pp. 580–3. Lausanne: International Olympic Committee.

Coubertin, P. 1936, 2000. 'Message to the Olympia-Berlin runners'. In ed. N. Muller, *Pierre de Coubertin 1863–1937 – Olympism: Selected Writings*, pp. 578–9. Lausanne: International Olympic Committee.

Coubertin, P. 1938a, 2000. 'The origins and limits of athletic progress'. In ed. N. Muller, *Pierre de Coubertin 1863–1937 – Olympism: Selected Writings*, pp. 195–202. Lausanne: International Olympic Committee.

Coubertin, P. 1938b. *Olympische Rundschau*, April 1938, p. 133.

Coubertin, P. 1976, 2000. 'The unfinished symphony'. In ed. N. Muller, *Pierre de Coubertin 1863–1937 – Olympism: Selected Writings*, pp. 751–3. Lausanne: International Olympic Committee.

Coubertin, P. 1979. *Olympic Memories.* Lausanne: International Olympic Committee.

Coubertin, P. 1997a, 2000. 'The 1921 maneuver'. In ed. N. Muller, *Pierre de Coubertin 1863–1937 – Olympism: Selected Writings*, pp. 486–91. Lausanne: International Olympic Committee.

Coubertin, P. 1997b, 2000. 'Budapest (1911)'. In ed. N. Muller, *Pierre de Coubertin 1863–1937 – Olympism: Selected Writings*, pp. 431–5. Lausanne: International Olympic Committee.

Coubertin, P. 1997c, 2000. 'The Capitol in Rome (1923)'. In ed. N. Muller, *Pierre de Coubertin 1863–1937 – Olympism: Selected Writings*, pp. 495–9. Lausanne: International Olympic Committee.

Coubertin, P. 1997d, 2000. 'The conquest of Greece'. In ed. N. Muller, *Pierre de Coubertin 1863–1937 – Olympism: Selected Writings*, pp. 321–5. Lausanne: International Olympic Committee.

Coubertin, P. 1997e, 2000. 'The fifth Olympiad (Stockholm 1912)'. In ed. N. Muller, *Pierre de Coubertin 1863–1937 – Olympism: Selected Writings*, pp. 435–41. Lausanne: International Olympic Committee.

Coubertin, P. 1997f, 2000. 'The first Olympiad (Athens 1896)'. In ed. N. Muller, *Pierre de Coubertin 1863–1937 – Olympism: Selected Writings*, pp. 321–5. Lausanne: International Olympic Committee.

Coubertin, P. 1997g, 2000. 'The inclusion of literature and the arts'. In ed. N. Muller, *Pierre de Coubertin 1863–1937 – Olympism: Selected Writings*, pp. 620–2. Lausanne: International Olympic Committee.

Coubertin, P. 1997h, 2000. 'Legends'. In ed. N. Muller, *Pierre de Coubertin 1863–1937 – Olympism: Selected Writings*, pp. 747–9. Lausanne: International Olympic Committee.

Coubertin, P. 1997i, 2000. 'The Paris Congress and the revival of the Olympic Games'. In ed. N. Muller, *Pierre de Coubertin 1863–1937 – Olympism: Selected Writings*, pp. 313–20. Lausanne: International Olympic Committee.

Coubertin, P. 1997j, 2000. 'The Olympic Congress at Le Havre (1897)'. In ed. N. Muller, *Pierre de Coubertin 1863–1937 – Olympism: Selected Writings*, pp. 369–72. Lausanne: International Olympic Committee.

Coubertin, P. 1997k, 2000. 'The seventh Olympiad (Antwerp 1920)'. In ed. N. Muller, *Pierre de Coubertin 1863–1937 – Olympism: Selected Writings*, pp. 471–6. Lausanne: International Olympic Committee.

Coubertin, P. 1997l, 2000. 'The four war years'. In ed. N. Muller, *Pierre de Coubertin 1863–1937 – Olympism: Selected Writings*, pp. 464–8. Lausanne: International Olympic Committee.

Coubertin, P. 1997m, 2000. 'The 20th anniversary of the Olympic Games (Paris 1914)'. In ed. N. Muller, *Pierre de Coubertin 1863–1937 – Olympism: Selected Writings*, pp. 458–64. Lausanne: International Olympic Committee.

Culpin, C. 1996. *Making History: World History from 1914 to the Present*. London: Collins Educational.

DaCosta, L. with A. Miragaya, M. Gomes, N. Abreu and O. Tavares. 2002. *Olympic Studies: Current Intellectual Crossroads*. Rio de Janeiro: Editora Gama Filho (available from http://www.1984foundation.org/SportsLibrary/Books/OlympicStudies.pdf).

Dacosta, L. P. 1997. 'The Olympic movement today and environmental protection'. In ed. International Olympic Academy, *37th Young Participants Session*, pp. 100–6. Olympia: International Olympic Academy.

Darby, P. 2000. 'The new scramble for Africa: African football labour migration to Europe'. *The European Sports History Review*, 3: 217–44.

Darby, P. 2002. *Africa, Football, and FIFA: Politics, Colonialism, and Resistance*. London; Portland, Or.: F. Cass.

Darnell, S. C. 2007. 'Playing with race: Right to play and the production of whiteness in "development through sport"'. *Sport in Society*, 10: 560.

Davies, T. 1997. *Humanism*. London: Routledge.

Day, D. 2011. 'Massaging the amateur ethos: Professional coaches at Stockholm in 1912'. In ed. D. Day, *Sports and Coaching: Pasts and Futures*. Crewe: Institute for Performance Research, Manchester Metropolitan University.

Dean, M. 1994. *Critical and Effective Histories: Foucault's Methods and Historical Sociology*. London: Routledge.

Dean, M. 1999. *Governmentality: Power and Rule in Modern Society*. London: Sage.

DeFrantz, A. 1989. 'Olympic movement: Youth and doping'. International Olympic Academy, *29th Young Participants Session*, pp. 106–11. Olympia: International Olympic Academy.

Diem, C. 1906, 1970. 'The Olympic Games 1906'. In ed. Carl-Diem-Institut, *The Olympic Idea. Discourses and Essays*, pp. 35–7. Verlag, Germany: Karl Hofmann.

Diem, C. 1912a, 1970. 'The International Olympic Committee'. In ed. Carl-Diem-Institut, *The Olympic Idea. Discourses and Essays*, pp. 27–30. Verlag, Germany: Karl Hofmann.

Diem, C. 1912b, 1970. 'Towards the Olympic Games'. In ed. Carl-Diem-Institut, *The Olympic Idea. Discourses and Essays*, pp. 38–9. Verlag, Germany: Karl Hofmann.

Diem, C. 1912c, 1970. 'VIth Olympiad'. In ed. Carl-Diem-Institut, *The Olympic Idea. Discourses and Essays*, p. 44. Verlag, Germany: Karl Hofmann.

Diem, C. 1914, 1970. 'The result of the Paris Sport Congress'. In ed. Carl-Diem-Institut, *The Olympic Idea. Discourses and Essays*, pp. 30–1. Verlag, Germany: Karl Hofmann.

Diem, C. 1920a, 1970. 'Germany's Olympic movement'. In ed. Carl-Diem-Institut, *The Olympic Idea. Discourses and Essays*, pp. 3–5. Verlag, Germany: Karl Hofmann.

Diem, C. 1920b, 1970. 'The Olympic idea'. In ed. Carl-Diem-Institut, *The Olympic Idea. Discourses and Essays*, pp. 1–2. Verlag, Germany: Karl Hofmann.

Diem, C. 1923, 1970. 'The stadium in Stockholm'. In ed. Carl-Diem-Institut, *The Olympic Idea. Discourses and Essays*, pp. 40–4. Verlag, Germany: Karl Hofmann.

Diem, C. 1925. 'Die Welt fur Deutschland fordern'. *Olympsiche Flamme*, p. 44.

Diem, C. 1926. 'Vonn deutschen Sinn der Deutschen Kampfspiele'. *Olympische Flamme*, p. 231.

Diem, C. 1927. 'Sport und Geist'. *Olympsiche Flamme*, p. 150.

Diem, C. 1929, 1970. 'Note on the future programme of the international Olympic Games'. In ed. Carl-Diem-Institut, *The Olympic Idea. Discourses and Essays*, pp. 53–6. Verlag, Germany: Karl Hofmann.

Diem, C. 1930, 1970. 'The opening of the Olympic Congress'. In ed. Carl-Diem-Institut, *The Olympic Idea. Discourses and Essays*, p. 33. Verlag, Germany: Karl Hofmann.

Diem, C. 1932, 1970. 'Olympic days of wandering, teaching and learning'. In ed. Carl-Diem-Institut, *The Olympic Idea. Discourses and Essays*, pp. 58–63. Verlag, Germany: Karl Hofmann.

Diem, C. 1933a, 1970. 'The Games of the XIth Olympiad, Berlin, 1–16 August 1936'. In ed. Carl-Diem-Institut, *The Olympic Idea. Discourses and Essays*, pp. 63–4. Verlag, Germany: Karl Hofmann.

Diem, C. 1933b, 1970. 'The meaning of the modern games'. In ed. Carl-Diem-Institut, *The Olympic Idea. Discourses and Essays*, pp. 6–9. Verlag, Germany: Karl Hofmann.

Diem, C. 1936a, 1970. 'Official report on the games'. In ed. Carl-Diem-Institut, *The Olympic Idea. Discourses and Essays*, pp. 75–6. Verlag, Germany: Karl Hofmann.

Diem, C. 1936b, 1970. '"Olympic Youth" Festival Play. In Official Report on the Games', ed. Carl-Diem-Institut, *The Olympic Idea. Discourses and Essays*, pp. 73–4. Verlag, Germany: Karl Hofmann.

Diem, C. 1937, 1970. 'Preparations for the 1936 Games'. In ed. Carl-Diem-Institut, *The Olympic Idea. Discourses and Essays*, pp. 67–72. Verlag, Germany: Karl Hofmann.

Diem, C. 1938a, 1970. 'Helsinki'. In ed. Carl-Diem-Institut, *The Olympic Idea. Discourses and Essays*, pp. 78–80. Verlag, Germany: Karl Hofmann.

Diem, C. 1938b, 1970. 'The International Olympic Institute in Berlin'. In ed. Carl-Diem-Institut, *The Olympic Idea. Discourses and Essays*, pp. 34–5. Verlag, Germany: Karl Hofmann.

Diem, C. 1940, 1970. 'Torch-race visions'. In ed. Carl-Diem-Institut, *The Olympic Idea. Discourses and Essays*, pp. 77–8. Verlag, Germany: Karl Hofmann.

Diem, C. 1941. 'Weltspiele?' *Olympsiche Flamme*, pp. 244–5.

Diem, C. 1942a, 1970. 'Appeal to the Berlin Reichstag'. In ed. Carl-Diem-Institut, *The Olympic Idea. Discourses and Essays*, pp. 49–50. Verlag, Germany: Karl Hofmann.

Diem, C. 1942b, 1970. 'Coubertin's heart in eternal Olympia'. In ed. Carl-Diem-Institut, *The Olympic Idea. Discourses and Essays*, pp. 9–11. Verlag, Germany: Karl Hofmann.

Diem, C. 1942c, 1970. 'Note on preparations for the VIth Olympiad 1916'. In ed. Carl-Diem-Institut, *The Olympic Idea. Discourses and Essays*, pp. 46–9. Verlag, Germany: Karl Hofmann.

Diem, C. 1942d, 1970. 'Olympia – Tokyo torch relay'. In ed. Carl-Diem-Institut, *The Olympic Idea. Discourses and Essays*, pp. 76–7. Verlag, Germany: Karl Hofmann.

Diem, C. 1942e, 1970. 'Olympic academy'. In ed. Carl-Diem-Institut, *The Olympic Idea. Discourses and Essays*, p. 113. Verlag, Germany: Karl Hofmann.

Diem, C. 1942f, 1970. 'The first step to the VIth Olympiad'. In ed. Carl-Diem-Institut, *The Olympic Idea. Discourses and Essays*, pp. 45–6. Verlag, Germany: Karl Hofmann.

Diem, C. 1947, 1970. 'Invitations'. In ed. Carl-Diem-Institut, *The Olympic Idea. Discourses and Essays*, p. 80. Verlag, Germany: Karl Hofmann.

Diem, C. 1948, 1970. 'In the Olympic spirit'. In ed. Carl-Diem-Institut, *The Olympic Idea. Discourses and Essays*, pp. 80–2. Verlag, Germany: Karl Hofmann.

Diem, C. 1949, 1970. 'Tasks of the National Olympic Committee'. In ed. Carl-Diem-Institut, *The Olympic Idea. Discourses and Essays*, pp. 82–8. Verlag, Germany: Karl Hofmann.

Diem, C. 1952, 1970. 'Competition for the Olympic youth tour to Helsinki 1952'. In ed. Carl-Diem-Institut, *The Olympic Idea. Discourses and Essays*, pp. 17–20. Verlag, Germany: Karl Hofmann.

Diem, C. 1954, 1970. 'An immortal idea'. In ed. Carl-Diem-Institut, *The Olympic Idea. Discourses and Essays*, pp. 20–1. Verlag, Germany: Karl Hofmann.

Diem, C. 1956, 1970. 'That's why it's Melbourne'. In ed. Carl-Diem-Institut, *The Olympic Idea. Discourses and Essays*, pp. 91–3. Verlag, Germany: Karl Hofmann.

Diem, C. 1957a, 1970. 'Criticism and thanks'. In ed. Carl-Diem-Institut, *The Olympic Idea. Discourses and Essays*, pp. 93–8. Verlag, Germany: Karl Hofmann.

Diem, C. 1957b, 1970. 'Farewell to the past – A greeting to the future'. In ed. Carl-Diem-Institut, *The Olympic Idea. Discourses and Essays*, pp. 98–101. Verlag, Germany: Karl Hofmann.

Diem, C. 1957c, 1970. 'From a letter to Eduard Spranger'. In ed. Carl-Diem-Institut, *The Olympic Idea. Discourses and Essays*, pp. 110–11. Verlag, Germany: Karl Hofmann.

Diem, C. 1957d, 1970. 'Raise Olympia to the light!'. In ed. Carl-Diem-Institut, *The Olympic Idea. Discourses and Essays*, pp. 109–10. Verlag, Germany: Karl Hofmann.

Diem, C. 1957e, 1970. 'The renewal of the Olympic Games'. In ed. Carl-Diem-Institut, *The Olympic Idea. Discourses and Essays*, pp. 21–7. Verlag, Germany: Karl Hofmann.

Diem, C. 1960, 1970. 'The balance sheet of the Rome Games'. In ed. Carl-Diem-Institut, *The Olympic Idea. Discourses and Essays*, pp. 104–9. Verlag, Germany: Karl Hofmann.

Diem, C. 1961a, 1970. 'An "Elis" of our times'. In ed. Carl-Diem-Institut, *The Olympic Idea. Discourses and Essays*, pp. 113–18. Verlag, Germany: Karl Hofmann.

Diem, C. 1961b, 1970. 'The final clearance of the stadium'. In ed. Carl-Diem-Institut, *The Olympic Idea. Discourses and Essays*, pp. 118–19. Verlag, Germany: Karl Hofmann.

Dimeo, P. and T. Hunt 2009. 'Leading anti-doping in the IOC: The ambiguous role of Prince Alexandre de Merode'. *Journal of Olympic History*, 17: 20–2.

Dimeo, P. 2007. *A History of Drug Use in Sport, 1876–1976: Beyond Good and Evil*. London: Routledge.

Dine, P. 1996. 'Un Héroisme problématique – Le sport, la littérature et la guerre d'Algérie'. *Europe*, 806–7: 177–85.

Dodds, K. 2000. *Geopolitics in a Changing World*. New York: Prentice Hall.

Donelly, P. 1996. 'Prolympism: Sport monoculture as crisis and opportunity'. *Quest*, 48: 25–42.

Donnelly, P. 1995. 'Sport monoculture: Crisis or opportunity?' *International Olympic Academy, 35th Young Participants Session*, pp. 55–68. Olympia: International Olympic Academy.

Dorsey, J. 2011. 'FIFA bans Jordanian women soccer players for wearing the hijab'. *Al Arabiya News*. Dubai.

Doward, J. 2011. 'David Cameron's attack on multiculturalism divides the coalition'. *The Observer*. London.

Dubberke, H. 1986. 'Critical remarks regarding sports aid for developing countries'. In eds. J. A. Mangan and R. B. Small, *Sport, Culture, Society: International Historical and Sociological Perspectives. Proceedings of the VIII Commonwealth and International Conference on Sport, Physical Education, Recreation and Dance*. London: E. & F. N. Spon.

Dussel, E. and A. Fornazzari. 2002. 'World system and "trans"-modernity'. *Nepantla: Views from South*, 3(2): 221–44.

Eichberg, H. 1984. 'Olympic sport: Neocolonialism and alternatives'. *International Review for the Sociology of Sport*, 19: 97–105.

Eichberg, H. 2004. 'The global, the popular and the inter-popular: Olympic sport between market, state and civil society'. In eds. J. Bale and M. K. Christensen, *Post-Olympism? Questioning Sport in the Twenty-first Century*, pp. 65–80. Oxford: Berg.

Eichenwald, K. 2005. *Conspiracy of Fools: A True Story*. New York: Broadway Books.

Espy, R. 1979. *The Politics of the Olympic Games*. Los Angeles: University of California Press.

European Commission. 2007. *White Paper on Sport*. Brussels: European Commission.

European Commission. 2011. 'Developing the European dimension in sport'. In *Communication from the European Commission to the European Parliament, the European Council, the European Economic and Social Committee and the Committee of the Regions*. Brussels: European Commission.

European Council. 2000. Presidency Conclusions – Nice European Council Meeting 7, 8, 9 December 2000. Brussels: European Commission.

Evanoff, R. 2000. 'The concept of "third cultures" in intercultural ethics'. *Eubios Journal of Asian and International Bioethics*, 10: 126–9.

Evans, J. and B. Davies. 2004. 'Sociology, the body and health in a risk society'. In ed. B. Davies and J. Wright J. Evans, *Body Knowledge and Control: Studies in the Sociology of Physical Education and Health*. London: Routledge.

Eyquem, M. T. 1981. *Pierre de Coubertin: L'Epoque Olympique*. Paris: Calman-Levy.

Fairclough, N. 2005. 'Critical discourse analysis, organizational discourse, and organizational change'. *Organization Studies*, 26: 915–39.

Ferris, D. 2000. *Silent Urns: Romanticism, Hellenism, Modernity*. Stanford, California: Stanford University Press.

Fichte, J. G. 1806. 'Address to the German nation (1806)'. Retrieved 30 July 2011, from http://www.historyman.co.uk/unification/Fichte.html.

Finley, N. and H. Pleket. 1976. *The Olympic Games: The First Thousand Years*. London: Chatto & Windus.

Foucault, M. 1972. *The Archaeology of Knowledge*. London: Tavistock.

Foucault, M. 1991. 'Governmentality'. In eds. G. Burchell, C. Gordon and P. Miller, *The Foucault Effect: Studies in Governmentality*, pp. 87–104. Hemel Hempstead: Harvester Wheatsheaf.

Foucault, M., L. H. Martin, H. Gutman and P. H. Hutton. 1988. *Technologies of the Self: A Seminar with Michel Foucault*. London: Tavistock.

Fukuyama, F. 1990. 'Are we at the end of history?', *Fortune*, p. 75.

Fukuyama, F. 1992. *The End of History and the Last Man*. New York: Free Press

Fukuyama, F. 1993. *The End of History?* London: Institute of Economic Affairs.

Fukuyama, F. 1995. 'Reflections on the end of history, five years later'. *History and Theory and Society*, 34: 27–43.

Fusaro, P. and R. Miller. 2002. *What Went Wrong at Enron: Everyone's Guide to the Largest Bankruptcy in U.S. History*. New York: Wiley.

Fusco, C. 2007. '"Healthification" and the promises of urban space: A textual analysis of place, activity, youth (PLAY-ing) in the city'. *International Review for the Sociology of Sport*, 42: 43–63.

Gafner, R. 1971. 'Olympism in the world of tomorrow'. In *International Olympic Academy, 11th Young Participants Session*, pp. 170–81. Olympia: International Olympic Academy.

Gafner, R. 1987. 'The activities of the International Olympic Committee'. In *International Olympic Academy, 27th Young Participants Session*, pp. 44–52. Olympia: International Olympic Academy.

Garcia, B. 2007. 'Living the multicultural Olympic city. Cultural policy and planning in the Sydney 2000 Olympic Summer Games'. In eds. J. R. Gold and M. M. Gold, *Olympic Cities: Urban Planning, City Agendas and the World's Games, 1896 to the Present*. London: Routledge.

Garcia, S. 1993. 'Barcelona und die Olympische Spiele'. In eds. H. Haubermann and W. Siebel, *Festivalisierung der Stadpolitik, Stuttgart: Leviathan-Westdeutcher Verlag* (English Version: (1994) *Big Events and Urban Politics: Barcelona and the Olympic Games*. Unpublished Paper, ISA World Sociology Congress, Bielefeld, Germany).

Ghannoushi, S. 2007. 'Return of the Muslim other: The far right is reviving the prejudices that used to dominate mainstream European politics'. In *Guardian*, London, Wednesday 24 October 2007, http://www.guardian.co.uk/commentisfree/2007/oct/24/thefarright.religion%20ForceRecrawl:%200 retrieved 20 October 2011.

Giddens, A. 1990. *The Consequences of Modernity*. Cambridge: Polity Press.

Giroux, H. 1994. 'Living dangerously: Identity politics and the new cultural racism'. In eds. H. Giroux and P. McLaren, *Between Borders: Pedagogy and the Politics of Cultural Studies*. New York and London: Routledge.

Giulianotti, R. 2004. 'Human rights, globalization and sentimental education: The case of sport'. *Sport in Society*, 7: 355–69.

Goksøyr, M. 1991. Idrettsliv i borgerskapets by. En historisk undersøkelse av idrettens utvikling og organisering i Bergen pa[o] 1800 tallet. Norges Idrettshøgskole.

Gold, D. 2011. 'Cameron labels Blatter re-election a "farce" during Prime Minister's question time', *Inside World Football*, http://www.insideworldfootball.biz/world-football/42-news/9338-cameron-labels-blatter-re-election-a-farce-during-pmqs (retrieved 20 October 2011).

Gold, T. 1986. *State and Society in the Taiwan Economic Miracle*. New York: Armonk.

Green, M. 2007. 'Governing under advanced liberalism: Sport policy and the social investment state'. *Policy Sciences*, 40: 55–71. doi: 10.1007/s11077-007-9034-y

Greenhalgh, P. 1988. *Ephemeral Vistas: Expositions Universelles. Great Exhibitions and Worlds Fairs 1851–1939*. Manchester: Manchester University Press.

Gruneau, R. 1989. 'Television, the Olympics and the question of ideology'. In eds. R. Jackson and T. McPhail, *The Olympic Movement and the Mass Media: Past, Present and Future Issues*. University of Calgary: Hurford Enterprises.

Gruneau, R. 1984. 'Commercialism and the modern Olympics'. In eds. A. Tomlinson and G. Whannel, *Five Ring Circus. Money, Power and Politics at the Olympic Games*. London: Pluto Press.

Gruneau, R. 1993. 'The critique of sport in modernity'. In ed. E. Dunning, J. Maguire and R. Pearton, *The Sport Process. A Comparative and Developmental Approach*. Leeds: Human Kinetics.

Guardian Newspaper. 2011. 'Transocean report blames BP for Gulf of Mexico oil disaster'. *Guardian*, 22 June 2011. London: Associated Press.

Guttmann, A. 1978. *From Ritual to Record*. New York: Columbia University Press.

Guttmann, A. 1988. *A Whole New Ball Game. An Interpretation of American Sports*. Chapel Hill: University of North Carolina Press.

Guttmann, A. 1992a. *The Olympics*. Urbana and Chicago: University of Illinois Press.

Guttmann, A. 1992b. *The Olympics: A History of the Modern Games*. Urbana: University of Illinois Press.

Guttman, A. 1994. *Games and Empires. Modern Sports and Cultural Imperialism*. New York: Columbia University Press.

Guttmann, A. 2002. *A History of the Modern Games, 2nd Edition*. Urbana and Chicago: University of Illinois Press.

Guttmann, A. and L. Thompson. 1984. *The Games Must Go On: Avery Brundage and the Olympic Movement*. New York: Columbia University Press.

Haag, H. 1982. 'Life and work of Carl Diem. The father of modern physical education in Germany'. *International Journal of Physical Education*, 19(2): 24–30.

Habermas, J. 1990a. *The Philosophical Discourse of Modernity: Twelve Lectures*. Massachusetts: MIT Press.

Habermas, J. 1985. *The Philosophical Discourse of Modernity*. Frankfurt: Suhrkamp Verlag.

Habermas, J. 1990. *Moral Consciousness and Communicative Action*. Cambridge, Mass.: MIT Press.

Haddad, Y. Y. 1998. 'Islam and gender: Dilemmas in the changing Arab world'. In Islam and Gender: Dilemmas in the Changing Arab World, eds. Y. Y. Haddad and J. Esposito, *Islam, Gender and Social Change*. Oxford: Oxford University Press.

Haggard, S. 1990. *Pathways from the Periphery: The Politics of Growth in the Newly Industrializing Countries*. Ithaca: Cornell University Press.

Hall, S., D. Held and A. McGrew eds. 1992. *Modernity and its Futures*. Cambridge: Polity Press.

Hargreaves, J. 1994. *Sporting Females: Critical Issues in the History and Sociology of Women's Sports*. London: Routledge.

Hargreaves, J. 2002. 'Globalisation theory, global sport and nations and nationalism'. In eds. J. Sugden and A. Tomlinson, *Power Games: A Critical Sociology of Sport*. London: Routledge.

Heinze, G. 1989. 'The concept of the IOC on doping as a counterpoint to the Olympic spirit'. *International Olympic Academy, 29th Young Participants Session*, pp. 60–6. Olympia: International Olympic Academy.

Held, D., A. McGrew, D. Goldblatt and J. Perraton. 1999. *Global Transformations: Politics, Economics and Culture*. Cambridge: Polity.

Helstein, M. T. 2005. 'Rethinking community: Introducing the "whatever" female athlete'. *Sociology of Sport Journal*, 22: 1–18.

Henry, I. 2007. 'Bridging research traditions and world views: Universalisation versus generalisation in the case for gender equity'. In I. Henry and Institute of Sport and Leisure Policy, *Transnational and Comparative Research in Sport: Globalisation, Governance and Sport Policy*. London: Routledge.

Henry, I. 2009. 'Strategies of the 2012 London Olympic Games in an era of global economic depression'. *Asian Association of Sport Management*. Taipei: Taiwan National Sport University.

Henry, I. 2012. 'The Olympics: Why we should value them'. In eds. H. Lenskyj and S. Wagg, *A Handbook of Olympic Studies*. Basingstoke: Palgrave.

Henry, I. and Institute of Sport and Leisure Policy. 2007. *Transnational and Comparative Research in Sport: Globalisation, Governance and Sport Policy*. London: Routledge.

Henry, I. and L. Robinson. 2010. *Gender Equity and Leadership in Olympic Bodies: Women, Leadership and the Olympic Movement 2010*. Lausanne: International Olympic Committee & Centre for Olympic Studies & Research, Loughborough University.

Henry, I. and N. Matthews. 1998. 'Sport policy and the European Union: The post-Maastricht agenda'. *Managing Leisure: An International Journal*, 3(1): 1–19.

Henry, I. P., M. Amara and M. Al-Tauqi. 2003. 'Sport, Arab nationalism and pan-Arab games'. *International Review for the Sociology of Sport*, 38(3): 295–310.

Henry, I., M. Amara and D. Aquilina. 2007. 'Multiculturalism, interculturalism, assimilation and sports policy in Europe'. In I. Henry and the Institute of Sport and Leisure Policy, *Transnational and Comparative Research in Sport: Globalisation, Governance and Sport Policy*. London: Routledge.

Henry, I. P., W. Radzi, E. Rich, E. Theodoraki and A. White 2004. *Women, Leadership, and the Olympic Movement*. Loughborough: Institute of Sport & Leisure Policy, Loughborough University and I.O.C.

Henry, I. and M. Al-Tauqi 2008. 'The development of Olympic solidarity: West and non-west (core and periphery) relations in the Olympic world'. *International Journal of the History of Sport*, 25: 355.

Heywood, A. 2002. *Politics*. London: Palgrave.

Hill, C. 1992. *Olympic Politics*. Manchester: Manchester University Press.

Hill, C. 1996. *Olympic Politics, 2nd edition*. Manchester: Manchester University Press.

Hoberman, J. 1984. *Sport and Political Ideology*. Austin: The University of Texas Press.

Hoberman, J. 1986. *The Olympic Crisis. Sport, Politics and the Moral Order*. New Rochelle, NY: Caratzas Publishing Co, Inc.

Hoberman, J. 1992. *Mortal Engines: The Science of Performance and the Dehumanization of Sport*. New York: The Free Press.

Hoberman, J. 1995. 'Toward a theory of Olympic internationalism'. *Journal of Sport History*, 22(1): 1–37.

Hoberman, J. 2004. 'Sportive nationalism and globalization'. In eds. J. Bale and M. K. Christensen, *Post-Olympism? Questioning Sport in the Twenty-first Century*, pp. 177–88. Oxford.

Hobsbawm, E. 1992. 'Mass-producing traditions: Europe, 1870–1914'. In eds. E. Hobsbawm and J. Ranger, *The Invention of Tradition*. Cambridge: Canto/Cambridge University Press.

Honeyball, M. 2011. 'Why corruption in FIFA matters to the EU'. Brussels: Public Service Europe – (downloaded 20 October 2011) http://www.publicserviceeurope.com/article/441/why-corruption-in-fifa-matters-to-the-eu

Hoogvelt, A. 1997. *Globalization and the Postcolonial World: The New Political Economy of Development*. Basingstoke: Palgrave.

Hoogvelt, A. 2001. *Globalization and the Postcolonial World: The New Political Economy of Development, 2nd edition*. Basingstoke: Palgrave.

Horton, P. A. 2001. 'Complex Creolization: The evolution of modern sport in Singapore'. In ed. J. A. Mangan, *Europe, Sport World. Shaping Global Societies*. London: Frank Cass.

Houlihan, B. 1994. *Sport and International Politics*. Brighton: Harvester-Wheatsheaf.

Houlihan, B. 1999. *Dying to Win: Doping in Sport and the Development of Anti-Doping Policy*. Strasbourg.

Houlihan, B. 2001. 'The world anti-doping agency: Prospects for success'. In ed. J. O'Leary, *Drugs and Doping in Sport: Socio-Legal Perspectives*, pp. 125–45. London: Cavendish Publishing Ltd.

Hughes, T. 1857, 1999. *Tom Brown's Schooldays*. Oxford: Oxford World's Classics.

Huntington, S. 1996. *The Clash of Civilizations*. London: Simon & Schuster.

Inglehart, R. 1997. *Modernization and Postmodernization*. Princeton, NJ: Princeton University Press.

Inglehart, R. and C. Welzel. 2005. *Modernization, Cultural Change and Democracy: The Human Development Sequence*. Cambridge: Cambridge University Press.

Inglehart, R. and P. Norris. 2009. *Cosmopolitan Communications: Cultural Diversity in a Globalized World*. Cambridge: Cambridge University Press.

International Olympic Committee. 2007. *Olympic Charter*. Lausanne: International Olympic Committee.

International Olympic Committee. 2008. *Singapore to Host the 1st Summer Youth Olympic Games in 2010*. Lausanne: International Olympic Committee http://en.beijing2008.cn/news/official/ioc/n214254189.shtml

International Monetary Fund. 2005. *The IMF's Approach to Promoting Good Governance and Combating Corruption – A Guide*. http://www.imf.org/external/np/gov/guide/eng/index.htm (retrieved 20 October 2011).

International Olympic Academy. 2011. *Mission of the International Olympic Academy*. Olympia: IOA. http://ioa.org.gr/en/ioa-information/mission (retrieved 21 October 2011).

International Olympic Committee. 1978. *Olympic Charter*. Lausanne: International Olympic Committee.

International Olympic Committee. 1996. *Olympic Charter*. Lausanne: International Olympic Committee.

International Olympic Committee. 2004. *The Olympic Movement's Agenda 21: Sport for Sustainable Development*. Lausanne: International Olympic Committee. http://www.olympic.org/Documents/Reports/EN/en_report_300.pdf (retrieved 21 October 2011).

International Olympic Committee. 2009. *Factsheet: The Environment and Sustainable Development*. Lausanne: International Olympic Committee, updated July 2009 http://www.olympic.org/Documents/Reference_documents_Factsheets/Environment_and_substainable_developement.pdf (accessed 21 October 2011).

International Olympic Committee. 2010a. *Shaping the Future: Interim Report 2009–10*. Lausanne: International Olympic Committee.

International Olympic Committee. 2010b. *The Olympic Charter*. Lausanne: International Olympic Committee.

International Olympic Committee. 2011. *The Olympic Charter*. Lausanne: International Olympic Committee.

Jäger, S and F. Maier 2009. 'Theoretical and methodological aspects of Foucauldian critical discourse analysis and dispositive analysis'. In eds. R. Wodak and M. Meyer, *Methods of Critical Discourse Analysis*. London: Sage.

James, H. 2001. *The End of Globalization: Lessons from the Great Depression*. Cambridge, MA: Harvard University Press.

Jennings, A. 2000. *The Great Olympic Swindle: When the World Wanted Its Games Back*. London: Simon & Schuster.

Jennings, A. 2010. 'How FIFA corruption empowers global'. In ed. C. Schulz Herzenberg, *Player and Referee: Conflicting Interests and the 2010 FIFA World Cup*. Pretoria, South Africa: Institute for Security Studies.

Jennings, A. and V. Simson. 1996. *The New Lords of the Rings: Olympic Corruption and How to Buy Gold Medals*. London: Pocket Books.

Jennings, A. and V. Simson. 1992. *The Lords of the Rings*. London: Simon & Schuster.

Jones, S. 1988. *Sport, Politics and the Working Class*. Manchester: Manchester University Press.

Jowell, T. 2006. *What Social Legacy of 2012?*, Speech at the Fabian Fringe in Manchester, 27 September 2006. http://www.labour.org.uk (retrieved 4 December 2007).

Kanin, D. B. 1981. *A Political History of the Olympic Games*. Boulder, CO: Awetview Replica.

Karam, A. M. 1998. *Women, Islamisms and the State: Contemporary Feminisms in Egypt*. Basingstoke: Palgrave.

Kastoryano, R. 2002. *Negotiating Identities: States and Immigrants in France and Germany*. Princeton, New Jersey: Princeton University Press.

Kidd, B. 1996. 'Taking the rhetoric seriously: Proposals for Olympic education'. *Quest*, 48: 82–92.

Killanin, L. and J. Rodda. 1976. *The Olympic Games. 80 Years of People, Events and Records*. London: Barrie & Jenkins.

King, A. D. 1995. *Global Modernities; The Times and Spaces of Modernity (or Who Needs Post-modernism?)*. London: Sage.

Klein, A. M. 1995. 'Culture, politics, and baseball in the Dominica Republic'. *Latin American Perspectives*, 22: 111–30.

Klein, N. 2001. *No Logo*. New York: Flamingo Books.

Kristof, N. 1999 'At this rate we will be global in another 100 years'. *New York Times*, 23 May.

Kruger, A. 1972. *Die Olympischen Spiele 1936 und de Weltmeinung*. Berlin: Bartels and Wernitz.

Kruger, A. 1999. 'The unfinished symphony: A history of the Olympic Games from Coubertin to Samaranch', in eds. J. Riordan and A. Kruger, *The International Politics of Sport in the 20th Century*, pp. 3–27. London: Taylor and Francis.

Krüger, A. and J. Riordan. 1996. *The Story of Worker Sport*. Champaign, IL: Human Kinetics.

Lalaoui, B. 1993. 'Olympism as a cultural phenomenon and a factor of social development and social policy: A link between society, sport and religion'. *International Olympic Academy, 33rd Young Participants Session*, pp. 102–8. Olympia: International Olympic Academy.

Landry, F. 1985. 'Olympic education and international understanding: Educational challenge or cultural hegemony?'. *International Olympic Academy, 25th Young Participants Session*, pp. 139–49. Olympia: International Olympic Academy.

Landry, F. and M. Yerles. 1994. 'The presidencies of Lord Killanin (1972–1980) and of Juan Antonio Samaranch (1980–)'. In ed. *The International Olympic Committee, The International Olympic Committee – One Hundred Years: The Idea – The Presidents – The Achievements*.

Lawler, P. 1994. 'Fukuyama versus the end of history'. In ed. T. Burns, *After History? Francis Fukuyama and His Critics*, pp. 63–80. London: Rowman & Littlefield Publishers.

Leiper, J. M. 1976. *The International Olympic Committee: Its Structure and Function, Past and Present Problems, and Future Challenges*. Unpublished PhD Thesis, University of Alberta.

Leiper, J. M. 1980. 'The evolution of the Olympic ideal since 1896'. *International Olympic Academy, 20th Young Participants Session*, pp. 89–96. Olympia: International Olympic Academy.

Lekarska, M. 1988. 'Olympism – Immutable values and outdated factors'. *28th Session of the International Olympic Academy*, pp. 73–80. Olympia.

Lenk, H. 1964. 'Values, aims, reality of the modern Olympic games'. *International Olympic Academy, 4th Young Participants Session*, pp. 205–11. Olympia: International Olympic Academy.

Lenskyj, H. 2000. *Inside the Olympic Industry: Power, Politics, and Activism*. Albany: State University of New York Press.

Lenskyj, H. 2002. *The Best Olympics Ever?: Social Impacts of Sydney 2000*. Albany: State University of New York Press.

Lenskyj, H. 2008. *Olympic Industry Resistance: Challenging Olympic Power and Propaganda*. Albany: State University of New York Press.

Link, J. 1982. 'Kollectivsymbolk und Mediendiskurse'. *Kultur Revolution*, 1: 6–21.

Liponski, W. 1992. 'Between Western concepts and East European reality: Some aspects of commercialization in Olympism sport of the 1980s and early 1990s'. *International Olympic Academy, 32nd Young Participants Session*, pp. 110–17. Olympia: International Olympic Academy.

Lipset, S. M. 1959. 'Some social requisites of democracy'. *American Political Science Review*, 53: 69–105.

Loland, S. 1994. 'Pierre de Coubertin's ideology of Olympism from the perspective of the history of ideas'. In *Second International Symposium for Olympic Research*. The University of Western Ontario, London, Ontario, Canada.

London Organising Committee of the Olympic Games and Paralympic Games. 2010. *International Inspiration: Transforming Lives Through Sport*. London: LOCOG.

Lovell, R. and J. Stokdyk. 2010. 'Ernst & Young sued over Lehman collapse'. *Accounting Web*, 22 December 2010: http://www.accountingweb.co.uk/topic/practice/ernst-young-charged-over-lehman-collapse/469322 (accessed 21 October 2011).

Lucas, J. 1980. *The Modern Olympic Games*. London: Thomas Yoseloff Ltd.

Lucas, J. 1992. *Future of the Olympic Games*. Champaign, Illinois: Human Kinetics.

Luton, F. and H. Fan. 2007. 'The polarization of sport: GANEFO – A case study. In ed. Hong Fan, *Sport, Nationalism, and Orientalism, The Asian Games*. London: Routledge.

MacAloon, J. 1981. *This Great Symbol: Pierre de Coubertin and the Origins of the Modern Olympic Games*. Chicago: University of Chicago Press.

MacAloon, J. 1986. *Intercultural Election and Olympic Sport: The 1986 Challenge Address to the Olympic Academy of Canada*. Quebec: Olympic Academy of Canada.

MacAloon, J. 1996a. 'Humanism as political necessity? Reflections on the pathos of anthropological science in Olympic contexts'. *Quest*, 48: 67–81.

MacAloon, J. 1996b. 'Humanism as political necessity? Reflections on the pathos of anthropological science in Olympic contexts'. *Quest*, 48: 67–81.

MacAloon, J. 2011. 'Scandal and governance: Inside and outside the IOC 2000 Commission'. *Sport in Society*, 14: 292–308.

Maguire, J. 1999. *Global Sport: Identities, Societies, Civilizations*. Oxford: Polity.

Mandell, R. 1971. *The Nazi Olympics*. London: Souvenir Press.

Mandell, R. 1974. 'Carl Diem on sport and war'. *Canadian Journal of History of Sport and Physical Education*, 5(1): 10–13.

Mangan, J. A. and C. Hickey. 2001. *Globalization, the Games Ethic and Imperialism: Further Aspects on the Diffusion of an Ideal*. London: Frank Cass.

Mangan, J. A. 2000. *Athleticism in the Victorian and Edwardian Public School*. London: Frank Cass.

Mangan, J. A. and H. Nam-gil. 2001. 'Confucianism, imperialism, nationalism: Modern sport, ideology and Korean culture'. In ed. J. A. Mangan, *Europe, Sport World. Shaping Global Societies*. London: Frank Cass.

Marwick, A. 1998. *The Sixties, Cultural Revolution in Britain, France, Italy and the United States c.1958–c.1974*. Oxford: Oxford University Press.

McGrew, A. 1992. *Global Politics: Globalisation and the Nation-State*. Cambridge: Polity Press.

Merkel, U. 2000. 'The hidden social and political history of the German Football Association (DFB), 1900–50'. *Soccer and Society*, 1: 167–86.

Mernissi, F. 1985. *Beyond the Veil: Male-Female Dynamics in a Modern Muslim Society*. London: Al Saqi Books.

Mernissi, F. and M. Lakeland. 1991. *The Veil and the Male Elite: A Feminist Interpretation of Women's Rights in Islam*. Wokingham: Addison-Wesley.

Metallinos, G. D. 1995. Orthodox and European Culture: Excerpts from the speech of Fr. Georgios Metallinos, Professor at the University of Athens, during the February '95 Theological Conference in Pirgos, Greece; http://www.romanity.org/mir/me04en.htm (accessed 21 October 2011).

Miller, T., G. Lawrence, J. McKay and D. Rowe. 2001. *Globalization and Sport*. London: Sage.

Milshstein, O. 1992. 'Commercialization in sport and the pedagogical aims of the Olympic movement'. *International Olympic Academy, 32nd Young Participants Session*, pp. 118–38. Olympia: International Olympic Academy.

Milton-Smith, J. 2002. 'Ethics, the Olympics and the search for global values'. *Journal of Business Ethics*, 35: 131–42.

Moller, V. 2004. 'Doping and the Olympic Games from an aesthetic perspective'. In eds. J. Bale and M. K. Christensen, *Post-Olympism? Questioning Sport in the Twenty-first Century*, pp. 201–10. Oxford: Berg.

Molokotos-Liederman, L. 2003. *The Religious Factor in the Construction of Europe: Greece, Orthodoxy and the European Union*, a paper delivered at the 1st LSE PhD Symposium on Modern Greece: 'Current Social Science Research on Greece'. London School of Economics.

Moltman, J. 1980. 'Olympism and religion'. *International Olympic Academy, 20th Young Participants Session*, pp. 81–8. Olympia: International Olympic Academy.

Mosse, G. 1981. *The Crisis of German Ideology: Intellectual Origins of the Third Reich*. New York: Schocken Books.

Müller, N. 1998. *The IOA Sessions of the International Olympic Academy: 1961–1998*. Olympia: International Olympic Academy.

Müller, N. 2000. *Pierre de Coubertin 1863–1937. Olympism, Selected Writings*. Lausanne: International Olympic Committee.

Muller, N. and R. Tuttas. 2000. 'The role of the YMCA: especially that of Elwood S. Brown, Secretary of physical education of the YMCA, in the worldwide expansion of the Olympic movement during de Coubertin's presidency'. *5th International Symposium for Olympic Research*, pp. 127–34. Sydney.

Müller, N. 1994. *One Hundred Years of Olympic Congresses (1894–1994)*. Lausanne: International Olympic Committee.

Munslow, A. 1997. *Deconstructing Reality*. London: Routledge.

Nafziger, J. 1985. 'Foreign policy in the sport arena'. In ed. J. Johnson, *Government and Sport: The Public Policy Issue*. New York: Rawmoin and Allanheld.

Neuendorff, E. 1910. *Volker Liederbuch der deutschen Turnerschaft*. Germany: Versandhaus der Deutschen Turnerschaft.

Neverkovich, S. 1987. 'Methods of Olympic education'. *International Olympic Academy, 27th Young Participants Session*, pp. 172–6. Olympia: International Olympic Academy.

Nielsen Media Research. 2008. *Nielsen Television Audience Measurement: AGB Nielsen Media Research (China) – News*. New York: Nielsen Media Research.

Nissiotis, N. 1984. 'Olympism and today's reality'. *International Olympic Academy, 24th Young Participants Session*, pp. 57–74. Olympia: International Olympic Academy.

Nixon, H. L. 1988. 'The background, nature and implications of the organisation of the "Capitalist Olympic"'. In J. Segrave and D. Chu, *The Olympic Games in Transition*. Champaign, Illinois: Human Kinetics, pp. 237–51.

Organisation for Economic Co-Operation and Development. 2005. *OECD Guidelines on Corporate Governance of State-owned Enterprises*. Paris: Organisation for Economic Co-Operation and Development.

Osterhoudt, R. G. 1981. 'Capitalist and socialist interpretations of modern amateurism: An essay on the fundamental difference'. In eds. J. Segrave and D. Chu, *Olympism*, pp. 42–6. Champaign, Illinois: Human Kinetics.

Papadoyanakis, Y. 1989. 'Legislative measures and penalization of doping'. *International Olympic Academy, 29th Young Participants Session*, pp. 81–6. Olympia: International Olympic Academy.

Parekh, B. 1992. 'The cultural particularity of liberal democracy'. *Political Studies Volume*, 40: 160–75.

Pariente, R. 1989. 'The end of doping: Utopia or reality?' *International Olympic Academy, 29th Young Participants Session*, pp. 116–25. Olympia: International Olympic Academy.

Parrish, R., S. Miettenen, B. Garcia and R. Siekman 2010. *The Lisbon Treaty and EU Sports Policy*. Brussels: European Parliament, Directorate General for Internal Policies.

Parry, J. 1994. 'The moral and cultural dimensions of Olympism and their educational application'. *International Olympic Academy 34th Session of Young Participants*. Olympia: International Olympic Academy.

Parry, J. 1988. 'Olympism at the beginning and end of the twentieth century – Immutable values and principles and outdated factors', *International Olympic Academy, 28th Young Participants Session*, pp. 81–94. Olympia: International Olympic Academy.

Parry, J. 2004. 'Olympism and its ethic'. *International Olympic Academy, 44th Young Participants Session*. Olympia: International Olympic Academy.

Paton, G. and R. Barney. 2002. 'Adolf Hitler, Carl Diem, Werner Klingeberg, and the Thousand Year Reich: Nazi Germany and its envisioned post-war Olympic world'. In ed. R Barney, *Sixth International Symposium for Olympic Research*, pp. 93–104.

Penney, D. and D. Chandler. 2000. 'A curriculum with connections'. *British Journal of Teaching Physical Education*, 31: 37–40.

Pouret, H. 1970. 'What are people demanding from Olympism?' *International Olympic Academy, 10th Young Participants Session*, pp. 100–6. Olympia: International Olympic Academy.

Preston, P. 2000. *Understanding Modern Japan*. London: Sage.

Prevelakis, N. 2003. The Spirit of Greek Nationalism: An Examination of the Greek case in the light of Greenfeld's conceptual framework. Paper presented at the 1st LSE PhD Symposium on Modern Greece: 'Current Social Science Research on Greece'. London School of Economics.

Prynn, J. 2011. 'Blatter is dragged into world football's corruption scandal'. *London Evening Standard*, May 27 2011, http://www.londonwire.co.uk/london-news/blatter-is-dragged-into-world-footballs-corruption-scandal/ (retrieved 21 October 2011).

Przeworski, A. and F. Limongi. 1997. 'Modernization: Theories and facts'. *World Politics*, 49: 155–83.

Ramazanoglou, C. and J. Holland. 2002. *Feminist Methodology: Challenges and Choices*. London: Sage Publications.

Read, K. 1989. The IOC Athletes Commission Anti-Doping Campaign. *International Olympic Academy, 29th Young Participants Session*, pp. 112–15. Olympia: International Olympic Academy.

Ren, H. 2008. 'Embracing Wushu: Globalisation and cultural diversification of the Olympic movement'. In eds. M. Price and D. Dayan, *Owning the Olympics: Narratives of the New China*. Ann Arbor: University of Michigan Press.

Right to Play. 2010. *History of Right to Play*. Toronto: Right to Play. http://www.righttoplay.com/International/about-us/Pages/History.aspx (accessed 21 October 2011).

Riordan, J. 1999. 'The impact of communism on sport'. In eds. J. Riordan and A. Kruger, *The International Politics of Sport in the 20th Century*, pp. 48–66. London: Taylor and Francis.

Riordan, J. and A. Krüger. 1999. *The International Politics of Sport in the Twentieth Century*. London: Spon.

Ritter, P. 1978. 'The Olympic movement in the service of peace and brotherhood'. *International Olympic Academy, 18th Young Participants Session*, pp. 179–84. Olympia: International Olympic Academy.

Ritzer, G. 2004. *The Globalization of Nothing*. Thousand Oaks, CA: Pine Forge Press.

Robertson, R. 1992. *Globalization: Social Theory and Global Culture*. London: Sage.

Roche, M. 2000. *Mega-events and Modernity: Olympics, Expos and the Growth of Global Culture*. London: Routledge.

Rodda, J. 1989. 'A drug testing system which protects the rights of the individual'. *International Olympic Academy, 29th Young Participants Session*, pp. 102–5. Olympia: International Olympic Academy.

Roesch, H. 1979. 'Olympism and religion. Idea and reality – An attempt to a new interpretation'. *International Olympic Academy, 19th Young Participants Session*, pp. 192–205. Olympia: International Olympic Academy.

Rogge, J. 2001. 'Governance in sports: A challenge for the future'. In European Olympic Committee, Fédération Internationale de l'Automobile and Herbert Smith, *The Rules of the Game: Europe's First Conference on the Governance of Sport*. Brussels: Governance in Sport Group.

Rose, N. 1999. *Powers of Freedom: Reframing Political Thought.* Cambridge: Cambridge University Press.

Rosenberg, J. 2000. *The Follies of Globalization Theory. Polemical Essays.* London: Verso.

Ruuska, P. 1999. 'Globalization, connections and dialogues'. *European Journal of Cultural Studies*, 2: 249–61.

Said, E. 1991. *Orientalism: Western Conceptions of the Orient.* London: Penguin.

Saliba, T., C. Allen and J. A. Howard. 2002. *Gender, Politics, and Islam.* Chicago: University of Chicago Press.

Sandiford, K. 1994. *Cricket and the Victorians.* Aldershot: Scholar Press.

Sargent, D. A. 1889. 'The physical development of women'. In *Scribners*, February 1889, pp. 172–84.

Sartre, J. 1965 'Preface' in F. Fanon The Wretched of the Earth: MacGibbon and Kee Sayer, A. 2000. *Realism and Social Theory.* London: Sage.

Sayer, A. 2000. *Realism and Social Theory.* London: Sage.

Schaffer, K. and S. Smith. 2000. *The Olympics at the Millennium: Power, Politics and the Games.* London: Rutgers University Press.

Schaffer, W., B. Jaffee and L. Davidson 1993. *Beyond the Games: The Economic Impact of Amateur Sports.* Indianapolis: Chamber of Commerce.

Scharenberg, S. 1999. 'Religion and sport in the international politics of sport in the twentieth century'. In eds. J. Riordan and A. Krüger, *The International Politics of Sport in the Twentieth Century.* London: Spon.

Scheinder, A. 1996. 'Women in the republic and the Olympic movement'. *International Olympic Academy, 36th Young Participants Session*, pp. 104–9. Olympia: International Olympic Academy.

Segrave, J. and D. Chu. 1981. *Olympism.* Champaign, Illinois: Human Kinetics.

Segrave, J. O. 2000. 'The (neo)modern Olympic Games'. *International Review for the Sociology of Sport*, 35: 268–81.

Segrave, J. and D. Chu, eds. 1988. *The Olympic Games in Transition.* Champaign, Illinois: Human Kinetics Books.

Seppanen, P. 1984. 'The Olympics: A sociological perspective'. *International Review for the Sociology of Sport*, 19: 113–27.

Sie, S. 1978. 'Sport and politics: The case of the Asian Games and GANEFO'. In Lowe, B. *et al.* (ed.) *Sport and International Relations.* Champaign, Ill., Stipes, 1978, Section 3, pp. 279–96; 296.

Silk, M. L. and M. Falcous. 2005. 'One day in September/a week in February: Mobilizing American (sporting) nationalisms'. *Sociology of Sport Journal*, 22: 447.

Simri, U. 1983. 'Israel and the Asian Games', paper presented at Sport and Politics, the 26th ICHPER World Congress, Wingate Institute, Israel.

Simson, Y. and A. Jennings, 1991. *The Lords of the Rings. Power, Money and Drugs in the Modern Olympics.* London: Simon and Schuster Ltd.

Singh, T. 2009. 'European Court rules against the Sikh turban in French schools'. *Sikh Business World.com*, http://www.sikhbusinessworld.com/f59/european-court-rules-against-sikh-turban-58655/ (accessed 21 October 2011).

Smith, D. A. 2001. *Nationalism: Theory, Ideology, History.* London: Polity.

Soysal, Y. and V. Antoniou 2000. A Common Religious Past? Portrayals of the Byzantine and Ottoman Heritages from Within and Without. 5th Workshop of the Southeast European Joint History Project Textbook Committee on 'Teaching Sensitive and Controversial Issues in the History of South-East Europe'.

St. Pierre, M. 1990. 'West Indian cricket: A cultural contradiction?' *ARENA Review*, 14(4): 13–24.

Standage, T. 1999. *The Victorian Internet.* New York: Berkeley Books.

Stanley, A. P. 1845. *The Life and Correspondence of Thomas Arnold*. London: Fellowes (original 1844).

Stephens, A. 1989. 'Socrates or chorus person? The problem of individuality in Nietzsche's Hellenism'. In ed. G. W. Clarke, *Rediscovering Hellenism*, pp. 237–60. Cambridge: Cambridge University Press.

Steyn, J. 2003. Guantanamo Bay: The legal black hole. Twenty-Seventh FA Mann Lecture. British Institute of International and Comparative Law and Herbert Smith. Lincoln's Inn Old Hall.

Stoddart, B. 1988. 'Caribbean cricket – The role of sport in emerging small-nation politics'. *International Journal*, 43: 618–42.

Stolyarov, V. 1995. 'The two world political evolution and its consequences for the Olympic movement. Can the Olympic movement influence political changes through Olympic education?' *International Olympic Academy, 35th Young Participants Session*, pp. 76–89. Olympia: International Olympic Academy.

Stowasser, B. 1998. 'Gender issues and contemporary Quran interpretation'. In eds. Y. Y. Haddad and J. Esposito, *Islam, Gender and Social Change*. Oxford: Oxford University Press.

Strenk, A. 1981. 'Amateurism: Myth and reality'. In eds. J. Segrave and D. Chu, *Olympism*. Champaign, Illinois: Human Kinetics.

Techshout. 2008. *IOC and YouTube in Collaboration to Broadcast Beijing Olympics 2008*. http://www.techshout.com/internet/2008/06/ioc-and-youtube-in-collaboration-to-broadcast-beijing-olympics-2008/ (accessed 21 October 2011).

Teichler, H. J. 1982. 'Coubertin und das Dritte Reich'. *Sportwissenschaft*, 12(1982), Heft 1, S. 18–55.

Tenenbaum, L. 2000. 'Image and reality in Sydney's Olympic opening ceremony'. World Socialist Website: International Committee of the Fourth International (ICFI). http:// www.wsws.org/articles/2000/sep2000/open-s22.shtml (accessed 21 October 2011).

Tesche, L. and A. B. Rambo. 2001. 'Reconstructing the Fatherland: German Turnen in Southern Brazil in the nineteenth and twentieth centuries'. In ed. J. A. Mangan, *Europe, Sport World. Shaping Global Societies*. London: Frank Cass.

The Official Home Page of the United States Army (2012) *The Evolution Of and Ever Evolving Sports Program*. http//www.army.mil/fmwrc/docs/history-army-sports-program.pdf. Retrieved 11 April 2012.

Thoma, J. E. and L. Chalip. 1996. *Sport Governance in the Global Community*. Morgantown, WV Sport Management Library: Fitness International Technology Inc.

Tibi, B. 2001. *Islam Between Culture and Politics*. Houndmills, Basingstoke, Hampshire; New York: Palgrave.

Tinning, R. and T. Glasby. 2002. 'Pedagogical work and the "cult of the body": Considering the role of HPE in the context of the "new public health"'. *Sport Education and Society*, 7: 109–19.

Tipton, F. B. and R. Aldrich. 1987. *An Economical and Social History of Europe from 1939 to Present*. Basingstoke: Macmillan.

Tomlinson, A. 2004. 'The Disneyfication of the Olympics? Theme parks and freak-shows of the body'. In eds. J. Bale and M. K. Christensen, *Post-Olympism? Questioning Sport in the Twenty-first Century*, pp. 147–64. Oxford: Berg.

Toohey, K. and A. J. Veal. 2000. *The Olympic Games. A Social Science Perspective*. London: CAB International.

Torres, C. T. 2002. 'Tribulations and achievements: The early history of Olympism in Argentina'. In eds. J. A. Mangan and L. DaCosta, *Sport in Latin American Society – Past and Present*. London: Frank Cass.

United Nations. 1987. *Our Common Future, Report of the World Commission on Environment and Development.* New York: United Nations.

United Nations. 2009. *The United Nations Sport for Development and Peace: Key Milestones.* Geneva: United Nations.

United Nations. 2011. We can end poverty 2015: Millennium development Goals. United Nations Summit 20–22 September 2010 http://www.un.org/en/mdg/summit-2010/ (accessed 21 October 2011).

United Nations ESCAP. 2007. What is Good Governance? United Nations Economic and Social Commission for Asia and the Pacific. http://www.unescap.org/pdd/prs/projectactivities/ongoing/gg/governance.asp (accessed 22 October 2011).

United Nations Organisation for Sport for Development and Peace. 2010. Sport for Development and Peace: The UN System in Action: Why Sport? Geneva: United Nations Organisation for Sport for Development and Peace. http://www.un.org/wcm/content/site/sport/home/sport (accessed 22 October 2011).

United States Olympic Committee. 1999. Report of the Special Bid Oversight Commission. Released by the Commission on 1 March 1999, chaired by Senator George Mitchell: Colorado Springs: USOC.

Veal, A. and S. Frawley. 2009. 'Sport for All' and Major Sporting Events: Trends in Sport Participation and the Sydney 2000 Olympic Games, the 2003 Rugby World Cup and the Melbourne 2006 Commonwealth Games, School of Leisure, Sport and Tourism Working Papers. Sydney: Australian Centre for Olympic Studies, School of Leisure, Sport and Tourism, Faculty of Business, University of Technology Sydney.

Volpp, L. 2001. 'Feminism versus multiculturalism'. *Columbia Law Review*, 101: 1181–218.

Von Laue, T. 1994. 'From Fukuyama to reality: A critical essay'. In ed. T. Burns, *After History? Francis Fukuyama and His Critics*, pp. 23–38. London: Rowman & Littlefield Publishers.

Voy, R. 1991. *Drugs, Sport and Politics.* New York: Leisure Press.

Vrijman, E. N. 2001. 'Harmonisation: A bridge too far? A commentary on current issues and problems'. In ed. J. O'Leary, *Drugs and Doping in Sport: Socio-Legal Perspectives*, pp. 147–65. London: Cavendish Publishing Ltd.

Waddington, I. 2000. *Sport, Health and Drugs: A Critical Sociological Perspective.* London: Taylor and Francis.

Wallerstein, I. 1974. *The Modern World-System.* New York: Academic.

Warren, B. 1980. *Imperialism, Pioneer of Capitalism.* London: New Left Books.

Weber, W. 1970. 'Pierre de Coubertin and the introduction of organised sport in France'. *Journal of Contemporary History*, 5: 3–26.

Weed, M., E. Coren, J. Fiore, L. Mansfield, I. Wellard, D. Chatziefstathiou and S. Dowse. 2009. *A Systematic Review of the Evidence Base for Developing a Physical Activity and Health Legacy from the London 2012 Olympic and Paralympic Games.* Canterbury: Centre for Sport, Physical Education & Activity Research (SPEAR), Canterbury Christ Church University.

Widlund, T. 1998. Commentary on 'Of Olympic Chains and Flags: The Debate Continues'. *Olympika*, Vol. VII, pp. 174–6.

Winter, B. 2001. 'Fundamental misunderstandings: Issues in feminist approaches to Islamism'. *Journal of Women's History*, 13: 9–41.

Wittgenstein, L. (1967). *Philosophical Investigations.* Oxford: Basil Blackwell.

Worden, M. (ed.) 2008. *China's Great Leap: The Beijing Games and Olympian Human Rights Challenges.* New York: Seven Stories Press.

World Bank. 2010. *Worldwide Governance Indicators.* Washington DC: World Bank. http://info.worldbank.org/governance/wgi/sc_country.asp (accessed 23 October 2011).

Xu, Guoqi. 2008. *Olympic Dreams: China and Sports*. Boston: Harvard University Press.
Young, D. C. 1984. *The Olympic Myth of Greek Amateur Athletics*. Chicago: Ares Publishers.
Young, D. C. 1996. *The Modern Olympics, a Struggle for Revival*. Baltimore and London: The Johns Hopkins University Press.
Zijjl, W. V. 1964. 'Weakness and strength of the Olympic movement'. *International Olympic Academy, 4th Young Participants Session*, pp. 212–22. Olympia: International Olympic Academy.

Index